AF723966

Illustrator
A Hands-On Introduction
VERSION 5.5

Illustrator

A Hands-On Introduction
Version 5.5

Suzanne Sayegh Thomas

I(T)P™ **Delmar Publishers™**
An International Thomson Publishing Company

Albany • Bonn • Boston • Cincinnati • Detroit • London • Madrid
Melbourne • Mexico City • New York • Pacific Grove • Paris • San Francisco
Singapore • Tokyo • Toronto • Washington

NOTICE TO THE READER

Publisher does not warrant or guarantee any of the products described herein or perform any independent analysis in connection with any of the product information contained herein. Publisher does not assume, and expressly disclaims, any obligation to obtain and include information other than that provided to it by the manufacturer.

The reader is expressly warned to consider and adopt all safety precautions that might be indicated by the activities herein and to avoid all potential hazards. By following the instructions contained herein, the reader willingly assumes all risks in connections with such instructions.

The publisher makes no representation or warranties of any kind, including but not limited to, the warranties of fitness for particular purpose or merchantability, nor are any such representations implied with respect to the material set forth herein, and the publisher takes no responsibility with respect to such material. The publisher shall not be liable for any special, consequential, or exemplary damages resulting, in whole or part, from the readers' use of, or reliance upon, this material.

Cover Design: Rob Clancy/Spiral Design

Delmar Staff
Administrative Editor: John Anderson
Project Editor: Barbara Riedell
Production Coordinator: Larry Main
Design Coordinator: Lisa Bower

Printed in the United States of America
For more information, contact:
Delmar Publishers
3 Columbia Circle , Box 15015
Albany, New York 12212-5015

International Thomson Publishing Europe
Berkshire House 168-173
High Holborn
London, WC1V7AA
England

Thomas Nelson Australia
102 Dodds Street
South Melbourne, 3205
Victoria, Australia

Nelson Canada
1120 Birchmont Road
Scarborough, Ontario
Canada M1K 5G4

International Thomson Editores
Campos Eliseos 385, Piso 7
Col Polanco
11560 Mexico D F Mexico

International Thomson Publishing GmbH
Königswinterer Strasse 418
53227 Bonn
Germany

International Thomson Publishing Asia
221 Henderson Road
#05 -10 Henderson Building
Singapore 0315

International Thomson Publishing - Japan
Hirakawacho Kyowa Building, 3F
2-2-1 Hirakawacho
Chiyoda-ku, Tokyo 102
Japan

Printed in the United States of America
Published simultaneously in Canada
by Nelson Canada,
a division of the Thomson Corporation

3 4 5 6 7 8 9 10 XXX 00 99 98 97

Library of Congress Cataloging-in-Publication data
Thomas, Suzanne Sayegh.
Illustrator a hands-on introduction : (version 5.5) / Suzanne Sayegh Thomas.
p. cm.
Includes index.

ISBN 0-8273-7004-0

1. Computer graphics 2. Adobe illustrator (Computer file)

I. Title

T385. T49537 1994

006.6' 869—dc20

94–32103
CIP

DEDICATION

To my sisters, Barbara and Marie,

whose love of design and color

have threaded my life with joy.

CONTENTS

LESSON 10 LAYERS, MASKS, AND COMPOUND PATHS 129

LESSON 11 WORKING WITH PATTERNS 153

LESSON 12 FILTERS 165

PREFACE

This textbook is written primarily for teachers, trainers, and students of Adobe Illustrator, especially for those who are new to a PostScript drawing program. Although it is helpful to have some drawing expertise when working with this application, you really don't need it to use Illustrator effectively. So powerful are its tools and so intuitive its interface that, with practice, you will soon find yourself comfortable with this remarkable program. Once you become familiar with the pen tool, for example, you can trace scanned images to generate any kind of illustration as well as create complex illustrations by modifying objects created with the basic shape tools.

With the release of version 5.5, Adobe has transformed Illustrator into an application capable of producing truly glorious documents. Text handling now includes tabs and a spell checker; filters allow for greater transformational effects; working in Preview mode lets you see changes as you make them; the Layers palette gives you control over viewing and printing every item in the document; and Illustrator's seamless interface with Adobe Photoshop make it possible for the artist and designer to translate even their most visionary ideas to the printed page.

The book is organized around the basic tools and functions in Adobe Illustrator. Since all the functions covered in the text are explained whenever they are used, you can either move sequentially from one lesson to the next, or easily jump from lesson to lesson and section to section. You may want to skim the section on layers and work with type effects. Or, you may choose to concentrate on learning how to use the drawing tools and leave type for later. Since this book is designed for students working in the graphics and design industries, the business-oriented chart and graph functions in Adobe Illustrator are not covered in this book.

The text is comprised of the explanation for a command or function followed by an exercise based on that function. You can always change the values given in the exercises to create many more exercises which will reinforce your learning—and sometimes produce exciting results!

The author wishes to extend her gratitude to a number of people who were helpful in putting this material together: to Adobe Systems Incorporated, which actively encourages and supports the development of ancillary materials for its applications, especially to Sonya Schaefer, Public Relations Coordinator, who graciously provided me with advance copies of Illustrator 5 and 5.5; to Joe Conrey, Coordinator of the Fine and Performing Arts Department at Ocean County College in Toms River, New Jersey, who insisted that Adobe Illustrator be part of the desktop publishing curriculum; to my students in that first and exciting class who punctuated every lesson with "Wow!"; to Virginia Asman of Illuminage Art and Design whose "a la Matisse" illustration made the lessons on layers and masking interesting while providing a professional illustration from which to work and learn; to Brooke Graves, the best copyeditor an author could have; and to Barbara Riedell at Delmar for her patience and encouragement.

LESSON 1

Introduction to Adobe Illustrator

WELCOME TO ADOBE ILLUSTRATOR

If your computer drawing experience has been limited to bitmapped programs like MacPaint, Fractal Design Painter, and Adobe Photoshop, your study of Adobe Illustrator will take you into a world where lines are perfectly straight and curves are perfectly smooth—even if you move or resize them. Because Adobe Illustrator is a PostScript-based drawing program, the mathematically precise definitions of lines and curves are maintained in the drawing and printing process. This allows you not only to draw precise lines and shapes, but also to draw them in any weight, to fill them with color and patterns, and to use type as an illustration element. There is no limit to what you can produce with Adobe Illustrator once you learn how to use its tools and functions.

WHY USE ADOBE ILLUSTRATOR?

Adobe Illustrator is an art production tool used by graphic designers, production artists, typesetters, and service bureaus. Artwork created in Illustrator can be imported into programs like QuarkXPress and Aldus PageMaker where it can be further manipulated. Illustrator files can be opened and placed in Adobe Photoshop for further manipulation. Because Illustrator files are Encapsulated PostScript (EPS) files, they move easily and without loss of color or detail to and from other PostScript applications.

WHAT THIS BOOK COVERS

Lessons in this book are designed to cover the main functions and features of Adobe Illustrator 5.5. The first lesson introduces you to the terms, tools, and viewing modes available in Adobe Illustrator. Lesson 2 will teach you how to make selections and work with closed and open paths. Lesson 3 covers the powerful Paint Style palette, from which all colors, fills, and line attributes are applied. Strokes, gradient fills, and more of the painting tools are discussed in Lesson 4. The pen tool, Illustrator's primary drawing tool, is covered in Lesson 5. You will learn how to trace templates and measure and move objects in Lesson 6, as well as how to work with rulers and guides. Lesson 7 covers the transformation tools for scaling, rotating, reflecting, shearing, and blending. Lessons 8 and 9 cover type effects, typography, and word processing. The new layers feature, Layers palette, and masking commands are discussed in Lesson 10. You will learn how to create and use patterns in Lessons 11 and how to apply filters in Lesson 12. Although you will be printing work throughout the book, selecting options for printing black-and-white and color separations are covered in Lesson 13. A glossary of terms appears after the last chapter and a cross-referenced index completes the book.

⌘-H View/Actual Size

HOW TO USE THIS TEXT

This text has been designed so you can easily lay it flat next to your computer and work directly from it. Each lesson ends with a Review Exercise which will help you to pull together the different kinds of material covered in the lesson. You will also find multiple-choice questions at the end of each lesson which will reinforce what you learned in the lesson.

Although different functions are presented in each lesson, you can move sequentially from one lesson to another or skip a lesson if you like. For example, if you want to begin creating complex illustrations right away and leave painting objects for later, begin with Lesson 5. Or, if you feel that Lesson 3 on most of the features of the Paint Style palette gives you enough information to work with, leave Lesson 4 until later and move on to something else.

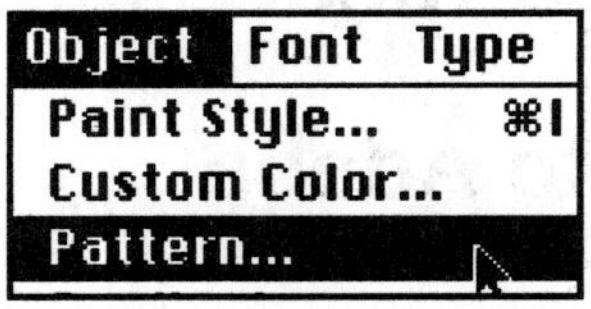

When you see "Choose Object/Pattern," click on the Menu Bar and drag to highlight the command.

To help you keep track of the various kinds of information you are working with, the narrow column on each page is where you will find much helpful information on using the features in Adobe Illustrator. All of the terms which appear on the first page of each lesson are found in the glossary at the end of the book.

In this book, menu commands appear followed by the keyboard command where they appear on the menu. When, for example, you are told to choose View/Actual Size (Command-H), either click on the View menu and drag down to select (highlight) Actual Size, or press the Command and H keys simultaneously. If a keyboard shortcut exists for a command, it will be given in the text and will also appear in the minor column. Learning to use these keyboard shortcuts will make your work in Illustrator faster and more efficient.

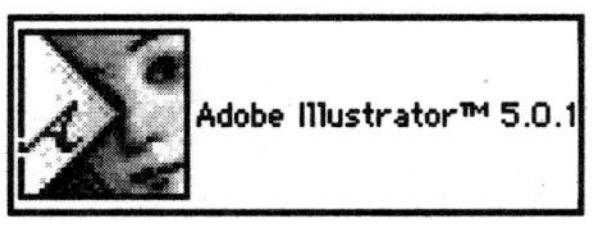

Double-click on the Adobe Illustrator application icon in the Adobe Illustrator folder on your hard drive to launch the program.

The disk accompanying this book contains tutorial files which you will use to do the exercises. Since all the files are locked, first move them to your hard drive. Then when you make changes to a file, save it under a new name. This will allow you to manipulate the file without losing the original file. The files needed for each lesson are listed on the first page of each lesson.

LAUNCHING THE PROGRAM

Launch (run) Adobe Illustrator either by double-clicking on the Adobe Illustrator icon or by double-clicking on an Adobe Illustrator document icon.

An Adobe Illustrator document can be a new document, a previously created Illustrator file, or a template. A template is a black-and-white bitmapped image which you trace or draw over to create artwork. For example, you could open a Paint file as a template and use Illustrator's tracing tool to trace the image; Illustrator will replace the template's jagged lines with smooth lines and curves.

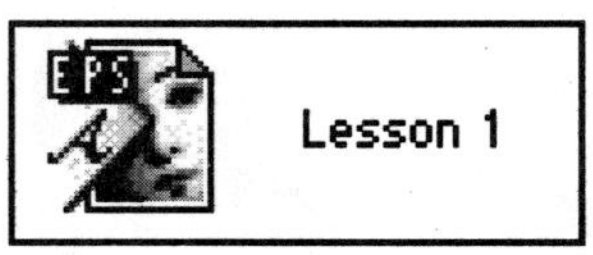

Double-click on any Illustrator document icon to launch the program.

When you launch Adobe Illustrator, a document labeled Untitled art 1 is created, the Menu Bar appears at the top of the screen, and the Toolbox appears on the left side of the screen (Figure 1.1). The Bar is used to access all the program's commands and functions. Click on a menu in the bar and drag down to display the commands under the menu. Then, without releasing the mouse button, drag down to highlight a command. Release the mouse button.

⌘-Control-T View/Show Toolbox

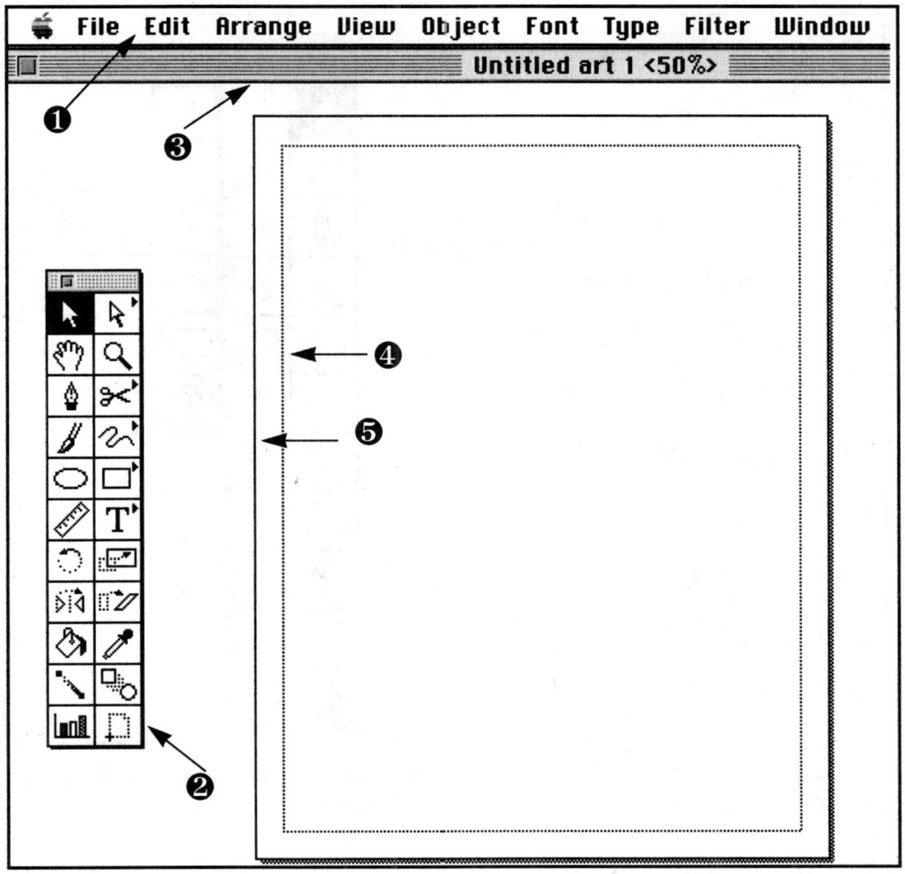

Figure 1.1—When you launch Adobe Illustrator, a drawing page appears. The Menu Bar (1) is displayed at the top of the screen and the Toolbox (2) appears at the left. The document's title bar (3) indicates that you are viewing the illustration page at 50% magnification. Click on the gray bars in the title bar to move the whole window around the screen. The dotted lines inside the page (4) indicate the page size; the shadow box on the outside of the page (5) displays the limits of the printable area.

Tip

Reset the Toolbox to its default settings by pressing the Command and Shift keys simultaneously while double-clicking on any tool.

THE TOOLBOX

The Toolbox, sometimes called the Tool palette, contains 22 default tools (Figure 1.2). However, if you click and drag out on these tools that display a black triangle (like the scissors and freehand tools), other tools will be displayed. You can drag the Toolbox around the screen and or close it by clicking on the Close button in its left corner. To display it again, choose Window/Show Toolbox (Command-Control-T).

SELECTING TOOLS

To select a tool, click once on the tool in the Toolbox. Then move the cursor onto the page and the crosshair will change to the appropriate cursor for that tool. When you double-click on certain tools like the scale tool, a dialog box appears where you can enter values for how the tool will function.

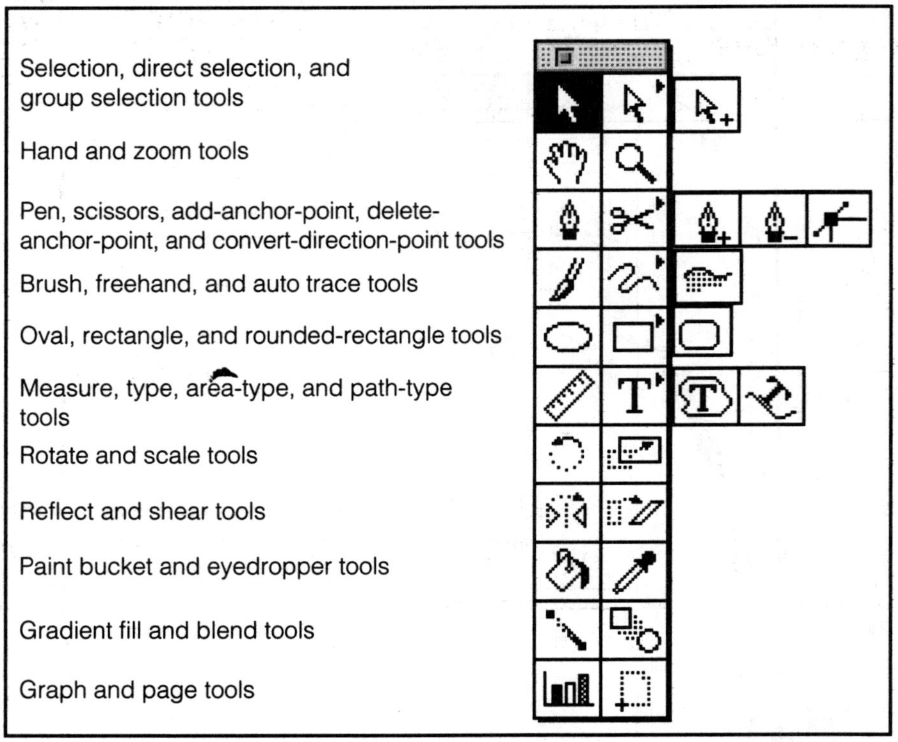

Figure 1.2—The Adobe Illustrator Toolbox displays 22 default tools. Click and drag on the black triangle in some of the tools to display other tools.

FYI

When you're told to work "on a clean drawing page," either select everything on the screen and delete it all or open a new document from the File menu.

THE DRAWING AREA

The drawing area is the large area in the center of the page (Figure 1.1). Once you save a document, the title bar displays the name of the document and the view percentage. If you're viewing a page at actual size, then the document's name followed by <100%> appears.

The dotted lines inside the drawing area mark the page size. The outside lines (drop shadow box) indicate the margins and define the printable or imageable area of the document.

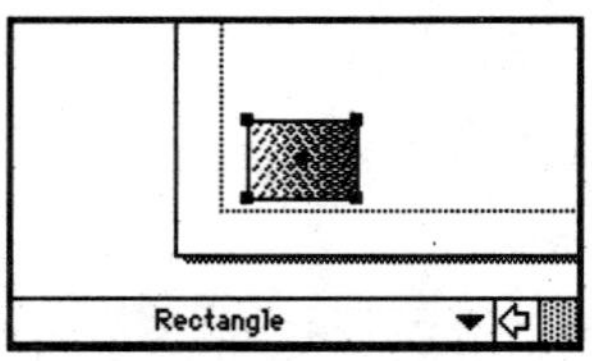

The information bar for this document indicates that a rectangle is currently selected.

The information bar in the lower right corner of the page displays information about the tools and their current function. Clicking on the black triangle in the information bar window displays four categories of information you may find useful.

NAVIGATING A DOCUMENT

Use the scroll bars on the right and bottom sides of the page to move quickly through the window or click on the scroll arrow to scroll through the window a little at a time. Drag the scroll bars to move even faster up, down, or from right to left.

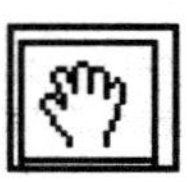

Hand tool

You can also select the hand tool, press the mouse button, and drag the hand around the screen to move to various areas of the document. If you're using another tool, press the spacebar to change that tool into the hand tool. Then click and drag with the mouse.

SAVING FILES

Once you have created a file, you can save it, then open it and modify the artwork again. To save a file, choose File/Save (Command-S). The first time you save a file, you will be asked to type a name for the file and select a preview format for viewing the file (Figure 1.3). You will usually choose Color Macintosh, which saves not only the file but also a preview color image of the file. Once a file has been named and saved, choosing File/Save overwrites the original file with the new information without prompting you to name it or choose a format.

⌘-S File/Save
⌘-W File/Close
⌘-O File/Open
⌘-M View/Fit in Window
⌘-Y View/Preview

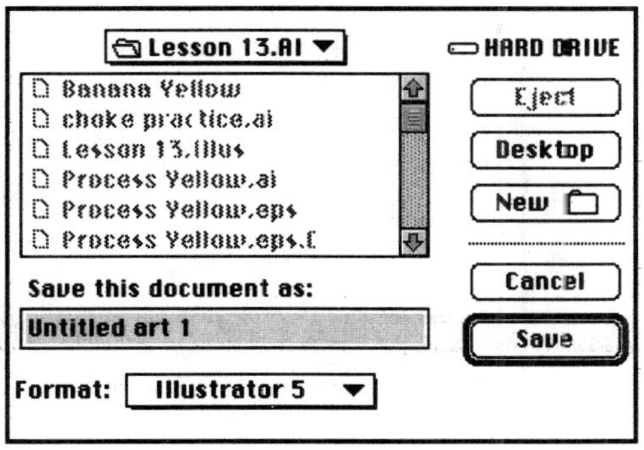

Figure 1.3—When you first save a file, this screen appears. Type a name for the document and select a preview format for the file.

CLOSING AND OPENING FILES

Files can be closed without quitting the program. When you have finished working on a document, choose File/Close (Command-W). If you haven't saved the file, you will be prompted to save any changes you made since you last saved that file.

To open a file, you must be in the Adobe Illustrator application. Choose File/Open (Command-O) and scroll through the drives and folders to locate the file. When the file appears in the scroll box, double-click on it or click once on the file and once on the Open button. The document will appear on the screen.

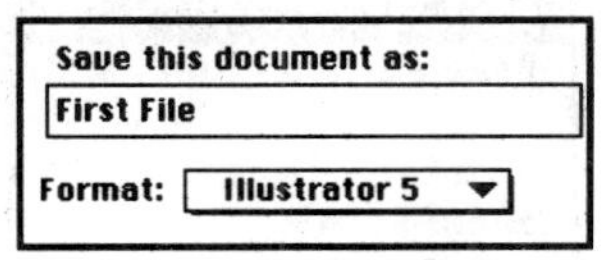

Use the Format menu to select a file format for the saved document. If you plan to bring the Illustrator file into a page layout program like PageMaker or QuarkXPress, save the document in EPS format.

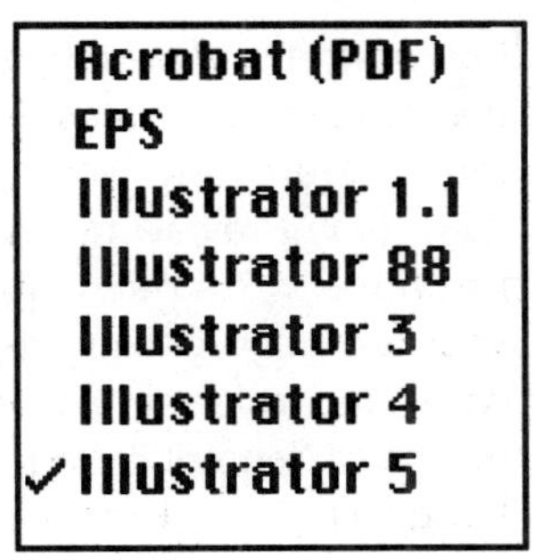

EXERCISE A

1. Double-click on the Adobe Illustrator application icon to launch the program.
2. When the blank page and Toolbox appear on the screen, choose View/ Fit in Window (Command-M). Choose View/Preview (Command-Y) to view the fill color.
3. Click on the rectangle tool (the fifth tool down in the right column of the Toolbox) and click and drag on the drawing area to create a rectangle. If a fill color was designated the last time the program was used, the rectangle will fill with that color. Don't worry if it doesn't fill.
4. Choose File/Save (Command-S) and type First File in the Save this document as field. Click on the black triangle in the Format field and drag down to highlight Illustrator 5. Make sure you are saving the file to the appropriate drive and folder, then click on the Save button.

⌘-O File/Open
⌘-W File/Close

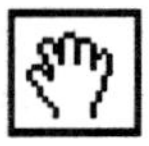

Hand tool

FYI

Tutorial files for each lesson are located on the Tutorial disk inside the folder for that lesson.

5. Choose File/Open (Command-O). Scroll to locate the First File document on the Tutorial disk. Double-click on it or click once to highlight First File and click on Open.The file opens and displays the file name and the rectangle that was saved with the file (Figure 1.4).
6. Click on the hand tool and then click and drag around the document to move to different areas of the document.
7. Choose File/Close (Command-W) to close the file.

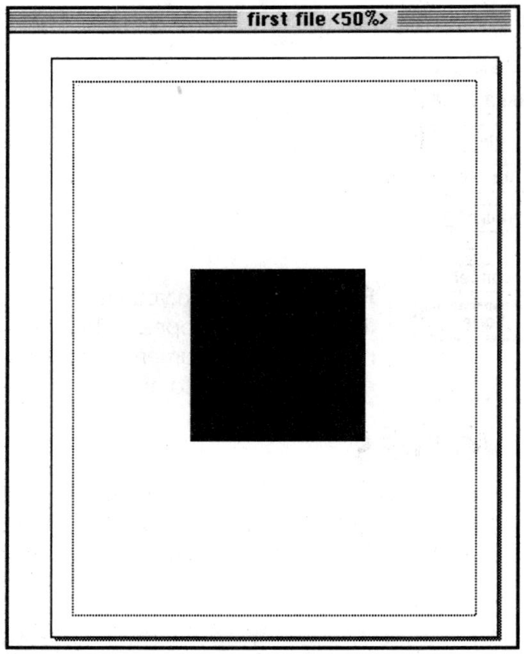

Figure 1.4—When you open a file, its name appears in the title bar along with the viewing percent. Any artwork that was saved with the file is also displayed.

VIEWING MODES

There are several different ways to view or display your illustration on the screen. To see how your artwork looks with all the color and stroke attributes applied, choose Preview from the View menu. You can edit the illustration in this mode, watching your changes take place on the screen as you make them.

Selecting Artwork from the View menu displays the illustration as a wireframe image (Figure 1.5). You can edit the image in this mode, but until you switch to Preview mode, you won't see the results of many editing commands. The advantage of working in Artwork view is that editing is much faster, since Illustrator doesn't have to generate all the fill and color commands on screen.

To preview only a selected area of the image, make the selection and choose View/Preview Selection. This is also a way of speeding up Illustrator, especially when you have a complicated illustration and are working with only a part of it.

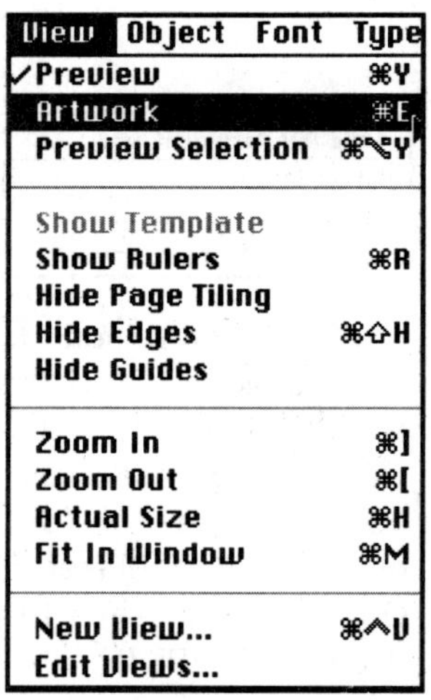

Pull down the View menu and drag to select a command. Here, the document is in Preview mode because Preview is checked. Highlighting Artwork and releasing the mouse button will change the view to Artwork mode.

⌘-O File/Open
⌘-E View/Artwork
⌘-Y View/Preview

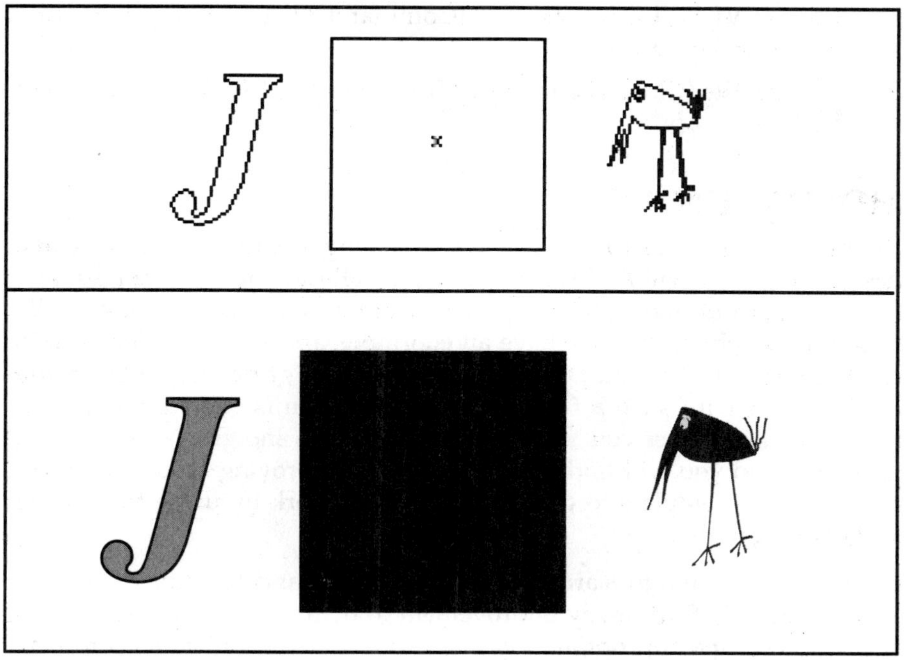

Figure 1.5—When you view an illustration in Artwork mode, a wireframe image appears (above) and does not display any of the color or fill commands (below). You can edit the image in either Artwork or Preview mode.

MAGNIFYING ARTWORK

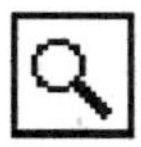

Zoom tool

The zoom-in tool and the zoom-out tool allow you to magnify or reduce the size of the display of any part of your document. Zooming in and out does not change the size of the image (you use the scale tool for that), but it does magnify and reduce the artwork display on the screen.

To enlarge the screen display, click on the zoom tool and click anywhere on the image. Once you move the zoom tool onto the image, a plus sign appears in the magnifier. To reduce the image display, press the Option key before clicking with the zoom tool. Once you press the Option key, a minus sign appears in the magnifier.

EXERCISE B

1. Insert the Tutorial disk and choose File/Open (Command-O). Double-click on the Lesson 1.ai file to open it.
2. Click on the hand tool to select it, then click and drag across the screen to center the orange barn at the right.
3. Click on the zoom tool and click on one of the yellow windows to magnify its display. Then click in the empty area above the barn and, keeping the mouse button pressed, drag a marquee around the entire barn to magnify just those elements of the image.
4. Choose View/Artwork (Command-E) and notice that only the wire-frame images appear. Choose View/Preview (Command-Y) to display the image with all the applied colors and line attributes.

⌘-M View/Fit in Window
⌘-W File/Close

5 Choose View/Fit in Window (Command-M) to display the entire image on the screen.

6. Choose File/Close (Command-W) to close the file. Don't save your changes.

MOVING ON

Adobe Illustrator is as complex as it is intriguing. If you have drawing and design skills, you will find that this program allows you to do almost anything you can do conventionally. If you are new to graphics, especially computer graphics, you will have an enormous amount of fun learning to create images in Illustrator. Either way, there is a great deal to learn and the best way with such a full-featured application is one step at a time. Don't worry if it takes you a while to master curves and gradients. Keep on practicing and you will find your illustrations improving. You can always use a scanned template to create PostScript artwork by using the tracing and drawing tools.

If you take the time to learn how the commands and functions are used, you will quickly find steady improvement in both your work and the ease of selection of the appropriate tools and functions. Don't be afraid to play with Illustrator, but keep in mind that this marvelous electronic art box is filled with thousands of tools. Learn how to choose the right ones to make your work "picture perfect."

LESSON 2

Drawing Paths

OVERVIEW

In this lesson you will learn how Adobe Illustrator defines lines and shapes, how to recognize points, paths, and segments, and how to select an object or part of an object. You will create objects and use the selection tools to edit open and closed paths.

TOPICS

Anchor points
Closed paths
Direct-selection tool to move segments
Selection tools
Direct-selection tool to move anchor points
Corner points and smooth points
Drawing an open path
Review Exercise
Review Questions

TERMS

anchor point
closed path
direct-selection tool
direction handles
endpoints
group-selection tool
join paths
line
object
open path
path
segment
selection tool
shape

⌘-N File/New
⌘-E View/View Artwork

ANCHOR POINTS

Before you can manipulate shapes in Illustrator, you have to understand how Illustrator creates those shapes. All lines and curves in a drawing exist between anchor points. The line or curve between those two anchor points is called a segment, and all of the connecting segments are called a path (Figure 2.1).

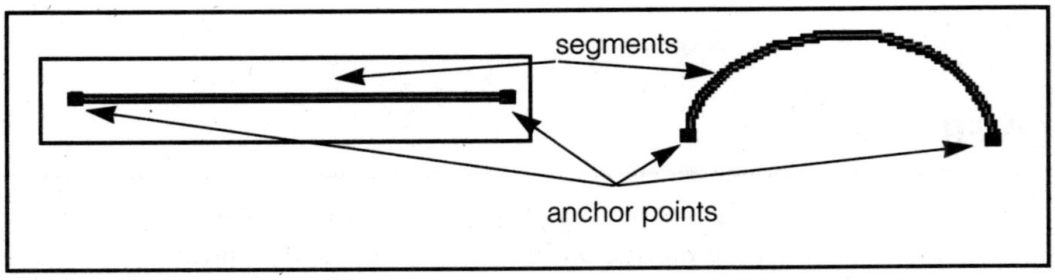

Figure 2.1—Displays two selected open paths with their anchor points visible. The line and curve between the anchor points are the segments.

If the last segment is connected to the first segment, the path is a closed path. A closed path is called a shape. If the last segment is not connected to the first segment, the path is an open path. An open path is called a line (Figure 2.2).

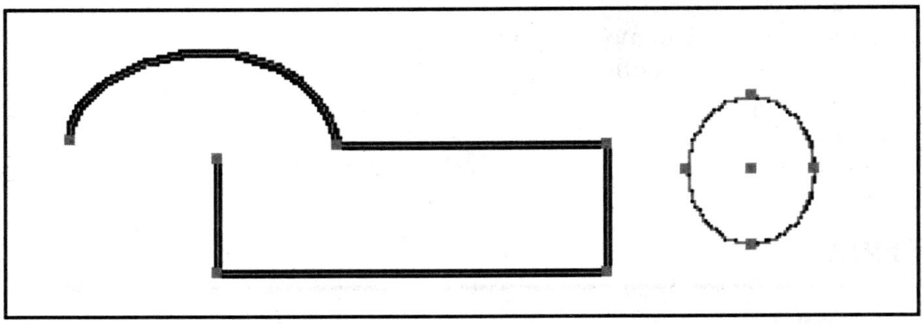

Figure 2.2—The path on the left is an open path because no segment connects the first and last segments. The path on the right is a closed path because the first and last segments are connected by another segment.

EXERCISE A

1. Choose File/New (Command-N) to create a new document.
2. Choose View/Artwork (Command-E) to display the illustration in Keyline mode. You will not be able to see fills and strokes in Artwork mode.

3. Click on the rectangle tool to select it. Move onto the drawing area and then click and drag to draw a rectangle. A rectangle with 5 points appears, one at each corner and one in the center. These points are called anchor points and the straight lines between these anchor points are called segments. The rectangle comprised of the four segments joined by the four points is called a path (Figure 2.3).

⌘-Shift-A Edit/Select None

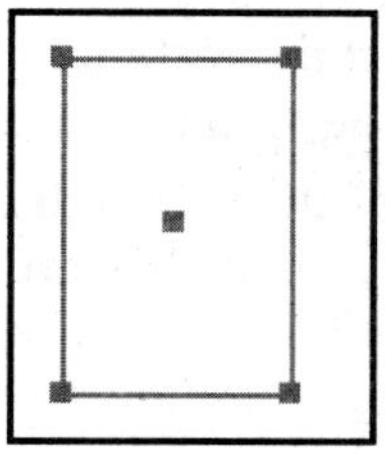

Figure 2.3—The rectangle is a closed path. Its anchor points are visible and solid, indicating that it was just drawn or that it has been selected with the selection tool.

4. The solid anchor points indicate that they are selected and therefore available for editing. Choose Edit/Select None (Command-Shift-A) to deselect the rectangle. Only the path comprised of the 4 segments and a center point appears.
5. Click on the selection tool (black arrow) and click on any segment of the rectangle. All 5 points appear solid, indicating that the object is selected and can be moved.

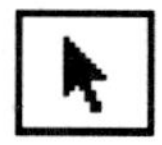

Selection tool

6. Click and drag on a segment to move the entire rectangle. Because every point is selected (solid), every segment moves. And since every segment is connected to form one object, the rectangle (the entire object), moves.
7. Click anywhere on the empty page to deselect the rectangle or choose Edit/Select None (Command-Shift-A). Click with the selection tool on another segment and drag the rectangle around the screen. Repeat deselecting, selecting, and moving until you get bored.

FYI

Clicking with the direct-selection tool on the center point of a basic shape closed path like a rectangle or circle selects the entire path, just as if you had used the selection tool.

CLOSED PATHS

A path is the entire group of connected segments. In a rectangle, the four segments form a path and, because the last segment is connected by an anchor point to the first segment, a closed path is created. When you moved the rectangle with the selection tool, you moved the whole path. In Illustrator, a closed path is also called a shape.

DIRECT-SELECTION TOOL TO MOVE SEGMENTS

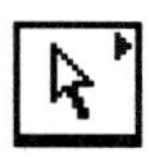

Direct-selection tool

When you used the selection tool (black arrow) to select the rectangle, it selected every anchor point and therefore every segment in the object. So, when you clicked and dragged to move the object, every segment moved simultaneously and the rectangle moved without becoming distorted. However, you can also choose to move only certain segments in an object. To do this, use the direct-selection tool, the white arrow. Selecting a segment with the direct-selection tool allows you to move only the segment or segments attached to the anchor points of the selected segment.

⌘-E View/Artwork
⌘-Shift-A Edit/Select None
⌘-Z Edit/Undo

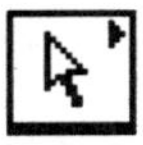

Direct-selection tool

EXERCISE B

1. Choose View/Artwork (Command-E). Use the rectangle tool to draw a rectangle, longer than it is wide.
2. When you release the mouse, the entire object is selected, as indicated by the filled anchor points. Click on any empty area of the page or choose Edit/Select None (Command-Shift-A) to deselect the rectangle.
3. Click on the direct-selection tool, the white arrow to the right of the selection tool, and click on any of the four segments of the rectangle. The rectangle is selected, but notice that now the anchor points are hollow (Figure 2.4). This means that you cannot move (edit) the anchor points, although you can edit (move) the segments between the anchor points.

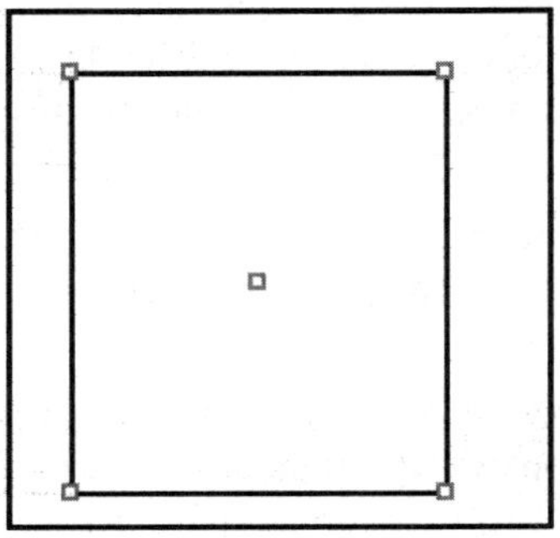

Figure 2.4—Displays a rectangle selected with the direct-selection tool. The anchor points are hollow, indicating that the object can't be moved without becoming distorted.

4. Click on the top segment of the rectangle and move it up and down and right and left. Notice that only the segments connected to the anchor points which anchor the top segment move. Those 3 segments are the top segment, the left segment, and the right segment. The bottom segment doesn't move because its anchor points are used to anchor only the bottom segment (Figure 2.5).

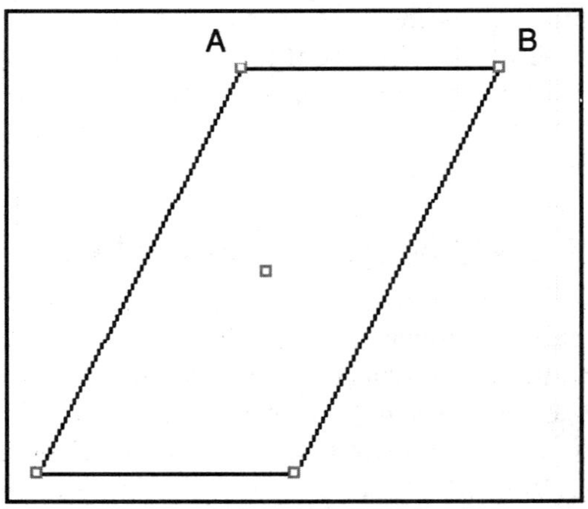

Figure 2.5—Displays a rectangle that was reshaped when the top segment between anchor points A and B was moved to the right.

5. Choose Edit/Undo (Command-Z) to return the rectangle to its original shape.

6. Click on the bottom segment and move it to the right and left. Notice that only the bottom segment, the left segment, and the right segment move. The top segment doesn't move this time because you didn't drag it, and its two anchor points are not connected to the bottom segment.
7. Click on the left segment of your distorted rectangle and move it around. Notice that only the left, top, and bottom segments move. The right segment doesn't move because its anchor points are not connected to the left segment which you are moving.
8. Continue to click and drag on each of the 4 segments and notice how the only segments that move are those whose anchor points are connected to the segment you are currently moving.

⌘-E View/Artwork
⌘-Shift-A Edit/Select None

SELECTION TOOLS

The three selection tools in Adobe Illustrator are the selection tool (black arrow), direct-selection tool (white arrow), and group selection tool (white arrow with plus sign). The selection tool selects an entire path, shape, or object. Any segments connected by anchor points are selected with the selection tool. The direct-selection tool, however, selects *individual segments* on a path or in a shape.

Just because you select a tool by clicking on it does not mean that any path is selected with that tool. For example, if you selected a path with the selection tool (black arrow), clicking on it with the direct-selection tool (white arrow) to select segments instead of the whole object would not select segments. To select segments with the direct-selection tool, first *deselect* the object (Command-Shift-A), *then* click on it with the direct-selection tool.

This is not true when a shape or path is first selected with the direct-selection tool. When this is the case, selecting the object with the selection tool overrides the direct selection and selects the whole path or shape.

Selection tool

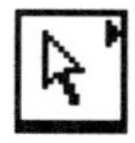

Direct-selection tool

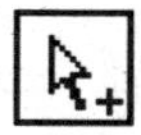

Group-selection tool

EXERCISE C

1. Choose View/Artwork (Command-E). Use the rectangle tool to draw a rectangle. Choose Edit/Select None (Command-Shift-A) to deselect it.
2. Click on the selection tool (black arrow) and click on the rectangle. Notice that the entire shape is selected. Click and drag on the selected shape to move it around the screen.
3. Keeping the rectangle selected, click on the direct-selection tool (white arrow) and click on the selected rectangle. Nothing happens. That's because the rectangle is still selected by the selection tool that selects the whole object.
4. Choose Edit/Select None (Command-Shift-A) or click on an empty area of the page to deselect everything.
5. Click on the direct-selection tool (white arrow) and click on the rectangle. It appears with its segments deselected, as indicated by the hollow anchor points. Click on any *segment*—not on an anchor point—and drag to reshape the rectangle.

Tip

Deselecting everything (Edit/Select None) is one of the most frequently used commands in Illustrator. To automate the function, use a macro program like QuicKeys from CE Software to assign a single keystroke to the Select None command. This allows you to deselect an entire illustration by pressing one key instead of the 3 (Command-Shift-A), or instead of pulling down the Edit menu.

⌘-Shift-A Edit/Select None

6. With the rectangle still selected, click on the selection tool (black arrow) and click on any segment of the rectangle. The entire shape becomes selected and can now be moved—but not reshaped.

DIRECT-SELECTION TOOL TO MOVE ANCHOR POINTS

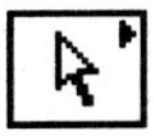

Direct-selection tool

When you select an object with the direct-selection tool, none of the anchor points are selected, which means that unless you select them, you can't move them. In the last exercise you clicked on a segment and dragged to move the segment. The segments between the anchor points moved and the anchor points moved with the segment, but only in relationship to the way the segment moved. The anchor points didn't move independently of the segment.

When you select an anchor point with the direct-selection tool, you can move that anchor point and force the segments connected to that anchor point to move with it. In other words, when you move a segment, the position of the segment determines the location of the anchor points. When you move an anchor point, the anchor point determines the position of the segment.

EXERCISE D

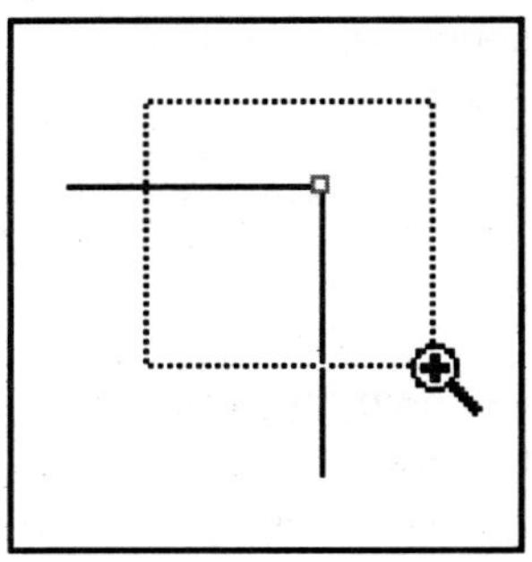

Drag the zoom tool around an area to magnify that area.

1. In a new or existing document, use the rectangle tool to create a rectangle. Choose View/Artwork (Command-E). The rectangle appears selected with all of its anchor points solid.
2. Click on the direct-selection tool to select it. Click on an empty area of the page or choose Edit/Select None (Command-Shift-A) to deselect everything. Then click on any segment of the rectangle to display its anchor points.
3. The anchor points are hollow, indicating that they are not selected and that they will move only in relation to a segment.
4. Use the zoom tool to draw a marquee around the upper right point to magnify it.
5. Use the direct-selection tool and click once on the upper right point to select it and release the mouse button. It becomes solid, indicating that it is selected and therefore can be edited (moved).
6. Click on the selected point and move it down and to the left until it meets the center point of the rectangle. You'll know you've reached the center point when the black cursor becomes hollow (Figure 2.6).

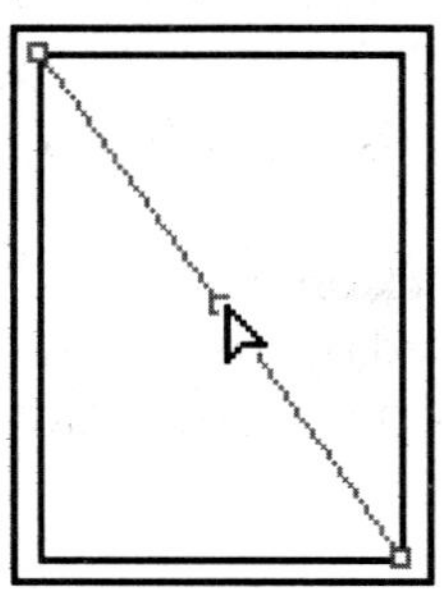

Figure 2.6—When you move the top right point down toward the center point, the cursor turns into a white arrow, indicating that both the top point and center point are touching.

7. Release the mouse button. Notice that by moving the point, you've also moved the segments related to that point and reshaped the rectangle into a triangle. However, the four segments of the original rectangle still exist. What happened is that when you moved the anchor point which connected those two segments, you positioned the segments so that they became tangential.

⌘-Z Edit/Undo

8. Choose Edit/Undo Move (Command-Z) to restore the rectangle to its original shape. Then use the direct-selection tool (white arrow) to drag the center point in the rectangle. Notice that once you clicked and dragged that center point, all of the points became selected and the entire object moved.

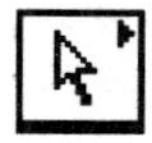

Direct-selection tool

CORNER POINTS AND SMOOTH POINTS

Points in Illustrator can be either corner points or smooth points. Corner points connect line segments and noncontinuous curve segments. Smooth points connect the segments of continuous curve paths, those paths which follow a continuous wavy shape (Figure 2.7)

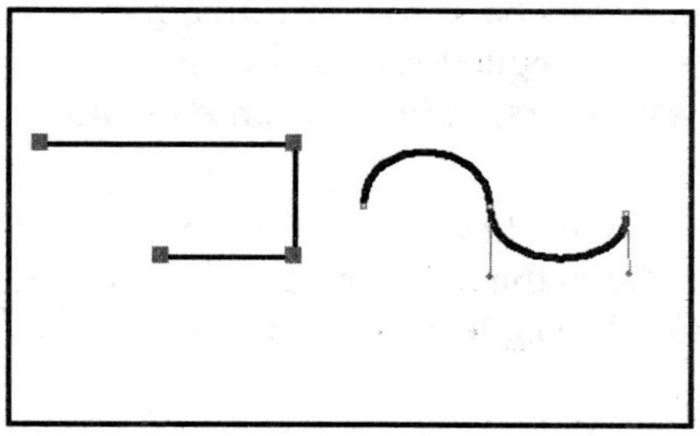

Figure 2.7—The path on the left is comprised of 4 corner points connecting the 3 line segments. The path on the right is comprised of 3 curve points connecting 2 curved segments.

When you click with the direct-selection tool (white arrow) on a segment connected to a smooth point, direction handles appear which allow you to manipulate the segments on either side of the anchor point. When you click on a corner point and move its direction handle, only the curve segment on the same side of the point as the direction handle is adjusted (Figure 2.8).

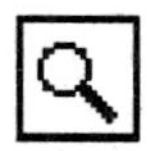

Zoom tool

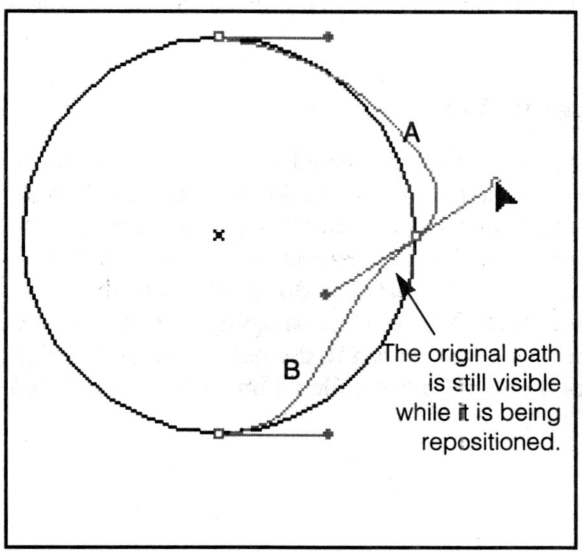

Figure 2.8—Moving the direction handle on a smooth point moves both segments (A and B) on either side of the point simultaneously. The anchor point does not move while the segments are being repositioned.

⌘-Shift-A Edit/Select None
⌘-E View/Artwork
⌘-Z Edit/Undo

Selection tool

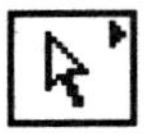

Direct-selection tool

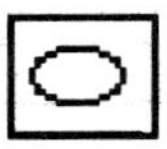

Oval tool

All gone!

If you inadvertently deselect the object and the direction handles disappear, use the direct-selection tool to click on the anchor point and they will reappear.

EXERCISE E

1. If necessary, double-click on the zoom tool to return the page to its actual display size. Choose Edit/Select All (Command-A) and press the Delete key to delete everything on the page.
2. Choose View/Artwork (Command-E). Click on the oval tool and press the Shift key before dragging to create a circle. It appears with all 5 of its points selected.
3. Click on the selection tool (black arrow) and click on any segment of the circle. Drag the entire circle around the page.
4. Choose Edit/Select None (Command-Shift-A) to deselect the circle. Click on the direct-selection tool (white arrow) and click on the upper right segment of the circle. It appears selected, with all of its points hollow. Notice, however, that the segment you clicked also displays two direction handles poking out from the two anchor points (Figure 2.8). This is because a circle is comprised of smooth points, whereas a rectangle is comprised of corner points. Corner points don't have direction handles, whereas smooth points have two direction handles. A direction handle is used to adjust the segments on either side of the anchor point. When you move these levers, only the segments move, not the anchor point (Figure 2.8).
5. With the direct-selection tool still active, click on the *tip* of the lower direction handle and move the handle to the right and left. Notice that the anchor point doesn't move; only the segments on either side of the anchor point move.
6. Choose Edit/Undo Move (Command-Z) to restore the circle to its original shape. Then click on the upper direction handle and move it up and down and right and left. Notice again how only the segments connected to the anchor point move; the anchor point itself doesn't move.
7. If you click on the center anchor point, you will select the entire object, just as if you had used the selection tool. If that happens, click on any blank area of the page, *then* click on a segment with the direct-selection tool.

DRAWING AN OPEN PATH

An open path is a segment or group of connected segments in which the last segment is not connected to the first segment. For example, a rectangle is a closed path because the last segment, the fourth segment in the object, shares the same anchor point as the first segment in the object (Figure 2.3). With an open path, however, the last segment does not share the same anchor point as the first segment. A line, for example, is an open path because the first anchor point is not connected to the last anchor point (Figure 2.1). In fact, in Illustrator an open path is called a line, whereas a closed path is called a shape.

EXERCISE F

1. Choose View/Artwork (Command-E). Click on the freehand tool and click and drag to draw a line. It doesn't have to be straight.
2. When you release the mouse button, the line (path) displays all the anchor points between the segments as hollow (deselected) except for the last anchor point, which appears filled (selected). Don't confuse the direction handles extending from the point with the point itself.
3. Click on the zoom tool and drag a marquee around that last point to enlarge the display of just that point. Click on the direct-selection tool and click on that last point (the endpoint). Drag the point to adjust the position of the last segment on the path.
4. Then click and drag on the top of the direction handle to change the slope of the segment.

⌘-E View/Artwork
⌘-T View/Hide/Show Toolbox
⌘-N File/New
⌘-S File/Save

Freehand tool

Direct-selection tool

REVIEW EXERCISE

1. Create a new document (File/New). Make sure the Tool palette is displayed (Command-Control-T). Choose View/Artwork (Command-E).
2. Click on the freehand tool to select it and move the cursor onto the page, where it changes into a pencil.
3. Click and drag to draw a heart, just as if you were drawing with a pencil. Don't worry if your heart looks like a coronary disaster; you'll fix it later.
4. When you release the mouse button, the heart appears with all its points deselected (hollow). Click on the direct-selection tool (white arrow) and click and drag on a segment to reposition it. Click on a hollow point to select that point and move the point. Continue to move segments and points to reshape the heart until it resembles an organ in the human body.
5. Choose File/Save (Command-S) and type Heart in the Save illustration as field. Choose Color Macintosh from the Preview pull-down menu. Scroll to select a drive and/or folder to store the file and click on Save.

FYI

The first and last anchor points of an open path are called endpoints.

REVIEW QUESTIONS

Read the following questions and choose the answer which best completes the statement.

1. To view an illustration with its applied colors, fills, and strokes, use the _____ mode.
   a. Artwork
   b. Preview
   c. Template
   d. Selection

2. To view an illustration as a wireframe image, use the _____ mode.
   a. Artwork
   b. Preview
   c. Template
   d. Selection
3. The line or curve between any two anchor points is called _____.
   a. an endpoint
   b. a segment
   c. a direction handle
   d. a closed path
4. Anchor points _____.
   a. are hollow when selected
   b. are solid when selected
   c. can be moved with the selection tool
   d. b and c
5. The selection tool selects _____.
   a. anchor points
   b. segments
   c. an entire path
   d. all of the above
6. To select only a path segment, use the _____.
   a. selection tool
   b. direct-selection tool
   c. group selection tool
   d. a and b
7. The direction handles on a smooth point affect only _____.
   a. the selected anchor point
   b. the segment on one side of a direction handle
   c. a and b
   d. the segments on either side of each direction handle
8. To move an anchor point, first _____.
   a. select it with the direct-selection tool
   b. select it with the selection tool
   c. drag the zoom tool around it
   d. b and c
9. An object in which the last segment is connected to the anchor point of the first segment is called a_____.
   a. line
   b. shape
   c. closed path
   d. b and c
10. An object in which the last segment is not connected to the anchor point of the first segment is called _____.
    a. a path
    b. an open path
    c. a line
    d. b and c

Answers: 1. b; 2. a; 3. b; 4. d; 5. d; 6. b; 7. d; 8. a; 9. d; 10. d

LESSON

3

The Paint Style Palette

OVERVIEW

In this lesson you will learn how to create and apply colors from the Paint Style palette. You will fill objects with colors and patterns and create custom process colors, as well as add colors to and delete colors from the Paint Style palette. You will also learn how to apply a painted stroke to an object.

TOPICS

Adobe Illustrator Preferences file
The Paint Style palette
Palette Display Menu
Applying a fill
Process colors
Storing colors in the Paint Style palette
Selecting multiple filled objects
Filling with Black, White, and None
The Stroke command
Applying a custom color
Defining a custom color
Pattern fills
Review Exercise
Review Questions

TERMS

custom color
fill
Paint Style palette
process color
stroke

TUTORIAL FILES

Stars.ai

ADOBE ILLUSTRATOR PREFERENCES

When learning Adobe Illustrator, it is best to start with the program's default settings, especially as they apply to the colors and patterns that ship with the program and appear in the Paint Style palette. To ensure that you are working with Illustrator's default settings, first quit Adobe Illustrator if you have already launched the program. Then open the System folder and scroll to locate the Preferences folder. Open the Preferences folder and drag the Adobe Illustrator Prefs file out of the folder and into the Trash icon. Be sure to empty the Trash icon. Now launch Adobe Illustrator, which will create a new Preferences file that includes all of the program's default settings.

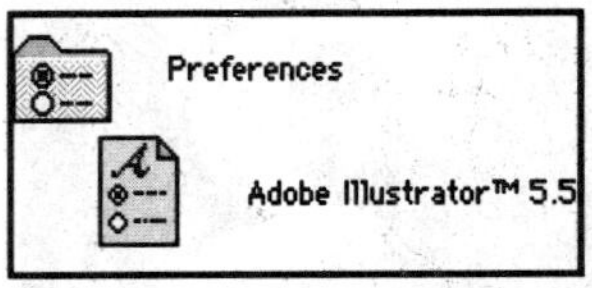

Locate the Adobe Illustrator Preferences file in the Preferences folder in the System folder.

THE PAINT STYLE PALETTE

So powerful is the Paint Style palette (Figure 3.1), that it is accessed from two menus, the Object and Window menus. This palette is the "command center" for all color application in Adobe Illustrator. Use it to define fill and stroke attributes for paths, to sample with the eyedropper tool and paint with the paint bucket tool, to define and clear a set of paint swatches, to define custom colors such as Pantone colors, to create gradients, and to fill paths with patterns.

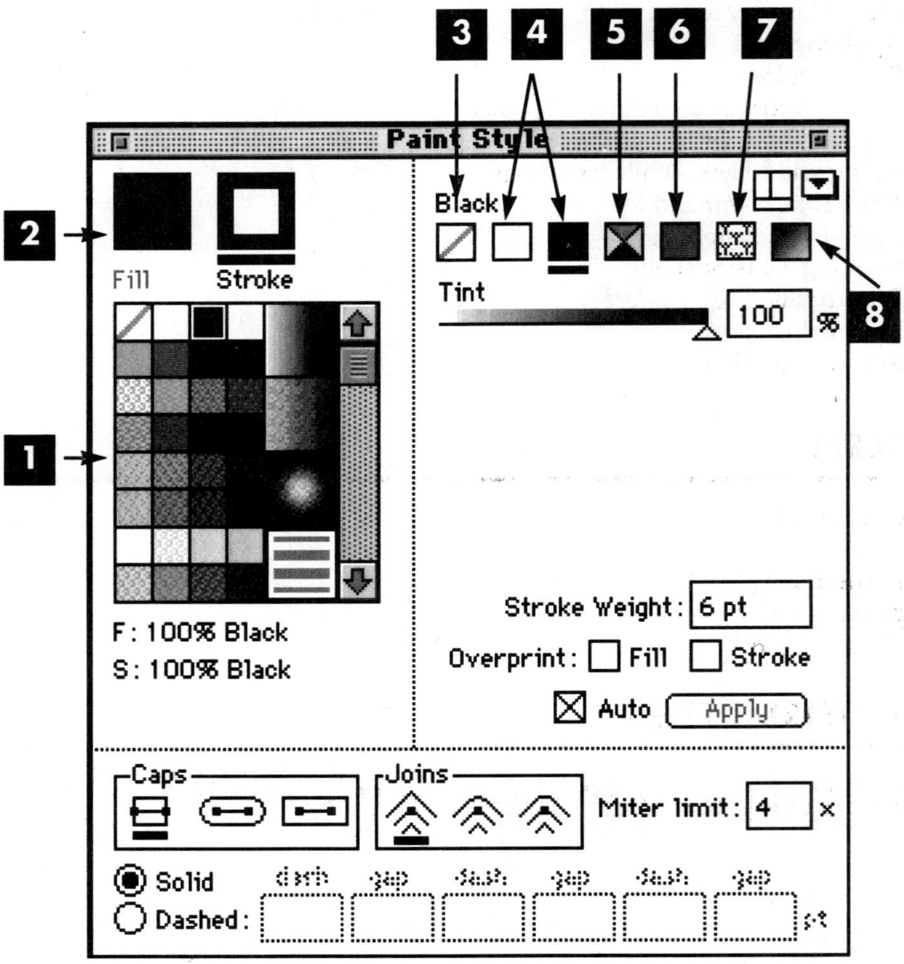

Figure 3.1—The Paint Style palette: **1. Paint swatches.** Click on the first box in the first row to remove a fill or stroke from a path, or click on one of the color swatches to apply a fill or stroke color to a path or object. **2. Fill and Stroke boxes**. Select before applying a fill or stroke to a path. The selected box displays a black line beneath it, indicating that color will be applied as a stroke or as a fill. **3. None option** for fills and strokes. **4. White or Black options**. **5. Process Color option** causes the Fill or Stroke box (whichever is selected) to display the composite process color and adjustment sliders. **6. Custom Color option** displays a list of the document's available custom colors. A custom color can be either a process color mix you've named and saved as a custom color or a predefined color from another color matching system. **7. Pattern option** for creating and using patterns. **8. Gradient option** for creating and applying gradient fills.

PALETTE DISPLAY MENU

Three major areas of the Paint Style palette (Figure 3.1) are accessed from the panel display menu. The left side of the palette is where you select the fill and stroke functions. You also select colors to be applied as fills and strokes to selected objects from the swatches, all of which are accessed by using the scroll bars to the right of the swatches.

The second area of the palette, on the right, is where you select the kind of color you will be applying, the pattern, or the gradient fill. If you are using process colors, the CMYK percentage sliders will appear. If you have imported or loaded custom colors such as Pantone colors, those colors will appear in a scroll box on this side of the palette. If you are applying a stroke to a line or path, the weight of that stroke is specified in the Stroke Weight field below the colors.

The lower area of the palette displays options for caps and joins, which affect the endpoints of lines and the way one line attaches to another. It is also from this part of the palette that you specify solid or dashed lines.

⌘-I Object/Paint Style
⌘-Y View/Preview

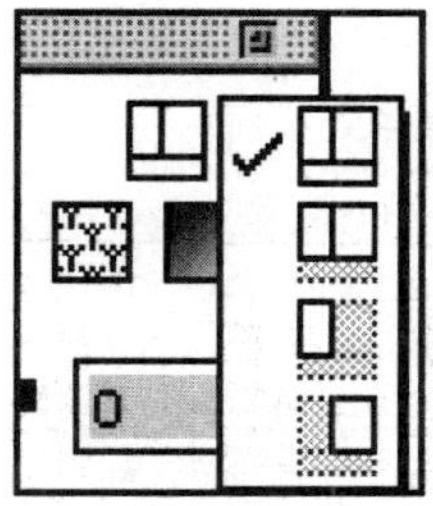

The panel display menu in the Paint Style palette allows you to determine how much of the palette will be displayed. The check mark before the three-part panel indicates that all three of the palette's areas are displayed on the screen.

APPLYING A FILL

You can apply a fill to both open and closed paths. The first time you create a path, that path automatically fills with black whether or not you are displaying the Paint Style palette. Before a path can be filled, however, it must be selected with any of the selection tools. If you're applying a fill and nothing happens, it's probably because you've forgotten to select the object.

To fill more than one object with the same fill, use any selection tool to select the first object, press the Shift key, and select the other objects you wish to fill. When you select a color from the Paint Style menu, all the selected objects will display that one fill.

FYI

You can fill both open and closed paths. However, when you fill a closed path, Illustrator will draw an invisible line between the two endpoints and fill in the entire object.

EXERCISE A

1. Choose Object/Paint Style (Command-I) to display the Paint Style palette. It appears with the right, left, and bottom panels visible.
2. Change the display by clicking on the black triangle in the upper right corner to display the four palette display options. The first one displays all three panels and is checked, indicating that it is the current display. Selecting the one below it displays only the left and right panels. Selecting the one below that displays the left panel. Checking the lowest icon displays only the right panel.
3. Practice changing the Paint Style palette display by selecting different icons from the panel display menu.

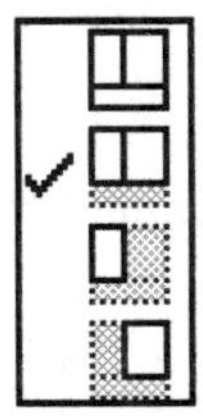

The check mark next to the double panel indicates that only the left and right panels of the Paint Style palette are currently displayed.

EXERCISE B

1. Choose View/Preview (Command-Y) to view the fill colors as you apply them. Use the rectangle tool to draw a rectangle. Choose Object/Paint Style (Command-I) to display the Paint Style palette. Use the panel display menu to display only the left and right panels.

⌘-Y View/Preview

2. Make sure the Auto button is selected in the lower right panel. Choose View/Preview (Command-Y) to view the fills and strokes as you apply them.
3. Select the rectangle and click on the Fill box in the upper right panel. A black line appears beneath the box, indicating that any color properties will be applied as a fill to the selected object.

WARNING!

If the Auto box is selected (checked) in the lower right panel, the objects will fill as soon as you click on the color swatch. If Auto is deselected (the box is empty), you have to double-click to apply the fill color, click on the Apply button in the lower right panel after clicking on one of the color swatches, or press the Enter key after clicking on the color swatch.

4. Click on the first of the seven color options icons, the one with the diagonal line. This is the None selector which removes any fill from the selected item if the Fill box is checked; otherwise, it removes a stroke if the Stroke box is selected.
5. With the rectangle still selected, click on the second color options icon, the white one. This fills (or strokes) with white.
6. Now click on the third color options icon, the black one. This fills (or strokes) with black.
7. Click on the fourth color options icon, the Process Color icon. Four sliders appear which allow you to create a color based on percentages of cyan, magenta, yellow, and black.
8. Draw a few rectangles and ovals and fill them with different colors by clicking on the small color swatches in the Paint Style palette.

PROCESS COLORS

Process colors are made up of varying percentages of cyan, magenta, yellow, and black. During the printing process, these colors will be printed on separate pages of film before going to a four-color printing press. If, for example, you assign a red process color to an object, that object will appear on both the magenta and yellow pages when the colors are separated, because red is a combination of magenta and yellow. The press will first print the yellow ink and then print the magenta ink on top of it to create the specified shade of red.

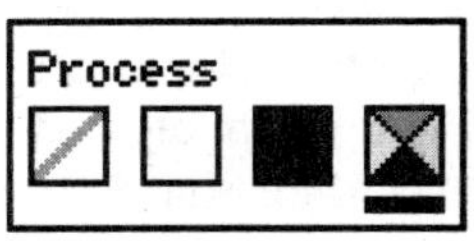

When the Process Color icon is selected, a bar is displayed beneath the icon and *Process* appears over the color options strip.

When you click on the Process Color icon at the top of the Paint Style palette—the fourth icon in the color options strip—four sliders appear (Figure 3.2). Use these sliders to define colors in percentages of cyan, magenta, yellow, and black by either moving the triangles under the sliders or typing values in the % fields on the right.

As you adjust the percentages, the new color appears in the Fill or Stroke box, depending on which one you have selected. Also, if you have an object or objects selected, that color will appear as a fill or stroke in the object(s).

FYI

To adjust color saturation when creating a process color, press the Shift key while moving any of the sliders. This adjusts all the triangles simultaneously and allows you to adjust the overall color value without affecting the individual CMYK proportions.

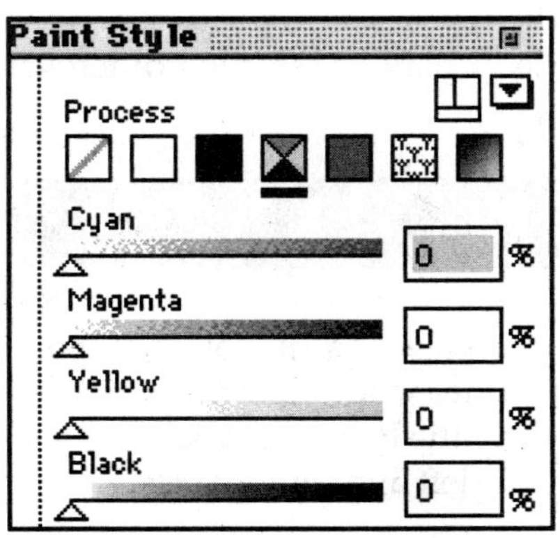

Figure 3.2—When the Process Color icon is selected, the four process color sliders appear. Type in a value or move the sliders to create a process color.

EXERCISE C

1. Choose Edit/Select All (Command-A) and press the Delete key to clear the screen. Choose View/Preview (Command-Y).
2. Display the Paint Style palette (Command-I) and click on the Fill icon on the left panel. Make sure the Auto box on the right panel is selected.
3. Use the rectangle and oval tools to draw objects on the screen. Use the selection tool to select one object.
4. Click on the Process Color icon on the right side of the Paint Style palette, the fourth icon, to display the CMYK sliders.
5. Click on the white triangles beneath each slider and drag to create a deep mauve process color. You can also create the color by typing the CMYK percentages in the % fields to the right of sliders (Figure 3.3). The color appears in the Fill box on the left panel and fills the selected object.

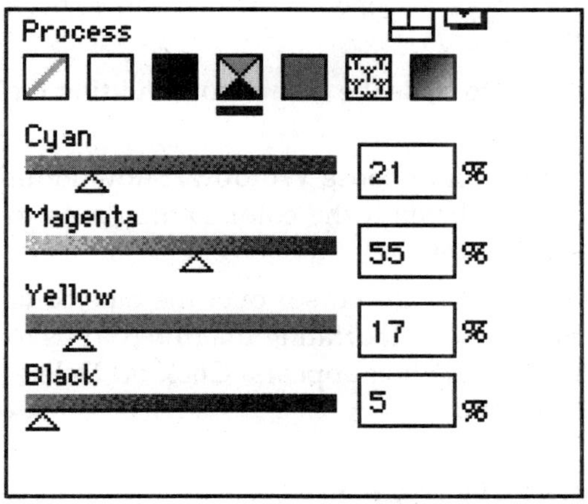

Figure 3.3—Displays the CMYK sliders and % fields which appear when the Process Color icon is selected.

6. With an object still selected, click on any of the small color swatches displayed in the left panel. The cursor changes to the eyedropper tool, and not only does the object fill, but the CMYK sliders also display the percentages of cyan, magenta, yellow, and black for that color. Because the Auto button is checked, the object fills immediately. If the Auto button were not checked, you would have to either double-click on the swatch or click on the swatch and then press the Enter key.

STORING COLORS IN THE PAINT STYLE PALETTE

Any color you create using the Paint Style palette can be stored in the palette and saved with the file. This means that the color will always be available whenever you open the file.

You can store a newly created color by dragging it from the Fill or Stroke box to an empty swatch box on the left panel. If you drag the new color over an existing color on the left panel, the new color will replace the previous color.

Use the scroll bars in the color swatch area to scroll down and locate the blank swatches which you can fill with your new colors.

⌘-A Edit/Select All
⌘-Y View/Preview
⌘-I Object/Paint Style

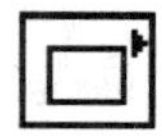

Rectangle tool

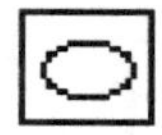

Oval tool

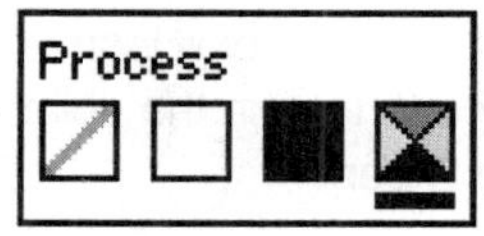

Process color icon selected in the color options strip

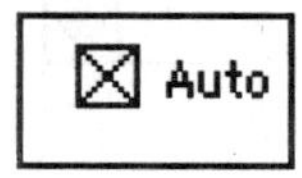

If Auto is selected (checked) in the right panel, colors will be applied to selected objects as soon as the color is selected or created.

Tip

You can quickly apply a color from the Fill or Stroke box to the paint swatch area by Option-clicking on one of the existing swatches or on an empty swatch.

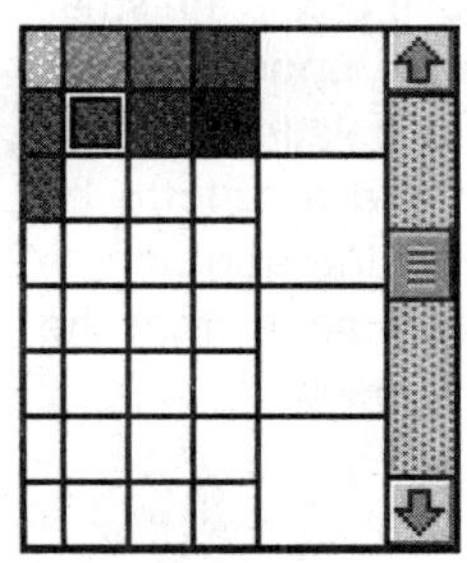

Use the scroll bars to find an empty swatch area to hold your new color.

⌘-I Object/Paint Style
⌘-S File/Save
⌘-W File/Close
⌘-O File/Open
⌘-Shift-A Edit/Select None

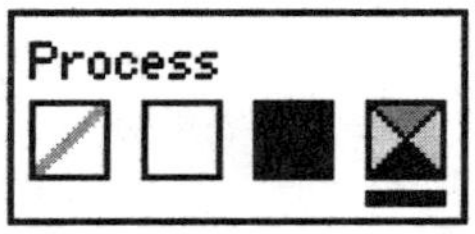

The Process Color icon is the fourth icon in the color options panel.

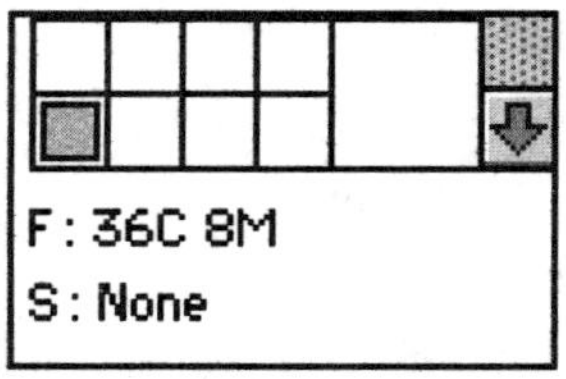

When a process color is selected for the Fill, its CMYK values appear below the color swatch area in the Paint Style palette. The stroke value for the currently selected object is None.

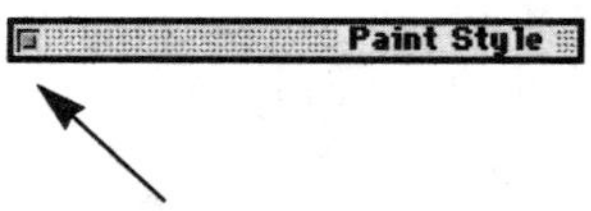

The close box is the small box in the upper left corner of a palette. You can also close a palette by choosing the appropriate Hide command from the Window menu.

EXERCISE D

1. Use the rectangle and oval tools to create a few objects. Display the Paint Style Palette (Command-I), click on the Fill box, and click on the Process Color icon in the color strip area.
2. *Deselect* the Auto option by clicking in the Auto box on the right panel until it is empty.
3. Type 36 in the Cyan % field and 8 in the Magenta % field. Leave the Yellow and Black fields at 0 to create a soft blue color.
4. Click on the Apply button next to the Auto button to apply the new blue color to the selected object.
5. Scroll in the paint swatch area in the left panel to display an empty swatch. Click in the Fill box and drag the blue color down to the empty swatch. Click on the Close box on the Paint Style palette to close the palette, or choose Window/Hide Paint Style.
6. Choose File/Save (Command-S), type a name for the file, and select a folder and drive. Click on Save.
7. Choose File/Close (Command-W) to close the file without quitting the program.
8. Choose File Open (Command-O) and choose Window/Show Paint Style or press Command-I. Scroll through the color swatch area to locate the blue color you saved with the file.
9. Press the Command key (⌘) and move the cursor over the blue color swatch. The cursor changes to a scissors, indicating that the color is to be deleted. Click the mouse. An Alert box appears. Click on Delete. The color is removed from the palette.

SELECTING MULTIPLE FILLED OBJECTS

When you select an object to which a fill has been applied, the color of the fill appears in the Fill box on the palette. But if you Shift-select objects to which different fills have been applied (Figure 3.4), a question mark appears in the Fill box on the palette. Since you can display only one color at a time in the Fill box, deselect the multiple selection (Command-Shift-A) and select only one object. The fill color for that one object is displayed in the Fill box.

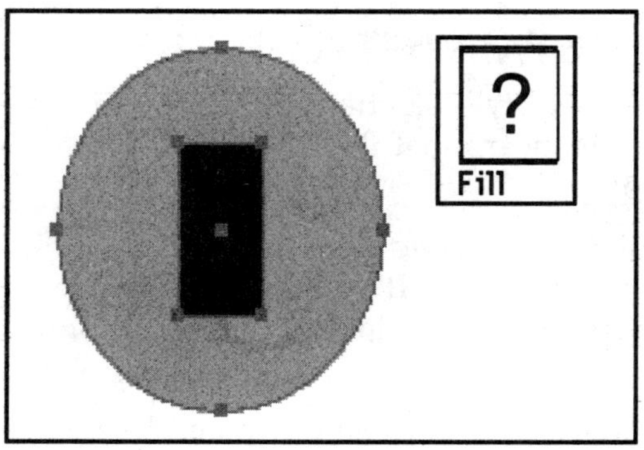

Figure 3.4—If multiple objects containing different fills are selected, a question mark appears in the Fill box on the right panel of the Paint Style palette.

FILLING WITH BLACK, WHITE, AND NONE

You can fill any object with black (or a tint of black) or white. To fill a selected object with black, click on the Black icon in the color options area on the right panel. When you do this, a Tint slider appears, allowing you to set the tint from 100% (black) to 0% (white). Likewise, to fill a selected object with white, click on the White icon in the color options area and use the Tint slider to create a tint anywhere from 100% (white) to 0% (black) (Figure 3.5).

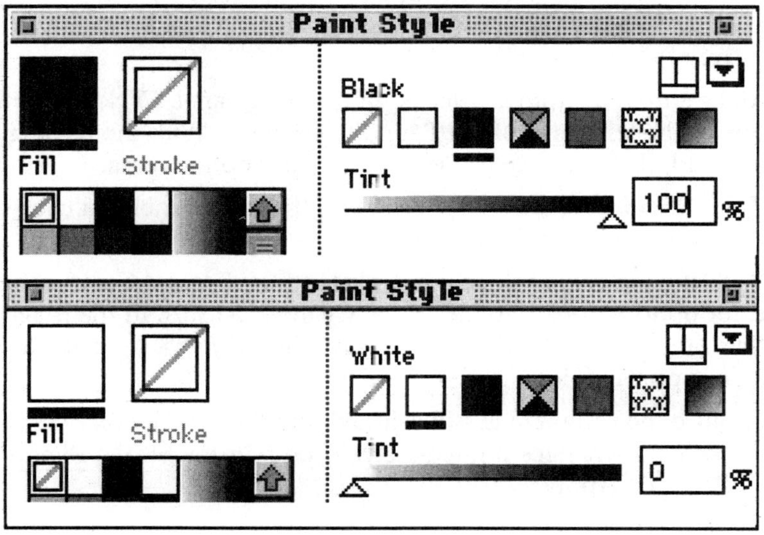

Figure 3.5—Clicking on the Black icon in the Color Options strip (top) changes the fill to 100% black and displays the Tint slider where you can reduce the tint value. To fill a selected object with whiter, click on the White icon in the Color Options strip and adjust the Tint slider.

To fill a selected object with nothing, click on the None icon in the color options panel. A diagonal line appears in the Fill box and the object becomes transparent (Figure 3.6).

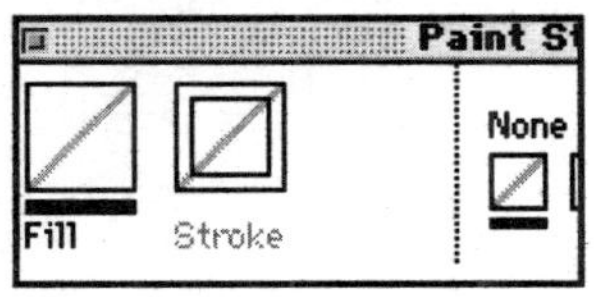

A diagonal line appears in the Fill box when None is selected from the color options.

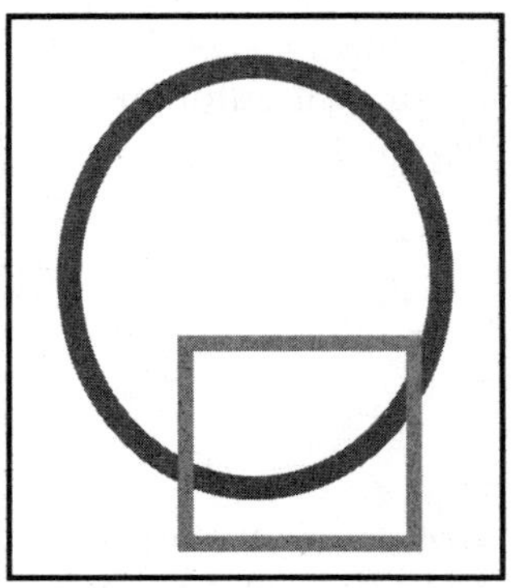

Figure 3.6—A fill of None was applied to the rectangle, making it transparent so that the circle filled with yellow shows through the rectangle.

⌘-Y View/Preview
⌘-N File/New
⌘-E View/Artwork
⌘-K File/Preferences/
General

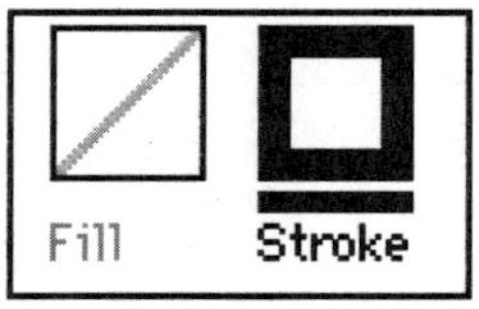

The Stroke box selected

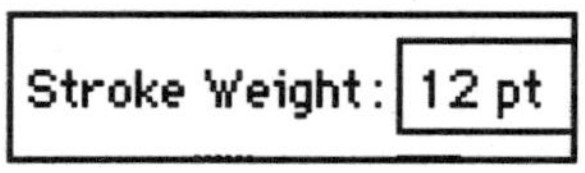

Type a value in the Stroke Weight field and click on the Apply button to apply the stroke to the selected object.

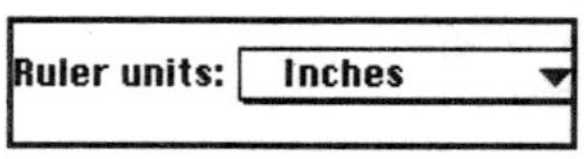

The unit of measure is selected in the General Preferences dialog box.

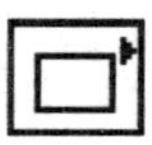

Rectangle tool

FYI

A value other than 0 in the Corner Radius field will result in rounded corners on the rectangle.

To create a square of specific dimensions, make both the Weight and Height values the same.

THE STROKE COMMAND

The Stroke command applies a stroke or border to the selected object. You can paint this stroke any color, just as you colored the fills. You can also specify a weight (in points) for the stroke from the Paint Style palette.

EXERCISE E

1. Choose View/Preview (Command-Y) and display the Paint Style palette. Use the rectangle tool to create a rectangle on the drawing page.
2. Make sure that Auto is selected in the right panel. Click on the Stroke box in the left panel of the Paint Style palette. With the rectangle still selected, click on the Black icon in the color options area.
3. Type 12 in the Stroke Weight field on the right panel and click on the Apply button to apply the stroke.
4. With the rectangle still selected, click on the Process Color icon in the color options area. Type 85 in the Cyan % field, 76 in the Magenta % field, and 6 in the Black % field. Leave the Yellow % field at 0 to create a deep purple color.
5. Because the rectangle is still selected and the Stroke box is active, the stroke color changes immediately. Type 5 in the Stroke Weight field and click on Apply.

EXERCISE F

1. Create a new document (Command-N) and choose View/Artwork (Command-E). Display the Paint Style palette (Command-I).
2. Choose File/Preferences/General (Command-K). In the lower part of the palette, use the Ruler Units pull-down menu to specify inches as the unit of measure. Click on OK.
3. Click on the rectangle tool to select it and then click in the center of the drawing page. When the Rectangle dialog box appears, type 3 in the Weight field and 5 in the Height field. Illustrator will automatically translate these values to inches. Click on OK (Figure 3.7).

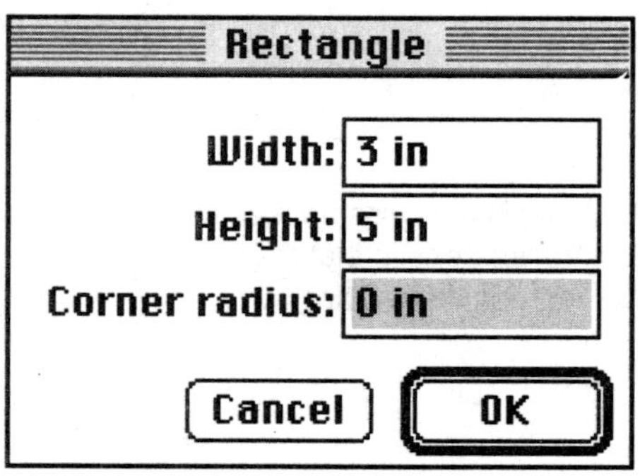

Figure 3.7—When you click with the rectangle tool on the drawing page, the Rectangle dialog box appears where you can specify a rectangle (or square) of specific dimensions.

⌘-Y View/Preview
⌘-= Arrange/Bring to Front

4. Click on the oval tool and click on the drawing page to display the Oval dialog box. Type 2 in the Weight field and 4 in the Height field. Click on OK.
5. Because you are in Artwork mode, you can see the outlines of the rectangle and the oval even though they have no fill or stroke. Use the selection tool to select the rectangle.
6. With the rectangle selected, click on the Fill button on the left panel, select the Auto button on the right panel, and then click on the Process Color icon in the color options area. Use the values in Figure 3.8 to create a deep turquoise color. You won't see the color because you are in Artwork mode, but it has been applied.

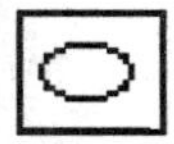

Oval tool

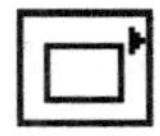

Rectangle tool

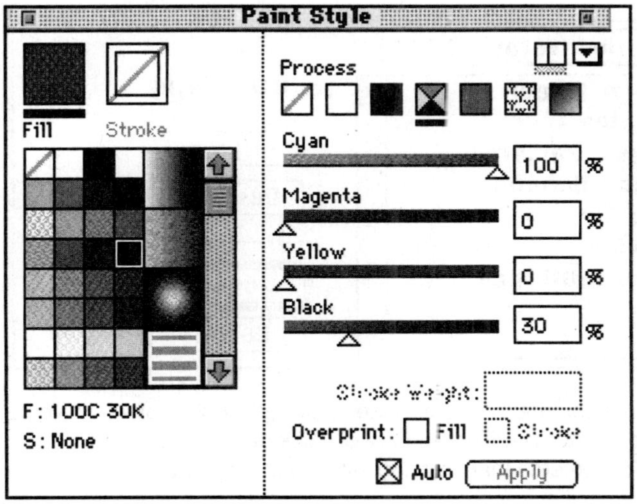

Figure 3.8—Use the Process Color options to create a deep turquoise color. Because the Auto button is checked, the selected object will fill as soon as the color is created or selected.

7. Use the selection tool to select the oval. Make sure the Fill box is selected in the Paint Style palette and click on the None icon in the color options strip.
8. Click on the Stroke box and click on the Black icon in the color options area. Type 10 in the Stroke Weight field and click the Apply button or press the Enter key to apply the stroke weight.
9. Select the rectangle and apply a 3-point black stroke. Click on Apply.
10. Choose View/Preview (Command-Y) and use the selection tool to move the oval on top of the rectangle so that only half of the oval is on the rectangle. With the oval still selected, choose Arrange/Bring to Front (Command-=). Because the None fill was applied to the oval, the rectangle is visible through the stroked oval. Your screen should resemble Figure 3.9.

Selection tool

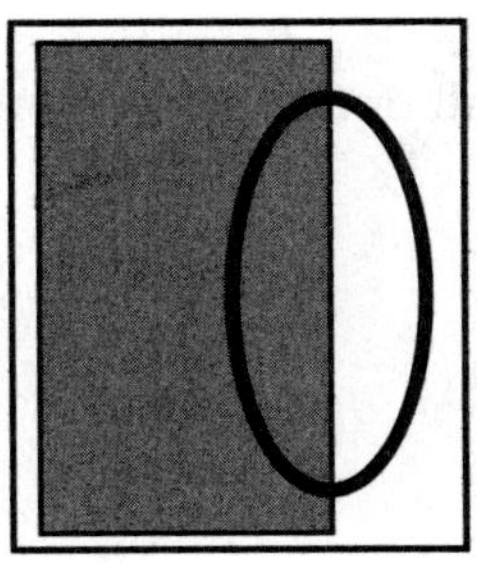

Figure 3.9—A stroke and fill was applied to the rectangle. A fill of None and a black stroke were applied to the oval. The None fill makes the oval transparent.

⌘-Y View/Preview

⌘-I Object/Paint Style

APPLYING A CUSTOM COLOR

A custom color is a process color you have mixed yourself then named and saved as a custom color. A custom color can also be a predefined color from another matching system, such as the Pantone Matching System. Any custom colors that you create in a document are saved with that document.

There are two ways to access custom colors. One way is to use the Open command to get to the Adobe Illustrator folder on your hard drive. Double-click on the Color Systems folder or highlight Color Systems and click on Open to select one of several color systems (Figure 3.10). Once the file is opened, resize it and position it in a corner of the screen since the colors have been loaded into the Paint Style palette.

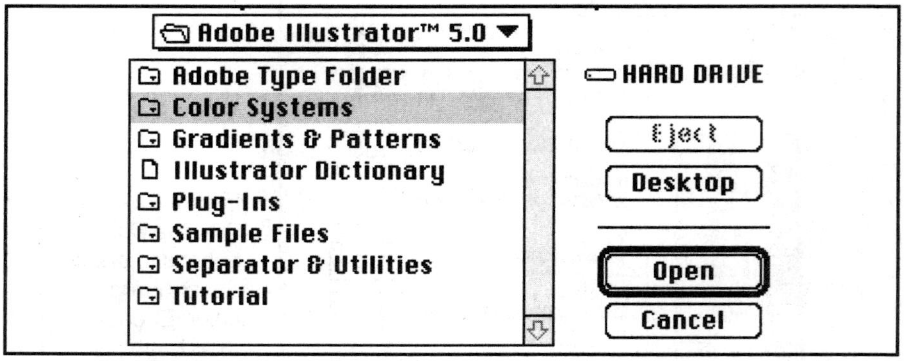

Figure 3.10—Use the Open command to get to the Adobe Illustrator folder on your hard drive where the Color Systems folder is located. Click on the Open button to access all the custom color systems that shipped with Adobe Illustrator.

Another way to access the different color systems is to use the Import Styles command under the File menu. The advantage of opening custom colors rather than importing them is that you can always close a custom color file after you select the colors you want. This frees up memory for the illustration itself or for other applications. Any custom colors you apply to the illustration are saved with that illustration even after you close the custom color file and the illustration file itself.

EXERCISE G

1. Choose View/Preview (Command-Y). Use any of the drawing tools to create a closed shape. Unless you trashed the Preferences file before launching Illustrator, the default paint attributes will be applied. Otherwise, the object will fill with black. Keep the object selected.

2. Choose Object/Paint Style (Command-I) to display the Paint Style palette. To select a custom color, first click on the Fill or Stroke box to indicate which attribute you want to change.

3. Select the Custom Color options box at the top of the palette. A list of the available custom colors appears (Figure 3.11). These are process colors which have been defined as custom colors and which ship with the Adobe Illustrator program.

⌘-O File/Open

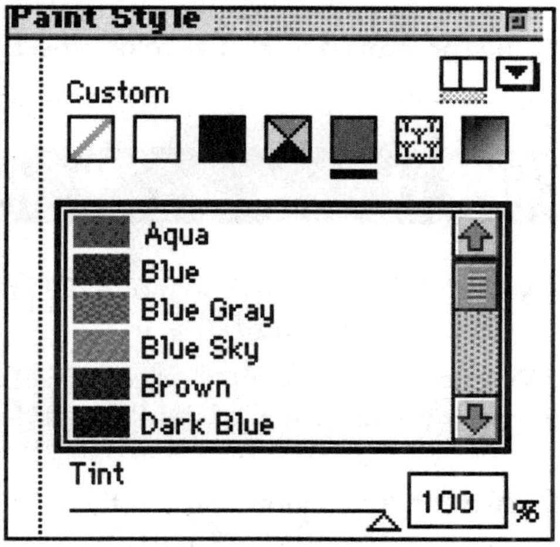

Figure 3.11—When you click on the Custom Color option, all of the predefined custom colors are loaded into the Paint Style palette.

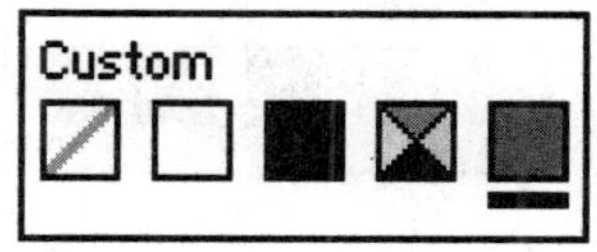

The word *Custom* appears over the Color Options strip when a custom color is selected.

4. Select the custom color by clicking either on the name or on its swatch. Then press either Enter or the Apply button on the palette if Auto is not selected. The color is applied as either a stroke or a fill to the selected object.

Selection tool

5. Use one of the drawing tools to draw another closed path. It automatically fills with the current custom color. Use the selection tool to Shift-select both objects.

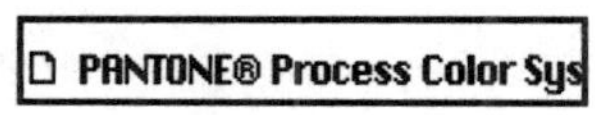

Pantone Colors for coated paper is one of the color models available that ships with Adobe Illustrator.

6. With the Custom Color icon still selected, scroll to select another custom color. Click on either the color swatch or the color's name. Press either Enter or the Apply button in the palette to apply the custom color to both objects.
7. Choose File/Open (Command-O) and scroll to the Adobe Illustrator folder on your hard drive. Open that folder and locate the Color Systems folder (Figure 3.10). Open that folder, then open the Pantone Colors (coated paper) file.
8. You may get an alert dialog box telling you that certain fonts are not available. Click on the Continue button.
9. Scroll through the color list on the right panel and notice that now the Pantone library of custom colors is available (Figure 3.12). You can apply these colors as a stroke or fill just as you would apply any other custom or process color.

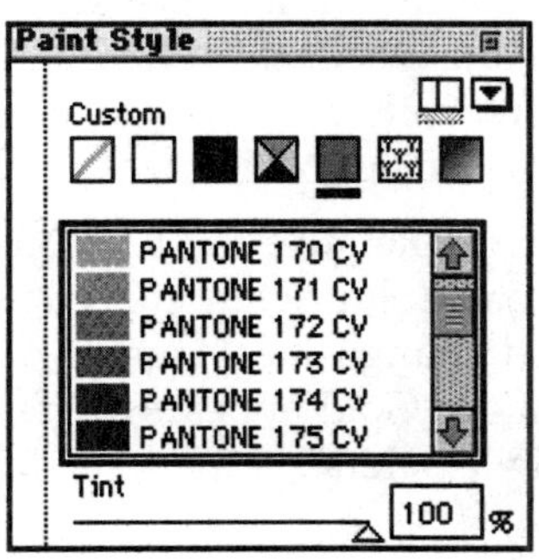

Figure 3.12—The Pantone System custom color library loads into the Paint Style palette and allows you to select a color and a Tint value for that color.

WARNING!

Any color *displayed* on the screen, whether it's a process color, custom color—or any color whatsoever—may not resemble the *printed* color. To match colors as precisely as possible, always select colors from the swatch book which is available for all the libraries in the Adobe Illustrator program.

⌘-N File/New
⌘-I Object/Paint Style
⌘-Y View/Preview

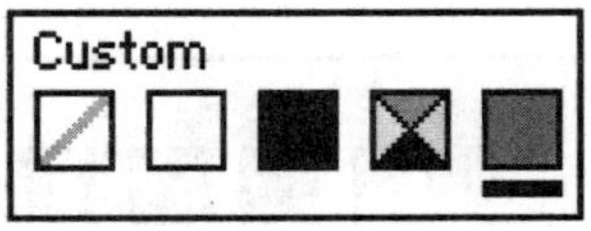

The Custom Color icon selected in the Paint Style palette.

DEFINING A CUSTOM COLOR

You can create colors, name them, apply them, store them, and edit them. Any custom color you create is saved with the file and available every time you open the file. You can also save the colors and then import them into another file. Whenever you make changes to a custom color, every object in the illustration which has been filled and/or stroked with that color reflects the change.

EXERCISE H

1. Create a new document (File/New) and select Preview mode (Command-Y). Display the Paint Style palette (Command-I).
2. Use the rectangle and oval drawing tools to draw three objects. Select one object and click on the Fill box in the left panel of the Paint Style palette.
3. Click on the Process Color icon in the colors option strip on the right panel of the Paint Style palette. A list of the available custom colors appears in the Colors scroll box.
4. Choose Object/Custom Color to display the Custom Color dialog box (Figure 3.13).

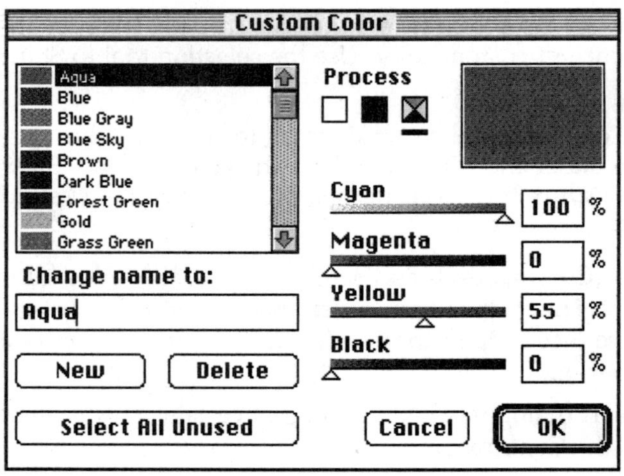

Figure 3.13—Use the Custom Color dialog box to define, rename, edit, and delete custom colors.

5. Click on Aqua and in the Change name to field below the color scroll box, type College Blue. Change the Magenta % value to 44 and the Yellow % value to 39 to create a deep blue-green color. Click on OK and notice that College Blue appears alphabetically in the color scroll box of the Paint Style palette. If you have Auto selected in the Paint Style palette, the selected object will automatically fill with College Blue. If not, press the Enter or the Apply button to apply the color.
6. Select another object on the drawing page. Make sure the Custom Color icon is selected. Choose Object/Custom Color again and click on Gold. Change Gold to College Gold and change the Magenta % value to 44. Click on OK and notice that College Gold appears alphabetically in the color scroll box of the Paint Style palette.

Tip

You can access the Custom Color dialog box by double-clicking on any custom color in the color scroll box in the Paint Style palette.

7. Click on the third object with the selection tool and choose Object/Custom Color. Click on New and type College Purple in the Change name to field. Change the % values to reflect those in Figure 3.14. Click on OK. If necessary, apply the new color to the third object on the drawing page.

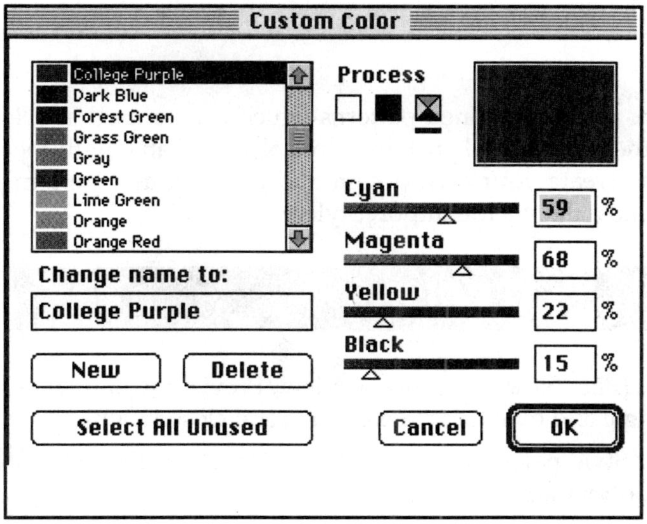

Figure 3.14—Create the College Purple color in the Custom Color dialog box by first clicking on New and then typing a name for the new color.

8. The colors scroll box on the right panel of the Paint Style palette should now include the three custom colors you created, College Blue, College Gold, and College Purple (Figure 3.15). You will now create a file with just those three colors and import them into a new file.

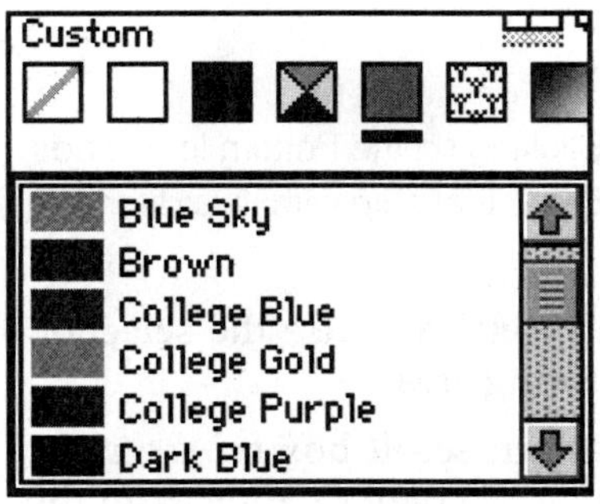

Figure 3.15—The three new colors are now included in the Colors scroll box on the right panel of the Paint Style palette and will appear when the Custom Color icon is selected.

9. Make sure that the three college colors and *only* those three colors have been applied to the three objects. Choose Object/Custom Color to display the Custom Color dialog box.

10. Click on the Select All Unused button. This selects every custom color in the file that was not applied as a stroke or fill in the illustration. Click on the Delete key to delete all the unused colors. Click on OK.

11. Choose File/Save (Command-S) and save the file as College Colors. Choose File/Close (Command-W). Choose File/Quit (Command-Q) to quit the program. If you don't quit, any file you open will contain only the three College Colors colors when you select the Custom Colors option.

⌘-S File/Save
⌘-W File/Close
⌘-Q File/Quit

Selection tool

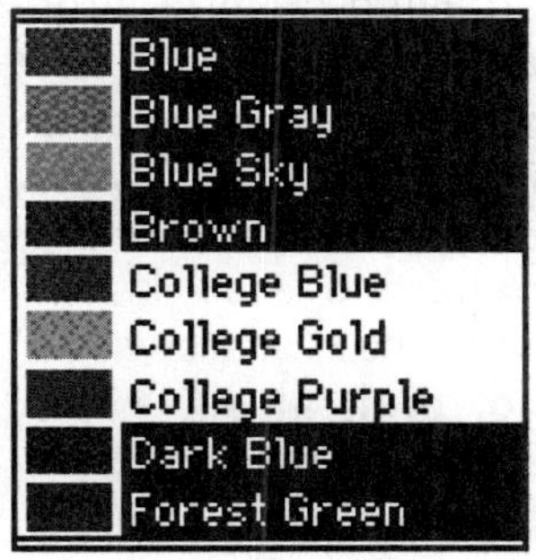

When you click on Select All Unused in the Custom Color dialog box, any color which has not been applied to an object is automatically selected and will be deleted from the Custom Colors scroll box when you click on the Delete button.

⌘-I Object/Paint Style
⌘-N File/New
⌘-Y View/Preview

12. Launch Adobe Illustrator, display the Paint Style palette (Command-I) and click on the Custom Colors icon in the color options strip.
13. Choose File/Import Styles and open the College Colors file you just saved. Notice that the three College Colors custom colors are now listed alphabetically in the custom colors scroll box and can be used in the new illustration.

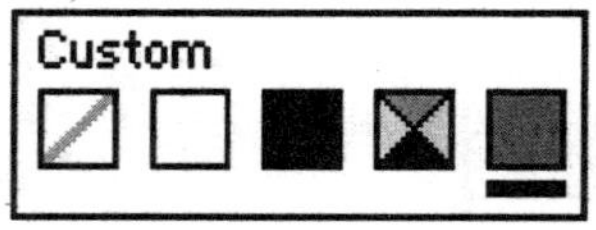

The Custom Color icon selected in the Paint Style palette.

PATTERN FILLS

Adobe Illustrator ships with predefined patterns which can be used as fill attributes, as well as the process and custom colors also available with the program. You can also create your own design and define it as a pattern which can be loaded into a file via the Import Styles command.

EXERCISE I

1. Create a new file (File/New) and choose View/Preview (Command-Y). Use the rectangle and oval tools to create several closed paths.
2. Display the Paint Style palette (Command-I) and click on the Pattern icon in the color options strip (Figure 3.16).

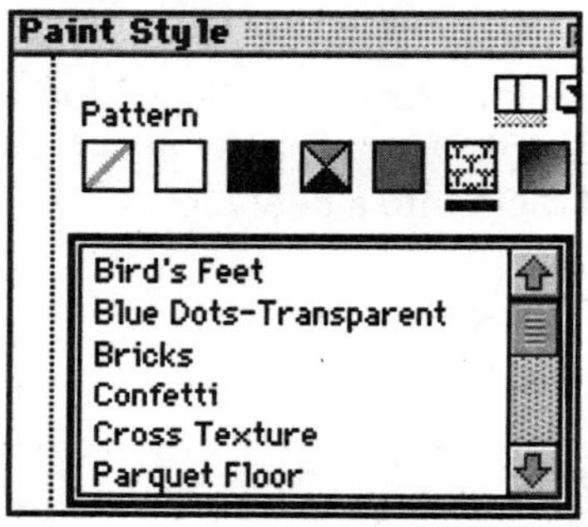

Figure 3.16—Clicking on the Pattern icon loads the various patterns that ship with Illustrator.

WARNING!

Patterns are pretty to look at on the screen, but applying them to large areas can slow down screen redraw and printing. If the pattern is too complicated and/or the patterned area is too large, the illustration might not print at all. Paths stroked with complicated patterns, for example, often will not print.

3. Click on the Fill box in the Paint Style palette and use the selection tool to select one of the objects on the drawing area.
4. Click on the Confetti pattern in the pattern scroll box on the right panel of the Paint Style palette. Notice that the pattern appears in the Fill box. If you have Auto checked, the selected object will fill immediately. Otherwise, press Enter or click on the Apply button to fill the object with the pattern.
5. Click on another object to select it and click on another pattern in the Paint Style palette to apply it to the selected object.
6. Choose File/Import Styles and get to the Adobe Illustrator folder on your hard drive. Open the folder and scroll to locate the Gradients and Patterns folder. Open that folder and open the Patterns folder. Scroll to select another pattern. Click on Import and notice that the pattern you selected is listed alphabetically in the pattern scroll box on the right panel.
7. Continue to import and apply patterns until you are comfortable with the procedure.

⌘-O File/Open
⌘-I Object/Paint Style

REVIEW EXERCISE

In this exercise you will open a file containing stars. Use the Paint Style palette to apply colors to the stars. Create custom colors and add them to the Paint Style palette. Then save the file under a new name, because you will make further color adjustments to the stars in the next lesson and you will use the stars to create an illustration of a landscape.

1. Open the Stars.ai file (Command-O) on the Tutorial disk. Display the Paint Style palette (Command-I).
2. Use the selection tool to select one star at a time and apply a different color to it.
3. Create at least one process color and apply it to one of the stars.
4. Create at least one custom color and apply it to one of the stars.
5. When you have applied colors to all the stars, save the file under a new name (File/Save As), because you will use it in a later lesson.

REVIEW QUESTIONS

Read the following questions and choose the answer which best completes the statement.

1. A diagonal line in the Fill or Stroke box indicates that _____.
   a. a custom color is selected in the illustration
   b. a diagonal line appears in the illustration
   c. the option is not selected
   d. the option is selected
2. To fill or stroke an object, _____.
   a. a custom color must be created
   b. the object must be selected
   c. use the direct-selection tool
   d. a and c
3. To apply a color immediately to a selected object, _____.
   a. select the Auto check box in the Paint Style palette
   b. press the Enter key
   c. click on the Apply button in the Paint Style palette
   d. click faster
4. Adjust the Paint Style palette display from _____.
   a. the keyboard
   b. the menu
   c. the Tool palette
   d. the Paint Style palette
5. Process colors are _____.
   a. a mix of cyan, magenta, yellow, and black percentages
   b. created via the Paint Style and Custom Color palettes
   c. loaded automatically into the Paint Style palette
   d. all of the above

6. Custom colors can be _____.
   a. saved with a file
   b. imported into a file
   c. process colors
   d. all of the above
7. A line weight is specified _____.
   a. in the Paint Style palette
   b. from the menu
   c. in the Line Tool dialog box
   d. a and c
8. Patterns _____.
   a. can be applied as fills and/or strokes
   b. are created in the Pattern dialog box
   c. are loaded into the Paint Style palette
   d. all of the above
9. When in Artwork mode, _____.
   a. shapes do not fill
   b. shapes are not stroked
   c. fills and strokes are not visible
   d. only anchor points are visible
10. A transparent object is created by _____.
   a. filling with White
   b. filling with None
   c. filling with a tint
   d. none of the above

Answers: 1. c; 2. b; 3. a; 4. d; 5. d; 6. d; 7. a; 8. d; 9. c; 10. b

LESSON 4

Gradients, Strokes, and Painting Tools

OVERVIEW

In this lesson you will learn how to apply gradient fills from the Paint Style palette and how to create, name, and edit custom gradient fills. You will be introduced to the pen tool, freehand tool, brush tool, eyedropper and paint bucket tools. You will also learn how to change the appearance of a line by changing its cap and join.

TOPICS

Gradient fills
The gradient fill tool
Creating a custom gradient fill
Line attributes
The freehand tool
Using the pen tool to draw dashed lines
Eyedropper and paint bucket tools
The brush tool
Review Exercise
Review Questions

TERMS

cap
dash/gap fields
gradient fill
join
line attributes
miter limit
start and stop indicators

TUTORIAL FILES

Caps & Joins.ai

⌘-N File/New
⌘-Y View/Preview
⌘-I Object/Paint Style

FYI

Before applying the Trap filter or manually trapping gradient fills, be sure to convert the custom colors to process colors.

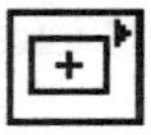

Double-clicking on the rectangle tool displays a plus sign, indicating that the rectangle or square will be drawn from its center outward.

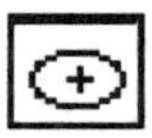

Double-clicking on the oval tool displays a plus sign, indicating that the oval or circle will be drawn from its center outward.

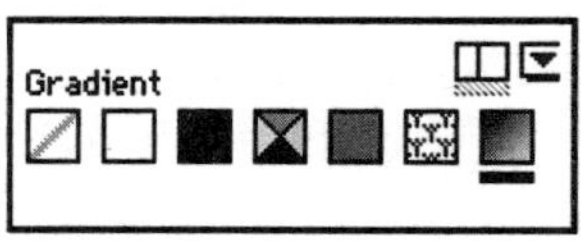

When the Gradient Color icon is selected, the word *Gradient* appears over the color options strip and a bar is displayed under the Gradient icon.

GRADIENT FILLS

A gradient fill is a graduated blend between colors. In the early days of the graphics industry (last year), you could only create a blend or gradient from one color to another. Illustrator 5 now allows you to blend up to 32 colors in one gradient fill.

Like color systems and patterns, several gradient fills are also loaded into the program when you select the Gradient icon in the color options strip on the Paint Style palette. Select a gradient and apply it to a selected object. A Gradient palette is also used to create custom gradient fills and the gradient tool is used to change the direction of the gradient fill within a selected object.

EXERCISE A

1. Create a new file (Command-N), choose View/Preview (Command-Y) and display the Paint Style palette (Command-I). Make sure that Auto on the right panel is selected.
2. Double-click on the rectangle tool. A plus sign appears in the center of the tool icon, indicating that the rectangle will be drawn from its center point.
3. Click and drag on the drawing page to draw a rectangle from its center outward. Leave the rectangle selected.
4. Click on the Fill box on the Paint Style palette. Click on the Gradient icon in the color options strip on the right panel of the Paint Style palette. The default gradient fills are loaded into the gradient scroll area (Figure 4.1).
5. Click on the name of a gradient and notice how it fills the selected rectangle. Change the Angle value to 45 and notice the different direction the gradient fill takes.
6. Double-click on the oval tool to display the centered-oval tool. The plus sign indicates that a circle or oval will be drawn from the center outward.

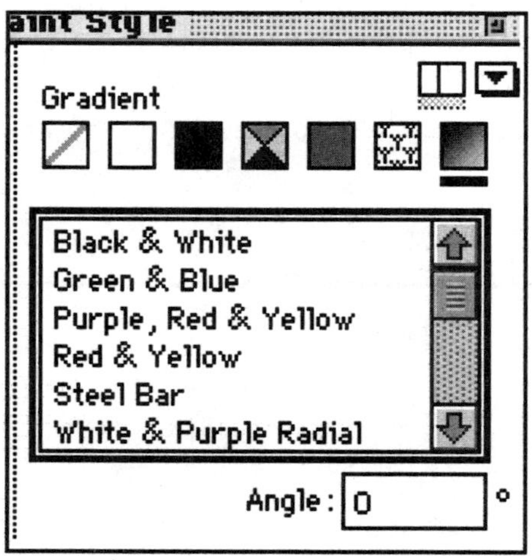

Figure 4.1—Clicking on the Gradient icon in the Paint Style palette loads the default gradient fills. Use the Angle field to specify an angle for the blend.

7. Click and drag to draw the oval, but before releasing the mouse button, press the Shift key to constrain the oval to a circle. Release the mouse button, *then* the Shift key.
8. Click on one of the radial fills in the gradient color scroll box. You cannot apply an Angle value for a radial fill but you can change the direction of the fill with the gradient fill tool.

⌘-A Edit/Select All
⌘-I Object/Paint Style
⌘-Y View/Preview
⌘-K File/Preferences/General

THE GRADIENT FILL TOOL

The gradient fill tool is used to change the direction of the blend in a selected object, to specify the starting and ending points of a gradient fill, and to apply a gradient fill across a group of selected objects.

EXERCISE B

1. Choose Edit/Select All (Command-A) to select all the objects on the screen and press the Delete key. Display the Paint Style palette (Command-I). Make sure that Auto is checked and that the Fill box is selected on the right panel.
2. Choose View/Preview (Command-Y).
3. Choose File/Preferences/General (Command-K) and use the Ruler Units pull-down menu to select inches. Click on OK.
4. Click once on the rectangle tool to select it and click in the center of the page. When the Rectangle dialog box appears, type 5 in the Width field and 3 in the Height field. Leave the Corner Radius field at 0. Click on OK. The rectangle will fill with the last selected fill.
5. Click on the Gradient icon in the color options strip to load the gradient fills.
6. With the rectangle still selected, click on the fill named Purple, Red, and Yellow. Make sure the Angle value is set to 0. The rectangle fills with a linear fill starting with purple, moving to red and ending with yellow.
7. Click on the gradient fill tool to select it. Click on the upper left corner of the rectangle and drag to the lower right corner. When the cursor changes to a white arrow, indicating that you have reached the end of the selected object, release the mouse button. The angle of the blend has been repositioned to 45° angle (Figure 4.2).

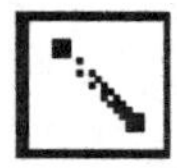

Gradient fill tool

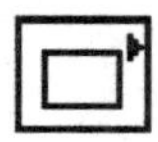

Rectangle tool

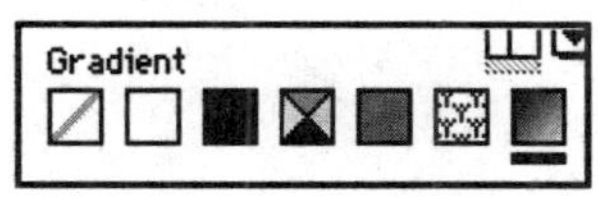

Gradient Color icon is selected in the color strip area.

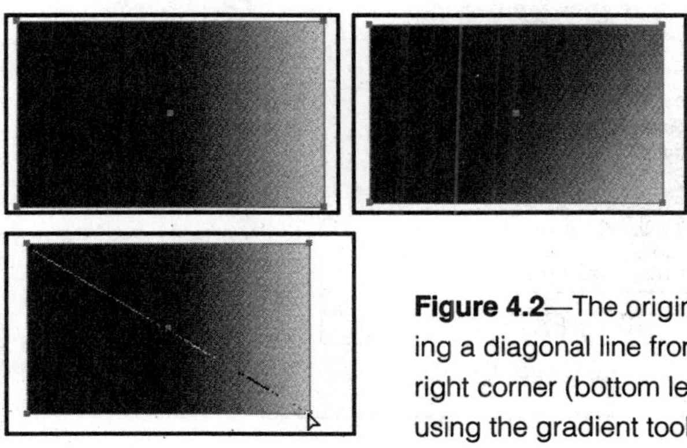

Figure 4.2—The original blend (top left), drawing a diagonal line from the top left to bottom right corner (bottom left), and the result of using the gradient tool (above).

⌘-Y View/Preview

8. Continue to click and drag with the gradient fill tool until you become comfortable with it.
9. Use the oval tool to draw ovals and circles (press the Shift key to constrain the oval to a circle), and fill with the radial fills. Then use the gradient fill tool to change the direction of the fills.

Gradient fill tool

10. Draw three circles and and use the selection tool to Shift-select them.
11. Select the Fill box on the left panel and click on the Red & Yellow fill on the right panel to fill all three circles with a red and yellow blend.
12. Select the gradient fill tool and click and drag from the first circle through the second and third circle. Instead of three separate red and yellow blends, the gradient distributes the blend among the three selected objects and fills from red to orange to yellow.

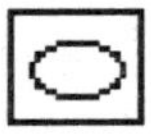

Oval tool

CREATING A CUSTOM GRADIENT FILL

Just as you created, named, and edited custom colors, so can you use the Gradient palette to create, name, and edit a linear or radial gradient fill. You can specify the starting and ending color of the fill as well as add other colors to the fill. When you create a radial fill, the starting point determines the filled object's highlighted (lighter) areas and the ending point defines its shadows (darker areas).

FYI

For the gradient fill tool to spread a fill among several objects, all of the objects must be selected with any selection tool.

EXERCISE C

1. Choose View/Preview (Command-Y) and display the Paint Style palette. Make sure that Auto is selected on the right panel. Use the rectangle tool to draw a large rectangle.
2. Click on the Gradient icon in the color options strip and click on Red & Yellow to fill the selected rectangle with a blend that goes from yellow to red.
3. Choose Object/Gradient to display the Gradient dialog box
4. The Gradient palette appears with a list of the currently available gradient fills. Click on the Red & Yellow gradient, then click on the Duplicate button to base the new fill on the existing Red & Yellow fill. Change the duplicate name to Mixed Red & Yellow by typing the new name in the highlighted field (Figure 4.3). Click on the Apply button.

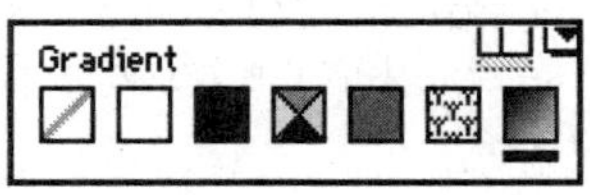

Gradient Color icon is selected in the color strip area

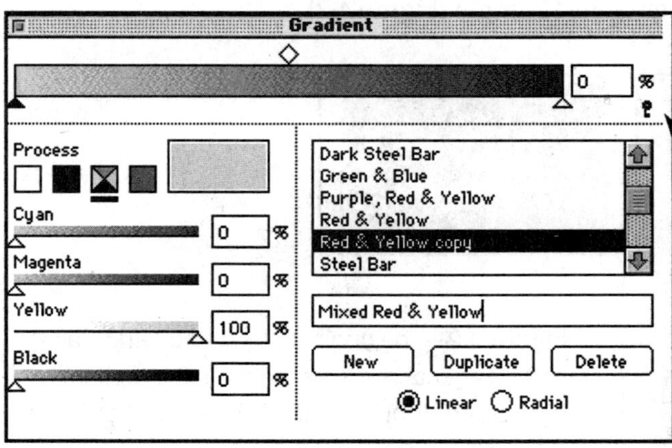

Figure 4.3—The Gradient dialog box. Click on the handle on the right to collapse the palette. Use the radio buttons at the bottom of the palette to select a linear or radial fill for new gradient fills.

5. The new name, Mixed Red & Yellow, appears not only in in the gradient scroll box, but also in the color scroll box on the Paint Style palette.
6. The current blend starts with yellow and blends into red. Notice the triangular color start and stop indicators at the beginning and end of the fade-out bar; these specify where the first color begins and where the second color ends. The diamond above the bar is the midpoint marker and indicates where the two colors mix in exactly the same amounts. The percentage field on the right displays the color percentage of the color at the start, midpoint, and end of the blend.

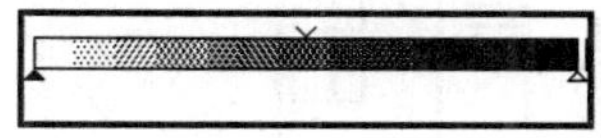

The triangle on the left is the start triangle and is currently selected. The triangle on the right is the stop triangle and indicates where the gradient fill ends.

7. Click on the left triangle beneath the start of the bar and notice that the % field remains at 0. Click on the midpoint marker and the % field reads 50. Click on the endpoint marker at the right end of the bar and the % field displays 100.
8. Begin by switching the start and stop colors. Click on the start triangle on the left and drag it to the right until it sits on top of the endpoint triangle. The red and yellow colors switch positions, and when the start triangle is selected, the % box will read 100 because the highest concentration of color has been moved to the beginning of the blend.
9. Switch the start and stop colors again by clicking on the endpoint triangle and moving it on top of the start triangle (Figure 4.4). The blend now moves from yellow to red, its default position.

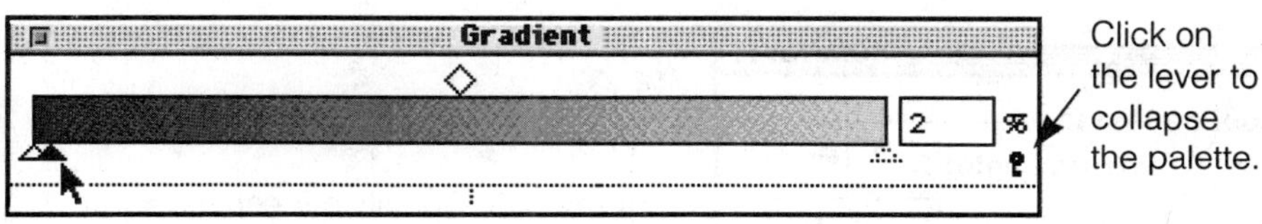

Figure 4.4—Clicking on the endpoint triangle selects it. When you move it to the left over the start triangle (white triangle), the start color in the blend becomes yellow and the end color becomes red.

10. To add a third color to this gradient, first click *beneath* the gradient bar about halfway along the bar. Use the sliders or type in the values in Figure 4.5 to create a green color which appears at the point where you just clicked. Click on the name of the color in the Gradient dialog box and change it to Mixed Red, Yellow, and Green. Click on the Apply button to activate the change in both the Gradient dialog box and the Paint Style palette.

FYI

When you save the file, the new gradient fill is saved with the file.

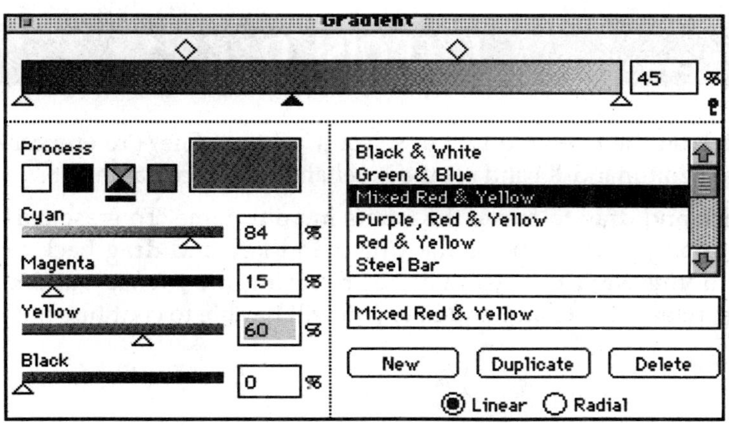

Figure 4.5—The black triangle appears when you click below the bar and indicates the start of green, the third color in the gradient.

⌘-Z Edit/Undo
⌘-K File/Preferences/ General

LINE ATTRIBUTES

When you stroke a path, you specify a Stroke Weight value in the Paint Style palette. However, a line can have other attributes. It can be solid or dashed; it can have three different kinds of caps which determine how the endpoints or line caps appear; and it can meet or join with another line in three different ways.

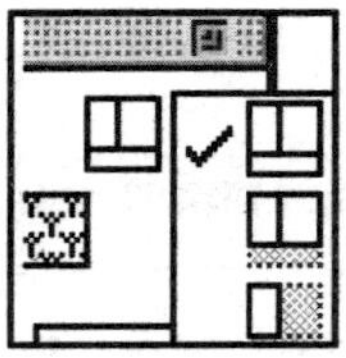

Use the full palette option to display the line attributes panel.

THE FREEHAND TOOL

The freehand tool thinks it's a drawing pencil, but it really is only a rough drawing crayon. It's hard to control, does not create straight lines, and renders curves as lumpy segments on a lumpy path. Once you learn to use the pen tool, you'll probably never use the freehand tool.

Freehand tool

When you draw with the freehand tool, Illustrator creates anchor points automatically. The longer and more complex the path, the more anchor points. The fewer anchor points used to create a path, the fewer bumps and lumps in the path, to say nothing about how much more easily a path with fewer anchor points will print! However, you can control the number of anchor points from the Freehand tolerance field in the General Preferences dialog box (Figure 4.6). The Freehand tolerance value defaults to 2, which gives you a fairly bumpy path. Increasing that value to its maximum of 10 pixels will result in a much smoother path.

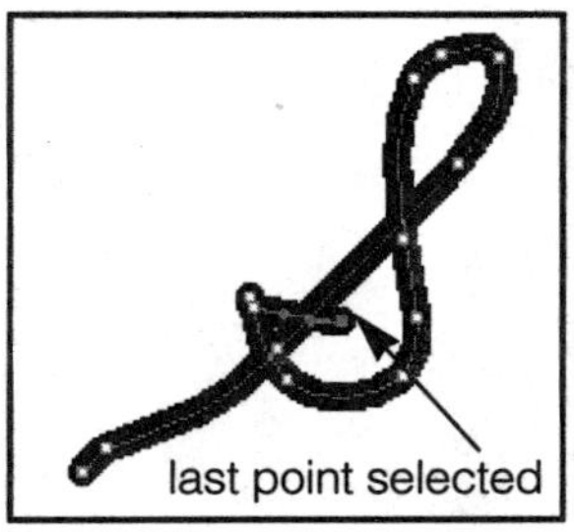

When using the freehand tool, releasing the mouse button leaves the last endpoint selected. Click on this point to continue the path.

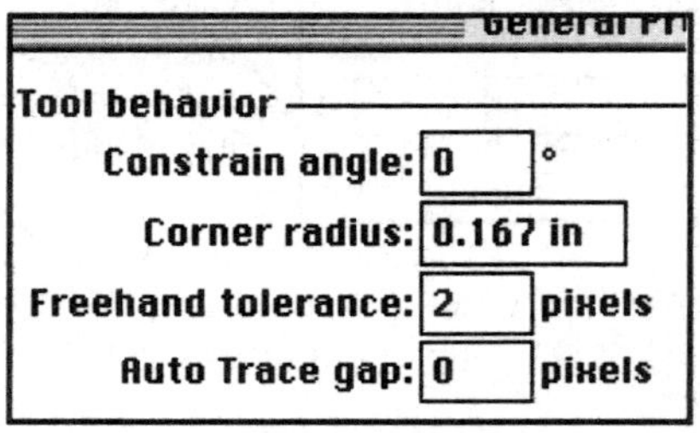

Figure 4.6—Specify a Freehand tolerance value in the General Preferences dialog box. The higher the number of pixels, the fewer the number of anchor points which will be created.

When you draw a freehand path, a dotted line appears behind the cursor as you are dragging. When you release the mouse button, anchor points will appear on the path with endpoints at each end of the path. The last endpoint is selected.

If you make a mistake while using the freehand tool, choose Edit/Undo (Command-Z) to undo the last segment drawn.

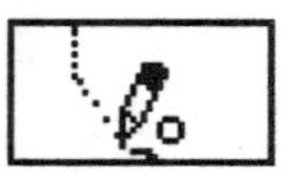

To close a path made with the freehand tool, move the cursor close to the first anchor point in the path. A loop appears next to the cursor indicating that the next time you click, you'll close the path.

EXERCISE D

1. Click on the freehand tool to select it. Choose File/Preferences/ General (Command-K) and set the Freehand tolerance value to 8.
2. Click and drag to create the letters in your name. To erase part of the path as you drag, press the Command key and drag back over the path you want to erase without releasing the mouse button. When you release the Command key, you will be able to continue the path.

EXERCISE E

1. Choose File/Open (Command-O) and open the Caps & Joins.ai file on the Tutorial disk. It displays nine L-shaped lines with different caps and joins (Figure 4.7). Display the Paint Style palette (Command-I).

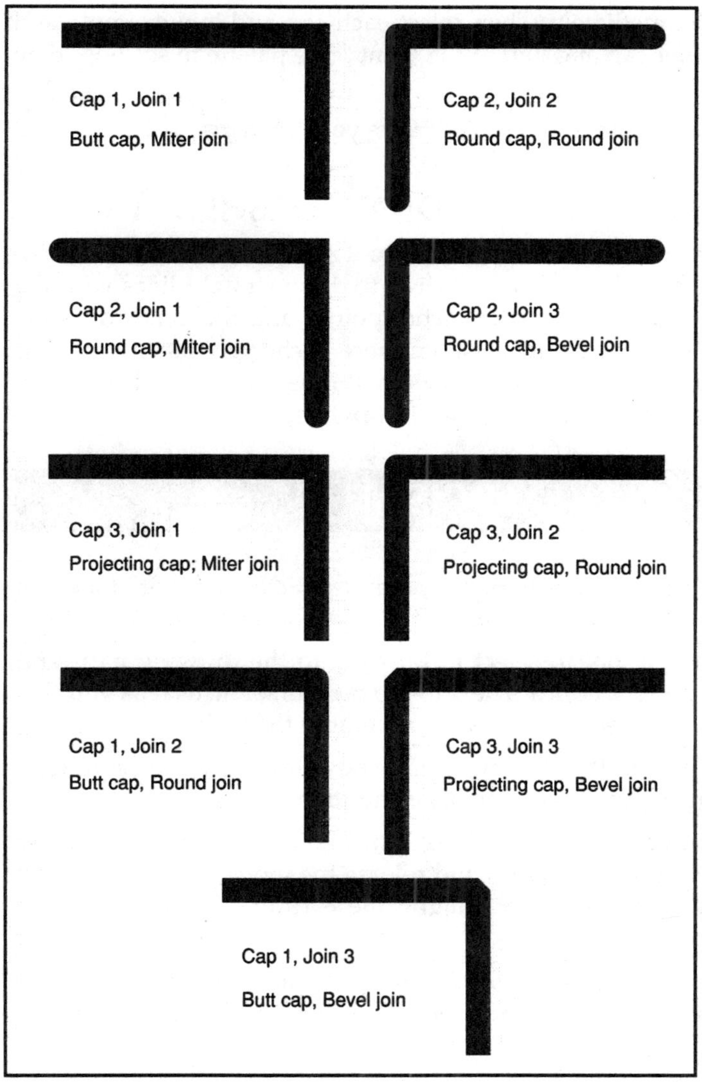

Figure 4.7—The various caps (end-points) and joins for lines, all of which are applied through the Paint Style palette.

2. The file is locked and all the objects are locked. In order to edit the objects, Choose File/Save As and type a new name for the file. Select Illustrator 5 from the Format pull-down menu and click on Save.
3. To unlock the objects, select them all and choose Arrange/Unlock All (Command-2). The objects appear selected. Choose Edit/Select None (Command-Shift-A) to deselect all the items.
4. Choose File/Save (Command-S) to save the file again under its new name with all the items unlocked.

⌘-O File/Open
⌘-I Object/Paint Style
⌘-2 Arrange/Unlock All
⌘-Shift-A Edit/Select None
⌘-S File/Save

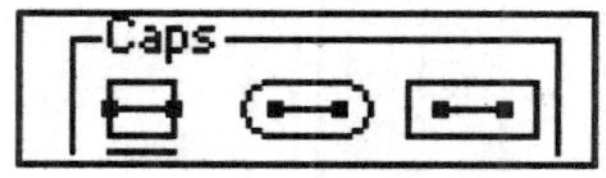

Cap 1 Cap 2 Cap 3

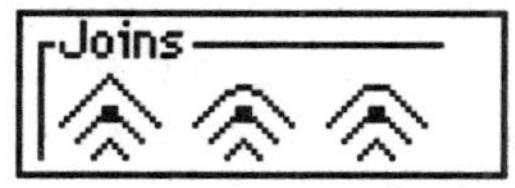

Join 1 Join 2 Join 3

FYI

The Miter Limit value defaults to 4. This means that when the point's length reaches four times its line weight, Illustrator will switch from a miter join to a bevel join.

WARNING!

Get into the habit of saving frequently. Anything can cause the program to crash, and you will lose everything that was not previously saved. (If this happens to you, don't cry over the keyboard or you'll cause it to short out!)

⌘-W File/Close
⌘-I Object/Paint Style

5. Make sure the lower panel of the Paint Style palette is visible. Use the selection tool to select the first item, Cap 1, Join 1. Cap 1 is called a *butt cap* and produces squared ends. Join 1 is a *miter join* and creates paths that meet with pointed corners. When this join is selected, you can enter a value between 1 and 500 in the Miter Limit field.
6. Click on each of the other items and notice the cap and join they use.
7. Be sure that Auto is selected in the Paint Style palette so that changes will appear immediately. Then select each cap and join example and click on another cap and join in the Paint Style palette to see how they change.
8. Close the file (Command-W). Don't save your changes.

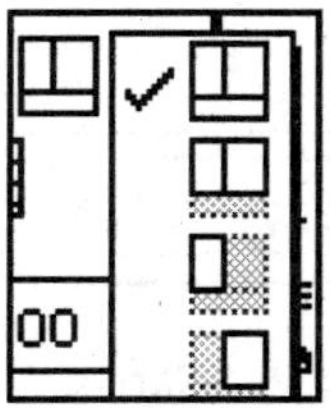

Use the panel display menu to select the first item, which will display the Line Attributes options.

USING THE PEN TOOL TO DRAW DASHED LINES

The pen tool is the most powerful drawing tool in Adobe Illustrator. Unlike the freehand tool, you don't click and drag to draw straight lines with the pen tool. Rather, you click to create anchor points, and Illustrator does the work of placing lines (segments) between those anchor points. If you press the Shift key while setting two anchor points, Illustrator will draw a perfectly straight line between those two anchor points.

Pen tool

EXERCISE F

1. Display the Paint Style palette (Command-I). Select a fill of None and a stroke of 10 points. Select black as the color for the stroke.
2. Click on the pen tool to select it. Move onto the drawing page and notice that a small *x* appears next to the pen cursor. This tells you that your first click will set the first anchor point in the path.
3. Click anywhere on the drawing page and release the mouse button. An anchor point appears on the page and the *x* disappears.
4. Move about two inches away from that first anchor point and press the Shift key. Then click again and release the mouse button. Another anchor point appears and a straight line is drawn between the two anchor points.
5. Move down a few inches, press the Shift key, and click to set another anchor point. Release the mouse button. A third anchor point appears and a second segment is created.
6. To complete the open path, move the cursor to the right a few inches and click to complete the path (Figure 4.8). Because this is an open path, anchor points 1 and 4 are called endpoints.

An *x* by the pen tool cursor indicates that it is ready to set the first anchor point in the path.

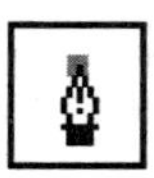

When you click the first time with the pen tool, an anchor point appears and the *x* disappears.

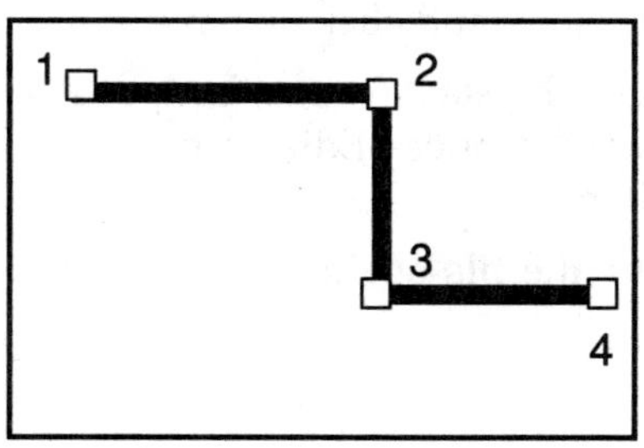

Figure 4.8—Click at 1 to set the first point, at 2 to create the first segment, at 3 to create the second segment, and at 4 to create the third segment of the open path.

7. With the line still selected, click on Dashed in the lower panel of the Paint Style palette. Type 3 in the dash field and press the Tab key. Type 5 in the Gap field and click on Apply to change the solid line into a dashed line (Figure 4.9). Change the Stroke Weight value to 2, and click on the Apply button.

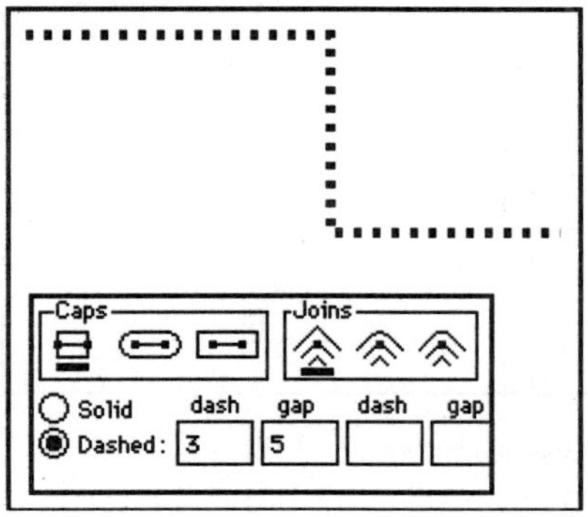

Figure 4.9—The dash value specifies the length of the dash in points. The gap value specifies the distance (in points) from one dash to another.

8. Use the zoom tool or press Command-} to enlarge the display. Increase the Stroke Weight to 10 points and select different Caps and Joins options. Notice how the *endpoints* change when you select different Caps options and how the points at which the segments meet change when you select the different Joins options.

EYEDROPPER AND PAINT BUCKET TOOLS

Thus far you have been applying paint and stroke characteristics to lines and paths directly from the Paint Style palette. You can also use the eyedropper tool to copy the fill and stroke attributes from an object to the Paint Style palette or use the paint bucket tool to copy the fill and stroke attributes from the Paint Style palette to an object.

EXERCISE G

1. Create a new file (File/New), display the Paint Style palette (Command-I), and choose View/Artwork (Command-E).
2. Use the rectangle tool to draw three rectangles on the page. Because you are in Artwork mode, none of the default fills and strokes will appear. Only the outline and center points of the objects are displayed.
3. Use the Paint Style palette to assign one rectangle a green fill and a purple stroke with a Stroke Weight of 8 points. Press the Apply button if necessary to apply the attributes.
4. Choose View/New Window to create another window of the same file. With the new window selected, choose View/Preview (Command-Y). Resize both windows so that they appear on your screen. The filled rectangle appears with its fill and stroke attributes displayed in the new window (Figure 4.10).

⌘-} View/Zoom In
⌘-N File/New
⌘-I Object/Paint Style
⌘-E View/Artwork
⌘-Y View/Preview

FYI

The Caps options apply only to endpoints; the Joins options apply only to anchor points that meet at a corner.

Eyedropper tool

Paint bucket tool

More info

Double-click on the eyedropper tool or on the paint bucket tool to access their dialog boxes where you can select which fill and stroke attributes the tool will select and apply.

Now you see it...

Using the New Window command allows you to see the changes made to objects in Artwork mode. It's easier to select objects and segments in Artwork mode because the stroked paths are easier to select and anchor points are more visible than in Preview mode, where the color and Stroke Weight values frequently make selection difficult.

⌘-Shift-A Edit/Select None
⌘K File/Preferences/General

Tip

Using the eyedropper tool to update the Paint Style palette is a lot easier than trying to figure out what colors were used, what the line weight is, what the Caps and Joins options are, and what the dash and gap values are for a dashed line.

Another tip

Select the filled rectangle in the Artwork mode window by clicking on its center point. This is easier than clicking all over the filled rectangle to find its center point.

You can also select the Area Select option in the General Preferences dialog box, which allows you to select a filled object by clicking anywhere inside the object.

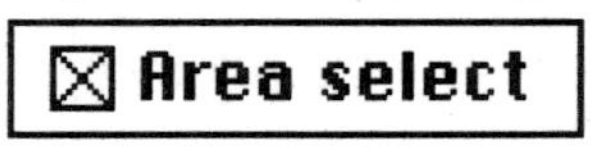

Eyedropper tool

Selection tool

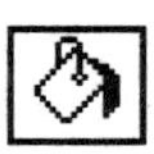

Paint bucket tool

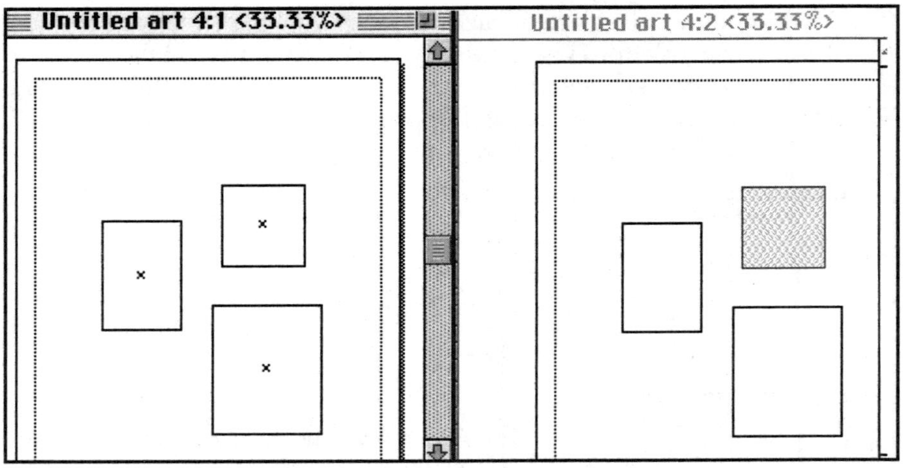

Figure 4.10—The New Window command allows you to view the color and stroke changes made in Artwork mode. You can, of course, make changes in both windows, and any changes you make in one window are updated in the other. Both windows belong to the same document.

5. Choose Edit/Select None (Command-Shift-A) and change the Fill and Stroke colors in the Paint Style palette to anything you did not use for the rectangle. Change the Stroke Weight value to 1. This will let you better see what happens when you use the eyedropper tool.
6. Use the selection tool to select the filled rectangle. Click on the eyedropper tool and notice that now the Fill and Stroke colors in the Paint Style palette change to reflect the fill and stroke values of the selected object and that the Stroke Weight value changes from 1 to 8.
7. Click anywhere on the page to deselect the filled rectangle. Use the selection tool and move to the window in Artwork mode. Shift-select only the two unfilled rectangles.
8. Click on the eyedropper tool and then *double-click* on the center point of the filled rectangle. Both of the selected rectangles now display the fill and stroke attributes of the first rectangle.
9. Choose Edit/Select None (Command-Shift-A) to deselect everything. Click on the Fill box in the Paint Style palette and click on the Pattern icon in the color options strip. Click on the Bricks pattern to designate it as the current fill. Click on any color to designate it as the current stroke. Because nothing is selected, these new fill and stroke attributes are not reflected in any of the objects in the illustration.
10. Click on the paint bucket tool to select it. The paint bucket tool automatically "fills" with the current fill and stroke attributes and becomes a selection tool. Click on one of the rectangles and notice that it fills with the current fill and stroke attributes.
11. Deselect everything (Command-Shift-A) and change the fill and stroke attributes, including the Stroke Weight value, in the Paint Style palette. Use the paint bucket tool to apply those new attributes to objects in the illustration.

THE BRUSH TOOL

⌘-I Object/Paint Style

The brush tool is very much like the freehand tool, in that you use it to draw freeform lines. However, where the freehand tool requires you to close the path by clicking on the first anchor point, paths created with the brush tool are automatically closed when you release the mouse button.

Paths drawn with the brush tool simulate those drawn with a paintbrush in that they display variable-width lines. You can specify the width of the brush stroke, or, if you have a pressure-sensitive tablet, vary the width of the brush stroke's lines by varying the pressure on the pen tip.

Brush tool

EXERCISE H

1. Double-click on the brush tool to display the Brush dialog box. If you are using a pressure-sensitive tablet, click in the Variable box. If not, type 4 in the Width field (Figure 4.11). Click on the first option in the Caps and Joins fields. Do not select Calligraphic. Click on OK.

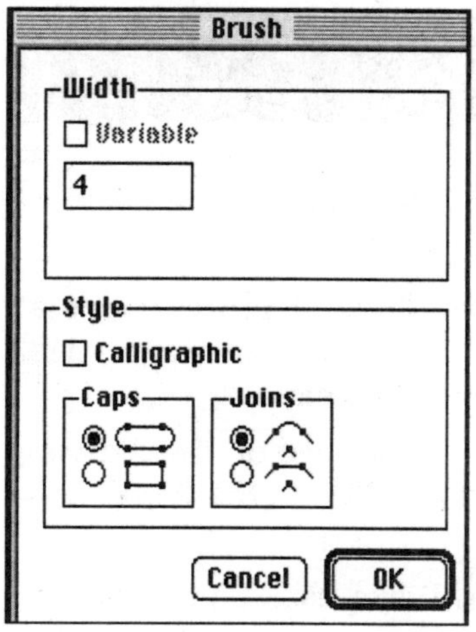

Figure 4.11—Type a value in the Width field to specify the width of the brush stroke as well as a cap style for the endpoints and a join for the points where a corner is created.

FYI

You cannot apply a different cap and join style to a path after it has been drawn with the brush tool. You must make the changes in the Style field of the Brush dialog box before drawing the path.

2. Use the brush tool to draw something resembling a flower. Notice that when you release the mouse button, a filled path appears and the end caps and joins reflect the selections made in the Brush dialog box. Use the Paint Style palette (Command-I) to apply a fill and stroke to the path.
3. Double-click on the brush tool again and select the butt cap and bevel join in the Style field. Click on OK.
4. Draw another shape and notice the difference in the end of the brush stroke (endpoints) and in the way the corners meet (Figure 4.12).

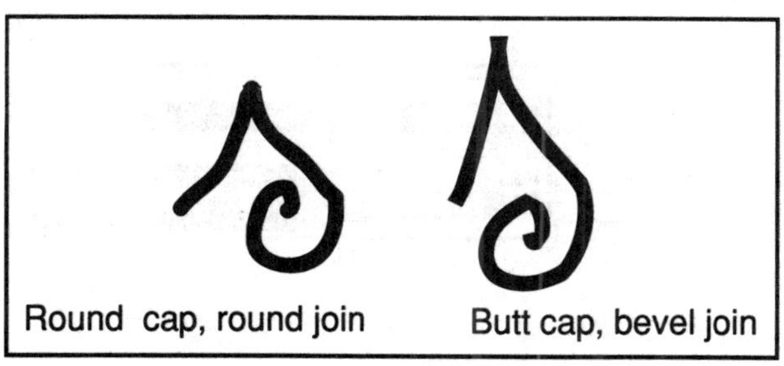

Figure 4.12—Change the Caps and Joins options in the Brush dialog box to create different effects with the brush tool.

⌘-N File/New
⌘-K File/Preferences/General
⌘-I Object/Paint Style

5. Double-click on the brush tool once more and click in the Calligraphic box in the Style field. Type 45 in the Calligraphic angle field. Click on OK. Use the brush to draw a letter. Then try drawing ribbons (Figure 4.13). Double-click on the brush tool and change the Calligraphic angle value to 120°. Click on OK. Notice how the change in angle creates a flatter stroke.

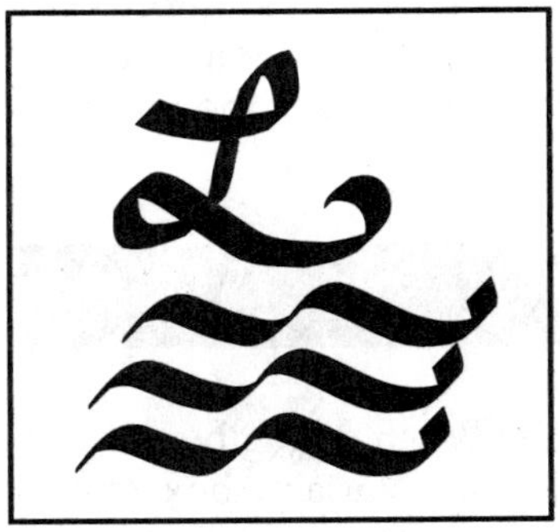

Figure 4.13—When the Calligraphic option is selected in the Brush dialog box, treat the cursor as if it were a pen with an angled nib.

True confessions

The Calligraphic option is frequently difficult to use. Sometimes it's easier to draw the object with the Calligraphic pen and then use the pen tool to draw a neater object over the original stroke—as in Figure 4.13.

REVIEW EXERCISE

In this exercise you will create a few more objects to be used in the final illustration of a mountain village.

1. Create a new file (Command-N). Choose File/Preferences/General (Command-K) and use the Ruler Units pull-down menu to select inches. Click on OK. Choose View/Preview (Command-Y).
2. Click on the rectangle tool to select it and click once on the drawing page to display the Rectangle dialog box. Type 7.25 in the Width field and 2 in the Length field. Click on OK.
3. Display the Paint Style palette (Command-I) and click on the Fill box on the left panel and on the Auto button on the right panel. Keep the rectangle selected. Click on the Gradient icon in the color strip area. Choose Object/Gradient to display the Gradient dialog box.
4. Click on New and type Santa Fe Sky for the name of the new gradient fill. Press the Enter key to add the name to the scroll boxes in the Gradient and Paint Style palettes.
5. Click on the Process Color icon to display the CMYK sliders. Click on the white triangle at the start of the gradient bar (Figure 4.14).
6. Type 17 in the Cyan field and press the Enter key. A 17% cyan color appears as the first color in the gradient.

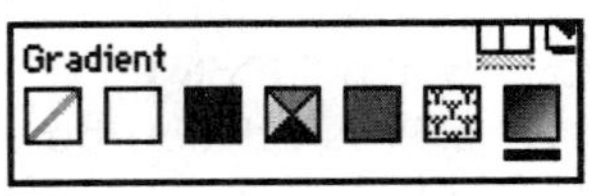

Gradient Color icon is selected in the color strip area.

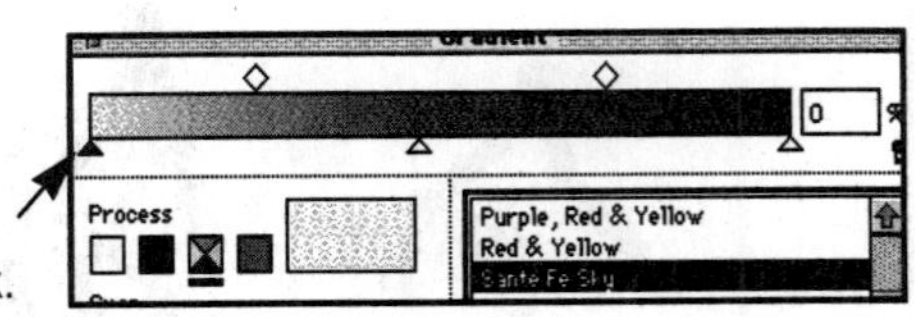

Figure 4.14—Clicking on the first white triangle selects it and changes it to black.

7. Click *below* the bar to set another triangle. Type 45 in the Cyan field; press the Tab key, and type 65 in the Magenta field. Press the Enter key. A purple color flows from the original cyan color in the gradient box (Figure 4.15).

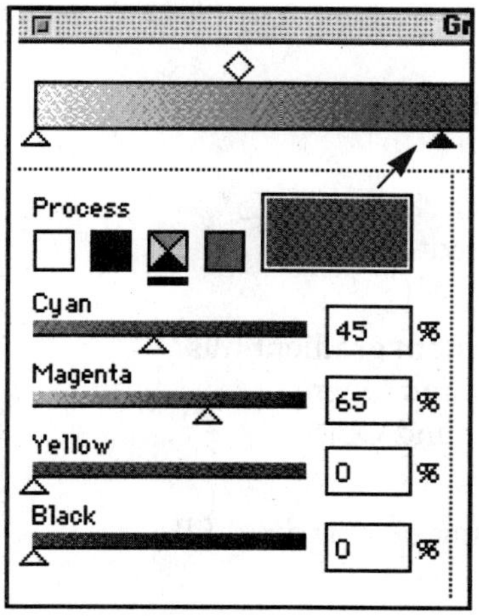

Figure 4.15—Click below the gradient bar to create a selected triangle which indicates the start of another color in the gradient fill.

8. Click on the last triangle under the gradient strip, the ending triangle, which will display 100% in the ending percentage field. Type 89 in the Cyan field and 69 in the Magenta field. Press the Enter button to create a deep blue color, the last of the three colors in the gradient fill.
9. Make sure the new gradient fill, Santa Fe Sky, is applied to the rectangle. Choose File/Save As and save the file as Sky & House. You will need it for a later exercise.
10. In the Paint Style palette, choose None for the fill and red for the stroke. Click on the pen tool and click once on the drawing page. Release the mouse button. Press the Shift key and click about two inches away from the first anchor point. Release the mouse button and then the Shift key to create a horizontal straight line.
11. Move about two inches above the second anchor point, press the Shift key, and click to create a vertical straight line. Continue to press the Shift key while clicking to draw the house (see sidebar).
12. When you close the path, the last anchor point will remain selected. Click on the direct-selection tool and click on that selected anchor point to move it and reposition the last segment of the path.
13. Choose Edit/Select None (Command-Shift-A) to deselect everything. Click on the selection tool and click on the house. Drag it a few inches to the right and left, but before you release the mouse button, press the Option key to create a duplicate of the selected object.
14. Choose File/Save (Command-S) to save the file under its current name.

⌘-Shift-A Edit/Select None
⌘-S File/Save

Check that strip!

When selecting triangles on the gradient bar, make sure that the Process Color icon is also selected above the CMYK sliders.

Selection tool

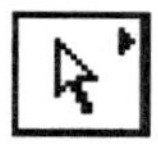

Direct-selection tool

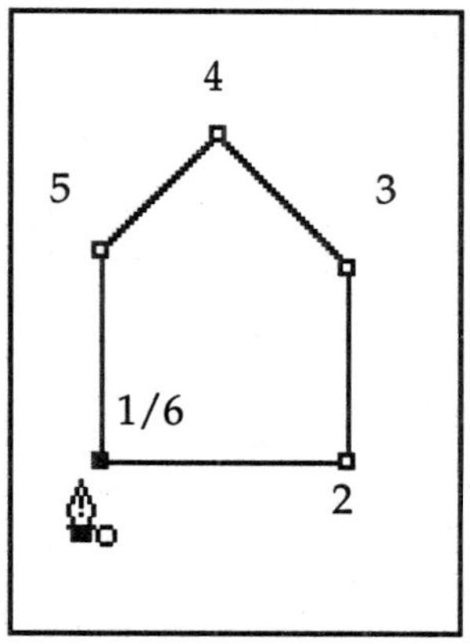

Start at 1 and move to 2, continuing around until you come back to 1 again. As you move the cursor onto the first point, a loop appears on the pen cursor, indicating that the next click (6) will close the path. The last point (6) remains selected.

REVIEW QUESTIONS

Read the following questions and choose the answer which best completes the statement.

1. A gradient fill is edited in the _____.
   a. Paint Style palette
   b. Gradient palette
   c. Menu Bar
   d. b and c
2. A gradient fill is repositioned in the object via the _____.
   a. Paint Style palette
   b. Menu Bar
   c. gradient fill tool
   d. a and c
3. Which commands allow you to access custom gradient fills?
   a. View and Place
   b. Open and Import Styles
   c. View and Open
   d. View and Object
4. Start and stop triangles _____.
   a. are triangles at the beginning and ending of a gradient fill
   b. appear in the Paint Style palette
   c. are drawn with the pen tool
   d are green and red lights on the information highway
5. Line attributes include _____.
   a. fill and stroke
   b. caps and joins
   c. shade and angle
   d. a and b
6. Freeform paths are created with _____.
   a. gradient fills
   b. the freehand and brush tools
   c. the brush and paint bucket tools
   d. a and b
7. Endpoints are edited with the _____ option.
   a. Joins
   b. Caps
   c. Miter Limit
   d. selection tool
8. Joins affect the way _____.
   a. lines curve
   b. lines end
   c. corners meet
   d. all of the above
9. Paths drawn with the _____ can be transformed into dashed lines.
   a. pen tool
   b. brush tool
   c. freehand tool
   d. all of the above
10. The eyedropper and paint bucket tools _____.
    a. copy attributes from the Paint Style palette to objects
    b. cannot be edited
    c. must be used together
    d. affect only paint attributes

Answers: 1. b; 2. c; 3. b; 4. a; 5. d; 6. b; 7. b; 8. c; 9. d; 10. a

LESSON 5

Drawing with the Pen Tool

OVERVIEW

In this lesson you will learn how to use the pen tool to draw straight and curved segments and open and closed paths. You will manipulate direction handles to reshape a curve and add and delete anchor points from a path. You will also learn how to split and join paths.

TOPICS

The pen tool
Drawing straight lines with the pen tool
Drawing an open path
Drawing curved segments
Editing paths
Changing the direction of a curve
Adding and deleting anchor points
Splitting paths
Joining endpoints
Converting anchor points
Review Exercise
Review Questions

TERMS

coincident points
corner points
direction handles
direction points
noncoincident points
noncontinuous curves
open path
Option-dragging
smooth points

TUTORIAL FILES

Mixed Template
Curve Template
Mouse Template

⌘-N File/New
⌘-I Object/Paint Style
⌘-E View/Artwork

THE PEN TOOL

The pen tool is the most powerful drawing tool in Adobe Illustrator. With it, you can draw straight lines in any direction and curved lines with any slope. You can resize, reposition, and reshape any straight or curved segment drawn with the pen tool by adjusting either its anchor points or the segments between the anchor points.

There's good news and great news about the pen tool. The good news is that it takes a little practice to learn how to use it skillfully; the great news is that once you learn—it's like climbing Mt. Everest—you never forget, and you don't have to think about what you're doing. You click a little, drag a little, and bingo! It's art!

DRAWING STRAIGHT LINES WITH THE PEN TOOL

In the last lesson you used the pen tool to draw dashed lines. In this lesson you will continue use the pen tool to draw straight lines. The important thing to remember about drawing lines is that *you do not drag to create the line*. You *click* to set the anchor points and Illustrator connects them for you. If you ever played "Connect the Dots," this is your tool!

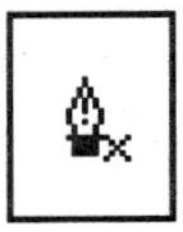

When you first click to select the pen tool and move onto the drawing page, a small *x* appears next to the cursor. This tells you that your first click will set the first anchor point in the path.

EXERCISE A

1. Create a new file (Command-N), choose View/Artwork (Command-E), and display the Paint Style palette (Command-I). Make sure that both Fill and Stroke are set to None.
2. Click once on the pen tool to select it. Move onto the drawing page and notice the *x* next to the cursor. This tells you that your first click will create the first anchor point in the path.
3. Click once in the middle of the page and release the mouse button. *Do not drag.* Move up or down a few inches and click again. Notice the line (segment) which appears between the first and second anchor points.
4. Move the cursor close to the second anchor point and notice that a caret appears to the right of the cursor. This tells you that the next segment will be connected to the selected anchor point (Figure 5.1).

FYI

Illustrator automatically fills an open path with the default fill and stroke colors unless you select None for the Fill and Stroke before drawing.

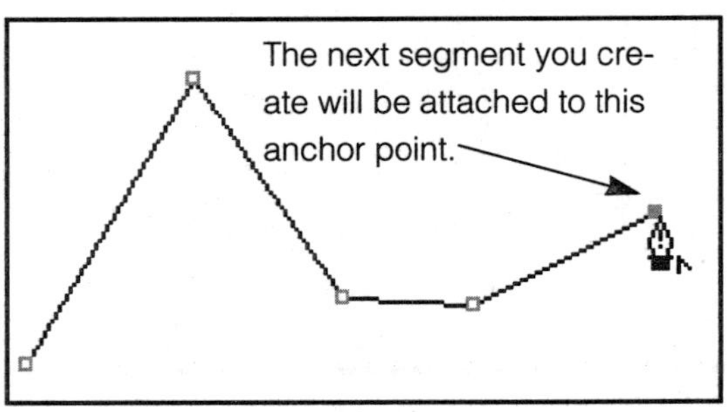

Figure 5.1—A caret appears next to the cursor when it is near a selected anchor point, indicating that the next time you click, the new segment will be anchored to the selected anchor point.

5. Click again to set another anchor point and create another segment.
6. Press the Shift key before clicking again to constrain the line to a 45° angle. You are now ready to deactivate (but not deselect) the pen tool.

7. Click once on the pen tool in the Tool palette to deactivate the pen tool and create an open path. All of the anchor points on the path are hollow except for the last one, which remains selected. The pen tool is still selected, and it will begin a new path the next time you click.
8. With the path still active and the pen tool selected, move the cursor onto the last, selected anchor point. Because you are going to *add a segment to a completed, open path,* the cursor displays a slant line to its right (Figure 5.2). This symbol tells you that when you click on the selected anchor point, you will continue to draw the original path.

⌘-Shift-A Edit/Select None
⌘-A Edit/Select All
⌘-I Object/Paint Style
⌘-Y View/Preview

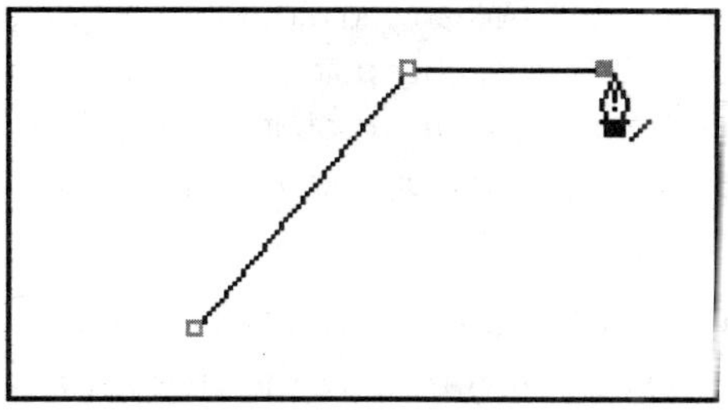

Figure 5.2—Clicking with the pen tool on the selected anchor point of a completed path displays a slant line to the right of the cursor, indicating that the next segment will be connected to the selected anchor point.

9. Continue to click and add a few more straight line segments to this path. When you have finished, click once on the pen tool.
10. Move the cursor around the drawing page, away from the selected endpoint of the path you just drew, and notice that the *x* is displayed next to the cursor. This tells you that you are ready to draw another path.
11. Choose Edit/Select None (Command-Shift-A) to deselect the path.

FYI

There are four ways to deactivate the pen tool: close the path with the loop-pen cursor; click once on the pen tool in the tool palette; press the Command key while clicking anywhere on the page; or choose Edit/Select None.

DRAWING AN OPEN PATH

A path with two endpoints (anchor points on each end of the path) is called an open path. This is the kind of path you created in Exercise A. You can also use the pen tool to create a closed path, a path in which you cannot see where one segment begins and another one ends.

EXERCISE B

1. Choose Edit/Select All (Command-A) to select all the objects on the screen. Press the Delete key. Display the Paint Style palette (Command-I). Make sure that None is selected for the Fill and Stroke options.
2. Choose View/Preview (Command-Y).
3. Click on the pen tool to select it and move onto the drawing page. You will draw a triangle. Click once to set the first anchor point. Release the mouse button. Move up and to the right and click to set the second anchor point and create the first segment. Release the mouse button. Move down and to the right and click to set the third anchor point and create the second segment. Release the mouse button.

Pen tool

4. Move to the left, onto the first anchor point. As you come onto it, the cursor displays a loop which tells you that the next time you click, you will be clicking on the first anchor point and you will close the path (Figure 5.3). Click on that first anchor point to close the path.

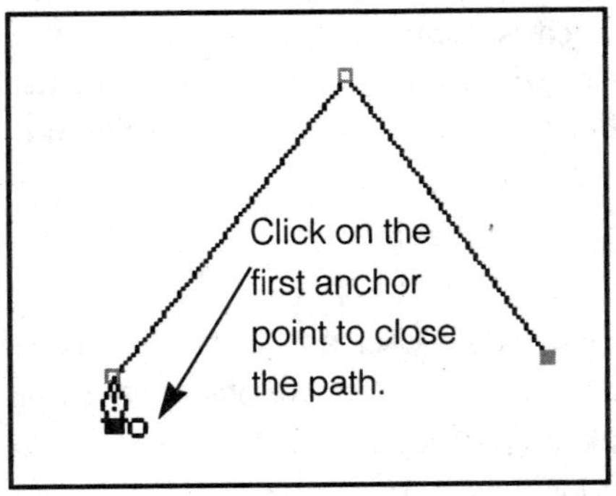

Figure 5.3—When you move the cursor onto the first anchor point, a loop is displayed next to the cursor, indicating that the next time you click, you'll close the path.

5. Not only have you closed the path, but you have returned the pen tool to its "start position." Notice that as soon as you click, the cursor displays the *x*, indicating that if you click again, you will start a new path (Figure 5.4). The completed, closed path, however, displays the selected last anchor point until you click to start another path.

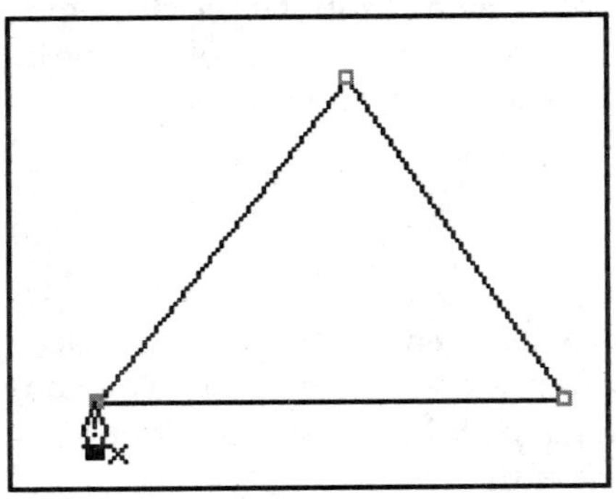

Figure 5.4—The cursor displays an *x* when it is ready to begin a new path.

6. Continue to draw closed paths until you are comfortable with drawing the straight lines and finding the first anchor point needed to close the path.

FYI

Remember: closing a path is one way to deactivate the pen tool, even though it remains selected.

Closed means shut!

You cannot add segments to a closed path in the same way as you continued to draw and add segments to an open path. The only way to reshape a closed path is to add anchor points along the segments.

DRAWING CURVED SEGMENTS

You don't drag when drawing straight lines because dragging with the pen tool produces curved segments. These segments are connected by anchor points which display direction handles and direction points. Use these handles to change the shape of a curve.

There are two ways to draw curves in Illustrator: the right way and the easy way. The right way is to click with the pen tool and drag in the direction of the curve; then click to complete the curve (Figure 5.5).

The other way is to click and release the mouse button, then click at the high point of the curve and drag to the right; and finally click at the endpoint to complete the curve (Figure 5.6).

⌘-E View/Artwork
⌘-R View/Show Rulers
⌘-I Object/Paint Style

The first way produces a more elegant curve (from a technical viewpoint) because it utilizes only two anchor points. The second way requires three anchor points, but many users find this a much easier and quicker way to create curves.

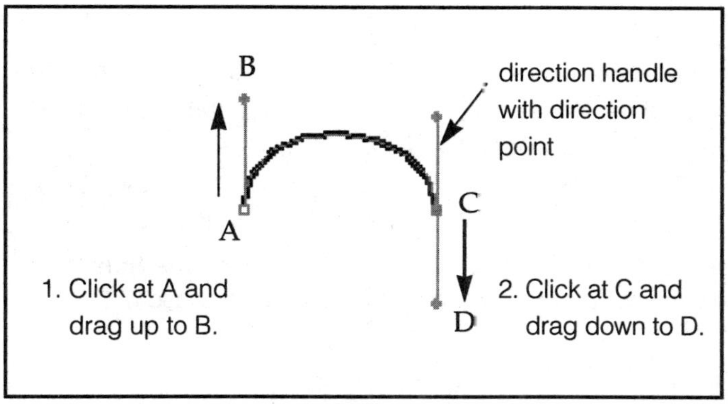

Figure 5.5—Direction handles appear when you drag to create a curve segment. Because this curve is an open path, A and C are endpoints.

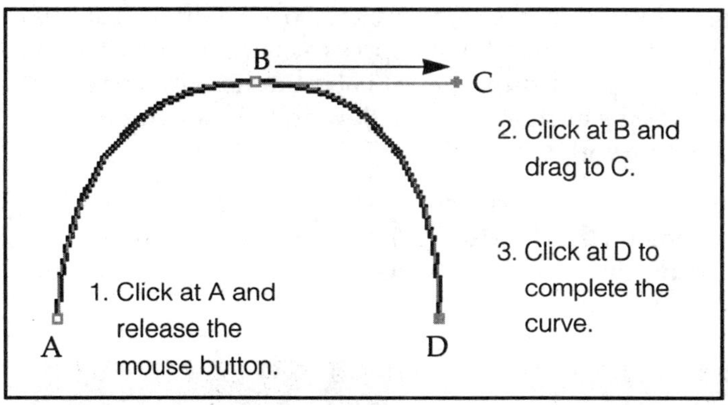

Figure 5.6—Dragging at B outward instead of dragging from A upward also sets the slope (arc) of the curve. The last endpoint remains selected.

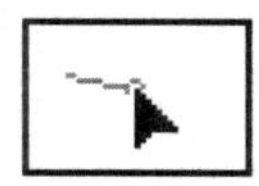

The cursor changes to an arrowhead when drawing curve segments.

EXERCISE C

1. Choose View/Artwork (Command-E) and display the Paint Style palette. Make sure that neither the Fill nor Stroke options are selected.
2. Choose View/Show Rulers (Command-R). Rulers will appear on the bottom and at the right side of the screen. Click in the horizontal ruler and drag a ruler guide up to the middle of the page. Drag another ruler guide up about two inches above the first guide.
3. Click on the pen tool to select it. Click on the bottom guide (A) and drag straight up to the top guide. Release the mouse button, the anchor point will appear selected (filled), and the direction handle will extend from the anchor point (A) to the top guide (Figure 5.7).

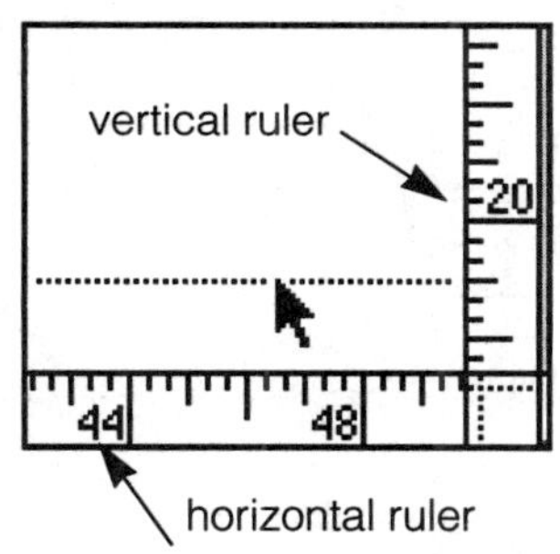

Click inside the horizontal ruler and drag a ruler guide up. Click inside the vertical ruler and drag a ruler guide out.

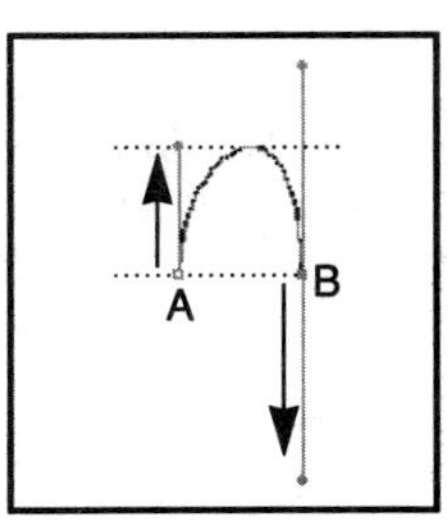

Figure 5.7—Click and drag *up* at A—always in the direction of the curve or the "hump"—and release the mouse button when the direction handle is about one third the size of the curve. Click and drag *down* at B to complete the curve.

⌘-Shift-A Edit/Select None
⌘-O File/Open
⌘-E View/Artwork

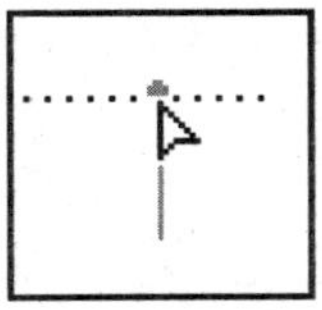

The cursor becomes hollow when it touches the ruler guide.

4. Notice the direction handle which appears when you release the mouse button. You'll use this handle later to adjust the slope of the curve.
5. Click on the bottom guide about two inches away from the selected anchor point and drag *down* to complete the curve. Always drag away from the "hump" to complete the curve.
6. When you release the mouse button, the selected anchor point displays two direction handles, one going up and one going down. You'll use these also to adjust the curve (Figure 5.7).
7. Repeat steps 3–5 until you are comfortable making "picket fence" curves. Don't worry if they're crooked, you'll fix them later.
8. Choose Edit/Select None (Command-Shift-A). Save the file (File/Save As) as Practice Curves. You will need it for the next exercise.

EDITING PATHS

Any path, whether it's a line or curve segment, may need editing. You may want to shorten or lengthen it, extend or compress a curve, or even remove part of it. All editing (except for duplicating) is best done with the direct-selection tool, as it leaves the anchor points hollow and allows you to select only the ones you want to work with.

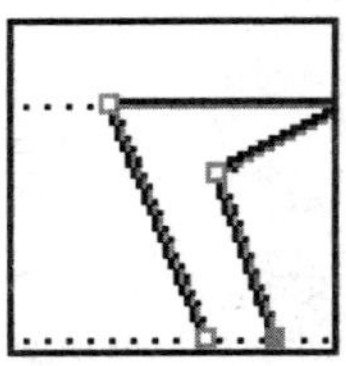

Corner points do not display direction handles.

A path can be edited by moving an anchor point or by adjusting the direction handles by dragging on the direction points. When you adjust a corner point, you have only the anchor point to work with, because corner points don't have direction handles.

EXERCISE D

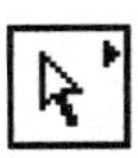

Direct-selection tool

1. If necessary, open the Practice Curves file (Command-O) and display the Paint Style palette. Make sure that the Fill and Stroke options are set to None and that nothing is selected. Choose View/Artwork (Command-E).
2. Click on the direct-selection tool to select it and click once on the first curve. It displays a direction handle on either side of the two anchor points. The endpoints are hollow because only the curve *segment* is selected, not the anchor points (Figure 5.8).

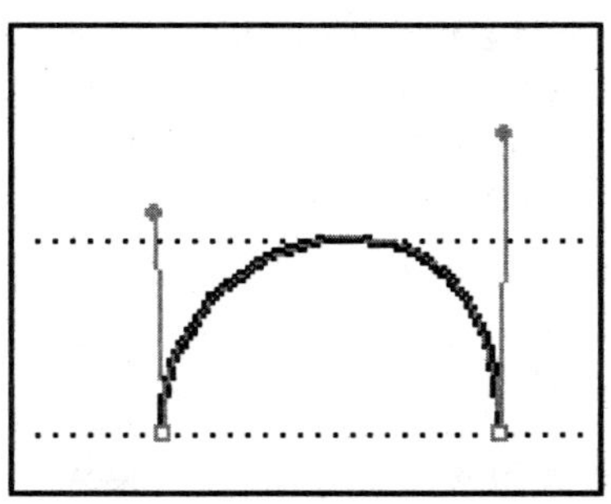

Figure 5.8—When you click on a curve path with the direct-selection tool, direction handles appear on each side of the curve.

3. With the direct-selection tool, click on the direction point of any direction handle. You move the handle by clicking and dragging this point. Notice that you can move the slope of the curve to the right and left as well as up and down (Figure 5.9). Notice also that only the curve *segment* moves; the anchor point remains stationary.

⌘-Z Edit/Undo

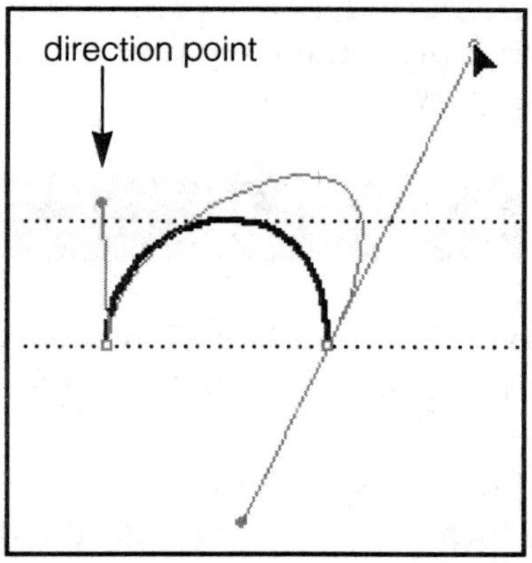

Figure 5.9—Click on the direction point and drag the direction handle to change the slope and height of the curve segment.

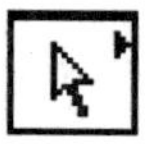

Direct-selection tool

4. Choose Edit/Undo (Command-Z) to return the curve to its original shape.
5. Click on the direction point extending from the other anchor point on the curve segment. Move it up and down and back and forth. Notice how the curve segment moves in the direction of the moving handle.
6. Choose Edit/Undo (Command-Z) to restore the curve to its original shape.
7. With the direct-selection tool, click on the left anchor point to display another direction handle from the anchor point (Figure 5.10). Click on its direction point and drag to the right and left. You cannot use this handle to move the curve up and down.

Now you see it...

If you click away from the segment when the direct-selection tool is active, the segment becomes deselected and the anchor points with their direction handles are no longer visible. If that happens, just click on the segment again *with the direct-selection tool* to make the anchor points and direction handles visible.

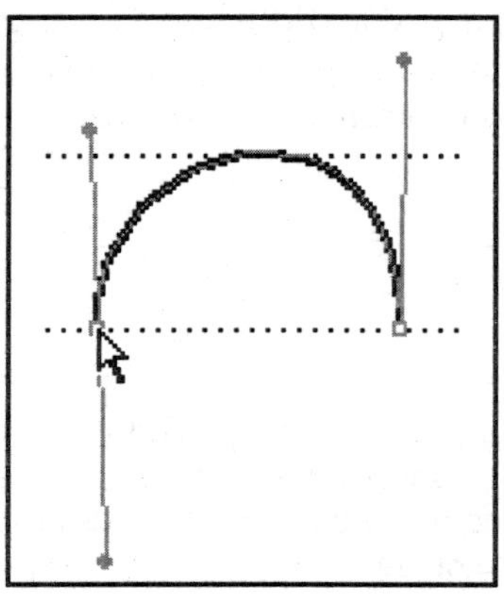

Figure 5.10—Click on the anchor point to display a second direction handle from the anchor point.

8. Click on the right anchor point to display its second direction handle. Use all four handles to adjust the shape of the curve.
9. Select the other curves and use their direction handles to adjust their arc and shape.

⌘-N File/New
⌘-I Object/Paint Style
⌘-R View/Show Rulers
⌘-Z Edit/Undo

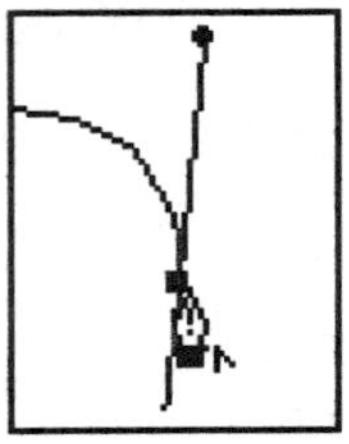

When you click on the smooth point, the cursor displays a caret, indicating that you can Option-click on this anchor point to create a corner point. The Info Bar in the lower left corner of the screen also displays Pen: Make Corner.

Pen: Make Corner

FYI

Option-clicking with the pen tool creates a corner point. Ordinarily, corner points don't display direction handles, but when they are set in conjunction with a smooth point, they will display the smooth point's first direction handle. It is the corner point's direction handle which appears when you Option-click and drag up.

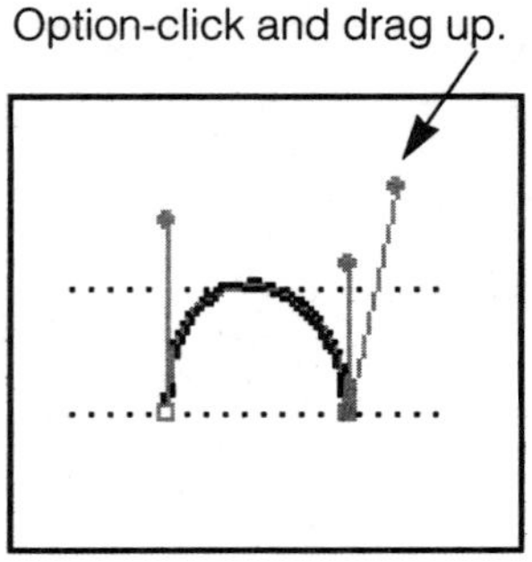

CHANGING THE DIRECTION OF A CURVE

Thus far, the curves you have been drawing are continuous curves—curves connected by smooth points. You drew the first segment, then placed the pointer where you wanted the next segment to end, and dragged in the opposite direction of the curve's hump. To create a noncontinuous curve—curves connected by corner points—like a series of curves in a picket fence, position the pointer on the last anchor point, press the Option key, and drag in the opposite direction to complete the curve.

EXERCISE E

1. Create a new file (Command-N). Choose View/Artwork (Command-E) and display the Paint Style palette (Command-I). Select None for the fill and any color for the stroke.
2. Choose View/Show Rulers (Command-R). Drag two horizontal rulers up onto the drawing page, about one inch apart. You will use these ruler guides as start and stop positions when creating curves.
3. Click on the pen tool to select it. Move onto the drawing page and notice that a small *x* appears next to the pen cursor. This tells you that your first click will create the first anchor point in the path.
4. Click on the lower ruler and drag up to begin the curve. Release the mouse button. You always drag in the direction of the curve when you set the first anchor point in the curve. Although nothing appears to happen, the next time you click, you will be able to complete the curve.
5. Click on the lower ruler and drag down to complete the curve. Always draw away from the "hump" when completing a curve.
6. Click and drag in the last anchor point you just created and drag up to start the next curve. Notice that when you click and drag in the same point, instead of moving to another position as you did when drawing continuous curves, the segment moves down and the curve becomes distorted (Figure 5.11). Choose Edit/Undo (Command-Z) to return to the original curve.

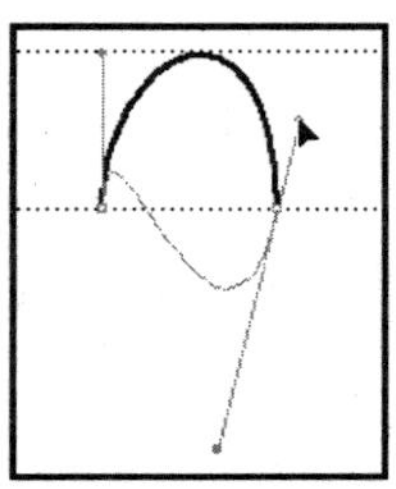

Figure 5.11—Clicking and dragging in the last placed anchor point causes the segment to flip. Option-click in the anchor point before dragging to set a corner anchor point and establish the direction (up) of the next curve.

7. Press the Option key, *then* click and drag up to set a *corner anchor point* and direction handle for the next curve. Move to the right and click and drag down to complete the curve.
8. Continue to create more sets of noncontinuous curves. When you're finished, click on the pen tool to deactivate it. Your screen should resemble Figure 5.12.

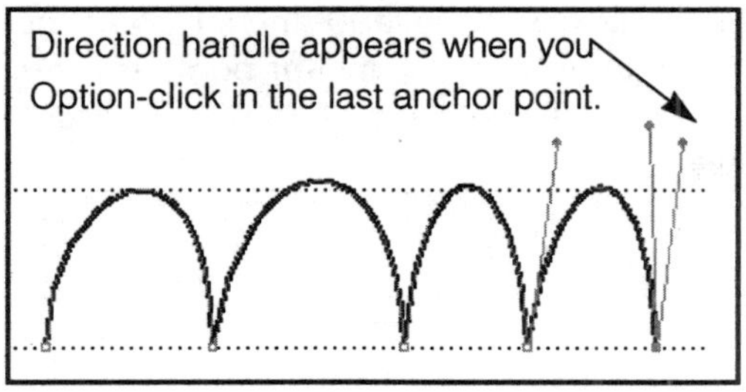

Figure 5.12—A series of noncontinuous curves connected by corner points and created by Option-clicking in the last anchor point of the previously completed curve.

⌘-O File/Open
⌘-E View/Artwork
⌘-N File/New
⌘-I Object/Paint Style

EXERCISE F

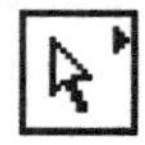

Direct-selection tool

1. Choose File/Open (Command-O) and open the Mixed Template file in the Templates folder on the Tutorial disk. Display the Paint Style palette and select None for the fill and a red color for the stroke. Choose View/Artwork (Command-E).
2. Use the pen tool to draw each of the straight and curved segments. Don't forget to click on the pen tool to select it when you have finished drawing each object.
3. Use the direct-selection tool to select a path. When you have finished drawing the path, use the direction handles to adjust the curves.
4. Save the file (File/Save As) as Mixed Templates.ai. The *ai* suffix tells you that the file contains the actual Illustrator artwork, not just the template. You will use this file later.

ADDING AND DELETING ANCHOR POINTS

No path is ever set in stone. You can always add and delete anchor points for reshaping a path. Illustrator provides you with an add-anchor point tool and a delete-anchor point tool. These tools are accessed from the Tool palette by clicking and dragging out on the black triangle on the scissors tool icon.

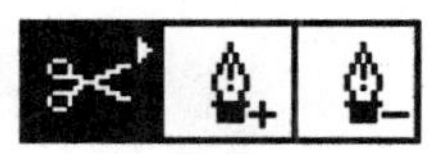

Add-anchor point tool (center) is accessed by clicking on the triangle on the scissors tool.

The delete-anchor point tool removes anchor points from a path. Deleting an anchor point simplifies the path and reshapes the object.

Add-anchor point tool

Adding anchor points is frequently an easy way to adjust a segment, since it gives you extra direction handles (smooth point) or just another corner point to manipulate. To add an anchor point, you must first select a path with either of the selection tools.

EXERCISE G

1. Create a new file (File/New). Display the Paint Style palette (Command-I) and select a light fill color. Leave the stroke at None. Choose View/Preview (Command-Y).
2. Reset the Toolbox by pressing the Command and Shift keys simultaneously and double-clicking on any tool.
3. Select the rectangle tool. Drag to draw a rectangle. Click and drag on the black triangle on the scissors tool to select the add-anchor point tool.

4. With the rectangle still selected, click with the add-anchor point tool on the top segment of the rectangle. A selected anchor point appears, and the other four anchor points on the rectangle become deselected (hollow) (Figure 5.13).

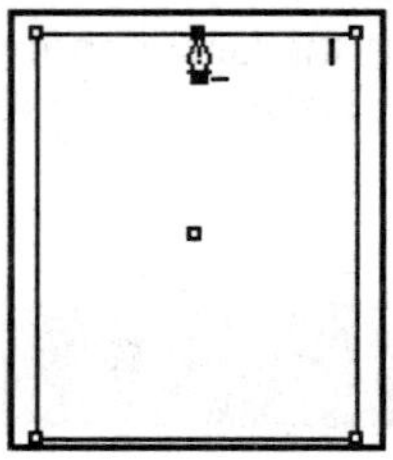

Figure 5.13—When you click with the add-anchor point tool, a selected anchor point appears on the path and the path becomes deselected.

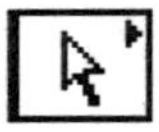

Direct-selection tool

5. Click on the direct-selection tool (hollow arrow) and click on the newly created selected point. Drag that point up to change the appearance of the rectangle to a roofed building (Figure 5.14).

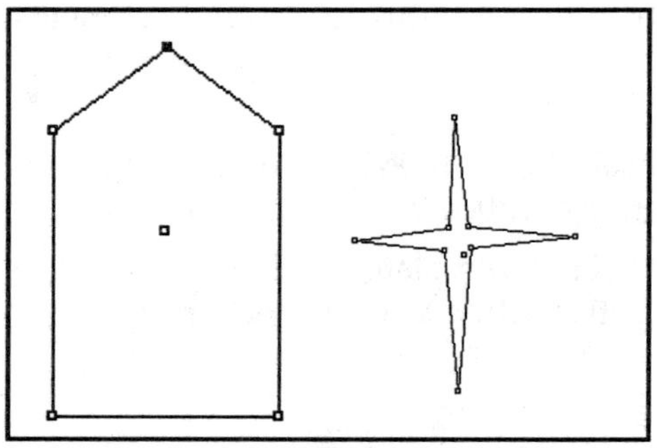

Figure 5.14—Use the direct-selection tool to drag the newly created anchor point up to reshape the rectangle. Adding another three anchor points, for a total of eight anchor points, lets you reshape the rectangle into a star.

FYI

The center point of an object created with the rectangle and oval tools is not an anchor point.

6. Click with the add-anchor point tool on the other three segments. Use the direct-selection tool to drag all four points outward to create a star similar to the one shown in Figure 5.14. The object now has a total of eight anchor points.
7. Use the direct-selection tool to select the star. Press the Command and Shift keys simultaneously and double-click on any tool to reset the Tool palette. Drag out the scissors tool and select the delete-anchor point tool.
8. Click on any of the anchor points with the delete-anchor point tool. Notice how the shape of the star changes as you delete anchor points.

Delete-anchor point tool

Scissors tool

SPLITTING PATHS

The scissors tool is used to split an open path into two separate paths or to split a closed path like a circle or rectangle so that it becomes an open path. If you split a path in the center of a segment, Illustrator creates two new endpoints, one on top of the other, and selects both endpoints (Figure 5.15).

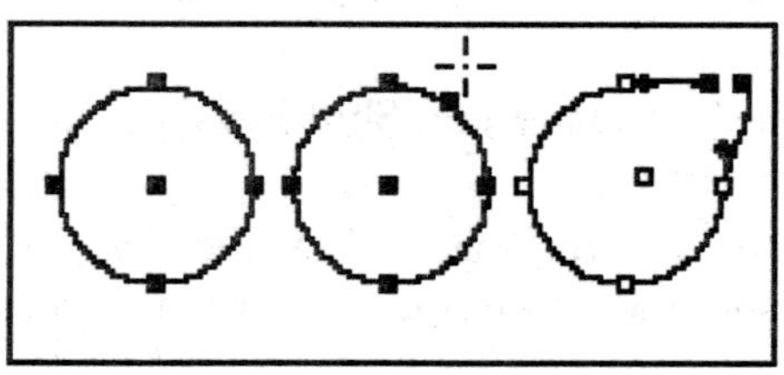

Figure 5.15—Clicking on the figure at the left with the scissors tool results in splitting the path and creating two new endpoints, one on top of the other (center), which can be moved independently (right).

JOINING ENDPOINTS

Just as you can split a path and create two endpoints, so you can join two endpoints of an open path. This creates a closed path. You can also join the endpoints of two open paths to create one open path.

There are two kinds of endpoints, coincident and noncoincident. Coincident endpoints are placed one on top of the other so that it appears that there is only one endpoint (see the center circle in Figure 5.15). When you join two coincident endpoints, both points are replaced by one endpoint. When you join two noncoincident endpoints, Illustrator draws a path between the two points.

EXERCISE H

1. Either create a new document (File/New) or choose Edit/Select All (Command-A) and press the Delete key to clear the screen.
2. Select the pen tool and click (don't drag) to create three segments (Figure 5.16). Click on the pen tool to deactivate it.
3. Use the selection tool to select the path. Press the Option key and drag the path a little to the right. Release the mouse button, *then* the Option key. Option-dragging creates a copy of the selected item. Choose Edit-Select None (Command-Shift-A) to deselect everything.
4. Using the direct-selection tool, drag a selection marquee around the two bottom points of the paths (Figure 5.16) to select those endpoints. The other anchor points on the two paths will appear, but they will be hollow (deselected).

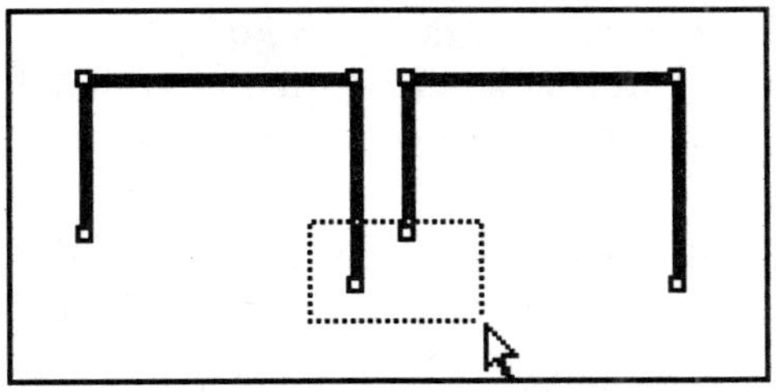

Figure 5.16—The two points being selected are noncoincident anchor points because they are not on top of each other. Illustrator will draw a path to join them.

5. Choose Object/Join (Command-J). Notice that Illustrator joined (connected) the two paths by drawing a segment from one noncoincident endpoint to the other.
6. Choose the selection tool and and click to select what is now one path. Drag it around the screen.
7. Click on the scissors tool and click on one of the anchor points connecting the new path. Then click on the other anchor point (Figure 5.17).

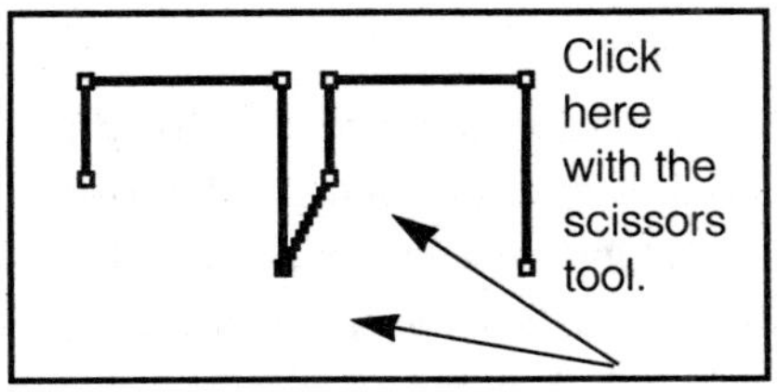

Figure 5.17—Click on both anchor points with the scissors tool to cut the newly created segment from the path.

⌘-N File/New
⌘-A Edit/Select All
⌘-Shift-A Edit/Select None
⌘-J Object/Join

Pen tool

Selection tool

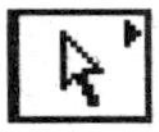

Direct-selection tool

Do a two-step

After using the scissors tool to cut an anchor point or several anchor points, deselect everything before using the selection tool to select and remove the severed segment.

⌘-Option-O File/Open Template
⌘-Shift-A Edit/Select None
⌘-W File/Close
⌘-I Object/Paint Style

8. Choose Edit/Select None (Command-Shift-A) or click on an empty area of the page to deselect everything. Use the direct-selection tool to select that small segment connecting the two paths, the one you just cut with the scissors tool, and drag it away from the paths. With the small segment still selected, press the Delete key to delete it.
9. Notice that when you cut the segment, you split the joined path into two separate paths. Close this file (Command-W). Don't save your changes.

CONVERTING ANCHOR POINTS

The third tool which appears when you drag the scissors tool out is the convert-direction point tool. Use this tool to convert a corner point (which has been selected with the direct-selection tool) to a smooth point by clicking on the corner point and dragging. Clicking on a smooth point with this tool converts the smooth point with its two direction handles to a corner point with no direction handles.

FYI

Templates are bitmapped images which exist on a background layer in Illustrator. You can't edit them, but you can choose to hide or display them from the View menu. Templates are used as guides for drawing with (most often) the pen tool or tracing with the auto trace tool.

REVIEW EXERCISE

In this exercise you will open two templates and use them to practice drawing curves with the pen tool and joining paths with the add-anchor point tool.

1. Open the Curve Template file in the Templates folder on the Tutorial disk (Command-Option-O). Display the Paint Style palette (Command-I) and select None for the fill and a red color for the stroke. Set the Weight value at 2 points.
2. Use the pen tool to practice drawing the different kinds of curves by drawing over the lines in the template. Remember, when drawing noncontinuous curves (second set of curves), that you must Option-click in the last created anchor point of the curve just completed (smooth point) to create a corner point so you can change the direction of the curve.
3. Open the Mouse Template file in the Templates folder on the Tutorial disk (Command-Option-O) to display a happy rodent (Command-O).
4. The base of the mouse's body is a circle drawn from the center. Click on the oval tool and press the Option key *before* clicking and dragging from the center of the body. When the oval is a close approximation of the template, release the mouse button.
5. Use the add-anchor point tool to add an anchor point to the front segment. Use the direct-selection tool to drag this anchor point out to create the head (Figure 5.18).

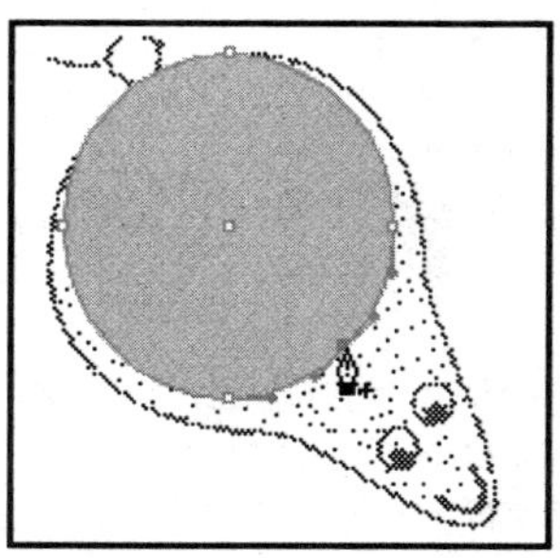

Figure 5.18—Use the add-anchor point tool to add another anchor point to the oval. Then use the direct-selection tool to select this new anchor point and drag it out. This reshapes the oval into the mouse's body.

6. Then move the direction handles and anchor points to adjust the curve of the body (Figure 5.19).

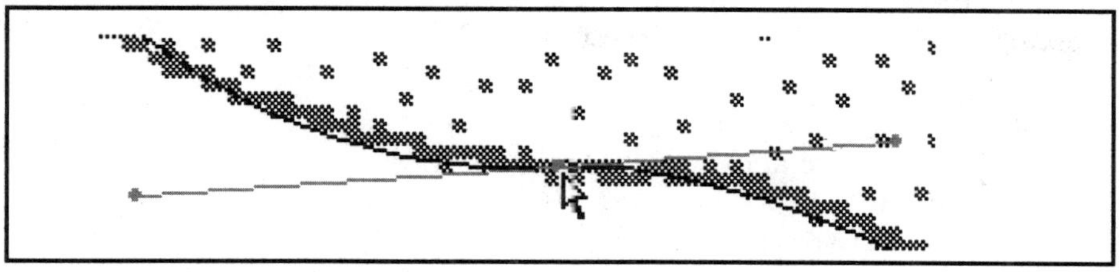

Figure 5.19—Select one of the anchor points on the body of the mouse and drag the direction handles out to make the curve conform to the line in the template .

7. Use the oval tool to create eyes and the freehand tool to create the tail and mouth.
8. When you've drawn the tail, make sure it's selected, and choose Arrange/Send to back (Command- – (hyphen)), so any part of the tail drawn over the mouse's body will appear behind it. Listen hard and you'll hear him squeak!

⌘- – Arrange/Send to Back

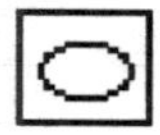

Oval tool

Freehand tool

REVIEW QUESTIONS

Read the following questions and choose the answer which best completes the statement.

1. The pen tool _____
   a. draws straight lines
   b. draws curved segments
   c. sets anchor points
   d. all of the above
2. Straight line segments are drawn _____
   a. by clicking and dragging
   b. by clicking
   c. by dragging
   d. with a ruler
3. Curved segments are drawn by _____.
   a. clicking and dragging
   b. by clicking
   c. by dragging
   d. with a compass
4. To adjust the slope of a curve, _____.
   a. move the anchor point
   b. drag a direction handle
   c. move the curve segment
   d. a and b
5. Edit paths with the _____.
   a. pen tool
   b. direct-selection tool
   c. add- and delete-anchor point tools
   d. b and c

6. Before drawing a noncontinuous curve, _____.
   a. draw a continuous curve
   b. Option-click in the previous anchor point
   c. create a smooth point with the pen tool
   d. use the direct-selection tool
7. In order to split a path, _____
   a. use the delete-anchor point tool
   b. select the path with the direct-selection tool
   c. use the scissors tool
   d. b and c
8. The add-anchor point and delete-anchor point tools _____.
   a. are accessed from the scissors tool
   b. appear when you press the Command key
   c. corners meet
   d. all of the above
9. In order to join two paths, _____.
   a. both paths must be selected
   b. both paths must be closed paths
   c. the endpoints of both paths must be selected
   d. use the selection tool
10. It's important to remember _____.
    a. to use the direct-selection tool
    b. to deactivate the pen tool when completing a path
    c. to select a path before adding or deleting anchor points
    d. b and c

Answers: 1. d; 2. b; 3. a; 4. d; 5. b; 6. b; 7. d; 8. a; 9. c; 10. d

LESSON

6

Tracing, Measuring, and Moving Objects

OVERVIEW

In this lesson you will learn how to use the auto trace tool to create Adobe Illustrator art from bitmapped templates. You will also learn how to use the ruler and ruler guides, how to measure and move objects, and how to hide and lock objects.

TOPICS

The auto trace tool
Setting Tolerance and Gap preferences
Templates
Tracing part of a shape
Displaying rulers
Ruler origin
Ruler guides
Creating guide objects
Measuring and moving objects
Moving objects
Grouping objects
Hiding and locking objects
Review Exercise
Review Questions

TERMS

Auto Trace gap
Freehand tolerance
group
guide
guide object
ruler origin
template

TUTORIAL FILES

Mushroom.PICT
Cake.Paint
Grouped Objects.ai
Cactus.Paint

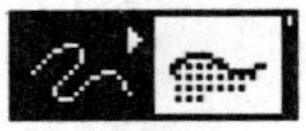

The auto trace tool is accessed by dragging on the triangle in the freehand tool icon.

THE AUTO TRACE TOOL

The auto trace tool is accessed from the tool palette by clicking and dragging out on the freehand tool. It is used to trace templates, thus creating PostScript art from bitmapped images. These templates exist on a background layer, cannot be edited in Illustrator, and will not print.

There's bad news and good news about the auto trace tool. The good news is that if the template you want to trace is big enough and simple enough—that is, if it contains hard edges which define the tracing area—the auto tracing works very well. The bad news is that if there are any open areas in the image—that is, if the image is somewhat complex, or if it is too small—the auto trace tool is useless. You're better off tracing the template with the pen tool or using a dedicated tracing program like Adobe Streamline.

SETTING TOLERANCE AND GAP PREFERENCES

The accuracy of the auto trace tool is affected by the values set in the Tool behavior field in the General Preferences dialog box (Figure 6.1). Both the Freehand tolerance and Auto Trace gap values determine what the auto trace tool does with the pixels it encounters on the template.

The Freehand tolerance value can be set from 0 to 10. A value of 0 tells Illustrator to skip zero pixels on the template. A value of 10 tells Illustrator to skip large jagged areas of the template and smooth out the line.

The Auto Trace gap value can be set from 0 to 2. A value of 1 tells Illustrator to trace the template by moving from one black pixel to the next, ignoring gaps created by one or less than 1 white pixel. A value of 2 specifies that the auto trace tool will ignore gaps existing between the black pixels of two or less than two white pixels.

FYI

There really isn't anything like a "white pixel," but it's helpful to think of the white areas between black pixels as white pixels.

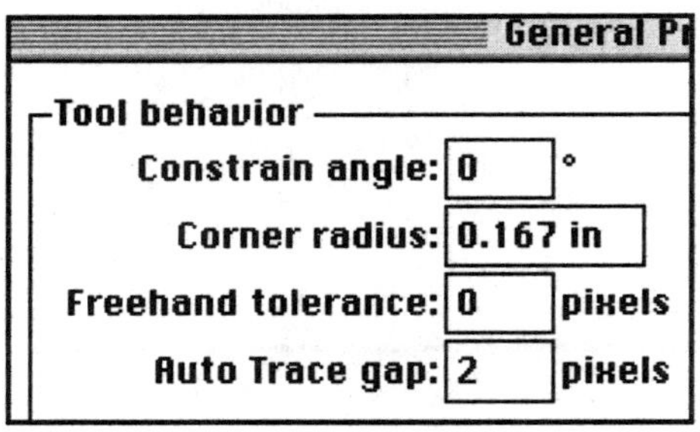

Figure 6.1—The higher the number in the Freehand tolerance field, the smoother the drawn line will be. Likewise, the higher the Auto Trace gap value, the smoother the line will be.

TEMPLATES

Illustrator will import as a template files saved in a bitmapped format such as PICT files and Paint files. When scanning images, save them in either of these formats. Much of the clip art on the market is in Paint or PICT format and can be imported into Illustrator and traced to create PostScript art. You cannot import TIFF files into Illustrator to use as templates.

EXERCISE A

1. Press Command-Option-N to display the Open template dialog box. Locate the Templates folder on the Tutorial files and open the Mushroom.PICT file. It appears on your screen as a gray image.
2. Display the Paint Style palette (Command-I) and choose None for the fill and black for the stroke. Choose View/Artwork (Command-E).
3. Click and drag on the scissors tool to select the auto trace tool.
4. Choose File/Preferences/General (Command-K) and type 6 in the Freehand tolerance field. Press the Tab key and type 0 in the Auto Trace gap field. Click on OK.
5. Click once with the crosshair cursor on the lower corner of the mushroom *cap* and release the mouse button.
6. Move the cursor to the bottom of the mushroom *stem* and click again. Both the cap and stem are outlined by a path (Figure 6.2).

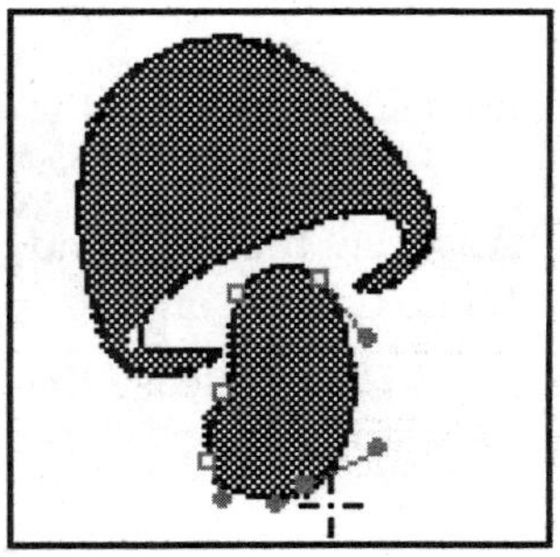

Figure 6.2—Click once on the outside edge of a template to begin tracing.

7. Choose View/Hide Template to display just the two paths.
8. Choose View/Preview (Command-Y). Use the selection tool to Shift-select both the cap and stem and change the fill to black (Figure 6.3).
9. Choose View/Artwork (Command-E) again, and use the direct-selection tool to adjust the curves on the mushroom so that it looks like something you would want to eat.
10. Choose File/Print (Command-P) and print the file. Then go back to the file and use the direct-selection tool to make any corrections in the mushroom's shape.

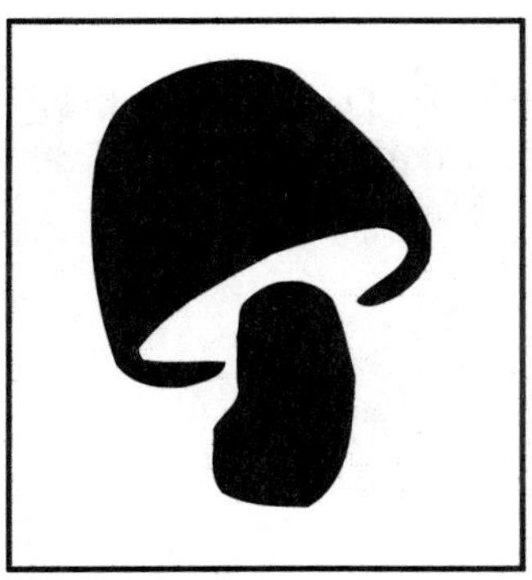

Figure 6.3—The traced mushroom after corrections were made to the paths and it was filled with black.

⌘-Option-N/File/Open/Template
⌘-I Object/Paint Style
⌘-E View/Artwork
⌘-K File/Preferences/General
⌘-Y View/Preview
⌘-P File/Print

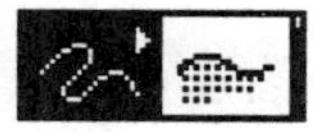

Auto trace tool

FYI

You must position the auto trace cursor within six pixels of the area you want to trace.

Double your view

Choose Window/New Window to display a duplicate of the current drawing page. This lets you work in Artwork mode while viewing the illustration in Preview mode. Any changes made in one window are automatically applied to the second window.

⌘-Option-N/File/Open/Template
⌘-I Object/Paint Style
⌘-K File/Preferences/General

TRACING PART OF A SHAPE

Sometimes you may want to trace only part of a path or trace the template one path at a time. This allows you to control the fill and stroke options for different parts of an image. To trace part of a template, drag the auto trace crosshair cursor from the point where you want the path to start to the position where the path should end. You must start and stop dragging within two pixels of the shape's edge.

EXERCISE B

1. Press Command-Option-N to open a template. Locate the Templates folder on the Tutorial disk and open the Cake.Paint template.
2. Press Command-} a few times to zoom in on the image. Although it appears to be a simple drawing, notice that there are lines at the top separating the top from the sides of the cake and that there are circles (probably big chocolate chip chunks!) inside the cake. This image lends itself to auto tracing one part at a time.
3. Display the Paint Style palette (Command-I) and select None for the fill and red for the stroke.
4. Choose File/Preferences/General (Command-K) and set the Freehand tolerance value to 10 and the Auto Trace gap value to 0. Click on OK.
5. Click at A on the left side of the cake and drag to B. Then release the mouse button (Figure 6.4). The top part of the cake is traced.

Tip

It's frequently easier to see the difference between the path created with the auto trace tool and the gray template line if you use a colored stroke.

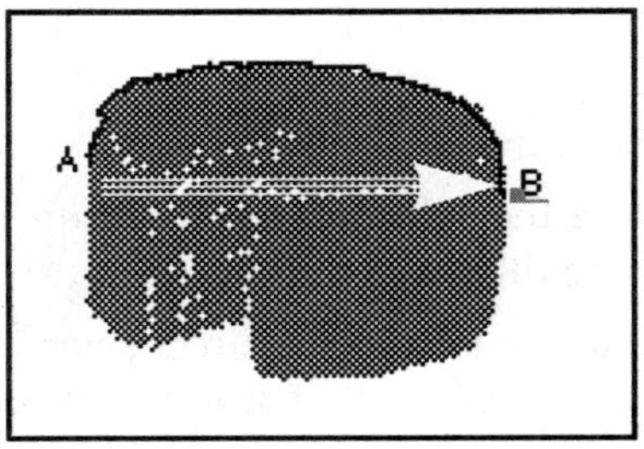

Figure 6.4—Click and drag from A to B to trace the upper part of the cake.

6. To trace the bottom part of the cake and connect the second traced path to the first, click with the crosshair on the anchor point created at A. Release the mouse button without dragging. This time the auto trace tool traced the available outline of the image, the lower part of the template, in a counterclockwise movement.
7. Now use the pen tool to complete the illustration. Draw one path of four segments to outline the center slice in the cake, pressing the Shift key to keep the vertical lines straight (Figure 6.5).

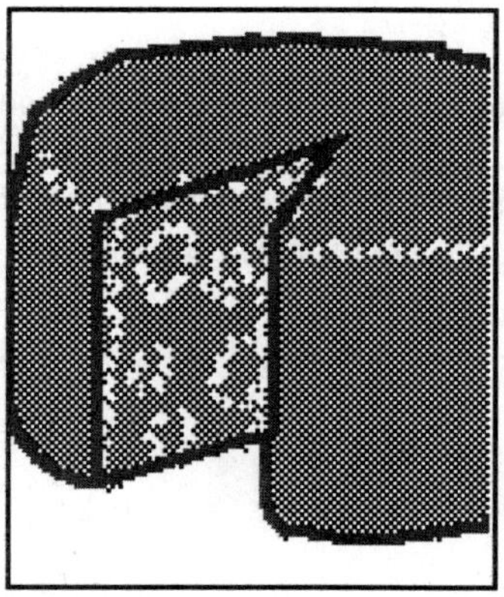

Figure 6.5—Use the pen tool to draw the four segments of the inside slice on the cake.

8. Then draw two curves to outline the curves to the left and right of the sliced area. Complete the illustration by using one of the drawing tools to outline the circles inside the cake.
9. Choose View/Artwork (Command-E) and use the direct-selection tool to correct the curves on the outside of the cake. Use the add-anchor point, delete-anchor point, and convert-anchor point tools to shape the paths so that they conform to the outline of the template.

DISPLAYING RULERS

When you first launch Illustrator, the rulers are not visible on the drawing page in the new document. To display the rulers, choose View/Show Rulers (Command-R). This command toggles between showing and hiding the rulers.

When you choose View/Show Rulers, a horizontal ruler displaying the unit of measure specified in the General Preferences dialog box appears along the bottom of the page. A vertical ruler appears on the right side of the page. The ruler origin, intersecting dotted lines, is displayed in the corner where the two rulers meet (Figure 6.6).

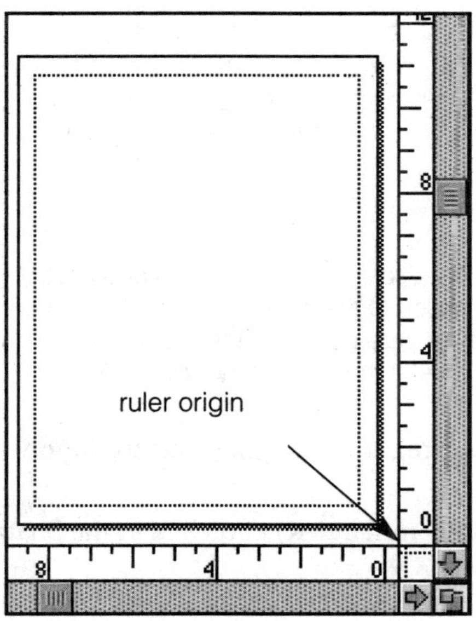

Figure 6.6—When rulers are displayed, they appear along the bottom and right edges of the drawing page.

⌘-E View/Artwork
⌘-R View/Show Rulers

FYI

The auto trace tool won't work on the rest of the template because there are no hard edges (black pixels) for it to latch onto. That's why you have to finish tracing the cake with the pen tool.

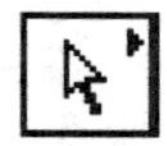

Direct-selection tool

⌘-7 Object/Guides/Unlock/Lock
⌘-R View/Show Rulers
⌘-I Object/Paint Style
⌘-Y View/Preview
⌘-K File/Preferences/General

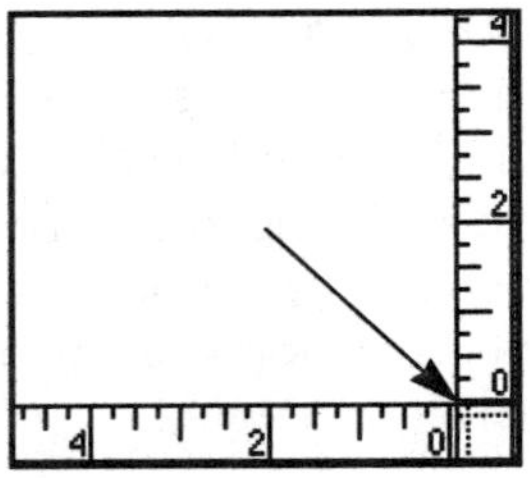

The ruler origin or zero point (dotted lines) is at the intersection of the horizontal and vertical rulers.

RULER ORIGIN

The ruler origin or zero point on the ruler is useful in establishing precise measurements in the illustration. For example, to position an object a certain distance from another object, you could use the Move command after drawing the object, or you could use a ruler guide and move the ruler origin so that the ruler guide would be at the 0 position for the x axis (horizontal) and 0 position for the y axis (vertical). This allows you to place a ruler guide at the precise point on the ruler.

RULER GUIDES

Ruler guides are nonprinting guidelines which are "stored" in the rulers. Click on the horizontal ruler and drag a ruler guide *up;* click on the vertical ruler and draw a ruler guide *out.*

The Guides option under the Object menu determines whether a guide is locked in place or unlocked. To unlock a guide so that you can reposition it or drag it off the page, choose Object/Guides/Lock (Command-7). This command toggles the Lock function on (default) and off.

FYI

Pressing the Option key while dragging a horizontal ruler guide switches it to a vertical ruler guide. The same switch occurs when you press the Option key while dragging a vertical ruler guide.

EXERCISE C

1. On a clean drawing page, choose View/Show Rulers (Command-R). Display the Paint Style palette (Command-I) and choose View/Preview (Command-Y).
2. Use the rectangle tool to draw a rectangle and fill it with any color.
3. Click on the ruler origin and drag the intersecting lines up and out of the rulers onto the drawing page so that they fit over the right and bottom segments of the rectangle (Figure 6.7). Notice that the zero points on the ruler are at the bottom and right sides of the rectangle.

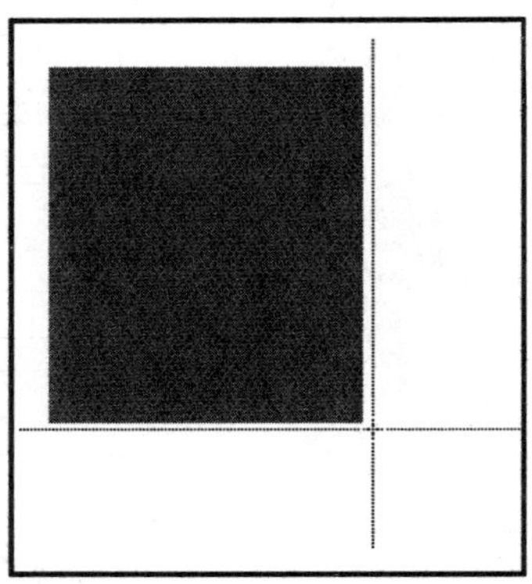

Figure 6.7—Click on the ruler origin and drag the intersection to the lower corner of the rectangle to set the zero points on the horizontal and vertical rulers at the point of the rectangle.

4. Click inside the vertical ruler and drag a ruler guide out to the one-inch mark on the horizontal ruler.
5. Choose File/Preferences/General (Command-K) and click in the Snap to point box to display an X. Click on OK.

More info

The Snap to point option allows you to snap an anchor point to a ruler guide. When this option is selected, dragging an object by its anchor points rather than by a segment causes it to snap to the guide whenever the cursor is within two pixels of the guide.

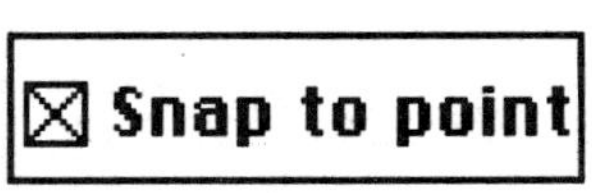

6. Draw another rectangle and fill it. While it is still selected, click on one of its *anchor points* and drag it to the ruler guide. The rectangle snaps to the guide and is positioned exactly one inch from the first rectangle (Figure 6.8). Remember that the center point is not an anchor point.

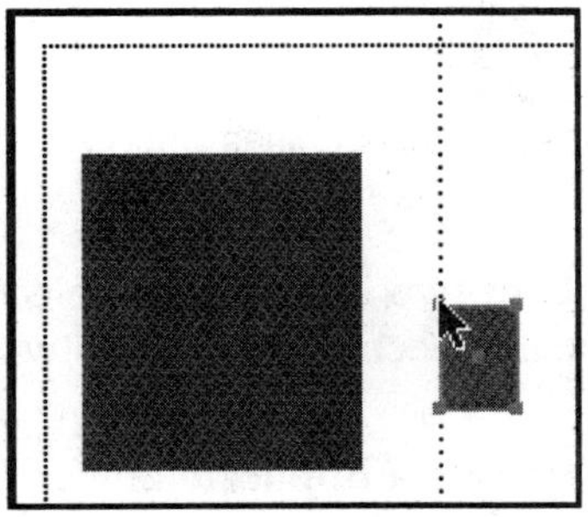

Figure 6.8—Drag by the anchor point to snap the object to the guide.

7. Choose Object/Guides/Lock (Command-7). This toggles the Lock command (default) to Unlock and allows you to move the ruler guide.
8. Move the ruler guide to the two-inch position on the horizontal ruler, and then select the second rectangle and move it against the guide at its new position.

CREATING GUIDE OBJECTS

A guide object is a ruler guide that started life as a path of any shape. When an object is changed into an guide, its path outline becomes a dashed line. Guide objects are useful when you want to align several objects.

EXERCISE D

1. On a clean drawing page, use the oval tool to draw a circle.
2. Choose File/Preferences/General (Command-K) and make sure that the Snap to Point option is checked. This allows you to drag an object *by an anchor point* and have it snap to a guide—whether it's a ruler guide or guide object.
3. Press the Option key and use the selection tool to drag the circle directly down. *Before releasing any keys,* press the Shift key. This creates a duplicate circle (Option-drag) and constrains its movement to the vertical axis (Shift-drag). When the second circle is directly below the first, release the mouse button, *then* release the Option key.
4. Shift-select both circles and choose Arrange/Repeat Transform (Command-D). This command repeats the last drawing action; in this case, it duplicates the first circle and moves it directly below the second circle.
5. Use the selection tool to drag a marquee around all four circles to select them. Choose Object/Guides/Make (Command-5). The outline of the circles changes from any stroke to a dashed line (Figure 6.9).

⌘-7 Object/Guides/Unlock/Lock
⌘-K File/Preferences/General
⌘-D Arrange/Repeat Transform
⌘-5 Object/Guides/Make

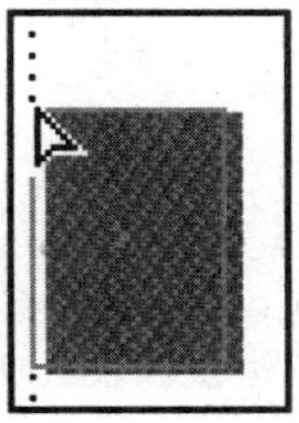

The cursor changes to a white pointer when the anchor point locks to the ruler guide.

FYI

You can override the Lock command and move a locked guide by pressing the Control-Shift keys simultaneously while moving the ruler guide.

More info

Pressing the Shift key constrains the movement to a horizontal or vertical move—depending on which way you moved first.

⌘-6 Objects/Guides/Release
⌘-K File/Preferences/General
⌘-I Object/Paint Style
⌘-E View/Artwork

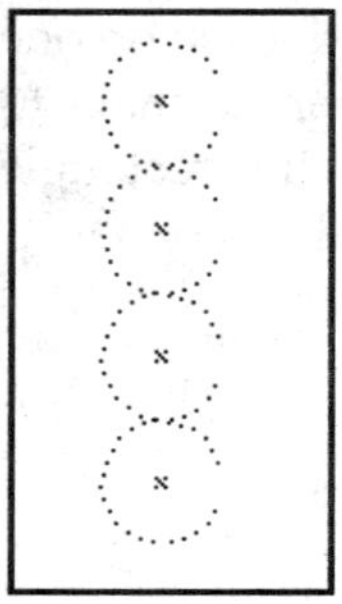

Figure 6.9—The four circles appear as dashed lines when you use the Make Guides command.

6. Use the pen tool to draw a straight line about two inches long. Select the line and drag it *by its anchor point* to the intersection of the first two circles. Make sure it snaps to the guide.
7. Drag the line and press the Option key to create a duplicate line and drag it *by the anchor point* to the center line of the center circle
8. Continue to duplicate and place lines, creating a design similar to that in Figure 6.10.

FYI

When pressing the Option key to duplicate an object, keep it depressed until you have released the mouse and/or any other modifier keys (like the Shift key). The Option key is the last key to be released.

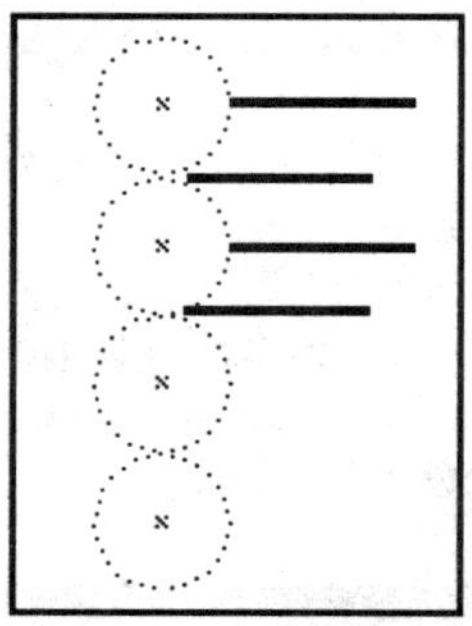

Figure 6.10—Drag a line by its anchor point to snap it to the guide.

9. When you have finished aligning the lines, use the selection tool to Shift-select the four circles. Choose Object/Guides/Release (Command-6). The selected circles return to being art objects and are no longer guides. You can now keep them or delete them.

MEASURING AND MOVING OBJECTS

Use the measure tool to calculate the distance between any two anchor points in an illustration. This value appears on the Info palette and is used as the default value in the Move dialog box. Always move an object immediately after measuring it, because any operation performed between measuring and moving changes the values in the Info palette and in the Move dialog box.

EXERCISE E

1. Begin with a clean drawing page and choose the Snap to Point option in the General Preferences dialog box (Command-K). This will force the measure tool to snap to anchor points and guide objects. Choose inches as the unit of measure from the Ruler Units pull-down menu.
2. Display the Paint Style palette (Command-I) and choose None for the fill and stroke options. Choose View/Artwork (Command-E).

3. Choose Window/Show Info (Command-Control-I) to display the Info palette (Figure 6.12). When you display the Info palette in a document where nothing is selected, the X and Y values display the horizontal (X) and vertical (Y) position of the cursor.
4. Choose Window/Hide Info palette (Command-Control-I) or click in the Close box of the Info palette to close it.
5. Click on the rectangle tool and click on the drawing page to display the Rectangle dialog box. Type 3 in the Width field and 4 in the Height field. Click on OK.
6. Use the selection tool and Option-drag the rectangle to create another rectangle. Move the second rectangle a few inches away from the original rectangle.
7. Click on the measure tool and click on the first rectangle. Then click on the second rectangle. The Info palette appears automatically and the distance between the rectangles is displayed in the W field on the Info palette (Figure 6.11).

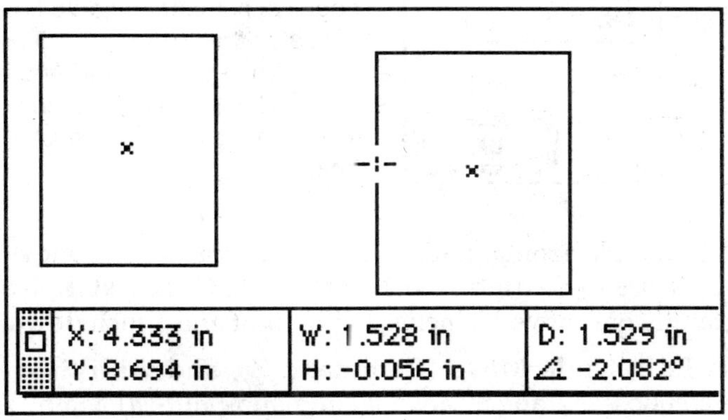

Figure 6.11—The W field indicates that the right rectangle is 1.528 inches to the right of the left rectangle. If you had clicked the right triangle first, then the left triangle, the W value would be represented as –1.528 inches.

8. The X and Y values indicate the right rectangle's horizontal (X) and vertical (Y) position from the x and y axes, or the zero point on the rulers. The W and H values indicate the absolute horizontal (W) and absolute vertical (H) distances measured. The D and Angle fields indicate that moving the rectangle 1.528 inches to the right and –0.056 inches down is the same as moving it 1.529 inches 2.082 degrees to the left.

MOVING OBJECTS

As helpful as the Info palette is, it's often much easier to use the Move command to specify the distance an object should be moved on the drawing page. You can also use the arrow keys to move an object the distance specified in the General Preferences dialog box. This is an excellent way of making lines straight, since you can't constrain a line segment to a 45 degree angle once it is drawn.

⌘-Control-I Show/Hide Info palette

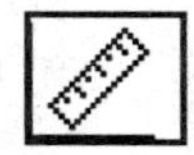

Measure tool

FYI

In both the Info palette and the Move dialog box, a positive number indicates that an object is moved up or to the right. A negative number indicates that an object is moved down or to the left.

⌘-K File/Preferences/General
⌘-Shift-M Arrange/Move
⌘-Z Edit/Undo

EXERCISE F

1. Choose File/Preferences/General (Command-K) and select Inches from the Ruler Units pull-down menu.
2. Use the two rectangles you drew in the last exercise or draw two new objects with any of the drawing tools.
3. Click on one of the objects and choose Arrange/Move (Command-Shift-M) to display the Move dialog box (Figure 6.12).

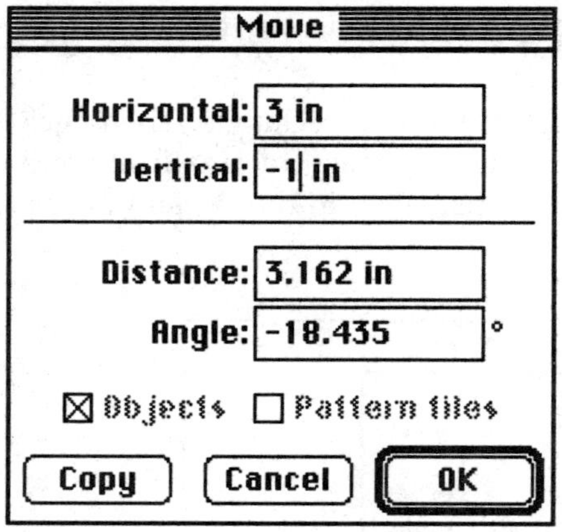

Figure 6.12—The positive number in the Horizontal field indicates that the object will be moved to the right; the negative number in the Vertical field indicates that the object will be moved down. The Distance and Angle fields are filled automatically once you input values in the upper panel of the dialog box.

4. Type 3 in the Horizontal and –1 in the Vertical field to move the rectangle 3 inches to the right and 1 inch down. Click on OK. Notice that the rectangle has moved 3 inches to the right and 1 inch down.
5. Choose Edit/Undo Move (Command-Z), and with the rectangle selected, choose Arrange/Move (Command-Shift-M) again. Type in a negative value in the Horizontal field and a positive value in the Vertical field. Click on Copy. Notice that a copy of the selected rectangle moves to the left and up on the drawing page.
6. Choose File/Preferences/General (Command-K) and type 0.001 in the Cursor key field under Keyboard increments (Figure 6.13). This specifies the distance the cursor will move when you press the arrow keys. The value of .001 means that the selected object or segment will move very little, giving you a great deal of control over its positioning.

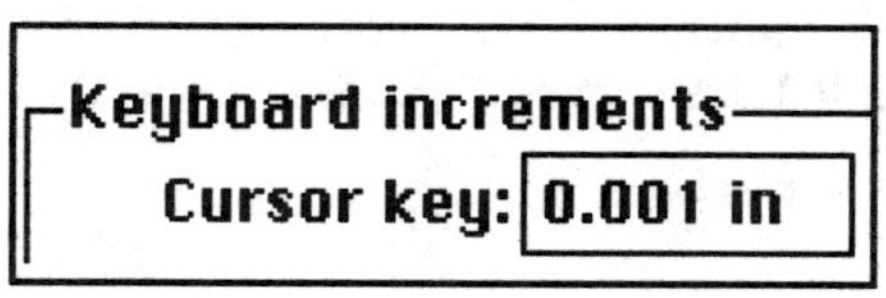

Figure 6.13—Set the Cursor key value for a fraction of an inch to limit the movement of the arrow keys.

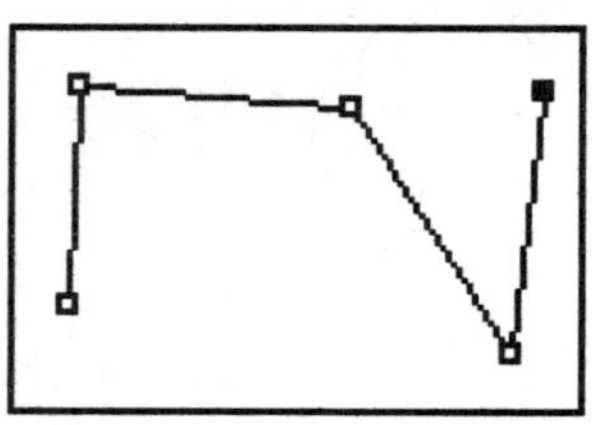

When you draw an open path, the last point remains selected.

7. Use the pen tool to draw a line with several segments. Don't press the Shift key before clicking; you don't want a perfectly straight line.
8. Zoom in on the last segment of the line. With the line's endpoint still selected, press the right arrow key and notice how the line moves almost imperceptibly. Press the arrow key again a few more times or until you have straightened out the line.

9. Choose Edit/Select None (Command-Shift-A) to deselect the line. Use the direct-selection tool to select the line again and Shift-click on two anchor points connecting a segment to select them. Use the arrow keys to move the segment right and left, up and down to change its position.

⌘-Shift-A Edit/Select None

GROUPING OBJECTS

Direct-selection tool

When you want to keep objects connected so they will move as a unit, group them. You can group one group with another, thus ensuring that many objects will move or be transformed simultaneously.

When you use the *selection tool* to select any object in a group, the entire group is selected, and any changes made will affect the entire group. Use the *direct-selection tool* to select a single path or single object in a group. If you have nested groups (a group within a group), select the next group up in the grouping order with the *group-selection tool*. Each time you click with the group-selection tool, you add another set of grouped objects to the selection (Figure 6.14).

In Figure 6.14, Group 1 and Group 2 (the arcs and balls) are grouped together and that new group is grouped to Group 3 (line).

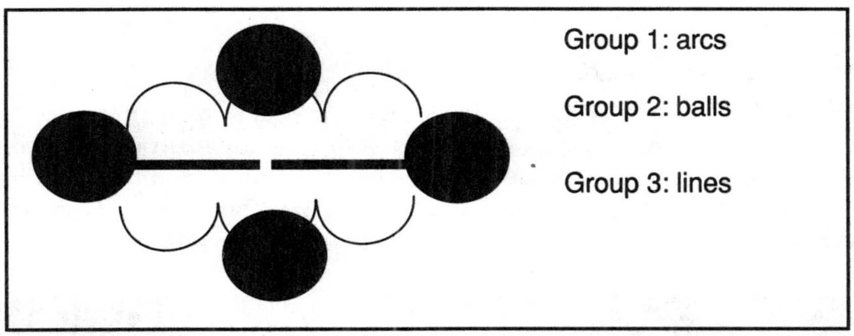

Figure 6.14—Three groups of objects. Use the group-selection tool to select each nested group in the illustration.

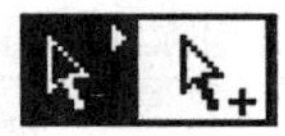

Drag on the triangle on the direct-selection tool icon to access the group-selection tool. The group-selection tool displays a + sign.

EXERCISE G

1. Open the Grouped Objects.ai file in the Tutorial folder. Choose File/Save As and save it under a different name. Choose View/Artwork (Command-E).
2. Click on the group-selection tool and click on one of the upper arcs. One arc is selected. Don't move the cursor. Click a second time and the other two arcs in the first group of arcs are selected. Click a third time and the entire group of lower arcs is selected. Both the upper and lower arcs are now selected.
3. Click a fourth time to select the four balls. Click a fifth time to select the bars. You have selected the three groups in the illustration, one group at a time.

⌘-Shift-A Edit/Select None
⌘-Z Edit/Undo
⌘-U Arrange/Ungroup
⌘-N File/New
⌘-I Object/Paint Style
⌘-Y View/Preview
⌘-1 Arrange/Lock
⌘-2 Arrange/Unlock
⌘-3 Arrange/Hide
⌘-4 Arrange/Show All

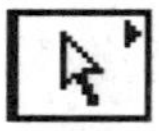

Direct-selection tool

FYI

When you select and ungroup, you must deselect everything before you can begin to work with the individual elements that were grouped. Always deselect everything before issuing another command or before selecting another object.

4. Choose Edit/Select None (Command-Shift-A) to deselect everything.
5. Use the group-selection tool and click on one of the balls. Click a second time to select all four of the balls. Drag the four balls away from the illustration. Choose Edit/Undo Move (Command-Z) to restore the illustration. Deselect everything (Command-Shift-A).
6. Use the direct-selection tool to select one of the arcs and move the direction handles to reshape the curve.
7. Choose Edit/Select None to deselect everything. Use the group-selection tool to select one of the balls. Click on the selection tool and drag the selected ball away from the illustration.
8. Deselect everything. Click anywhere on the illustration with the selection tool. Choose Arrange/Ungroup (Command-U). You have ungrouped only the arcs from the larger illustration.
9. Click anywhere on the page to deselect everything. Click on the balls with the selection tool, and choose Arrange/Ungroup (Command-U) again. You have ungrouped the four balls. Deselect everything. Click with the selection tool on one of the balls and move it away from the group. Deselect everything.
10. Click with the selection tool on one of the bars. Press Command-U to ungroup the bars. Deselect everything.

HIDING AND LOCKING OBJECTS

When you're working with a complex illustration, it's frequently easier to see what you're doing when only the part of the illustration you're working with is visible. You can choose to hide objects while working with other illustration elements and then display them. You can also lock objects, which prevents you from accidentally selecting and editing them.

EXERCISE H

1. Create a new file (File/New). Choose View/Preview (Command-Y).
2. Reset the Toolbox by pressing the Command and Shift keys simultaneously while double-clicking on any tool.
3. Select the rectangle tool and draw two rectangles. Fill each with a different color.
4. Use the selection tool to select one rectangle. Choose Arrange/Hide (Command-3) to make the selected rectangle disappear.
5. Choose Arrange/Show All (Command-4) to make the hidden rectangle visible on the screen.
6. Select the other rectangle. Choose Arrange/Lock (Command-1). Now try selecting it—you can't. Although the locked object is visible, it is not available for editing.
7. Choose Arrange/Unlock All (Command-2) to unlock the object and make it available for editing.

REVIEW EXERCISE

⌘-O File/Open
⌘-I Object/Paint Style
⌘-K File/Preferences/General
⌘-D Arrange/Repeat Transform
⌘-G Arrange/Group
⌘-2 Arrange/Unlock

In this exercise you will trace a template, then use the various tools to create an illustration from one object.

1. Press the Option key and choose File/Open. Locate the Cactus.Paint file in the Tutorial folder and click on Open. The cactus appears as a grayed-out image in the background of the illustration page.
2. Display the Paint Style palette (Command-I) and choose none for the fill and a red color for the stroke.
3. Click on the auto trace tool and click at the top of the cactus to trace it. If you're not happy with the resulting artwork, make changes in the Auto Trace gap and Freehand tolerance fields in the General Preferences dialog box (Command-K).
4. Use the direct-selection tool to select the cactus and then use the add-anchor point, delete-anchor point, and convert-anchor point tools to edit the drawing.
5. Select the cactus with the selection tool, press the Option key, and drag to duplicate it.
6. Use the Arrange/Repeat Transform again (Command-D) to "grow" a whole field of cacti.
7. Shift-select three cacti and group them (Command-G). Select another cactus and hide it (Arrange/Hide). Select another cactus and lock it (Arrange/Lock).
8. While the cacti are hidden and locked, edit other cacti. Use the brush tool and freehand tool to draw desert objects.
9. Choose Arrange/Show All (Command-4) and Arrange/Unlock All (Command-2).
10. Choose File/Save (Command-S) and save this file as Desert Scene. You will use it in a later lesson.

REVIEW QUESTIONS

Read the following questions and choose the answer which best completes the statement.

1. A template _____.
   a. appears as a gray image
   b. is loaded into the background of the illustration
   c. cannot be edited
   d. all of the above
2. Templates must be _____.
   a. Paint Files
   b. TIFF files
   c. PICT files
   d. a and c

3. The auto trace tool is affected by the _____.
   a. Freehand tolerance preference
   b. Auto Trace gap preference
   c. speed of dragging
   d. a and b
4. The ruler origin is _____.
   a. the zero point on the horizontal ruler
   b. the zero point on the vertical ruler
   c. the intersection of the horizontal and vertical rulers
   d. displayed as a single line
5. Ruler guides cannot be _____.
   a. printed
   b. hidden
   c. locked
   d. all of the above
6. A guide object is made _____.
   a. with the rectangle tool
   b. with the oval tool
   c. with the freehand tool
   d. from any path
7. Objects that are hidden _____
   a. cannot be selected
   b. cannot be seen
   c. appear as gray objects
   d. a and b
8. Objects that are locked _____.
   a. cannot be selected
   b. cannot be seen
   c. appear as gray objects
   d. a and b
9. The group-selection tool _____.
   a. selects every group automatically
   b. selects one group at a time
   c. creates groups
   d. a and c
10. The Move dialog box is used to _____.
   a. move objects from one document to another
   b. repeat the duplicate function
   c. move objects a specific distance
   d. b and c

Answers: 1. d; 2. d; 3. d; 4. c; 5. a; 6. d; 7. d; 8. a; 9. b; 10. c

LESSON 7

Transforming Objects

OVERVIEW

This lesson will show you how to transform objects. You will learn how to use the scale, rotate, reflect, and shear tools to change the appearance of objects. You will also learn how to create blends between objects.

TOPICS

Scaling objects
Rotating objects
The reflect tool
The shear tool
The blend tool
Blending dissimilar objects
Blending similar closed paths
Creating guide objects
Review Exercises
Review Questions

TERMS

blend
point of origin
reflect
rotate
scale
shear

TUTORIAL FILES

Face.ai
Half Heart.ai
Mushroom.ai
Planes.ai
Desert Scene.ai
House.ai

⌘-N File/New
⌘-I Object/Paint Style
⌘-E View/Artwork

SCALING OBJECTS

You can reduce or enlarge an object by scaling it either horizontally, vertically, or both horizontally and vertically. Unless you specify a point of origin, all scaling takes place from the center point of an object.

To specify exact scaling dimensions, use the Scale dialog box. To scale visually, click and drag an object with the scale tool.

EXERCISE A

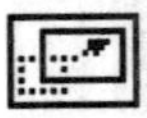

Scale tool

1. Choose File/New (Command-N) and display the Paint Style palette (Command-I). Choose fill and stroke colors. Choose View/Artwork (Command-E).
2. Choose Filter/Create/Star to display the Create Star dialog box. Create a five-pointed star and click on OK. A star appears selected on the drawing page.
3. With the star still selected, click on the scale tool. Then click on one of the points of the star and drag *away* from the object to *enlarge* it; drag *toward* the object to *reduce* it. Notice that in dragging this way, the star is becoming distorted. Choose Edit/Undo (Command-Z) to restore the star to its original shape.
4. This time you will set a point of origin for the scale. Select the scale tool and click in the center of the star. The cursor changes to an arrowhead (Figure 7.1).

FYI

If you released the mouse button more than once while scaling, choose Edit/Undo a few times to restore the original shape. You'll know you undid the correct number of times when Undo Filter appears in the Edit menu.

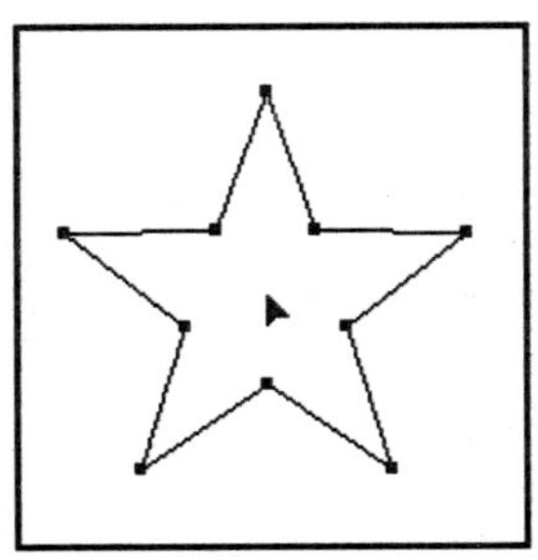

Figure 7.1—One click with the scale tool sets the point of origin for the scale. The object will be enlarged or reduced from this point.

5. Click on one of the star points and drag away from the center. The original star is displayed as the object is enlarged (Figure 7.2). Release the mouse button.

Make a point

Objects drawn with the drawing tools like the pen and brush tools do not display center points. To create a center point, choose Object/Attributes (Command-Control-A) and select the Show center point option in the Attributes dialog box.

☒ **Show center point**

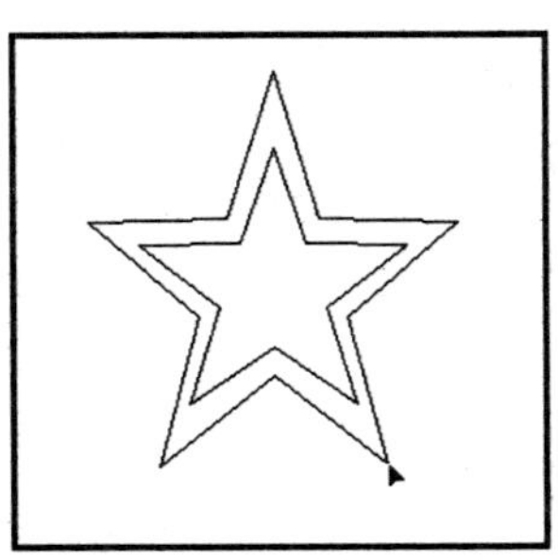

Figure 7.2—When you drag with the scaling cursor, the original object (inside star) remains displayed as it is reduced or enlarged.

6. Choose Edit/Undo Scale (Command-Z) to restore the original image.
7. Click with the scaling cursor on any star point and drag *away* from the star. Notice that dragging away from the object enlarges it; dragging toward the object reduces it. Likewise, depending on the direction in which you drag, the star can become distorted.
8. Choose Undo Scale (Command-Z) until you return to the original star. Double-click on the scale tool to display the Scale dialog box. Click the Uniform button to select it and type 50 in the percent field to reduce the object to half its current size. Click on the Copy button to create a copy of the selected object without changing the original object (Figure 7.3).

⌘-Z Edit/Undo

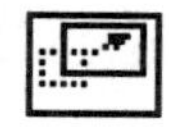

Option-click on the object with the scale tool to set the point of origin and display the Scale dialog box.

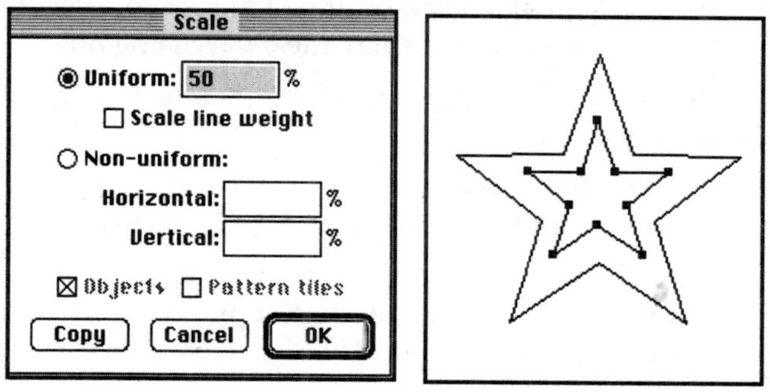

Figure 7.3—Double-clicking on the scale tool displays the Scale dialog box (left). Click on Copy to exit the dialog box and display a copy of the selected object, now scaled to the specified size (right)

9. Use the selection tool to move the small star onto a blank area of the drawing page. Double-click on the scale tool again to display the Scale dialog box.
10. Click on the Non-uniform button and type 150 in the Horizontal field to enlarge the object 50% beyond its current size in a horizontal (wide) direction. Type 25 in the Vertical field to reduce the object 25% of its current size in a vertical (high) direction. Click on OK. Your screen should resemble Figure 7.4.

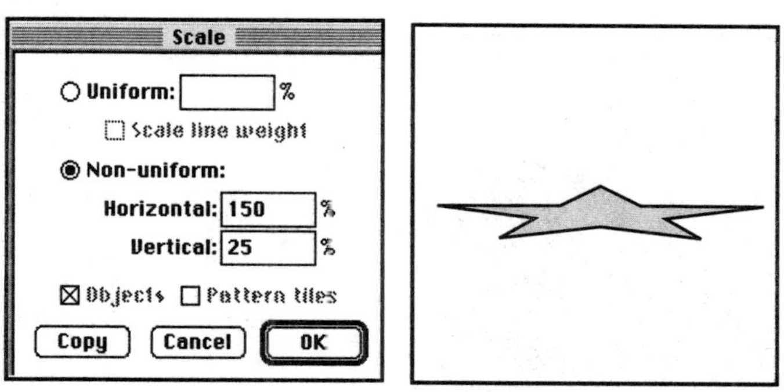

Figure 7.4—When you select the Non-uniform option, you can scale an object horizontally and/or vertically to different percentages of the object's current size.

FYI

When dragging with the scale tool, press the Shift key to scale the object uniformly. Release the mouse button *before* releasing the Shift key.

More info

If you click in the Scale line weight box, the stroke of any stroked path will be scaled along with the scaled object.

⌘-K File/Preferences/General

⌘-D Arrange/Repeat Transform

Rotate tool

ROTATING OBJECTS

As with the scale function, there are several ways to rotate an object in Illustrator. You can rotate by dragging a selected object around the object's midpoint with the rotate tool or by specifying an angle of rotation in the Rotate dialog box.

EXERCISE B

1. Choose File/Preferences/General and select inches from the Ruler units pull-down menu.
2. On a clean drawing page, click on the oval tool to select it, and click once on the drawing page to display the Oval dialog box.
3. Type 1 in the Width field; press the Tab key and type 2 in the Height field. Click on OK.
4. Click once on the rotate tool and click on the lower point of the oval. This sets the point around which the oval will rotate.
5. Move the arrowhead cursor away from the oval, press the Option key, and click and drag to rotate the oval about 30 degrees to the left. Release the mouse button (Figure 7.5).

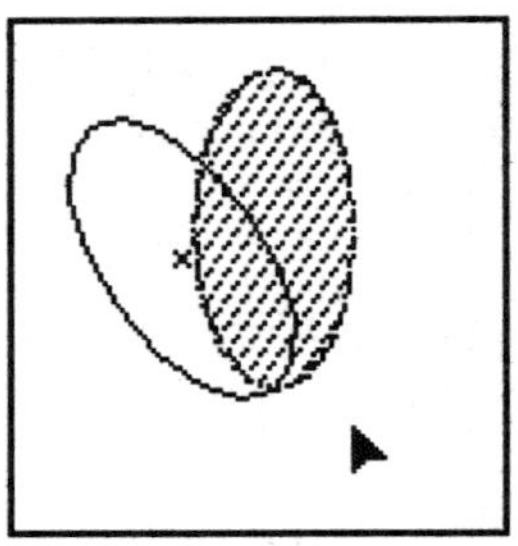

Figure 7.5—To rotate an object from a specific point, first click that point with the rotate tool, then move away from the object and drag. Pressing the Option key while dragging creates a rotated copy of the original object.

6. Choose Arrange/Repeat Transform (Command-D) to repeat the copy/rotate action. Continue to press Command-D until the rotated ovals create a flower (Figure 7.6).

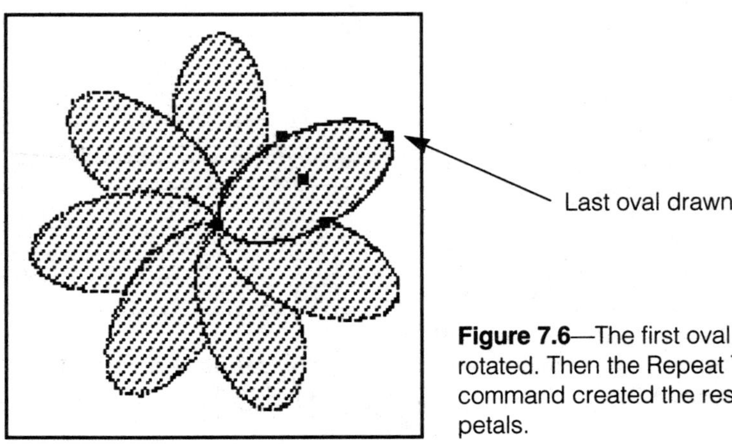

Figure 7.6—The first oval was Option-rotated. Then the Repeat Transform command created the rest of the flower's petals.

EXERCISE C

⌘-A Edit/Select All

⌘-Shift-A Edit/Select None

⌘-G Arrange/Group

1. Choose Edit/Select All (Command-A) and press the Delete key.
2. Use the rectangle tool to draw a square (Shift-drag). Deselect it (Command-Shift-A).
3. Use the direct-selection tool to select the square and click on one of the corner anchor points to select it. Drag that anchor point out so that the square becomes reshaped into a kite (Figure 7.7). Use the freehand tool to draw a tail on the kite.

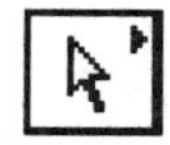

Direct-selection tool

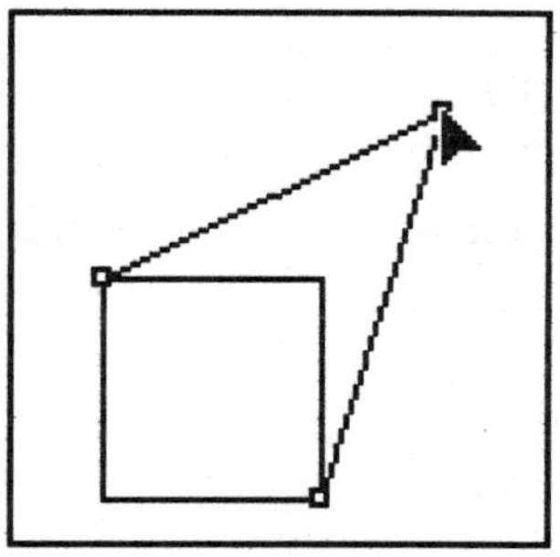

Figure 7.7—Select the square with the direct-selection tool. Then select one anchor point and drag it to reshape the square into a kite.

FYI

Before selecting with the direct-selection tool, always deselect first. You cannot select individual paths while an object is still selected with the selection tool.

4. Choose Edit/Select All (Command-A) and group all the objects (Command-G). Leave the group selected.
5. Click on the rotate tool to select it. Click anywhere on the page and drag to rotate the kite from its center point. Release the mouse button.
6. Now click with the rotate tool on one of the selected anchor points of the kite. This sets the point of origin around which the kite (object) will rotate.
7. Move the arrowhead away from the point you just clicked and drag in a circular motion to rotate the kite.
8. Press the Shift key while rotating to constrain the rotation to 45 degrees.

Rotate tool

EXERCISE D

1. Use any of the drawing tools to create an object. Keep the object selected.
2. Double-click on the rotate tool to display the Rotate dialog box.
3. Type 35 in the Angle field. Click on the Copy button to rotate a copy of the original object 35 degrees from its center point to the left.
4. With the copy still selected, double-click on the rotate tool again. Type –75 in the Angle field and click on OK to rotate the selection 75 degrees to the right.

⌘-O File/Open
⌘-E View/Artwork
⌘-W File/Close

THE REFLECT TOOL

Use the Reflect command to create a mirror image of an object. Illustrator reflects across the axis which runs through the selected anchor point. Press the Option key or click on the Copy button in the Reflect dialog box to create the mirror image.

Since the Reflect command flips only what is selected, you can select part of a path with the direct-selection tool and flip only that section. Or you could Shift-select several objects in a drawing and flip (reflect) only them.

EXERCISE E

1. Open (Command-O) the Face.ai file in the Tutorial folder. Choose View/Artwork (Command-E). Select the object with the selection tool.
2. Click once on the reflect tool. Click with the crosshair cursor on the top of the head (Figure 7.8).

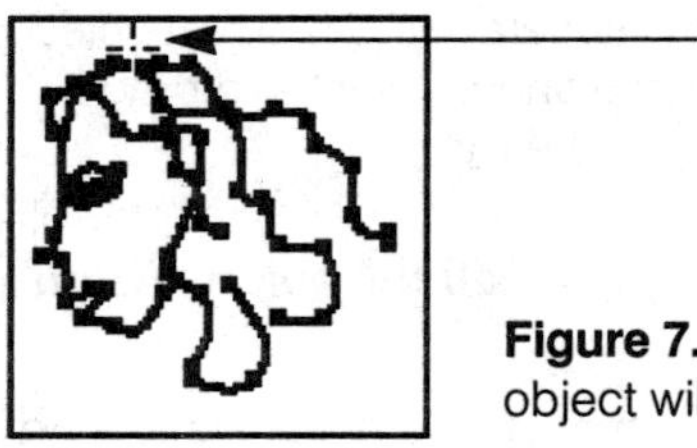

Click here with the reflect tool to set the flipping point of origin.

Figure 7.8—Click at a point to set the axis around which the object will flip.

3. Position the arrowhead on the chin and click. The object is reflected (flipped) horizontally across an invisible axis.
4. With the object still active, click with the reflect tool on the top of the head again.
5. Move the arrowhead pointer away from the object and drag to reflect (reposition) the object. As you drag, the axis of rotation you set in step 4 rotates around the point you clicked in step 3.
6. Continue to click and flip on other areas of the path with the reflect tool until you are comfortable with it.
7. Close this file (Command-W). Don't save your changes.

FYI

Option-clicking with the scale, rotate, reflect, and shear tools displays their respective dialog boxes and sets the point of origin for that function at the point where you clicked.

EXERCISE F

1. Open (Command-O) the Half Heart.ai file in the Tutorial folder. Choose View/Artwork (Command-E).
2. Select the half heart with the selection tool. Click once on the reflect tool.
3. Press the Option key and click with the crosshair pointer on the center point of the heart to display the Reflect dialog box.
4. Click on Vertical and click on Copy. The half heart is copied and flipped vertically from the center point to complete the shape of the heart (Figure 7.9).

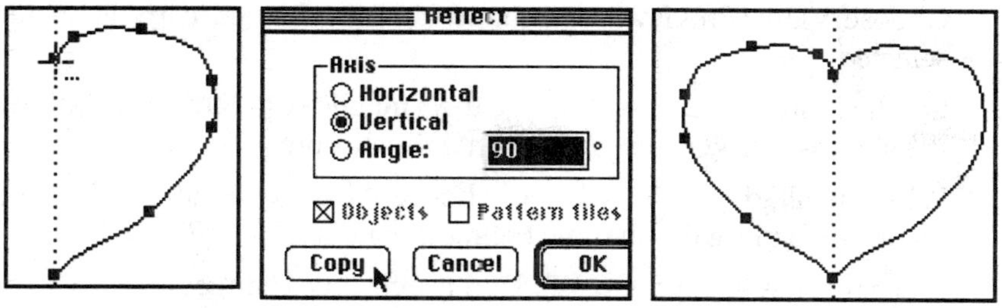

Figure 7.9—Option-clicking with the reflect tool on the center point of the object (left) displays the Reflect dialog box (center). Choosing Vertical and clicking on Copy produces a mirror image of the orig nal path (right).

5. Choose Edit/Select All (Command-A) and group the two paths into a single object (Command-G).
6. Close this file (Command-W). Don't save your changes.

THE SHEAR TOOL

What the rest of the world calls "skew," Adobe Illustrator calls "shear." The shear tool is used to slant an object along a specified axis. It is most useful for creating shadows when the Option-skew command is used.

The shear tool is tricky to use, especially when you are skewing a path with many segments. It's sometimes easier to access the Shear dialog box, plug in a small angle like 10 degrees and then repeat the transformation until the object is slanted properly.

Another way to control the skewing is to shear along an angle that is a multiple of 45 degrees in relation to the current x axis by pressing the Shift key while dragging with the shear tool. Pressing the Shift and Option keys while dragging with the shear tool will create a copy of the original object (Option) and constrain the shearing (Shift).

Unlike the other transformational tools, which calculate the transformation (scale, rotate, and reflect) counterclockwise from the selected axis, the shear tool calculates the skew angle clockwise from the current axis.

EXERCISE G

1. Open the Mushroom.ai file (Command-O). Display the Paint Style palette (Command-I) and select Artwork mode (Command-E).
2. Choose Edit/Select All (Command-A) and choose Arrange/Group (Command-G) to group the mushroom stem with the cap.
3. Click on the shear tool and click on the lower left corner of the mushroom stem. This sets the point of origin from which the object will slant.
4. Move the cursor away from the object and press the Option key. Click and Option-drag very slowly down and to the left. You can see the copy slanting up and to the left. When it is slanted enough to look like a shadow cast by the mushroom, release the mouse button, *then* the Option key.

⌘-A Edit/Select All
⌘-G Arrange/Group
⌘-W File/Close
⌘-I Object/Paint Style
⌘-E View/Artwork

Another way

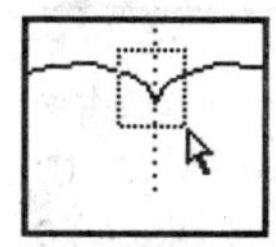

You could also connect the two pieces of the heart by first deselecting everything and using the direct-selection tool to draw a selection marquee around the two top endpoints. Then choose Object/Join. Do the same with the bottom endpoints to complete the connection.

FYI

The further away from the point of origin that you start dragging with the shear tool, the more control you have over it.

⌘-Y View/Preview
⌘-- (hyphen) Arrange/ Send to Back
⌘-W File/Close

5. Choose View/Preview (Command-Y). The skewed copy is currently selected.
6. On the Paint Style palette, move the Tint slider to 50%. This will make the shadow darker than the original mushroom.
7. With the shadow still selected, choose Arrange/Send to Back (Command--) to place the shadow behind the mushroom (Figure 7.10).
8. Close this file (Command-W). Don't save your changes.

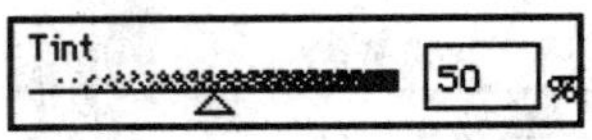

Use the Tint slider on the Paint Style palette to reduce the 100% black to 50% for the shadow.

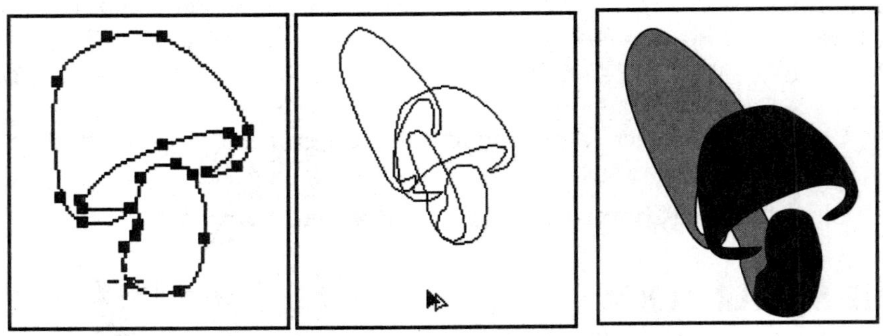

Figure 7.10—Click with the shear tool on a path to create the shearing point of origin (left). Pressing the Option key while dragging the cursor creates a sheared copy of the mushroom (center). Send the sheared copy to the back to create the shadow effect (right).

THE BLEND TOOL

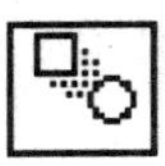

Blend tool

Blending objects creates a series of intermediate objects and colors between two selected objects. Two open paths like lines can be blended to create different graphic effects. You can also blend overlapping shapes to create a smooth blend between two different colors. Blending dissimilar shapes creates multiple objects with different shapes and colors.

There are a few rules to observe when blending:

1. Blend only two objects at a time. You cannot use the blend tool on groups of objects, although you can use the direct-selection tool to select parts of a group and blend between those two paths.
2. You cannot blend between an open and a closed path or between compound paths. Both paths must be either open or closed.
3. When blending objects to which color has been applied, the colors in both objects must be either process colors *or* custom colors. If you use the blend tool on differently colored objects, Illustrator will paint the blended shapes with a process color. If you blend between two different custom colors, Illustrator will substitute a process color for the intermediate objects. Blending between tints of the same custom color results in the steps being painted with the custom color.
4. When preparing illustrations containing blends to be color separated, use tints to reduce the number of separations. When blending a custom color with white, do not use process white. Instead, use a zero percent tint of the same custom color.
5. If you blend between patterns, both patterns must be the same.

FYI

Version 5.5 contains a Custom to Process filter that converts custom colors to the equivalent CMYK process colors.

To convert custom colors to process colors, choose Filter/Colors/Custom to Process.

EXERCISE H

1. On a clean drawing page, choose View/Preview (Command-Y) and display the Paint Style palette (Command-I).
2. Use the pen tool to draw a straight horizontal line about 3 inches long.
3. With the line still selected, choose Arrange/Move (Command-Shift-M) to display the Move dialog box (Figure 7.11). Type –3 (inches) in the Distance field. This displays 216 pt in the Horizontal field. Since you want to move a copy of the selected line 3 inches *down*—a negative number in the Vertical field moves an object *down*—type 216 in the Distance field and –3 (inches) in the Vertical field.
4. Click on Copy to move a copy of the selected line 3 inches *down* on the page (Figure 7.11).

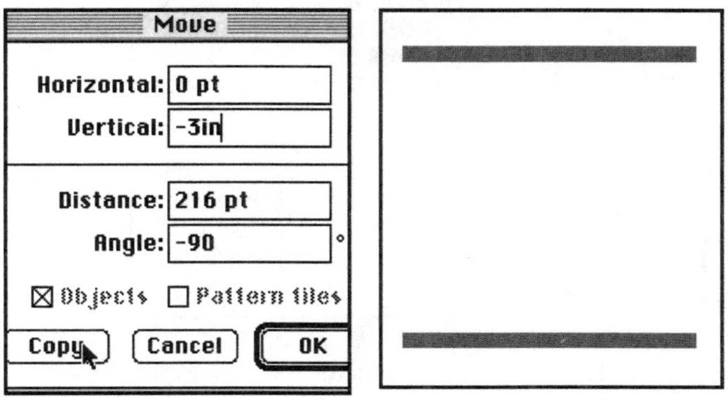

Figure 7.11—Use the Move command to create a copy of the selected line and position it 3 inches below it.

5. Click on the Process Color icon on the Paint Style palette to display the CMYK sliders. Choose None for fill, but click on the Stroke icon.
6. Use the selection tool to select the top line. Move the Magenta slider to the 100% position to stroke the line with 100% magenta; leave the CYK values at 0%.
7. Click on the second line and stroke it with 100% yellow.
8. Deselect everything (Command-Shift-A). Use the direct-selection tool to drag a selection marquee around the right endpoints of both lines (Figure 7.12).

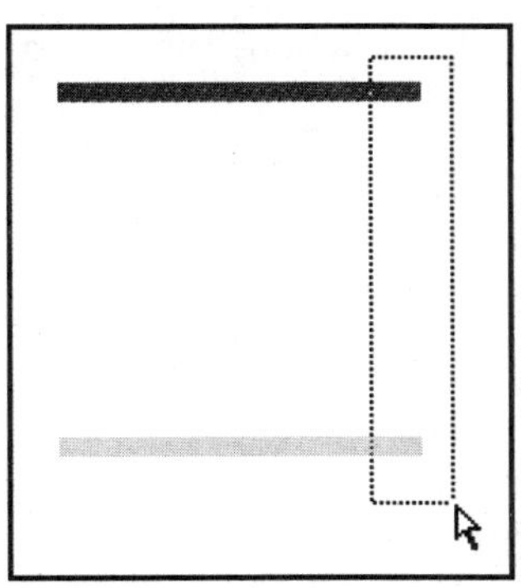

Figure 7.12—The blend tool must be applied to the endpoint of each open path. Dragging a selection marquee is an easy way to select both endpoints.

⌘-Y View/Preview
⌘-I Object/Paint Style
⌘-Shift-M Arrange/Move
⌘-Shift-A Edit/Select None

Sneaky info

Illustrator defaults to translating values in the Distance field to the Horizontal field in the Move dialog box. When you want to move an object vertically a specific distance, type that value in the distance, then cut and paste the displayed translated value (inches to points) from the Horizontal field to the Vertical field.

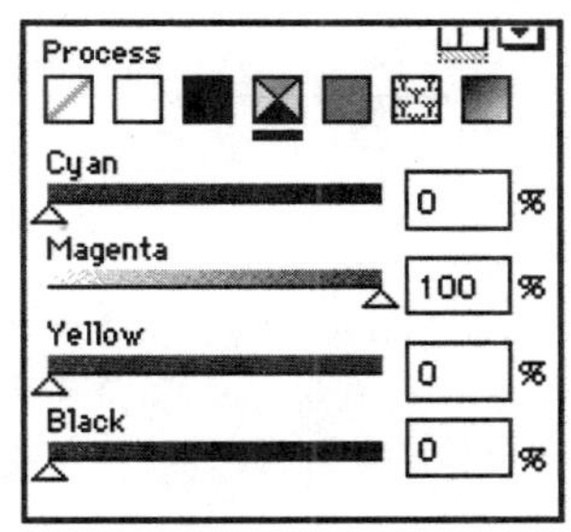

When the Process Color icon is selected, the CMYK sliders are displayed.

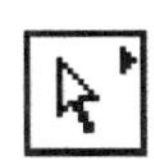

Direct-selection tool

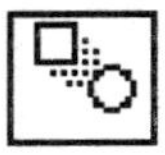

Blend tool

Endpoint Alert!

Sometimes it's hard to see the selected endpoint when you're trying to click with the blend tool. If you get an Alert message, click OK, switch to Artwork mode where you can more easily see selected anchor points, and click on the first endpoint again. The Alert message cancels the first click.

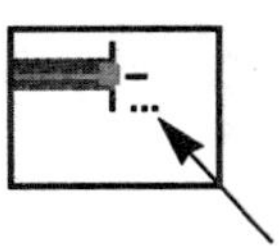

The blend tool cursor displays a small horizontal dotted line when you click on an endpoint.

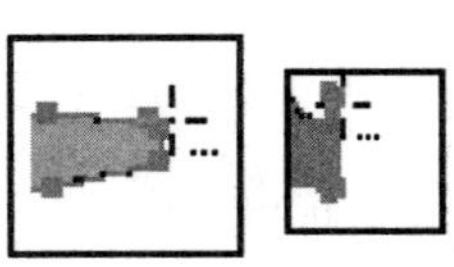

When creating a blend, it's sometimes easier to select both objects; this will display all of their anchor points. Then you can just click on one anchor point with the blend tool.

9. Click on the blend tool. Click once on the right endpoint of the top line and release the mouse button.
10. Click once on the right endpoint of the bottom line and release the mouse button. When the second of the two necessary endpoints is selected, the Blend dialog box is displayed. Type 10 in the Steps field to override Illustrator's recommended number. Illustrator calculates the percentage of change in the first and last steps on the basis of the two colors you are blending. Click on OK.
11. Illustrator draws 10 lines between the two selected lines, with the colors gradually blending from solid to pale magenta and pale to solid yellow (Figure 7.13).
12. Save this file (File/Save As) with the name of Blend.ai as an Adobe Illustrator 5 file.

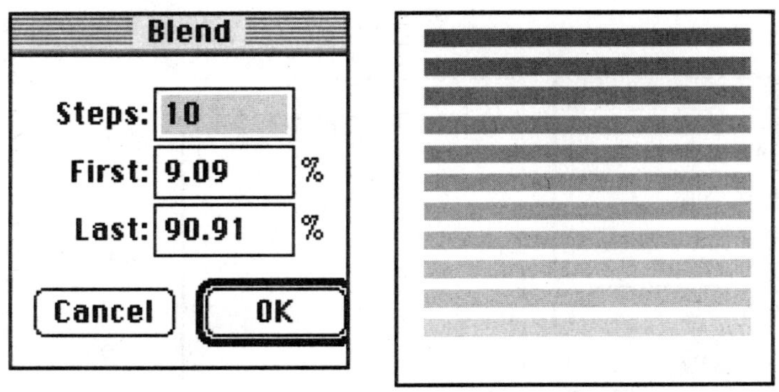

Figure 7.13—Specifying 10 in the Steps field causes 10 lines, graduating from magenta to yellow, to appear between the selected lines.

BLENDING DISSIMILAR OBJECTS

When you blend two dissimilar objects, Illustrator transforms the first selected object into the second. The subtlety or obviousness of this transformation depends on the number of steps specified for the blend. The greater the number of steps, the more subtle the transformation.

Remember, however, that because the blend command creates a series of intermediate objects, these steps take time, memory, and processing power to create. If, for example, you accept Illustrator's suggestion of 260 steps for a blend, you have to wait for it to draw each of those 260 objects. You may be just as happy with significantly fewer steps. That's where the Undo command (Command-Z) comes in handy.

⌘-O File/Open
⌘-A Edit/Select All
⌘-I Object/Paint Style

EXERCISE I

1. Open the Planes.ai file (Command-O) on the Tutorial disk. Choose Edit/Select All (Command-A) to display both planes.
2. Click on the blend tool and click on one of the selected points on the wing tip of the top plane. Click on a selected endpoint on the wing tip of the bottom plane to display the Blend dialog box.
3. Type 5 in the Steps field to create a blend of five intermediate planes (objects), which transform from a twin-engine plane to a fighter plane (Figure 7.14).

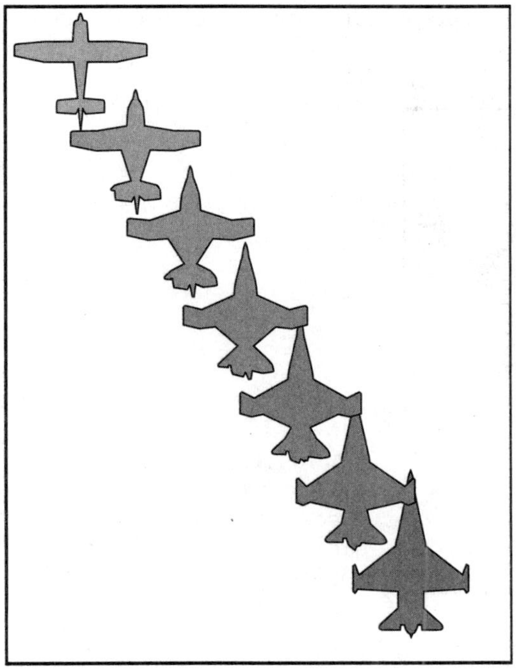

Figure 7.14—Specifying 5 in the Steps field of the Blend dialog box creates five intermediate shapes between the top and bottom objects.

BLENDING SIMILAR CLOSED PATHS

Blending similar closed paths creates interesting three-dimensional effects. Because the blend creates a series of intermediate objects, any of these objects can be selected and manipulated individually.

EXERCISE J

1. On a clean drawing page, choose Filter/Create/Star to display the Create Star dialog box. Type 5 in the Points field and click on OK.
2. The star appears, displaying the last selected fill and stroke options. Display the Paint Style palette (Command-I) and click on the Process Color icon to display the CMYK sliders. Use the sliders to create fill and stroke colors for the star.

⌘-Shift-M Arrange/Move
⌘-A Edit/Select All
⌘-O File/Open
⌘-Z Edit/Undo

3. With the star still selected, choose Arrange/Move (Command-Shift-M) to display the Move dialog box. Type 1 (inch) in the Horizontal field and 1 (inch) in the Vertical field and click on Copy. Another star appears, 1 inch to the right and 1 inch above the original star.
4. With the second star selected, click on the Process Color icon in the Paint Style palette and create another fill and another stroke color for that star.
5. Choose Edit/Select All (Command-A) to select both stars.
6. Select the blend tool and click on the right tip point of the lower star. Then click on the right tip point of the star above it to display the Blend dialog box.
7. Type 10 in the Steps field and click on OK. Your screen should resemble Figure 7.15.

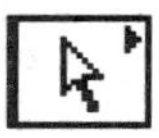

Direct-selection tool

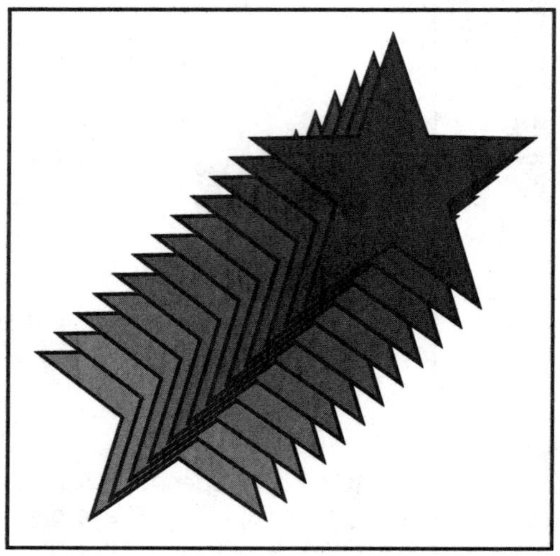

Figure 7.15—A blend between two stroked objects creates a 3D effect. Try this blend without stroking the stars for a very different effect.

FYI

You can change the effect of the blend by clicking on dissimilar points. For example, clicking with the blend tool on a selected lower point in one object and clicking on a selected higher point in the second object creates an entirely different effect.

REVIEW EXERCISE #1

In this exercise you will use the Desert Scene file created in Lesson 6 and apply the various transformation tools to the cacti and other objects.

1. Choose File/Open (Command-O) and open the file you saved as Desert Scene. If you wish, open the Desert Scene.ai file in the Tutorial folder. Save the file under a new name (File/Save As).
2. Use the various transformation tools to resize, rotate, reflect, and shear the individual cactus plants.
3. Select two objects and use the blend tool to create a different effect. Remember to use the Undo command (Command-Z) when you're not happy with the way an object looks.

⌘-O File/Open
⌘-I Object/Paint Style
⌘-Y View/Preview

REVIEW EXERCISE #2

1. Open the House.ai file (Command-O) on the Tutorial disk. Display the Paint Style palette (Command-I). Choose View/Preview (Command-Y).
2. Use the rectangle tool to draw a rectangle about 2 inches wide and 1 inch high. Click on the Fill icon in the Paint Style palette and click on the Patterns icon in the color strip. Select the Transparent Waves pattern.
3. Use the direct-selection tool to select just the brown house.
4. Click on the reflect tool and Option-click on the bottom of the house, its base, to display the Reflect dialog box.
5. Click on Horizontal and click on Copy to create a mirror image of the house. It appears beneath the waves and is selected.
6. Use the Tint slider on the Paint Style palette to reduce the tint to 30%. Your screen should resemble Figure 7.16.

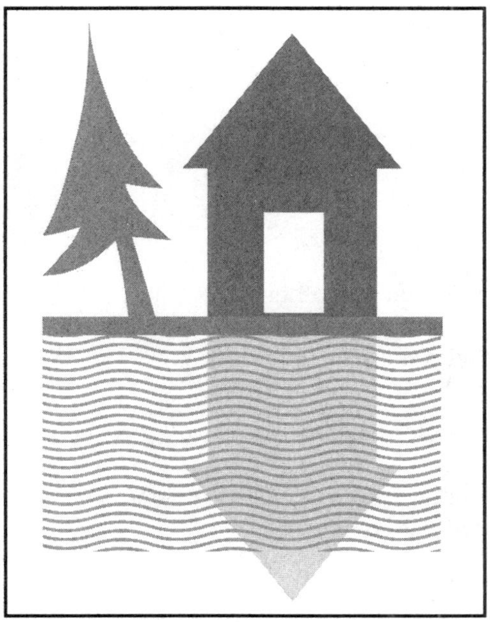

Figure 7.16—Use the reflect tool to create a mirror image of a selected object. You could also reflect the tree and apply some skewing to the reflected objects to make the image more realistic.

REVIEW QUESTIONS

Read the following questions and choose the answer which best completes the statement.

1. To scale an object, _____.
   a. resize it from a dialog box
   b. use the Object menu
   c. enlarge or reduce it with a cursor
   d. a and c

2. The Repeat Transform command _____.
   a. repeats a drawing command
   b. repeats a resizing command
   c. repeats a move command
   d. all of the above
3. Objects can be rotated _____.
   a. at any angle
   b. at constrained angles
   c. with the Arrange command
   d. a and b
4. To create a mirror image, use the _____.
   a. scale tool
   b. reflect tool
   c. shear tool
   d. b and c
5. To slant the sides of an object, use the _____.
   a. rotate tool
   b. reflect tool
   c. shear tool
   d. scale tool
6. To blend two open paths, _____.
   a. two endpoints must be selected
   b. the entire object must be selected
   c. all the anchor points must be joined
   d. none of the above
7. When blending two dissimilar paths, _____.
   a. one object becomes transformed into the other
   b. only one path must be selected with the blend tool
   c. both paths must be selected with the selection tool
   d. the paths appear as gray objects
8. When blending objects to which color has been applied, _____.
   a. both colors must be the same tint
   b. both colors must be either process colors or custom colors
   c. at least one color must be a process color
   d. a and c
9. Blending creates _____.
   a. a graduated fill
   b. a series of intermediate objects
   c. a pattern
   d. harmony
10. You cannot blend _____.
   a. two closed paths
   b. an open and closed path
   c. by clicking on anchor points
   d. b and c

Answers: 1. d; 2. d; 3. d; 4. b; 5. c; 6. a; 7. a; 8. b; 9. b; 10. b

LESSON 8

Type Effects

OVERVIEW

Because type manipulation in Adobe Illustrator is so powerful, this lesson will concentrate on showing you how to use the three type tools to create and edit type without reference to any of the typographical and word processing commands in the program. You will learn how to create and edit point type, rectangle type, and area type. Creating type on open and closed paths and converting text characters to outlines is also covered.

TOPICS

The type tool
Editing type
Rectangle type
Linking text boxes
The area-type tool
Editing path areas
The path-type tool
Resizing/reshaping an open path text object
Moving and flipping type on a path
Creating type around circular paths
Copyfitting text
Importing text files
Text wrap
Converting text to paths
Review Exercise
Review Questions

TERMS

area type
blend
overflow indicator
path type
point type
rectangle type
text object

TUTORIAL FILES

Path Type Practice.ai
Lesson 8.Text

⌘-Y View/preview

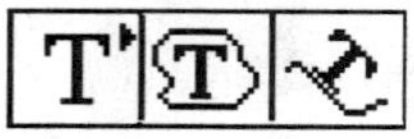

The type tool (left) is the default tool. Drag on the black triangle on the icon to access the area-type tool (center) or the path-type tool (right).

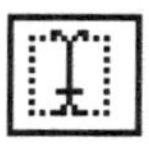

Type tool cursor displays a horizontal bar and is surrounded by a dotted box when it is not on or near any path.

Selection tool

FYI

When you click on the selection tool after creating point type, all the type becomes selected and can be edited.

Oops!

If you should inadvertently deselect the text object, use the selection tool to click on its baseline or on the alignment point. You can see the alignment point in Artwork mode.

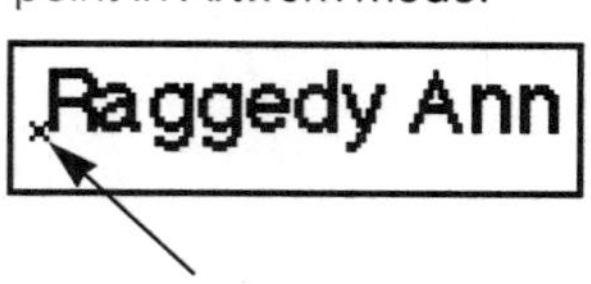

alignment point visible in Artwork mode

THE TYPE TOOL

There are four kinds of type which can be created with three type tools in Adobe Illustrator:

1. *Point type* is type you create with the type tool anywhere on the drawing page. Click with the type tool and type the text, which appears with its baseline visible. Point type does not exist in relation to any path.
2. *Rectangle type* is created with either the type tool or the area-type tool. Use the type tool to draw an imaginary rectangle into which the text fits, or draw a rectangle first with the rectangle tool and type with the type tool inside that rectangle. The rectangle acts as a bounding box for the text.
3. *Area type* turns any path into a text path. This allows you to enter text inside an open or closed path of any shape. The area-type tool (as well as the type tool) creates area type.
4. *Path type* is type placed along an open or closed path with either the type tool or the path-type tool.

The type tool is the default tool. Drag on the black triangle in the Type tool icon to access the area-type and path-type tools.

EXERCISE A

1. On a clean drawing page, choose View/Preview (Command-Y).
2. Click once on the type tool to select it. Move onto the drawing page and notice that the cursor is an I-beam which displays a dotted box around it, indicating that it will create point type—type that does not exist in relation to any path.
3. Click at any point on the page and the I-beam changes to a flashing cursor. Type your name using upper- and lower- case letters.
4. When you finish typing, click once on the selection tool. This deselects the type tool and selects the text, which is now a text object. Notice that the baseline is displayed and an alignment point appears to the left of the first character (Figure 8.1).

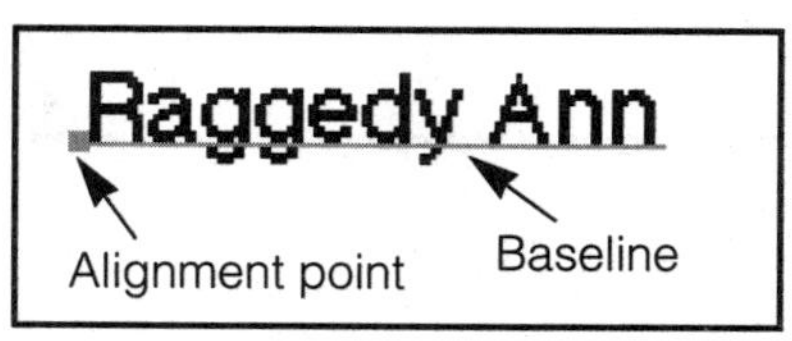

Figure 8.1—Point type appears in 12-point Helvetica. Use the alignment point to move the text object around the page.

5. With the selection tool active, click on the alignment point at the left end of the baseline and move the text around the page.
6. Pull down the Font menu and select another typeface. Because the *text object* is selected, as opposed to selected characters and words, the entire text object reflects the new typeface.
7. Pull down the Type menu and select a larger size. Again, the entire text object reflects the size change.

EDITING TYPE

Edit point type just as you would any type in a word processor. Double-click with the type tool to select a word, drag to select text, or position the I-beam and press the delete key.

Once text is selected, you can change its typeface and size as well as add other paint characteristics. And because type in Illustrator is a text object, it can be manipulated with the transformation tools.

⌘-Y View/Preview
⌘-I Object/Paint Style
⌘-Shift-S-Type/Size/Other
⌘-E View/Artwork

EXERCISE B

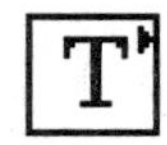

Type tool

1. Choose View/Preview (Command-Y) and display the Paint Style palette (Command-I). Use the selection tool to select the type you just created, or use the type tool to type your name again.
2. Click on the type tool and place the I-beam after the last letter in your name. Click once. The baseline and alignment point disappear and a flashing cursor appears. Press the spacebar to leave a space between the last word in the text object and the next character. Type another word or two.
3. Double-click on one word in the text object. Click on the Fill box in the Paint Style palette and click on a color. If the Auto button is checked, the color is automatically applied to the selected text. Otherwise, press the Enter key.
4. Drag to select the first letter in the text object. Choose Type/Size/Other (Command-Shift-S) to display the Character palette. Type 90 in the Size field and press Return. You must press Return or Enter to accept any changes typed in any of the palettes.
5. Change the fill color and apply a stroke to the capital letters from the Paint Style palette.
6. Choose View/Artwork (Command-E). Click with the selection tool on the alignment point to select the text object.
7. Double-click on the reflect tool to display the Reflect dialog box. Click on Horizontal and click on Copy. The reflected text object appears selected.
8. Use the selection tool to grab its alignment point and move it down below the original text.
9. Apply a fill of black and use the Tint slider to make it 50% black. Click on the Stroke box and select None. Your screen should resemble Figure 8.2.

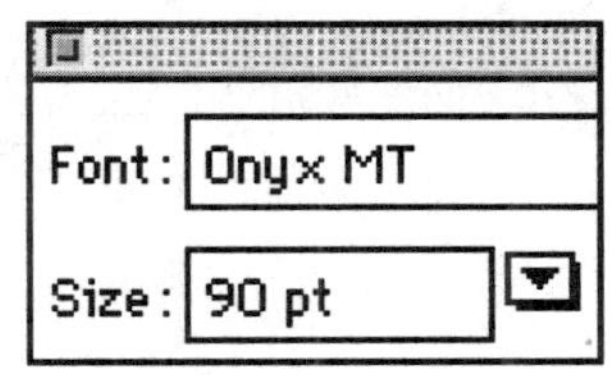

Use the Size pull-down menu to select a size or type the new size in the Size field and *press Return.*

FYI

When creating point type, the text will move along a straight line right off the page. To control its placement, press the Return or Enter keys. This causes the text to drop to the next line.

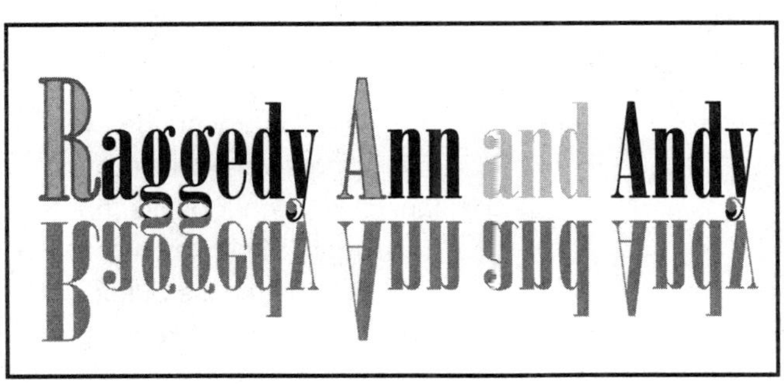

Figure 8.2—A text object where individual characters and words were edited before the object was reflected.

Tip

Press the Command key to change the current tool into the most recently used selection tool.

⌘-E View/Artwork
⌘-Shift-A Edit/Select None

RECTANGLE TYPE

Use either the type tool or the area-type tool to create type in a rectangle. The text automatically wraps to fit the boundary of the rectangular path, and if the text overflows, you can either duplicate and link the rectangles or create another rectangle into which the text will flow.

EXERCISE C

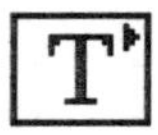

Type tool

1. On an empty drawing page, choose View/Artwork (Command-E).
2. Select the type tool. Click and drag with the type tool to create a small rectangle. When you release the mouse button, the flashing cursor appears in the upper left corner.

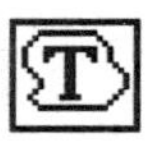

Area-type tool

3. Choose a font (Font menu) and small type size (Type menu) and type a few words inside the rectangle. Notice how the text automatically wraps within the confines of the rectangular path. Click on the type tool again to indicate an end to typing and to select both the text and the rectangle (Figure 8.3).

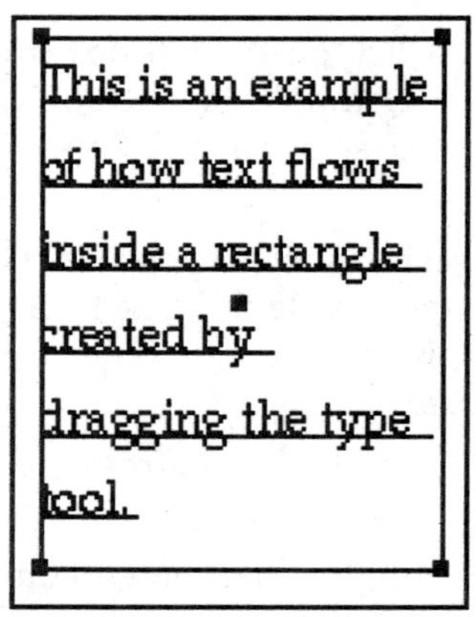

Figure 8.3—When you create rectangle type, both the type and the rectangle can be filled and stroked.

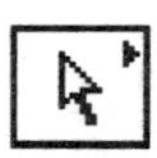

Direct-selection tool

4. Choose Edit/Select/None (Command-Shift-A) to deselect everything. Click on the direct-selection tool.
5. Because you are in Artwork mode, the outline of the rectangle is visible even though it has not been stroked. Drag a selection marquee around the two bottom corners to select them. Then click on the bottom line of the rectangle, press the Shift key, and drag it up or down to resize the rectangle (Figure 8.4). Release the mouse button.

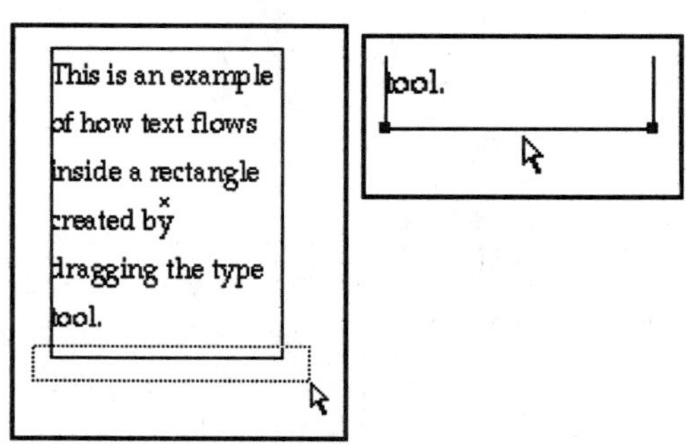

Figure 8.4—First drag a selection marquee around the two bottom corners (left) to select just those two anchor points (right). Pressing the Shift key before releasing the mouse button constrains the path to a rectangle.

6. Click on the bottom bar of the rectangle again, press the Shift key, and drag up with the direct-selection tool, making the rectangle too small to contain the text. A box with a plus sign appears above the lower right point of the rectangle, indicating text overflow.
7. With only the rectangle selected—not the text—apply a stroke and fill from the Paint Style palette. Choose View/Preview (Command-Y) and click on an empty area of the page to deselect everything and view the effects of the fill and stroke (Figure 8.5).
8. Save this file as Rectangle Text. You will need it for the next exercise.

⌘-Y View/Preview
⌘-E View/Artwork

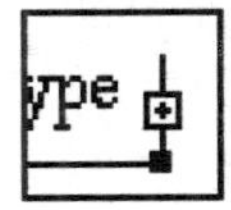

Overflow indicator appears when a path is too small for the amount of text inside or around it.

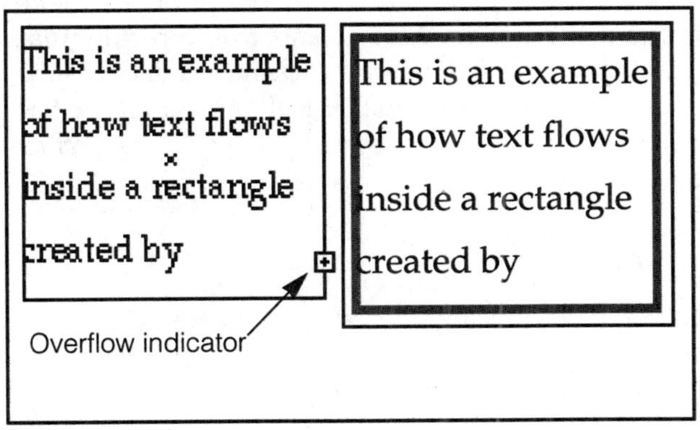

Figure 8.5—Apply fill and stroke attributes to the rectangle in Artwork mode; view them by deselecting everything in Preview mode.

LINKING TEXT BOXES

When the overflow indicator appears on a path which has been filled with text, link the text boxes so that the text will flow from one text box to another. You create new text boxes (paths) by using the group-selection tool and Option-dragging to copy the original text box, which creates an automatic link. You can also create another text box (path) and link the two boxes manually.

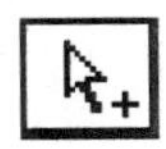

Group-selection tool

EXERCISE D

1. If necessary, open the Rectangle Text file. Choose View/Artwork (Command-E).
2. Use the group-selection tool to select the rectangle with the overflow indicator. Press the Option key and drag to the right to create a copy of that rectangle, which fills with the overflow text (Figure 8.6). Using the group-selection tool selects the path, not the text.

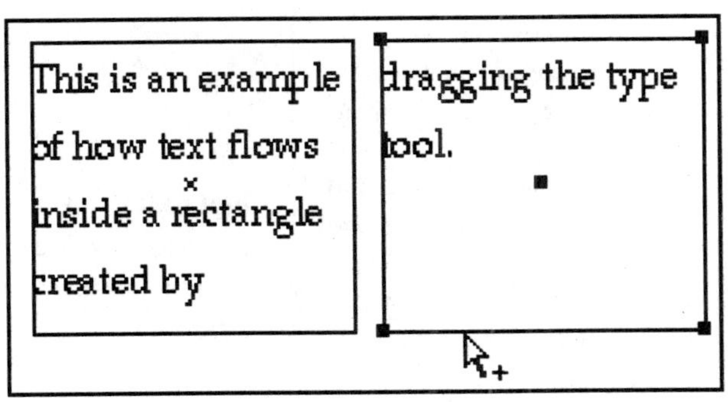

Figure 8.6—Use the group-selection tool to Option-drag the first box and create a second box which displays the overflow text.

FYI

If one additional path is not enough to display all the text, a plus sign will appear on the second rectangle. You can either repeat the Option-drag with the group-selection tool or choose Arrange/Repeat Transform until all the text is displayed.

⌘-Z Edit/Undo
⌘-E View/Artwork
⌘-Shift-G Type/Link Blocks
⌘-Y View/Preview
⌘-I Object/Paint Style
⌘-Shift-J Type/Alignment/Justify
⌘-A Edit/Select All

3. Choose Edit/Undo (Command-Z) to return to the original path displaying the overflow indicator. Choose View/Artwork (Command-E).
4. Click on the text tool and draw another small rectangle next to the original rectangle. Its outline appears in Artwork mode.
5. Use the selection tool to select the first rectangle. Both the path and the text are selected, as indicated by the visible baselines. Press the Shift key and click on the second rectangle to Shift-select it.
6. Choose Type/Link Blocks (Command-Shift-G). The overflow text flows from the original to the second rectangle.
7. Choose View/Preview (Command-Y) and use the Paint Style palette to apply fill and stroke attributes to the text and to the rectangular paths. *Use the type tool to select the individual text characters* and change their fill and stroke attributes. *Use the selection tool to select all the text* before applying global fill and stroke attributes. *Use the direct-selection tool to select just each path* (rectangle).

THE AREA-TYPE TOOL

Area-type tool

Use the area-type tool to enter type in any closed path or along an open path. If you use this tool on an open path, Illustrator creates an imaginary line between the endpoints of the path to define the path for type to follow.

To edit the path, use the direct-selection tool. To edit the text, use the type tool (selected text) or the selection tool (all of the text).

EXERCISE E

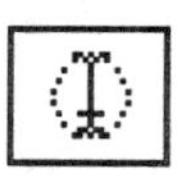

The area-type cursor displays a round dotted line when it is not on a path.

1. On a clean drawing page, use the oval tool to draw a circle by pressing the Shift key while dragging.
2. Choose View/Artwork (Command-E). Use the Paint Style palette (Command-I) to assign the circle a fill and stroke of None.
3. Click on the area-type tool to select it. Click *on* the circular path to begin entering type inside the path (Figure 8.7). After typing a few words, choose Type/Alignment/Justify (Command-Shift-J) to justify the type.
4. With the area-type tool still selected, choose Edit/Select All to select all of the text. Format the text from the Font and Type menus.
5. Save this file as Circular Path. You will use it in the next lesson.

Tip

To select all of the text automatically when the area-type tool is selected, click on the selection tool. Any changes you now make will be applied to all the text inside the path.

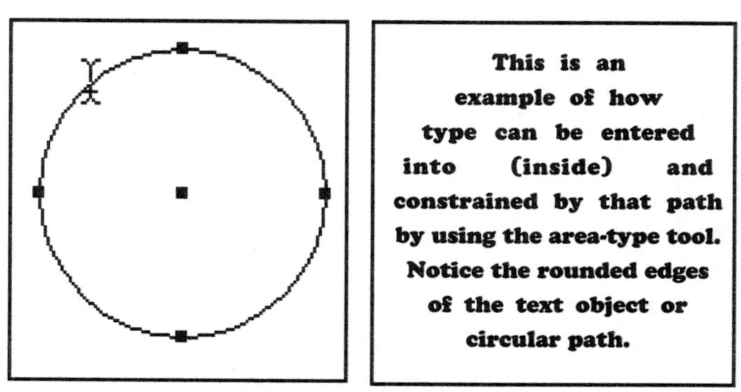

Figure 8.7—Use the area-type cursor to enter text inside a closed path.

EDITING PATH AREAS

In the last exercise, once the circle was drawn and the type entered inside the path, only the *type* was edited using the type tool, area-type tool, or the selection tool. To edit the *path,* use either the direct-selection tool or the group-selection tool to select the path.

When working with type in or along paths, it's a good idea to use Artwork mode, at least until you have the path selected. This allows you to see the path's outline even though it has not been stroked. Once the path is selected, you can always switch to Preview mode.

⌘-O File/Open
⌘-I Object/Paint Style
⌘-E View/Artwork
⌘-Y View/Preview
⌘-Shift-A Edit/Select None

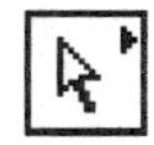

Direct-selection tool

Group-selection tool

EXERCISE F

1. If necessary, open (Command-O) the Circular Path file you created in the last exercise or create text inside a circular path. Display the Paint Style palette (Command-I).
2. Choose View/Artwork (Command-E). Click on the group-selection tool and click on the path to select it. Then choose View/Preview (Command-Y).
3. Apply a radial fill to the background of the circle. Apply a stroke to the outside of the path.
4. Choose Edit/Select/None (Command-Shift-A) to deselect everything. Use the selection tool to select the text object. All of the text is selected.
5. Choose Type/Leading and drag to select a leading value greater than the type size. This will help to vertically justify the text in the circle. Your screen should resemble Figure 8.8.

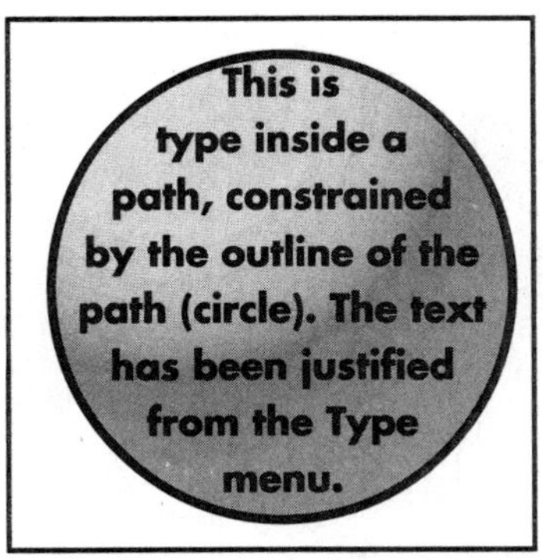

Figure 8.8—Use either the direct-selection tool or the group-selection tool to select only the path of a text object (a path in which or on which you have entered text).

Tip

Don't use the selection tool to select a text object unless you want to select all of the text. You cannot use the selection tool to select just a path into which or on which type has been entered.

THE PATH-TYPE TOOL

Use the path-type tool to place type along an open or closed path. Once you click with this tool on a path, that path becomes a text path, allowing you to individually manipulate the text and its path.

To use this tool, first create the path. If you paint and/or stroke the path before entering the text, those paint and stroke attributes will be reset to None once you enter the text. You can always use the direct-selection or group-selection tool to select and edit the path later.

Path-type tool

⌘-E View/Artwork
⌘-I Object/Paint Style
⌘-Shift-A Edit/Select None
⌘-Shift-L Type/Alignment/Left

Freehand tool

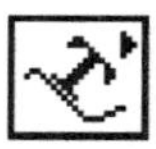

Path-type tool

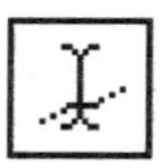

The path-type cursor displays a slant line when it is not on a path.

FYI

When you select a text object like an open path with type running along it with the selection tool, the path *appears* to be selected, but it is not. Only the text is selected.

Tip

You can also resize type and/or use the Letter spacing and Word spacing fields in the Paragraph palette to copyfit type on a path.

EXERCISE G

1. On a clean drawing page, choose View/Artwork (Command-E). Display the Paint Style palette (Command-I).
2. Use the freehand tool to draw a curvy path about six inches long.
3. Deselect everything (Command-Shift-A).
4. Click on the triangle in the Type tool icon and drag to select the path-type tool.
5. Choose Type/Alignment/Left (Command-Shift-L) and click at the beginning of the path. The cursor changes from an I-beam with a slant line to a flashing cursor. Type a few words on the path.
6. Click on the selection tool to indicate that the typing has stopped and to select all of the text.
7. Use the Font and Type menus to select a typeface and type size.
8. Deselect everything (Command-Shift-A). Click on the path-type tool and double-click to select one word on the path. Use the Font and Type menus to change its typeface and type size.
9. Deselect everything. Click on the group-selection tool and click on the path to select only the path. Apply a stroke from the Paint Style palette. Your screen should resemble Figure 8.9.

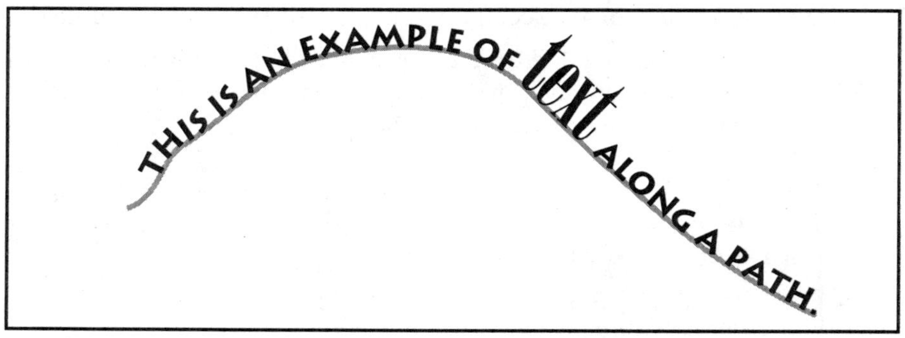

Figure 8.9—Text created with the path-type tool running along a path created with the freehand tool. Once the text was created, the path was selected with the group-selection tool and stroked.

RESIZING/RESHAPING AN OPEN PATH TEXT OBJECT

Once you have added text to an open path, you can resize it and reshape the path. Reshape the path and thereby change the shape of the text path by first using the direct-selection tool to select the path and then selecting and moving anchor points and direction handles.

Resizing the text object is a little more complicated. If the path is too long and is not stroked, it really doesn't matter how long it is, because it won't display or print. But if the path is to be stroked, then length is an issue.

To shorten the text path, you must add an anchor point and then delete *it and all the subsequent anchor points*. To lengthen the path, simply drag one of the endpoints out until the text fits the path.

EXERCISE H

1. Open the Path Type Practice.ai file on the Tutorial disk (Command-O).
2. Choose View/Artwork (Command-E). Notice that the path is too short to fit the text, "Lend a helping hand." Click on the right endpoint with the zoom tool to magnify it.
3. Use the direct-selection tool to select the path. Then click on the right endpoint. Drag the endpoint to the right until the overflow indicator disappears and all the text is displayed (Figure 8.10). Deselect everything (Command-Shift-A).

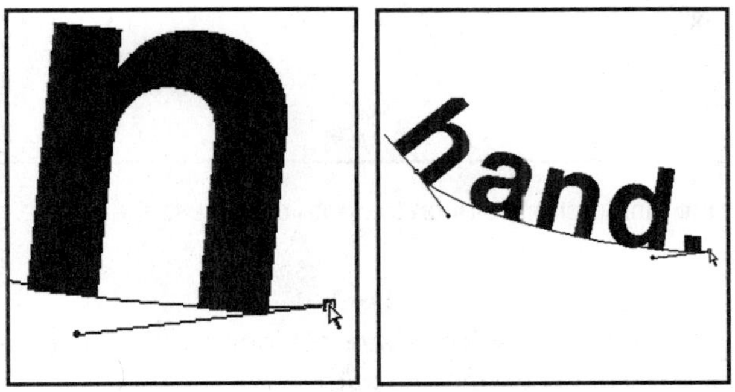

Figure 8.10—Use the direct-selection tool to stretch a path object (left) until it can display all of the text (right).

4. Once all the text is displayed, use the direct-selection tool again to select the path. Click on the right endpoint again and drag it out a few inches so that it is longer than necessary (Figure 8.11).

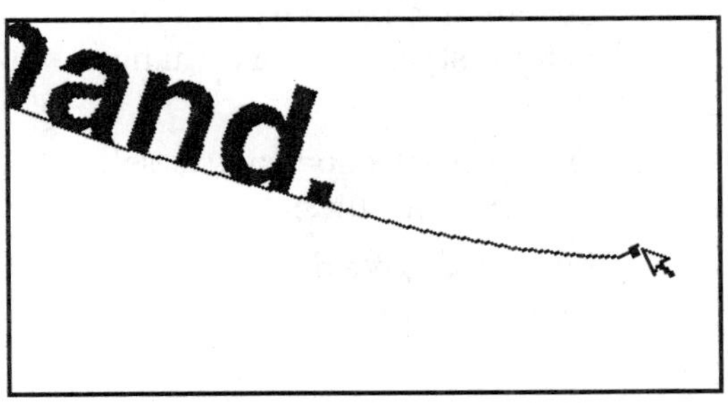

Figure 8.11—Use the direct-selection tool to stretch the path beyond the last text character, the period.

5. To cut the excess path, drag out on the scissors tool and select the add-anchor point tool.
6. With the add-anchor point tool selected, click once on the path *after the period in the text.* An anchor point appears (Figure 8.12).

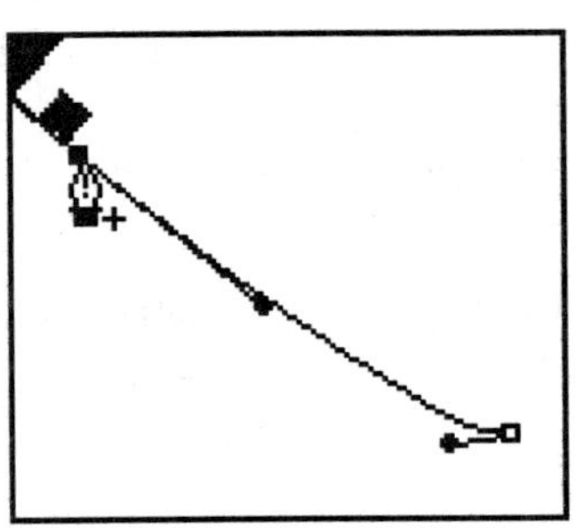

Figure 8.12—Use the add-anchor point tool to add an anchor point to the path you want to shorten. You can then use the direct-selection tool to delete the new anchor point and all subsequent anchor points to shorten the path.

⌘-O File/Open
⌘-E View/Artwork
⌘-Shift-A Edit/Select None

Zoom tool

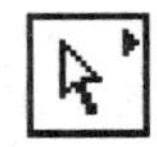

Direct-selection tool

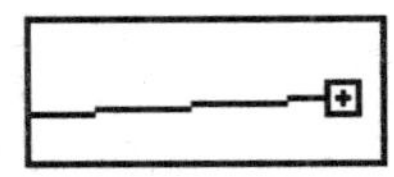

When a path is too short to display all of the text, an overflow indicator (plus sign) appears at the end of the path.

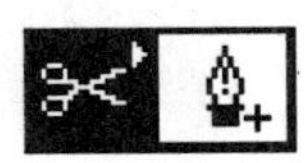

Drag on the scissors tool to access the add-anchor point tool.

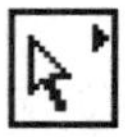

Direct-selection tool

7. Use the direct-selection tool to draw a selection marquee around the new anchor point and all subsequent anchor points in the path. Or use the direct-selection tool to Shift-select each of the anchor points individually. Be sure to leave one anchor point deselected, because it's the endpoint of the path, and every open path must have an endpoint (Figure 8.13).

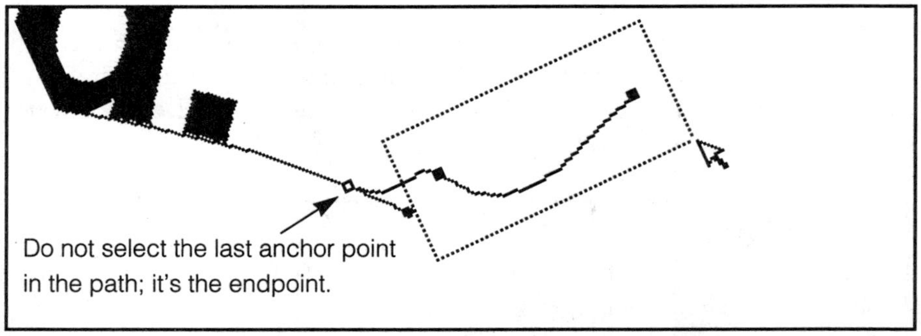

Figure 8.13—Select all but the last anchor point on the path and press the Delete key to shorten the path.

Tip

You can always use the Undo command (Edit/Undo) and try again.

8. Press the Delete key to delete the selected anchor points and the segments they connect, thereby shortening the path.
9. Use the direct-selection tool to select anchor points and direction handles and move them to reshape the path. Remember, using the direct-selection tool selects the path, not the text.
10. You can now use the type tool to select the text and apply font, size, and paint attributes to the text. You can also use the selection tool to select the entire text object so that font, style, and size changes will apply to all the text in the text object.
11. Use the direct-selection tool or the group-selection tool to select the path (use Artwork mode) and apply paint attributes.
12. When you have the path and text formatted, save the file as Path Practice.Finished. You will use it in the next exercise.

MOVING AND FLIPPING TYPE ON A PATH

In the last exercise you worked with type positioned on top of the path. You can also move the type along the path and flip the type so that it runs along the bottom of the path. Flipping is a useful maneuver when you want to create text above and below a circle.

Selection tool

When moving and flipping type, be careful not to drag the type across the path. If you find that the type is getting out of control, release the mouse button, then click with the selection tool again on the I-beam and move the type into position on the path. All moving and flipping is done with the selection tool on the I-beam.

If you click and drag and are dissatisfied with the way the type looks, use the Edit/Undo command (Command-Z) to undo the last command.

EXERCISE I

⌘-O File/Open
⌘-E View/Artwork
⌘-I Object/Paint Style
⌘-Shift-C Type/Alignment/Center
⌘-A Edit/Select All

1. If necessary, open the Path Practice.Finished file (Command-O) or create text on an open path.
2. Use the selection tool and click on the path to select it. Click on the I-beam. Drag it to the right across the path and release the mouse button (Figure 8.14).

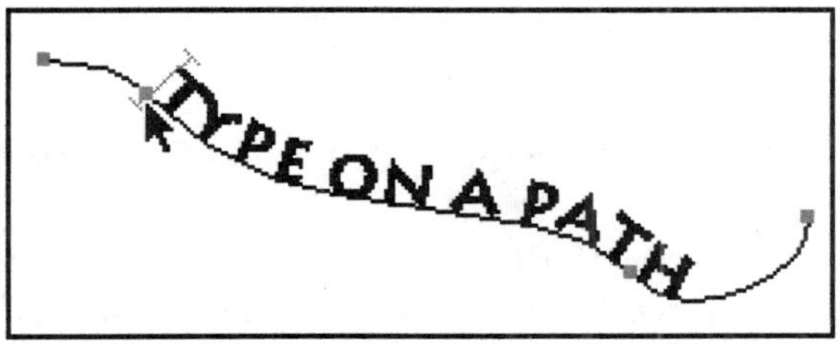

Figure 8.14—Use the selection tool to click and drag the type along the path.

Selection tool

3. Double-click with the selection tool on the I-beam. The type flips to the bottom of the path and the overflow indicator appears.
4. Click on the I-beam and drag it to the right (or left) until the text is fully displayed.

CREATING TYPE AROUND CIRCULAR PATHS

To create type above or below a circle, you need only one circle. However, to create type both above *and* below the circle, you must use two circles as paths and then position one circle on top of the other to create the illusion of type above and below one circle.

EXERCISE J

1. On a clean drawing page, choose View/Artwork (Command-E). Display the Paint Style palette (Command-I).
2. Use the oval tool to draw an oval or circle about two inches wide. While it is selected, click on the path-type tool to select it.
3. Choose Type/Alignment/Center (Command-Shift-C) to center the type along the path.
4. Click on the top anchor point and type a few words. If the Alert message is displayed, try again, making sure that the dotted line on the path-type tool crosses the oval's path.
5. With the path-type tool still active and the insertion bar flashing in the text (click with the path-type tool to make it flash), choose Edit/Select All (Command-A) to select all the text. Format it from the Font and Type menus.
6. Use the direct-selection or group-selection tool to select the path—not the text.

⌘-A Edit/Select All

7. Use the Paint Style palette to apply fill and stroke attributes. Try filling the oval with a pattern by clicking on the Pattern icon in the Paint Style palette to display Illustrator's default patterns.
8. To move the text above the path, use the Baseline shift command. First, use the magnifier to zoom in on the text.

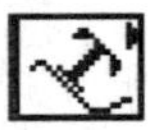

Path-type tool

9. Select the path-type tool, click on the text, and choose Edit/Select All (Command-A).
10. With the text selected, press the Command and Option keys simultaneously, then press the up arrow key on the keyboard. The text moves up two points. Press Command-Option-Up Arrow again and the baseline of the text shifts another two points.
11. Press Command-Option-Down Arrow to shift the text down two points.
12. Choose Window/Show Character to display the Character palette. Click on the lever in the lower right corner to expand the palette and display the Baseline shift field (Figure 8.15). It reflects the changes you made with the Command-Option-Arrow keystroke.

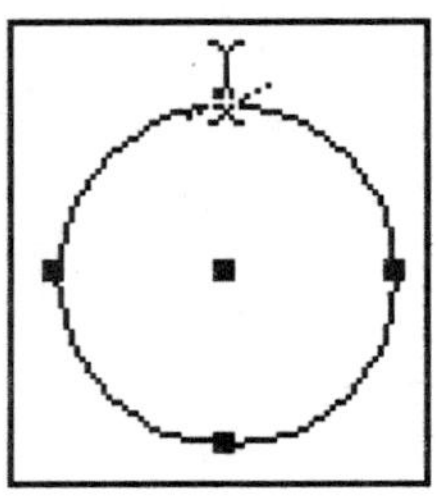

When using the path-type tool, make sure the dotted line on the cursor *crosses the path* before you click.

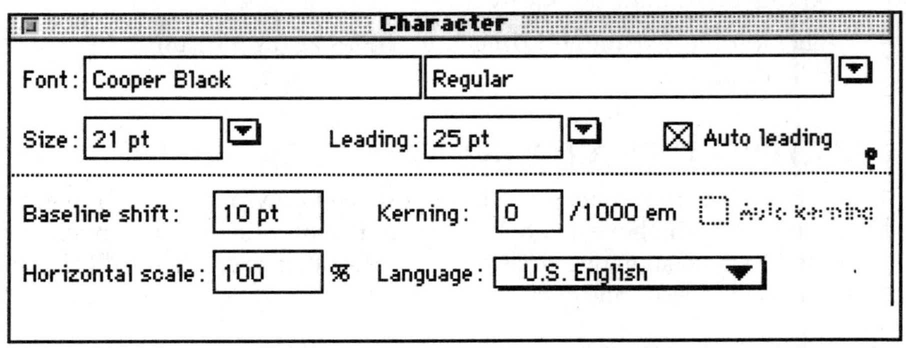

Figure 8.15—The Character palette controls the Baseline shift command.

13. Type *positive* values in the Baseline shift field to move text *up* from the path. Type *negative* numbers in the Baseline shift field to move text *down* from the path. Continue to adjust the Baseline shift values until you are satisfied. Your screen should resemble Figure 8.16.

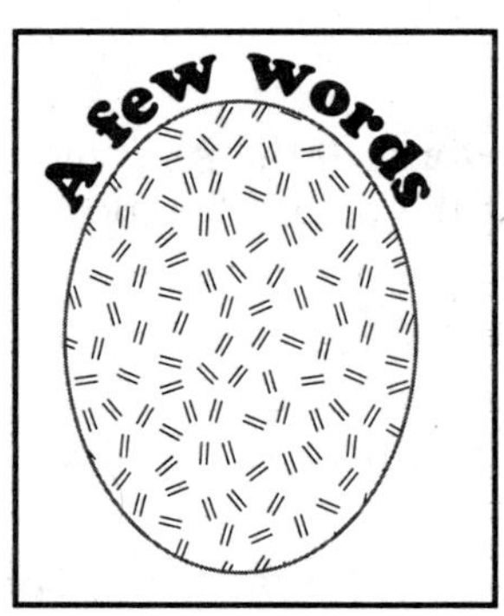

Figure 8.16—The type on this circular path has been shifted four points above the baseline.

COPYFITTING TEXT

The Fit Headline command is used to fit type across the width of a text path in a text object. The command is available only when type is entered into a text rectangle or into a text area. You cannot use this command for text on an open path.

IMPORTING TEXT FILES

To import a text file from another application like a word processor, create an insertion point with any of the three type tools, and use the Import Text command. If the Import Text command is unavailable (dimmed), make sure you have clicked on a point or path with one of the type tools.

TEXT WRAP

The text wrap or text runaround function in Illustrator works in a manner similar to the way it works in a page layout program. The Make Wrap command allows you to wrap text around a rectangle or around area type. When wrapping text, the object must be in front of the type in the stacking order on the drawing page. If you find the Make Wrap command not available (dimmed), select the object and choose Arrange/Bring to Front.

Once text has been wrapped around an object, it can be unwrapped by selecting the entire object (text object and graphic object) and choosing Release Wrap from the Type menu.

EXERCISE K

1. On a new drawing page, choose View/Artwork (Command-E). Display the Paint Style palette (Command-I).
2. Select the rectangle tool and click once on the page to display the Rectangle dialog box.
3. Type 3 in the Width field. Press the Tab key and type 4 in the Height field. Click on OK.
4. Use the Paint Style palette to assign it a fill of None and any stroke.
5. Choose Type/Alignment/Left (Command-Shift-L).
6. Select the area-type tool and click on the top of the rectangle. You must click *on the path* with this tool (Figure 8.17).

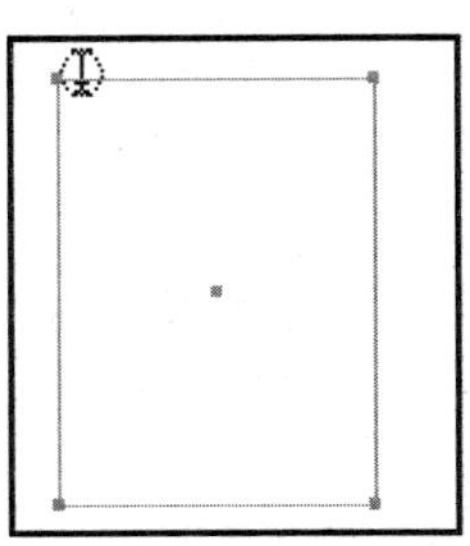

Figure 8.17—Click with the area-type cursor on the path, not inside the path.

7. Choose File/Import Text. Locate the Lesson 8.Text file on the Tutorial disk and click on Open. The text is displayed inside the rectangle.

⌘-E View/Artwork
⌘-I Object/Paint Style
⌘-Shift-L Type/Alignment/Left
⌘-A Edit/Select All

Tip

Type can be offset from the graphic object by selecting the text and inputting values in the Left and Right Indentation fields on the Paragraph palette.

Another way to achieve type offset is to wrap the type around a path to which you have applied a fill and stroke of none. The graphic object is then positioned on top of the "dummy" path.

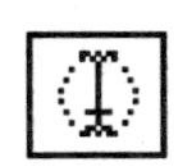

The area-type cursor displays a circular dotted line when placed on a path.

⌘-A Edit/Select All
⌘-Shift-J Type/Alignment/Justify

8. With the area-type tool still active, choose Edit/Select All (Command-A) to select all the text and format it in 10-point (Type/Size/10 pt) Helvetica (Font/Helvetica).
9. Click with the area-type cursor just before the *L* in *Let's.* Press the Return key to move down one line. Then click in the empty line above the first line of text.
10. Type *MACINTOSH* in capital letters. Double-click on the word to select it. Choose Type/Fit Headline to stretch the word across the width of the text block. Double-click on the headline with any type tool and press the Delete key.
11. Use the selection tool to select the rectangle (text object).
12. Choose Filter/Text/Rows & Columns to display the Rows & Columns dialog box. Type 2 in the Columns field. Click on OK.
13. Click with any type tool just before the *L* in *Let's* again. Press the Delete key to delete the extra line at the top of the text object.
14. Choose Edit/Select All (Command-A) and change the type size to 14 points. Change the alignment to Justified (Command-Shift-J).
15. Use the rectangle tool to draw a small rectangle in the middle of the large rectangle between the two columns. Fill it with a pattern.
16. Use the selection tool to Shift-select the small rectangle and the larger text object (rectangle). Choose Type/Make Wrap. The type in the larger rectangle (text object) wraps around the smaller rectangle (graphic object), which it treats as a graphic element. Your screen should resemble Figure 8.18.

FYI

You should format the headline before applying the Fit Headline command, because this command applies a specific tracking value to the type, and changes you make to the type will affect the width of the headline.

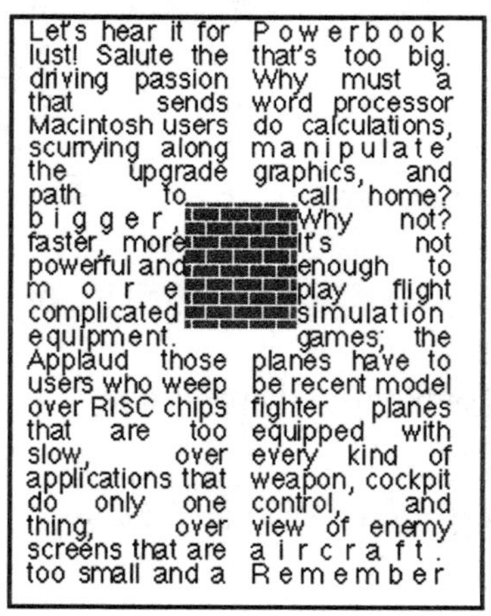

Figure 8.18—Use the Make Wrap command to wrap text around a graphic. Drawing a rectangle (no stroke/no fill) around the graphic will set the text off from the graphic object. Obviously, this text object needs letter spacing and/or word spacing adjustments.

The icon for Adobe's Type 1 (PostScript) font. The outline font (sometimes called the printer font) must be installed in your system.

CONVERTING TEXT TO PATHS

One of the most versatile functions in Illustrator is the Create Outlines command, which transforms type into editable artwork. For this command to be available, however, the Type 1 or TrueType font outline for that typeface must be installed in your system.

Once type has been converted to an outline, it is no longer text. Rather, it becomes an Adobe Illustrator graphic object, just as if you had drawn it with any of the tools, and any of the commands—paint, transform, etc.—that are applied to artwork can now be applied to the converted type.

EXERCISE L

1. On a clean drawing page, choose View/Preview (Command-Y).
2. Select the type tool and click anywhere on the page. Type *PLOP.* Click on the selection tool to select the text.
3. Format it in a large-point typeface. Be sure to choose a typeface with the outline font installed in your System.
4. With the type still selected by the selection tool (the baseline and alignment point are visible), choose Type/Create Outlines. The type appears as four selected paths.
5. Click on an empty area of the page to deselect everything.
6. Use the selection tool to select the second *P.* Apply a fill and stroke to just that object (it isn't a text character anymore!).
7. Click on the rotate tool and click on the upper left corner of the *P.* Move the cursor away from the object and drag to rotate it to the right. Press the Shift key to constrain the rotation to 45 degrees.
8. Use the selection tool to move the rotated object a little below the other objects. Your screen should resemble Figure 8.19.

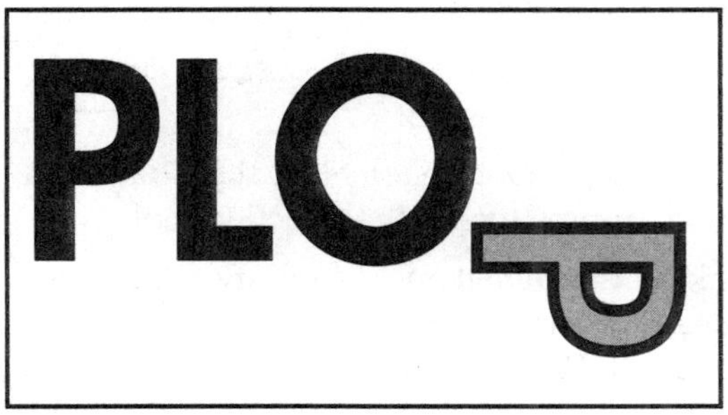

Figure 8.19—The four letters were converted to outlines, and the last object was painted and transformed.

REVIEW EXERCISE

In this exercise you will place type above one circle and below another circle, and then join the circles to create the illusion of a single path.

1. On a clean drawing page, choose View/Artwork (Command-E). Display the Paint Style palette (Command-I). Choose File/Preferences/General (Command-K) and select inches from the Ruler units pull-down men. Click on OK.
2. Click on the oval tool and click on the page to display the Oval dialog box. Type 2 in the Width field. Press the Tab key and type 2 in the Height field. Click on OK to create a circle with a 2-inch diameter. The circle appears selected.
3. Use the Paint Style palette to assign it a fill of None and a stroke of black.

⌘-Y View/Preview
⌘-E View/Artwork
⌘-I Object/Paint Style
⌘-K File/Preferences/General

FYI

Most computers have Times and Helvetica printer fonts installed in the system.

⌘-Shift-C Type/ Alignment/Center

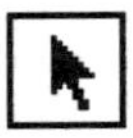

Selection tool

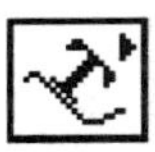

Path-type tool

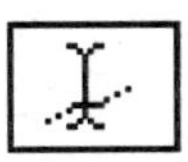

The dotted line on the path-type tool must cross the line of the path.

4. Press the Option *and* Shift keys, click on the circle with the selection tool, and drag down to create a copy of the circle (Option) which is placed directly below the original (Shift) (Figure 8.20).

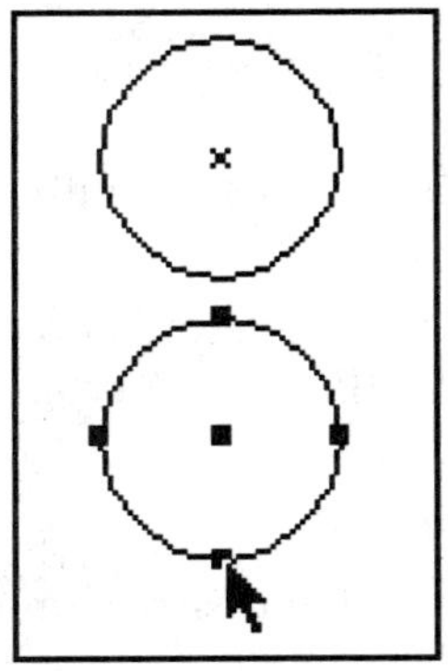

Figure 8.20—Option-Shift-drag with the selection tool to create a copy of the circle directly beneath it.

5. Choose Type/Alignment/Center (Command-Shift-C) to center the type along the top of one circle and along the bottom of the second circle.
6. Choose Font/Helvetica and Type/Size 14.
7. Use the selection tool to select the first circle. Its anchor points and center point should be displayed.
8. Select the path-type tool and click on the top anchor point of the first circle.
9. Type *TYPE ABOVE A CIRCLE.*
10. Click on the lower circle with the selection tool or press the Command key to temporarily change the path-type tool to the selection tool.
11. Use the path-type tool to click on the *bottom* anchor point of the lower circle. If you get an Alert message, make sure the dotted line on the path-type tool crosses the circle's path.
12. Type *TYPE BELOW A CIRCLE.* The type appears on the bottom of the circle. Double-click on the I-beam to flip it to the top of the circle. Your screen should resemble Figure 8.21.

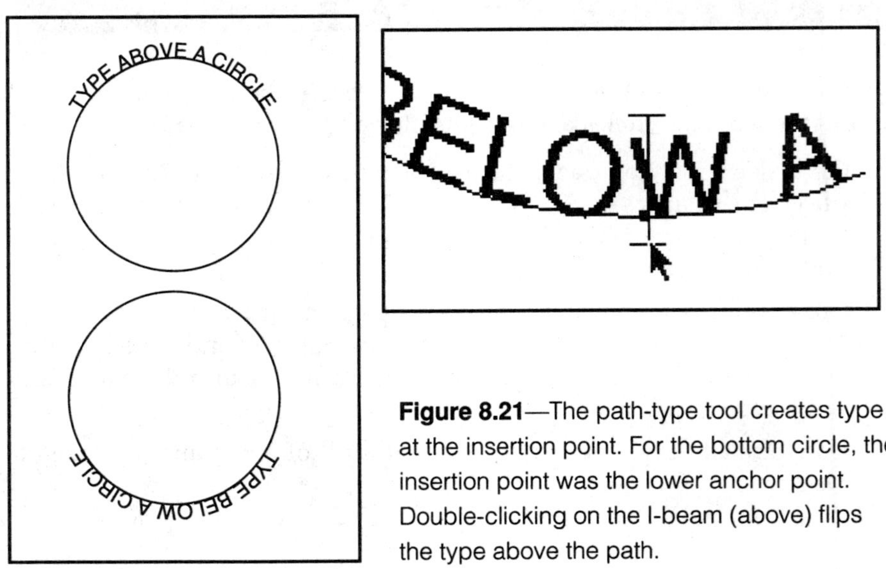

Figure 8.21—The path-type tool creates type at the insertion point. For the bottom circle, the insertion point was the lower anchor point. Double-clicking on the I-beam (above) flips the type above the path.

13. Use the type tool to select all the text on the lower circle by clicking on the text and choosing Edit/Select All (Command-A) or by triple-clicking on the text.
14. Choose Window/Show Character to display the Character palette. Click on the lever in the lower right corner of the palette to expand it. Type –14 in the Baseline shift field and press Return. This negative number drops the baseline of the text 14 points below the path.
15. Triple-click with the type tool on the text over the upper circle. Use the Character palette to change the Baseline shift value to 6. The positive number moves the text 6 points above the path.
16. Choose Edit/Select None (Command-Shift-A) to deselect everything.
17. Be sure you are in Artwork mode. Use the selection tool and click on the center point of the lower circle. Press the Shift key and drag the lower circle by the center point up until it matches the center circle of the upper circle. The cursor will turn to a white arrowhead when it does.
18. Choose View/Preview (Command-Y) to view the illustration. Your screen should resemble Figure 8.22.

⌘-A Edit/Select All
⌘-Y View/Preview
⌘-Shift-A Edit/Select None

The white arrowhead appears when the centers of the two circles are on top of each other.

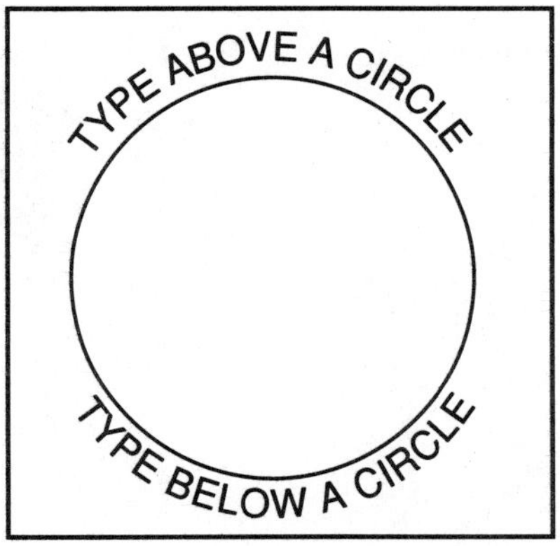

Figure 8.22—The lower circle is moved on top of the upper circle to display a single circle with text running above and below it.

REVIEW QUESTIONS

Read the following questions and choose the answer which best completes the statement.

1. The tool which sets type inside a rectangle is the _____.
   a. path-type tool
   b. area-type tool
   c. type tool
   d. b and c
2. To edit type, use ____.
   a. any type tool
   b. only the type tool
   c. only the area-type tool
   d. only the path-type tool

3. To flip type on a path, use the _____.
   a. type tool
   b. selection tool
   c. direct-selection tool
   d. rotate tool
4. To create type around a circle, use the _____.
   a. path-type tool
   b. type tool
   c. area-type tool
   d. all of the above
5. In order to wrap text around an object, _____.
   a. the object must be inside a path
   b. the text must be formatted
   c. the object must be first in the stacking order
   d. you need a ribbon
6. Before type can be converted to outlines, _____.
   a. the outline font must be installed in the system
   b. it must be formatted
   c. the paint attributes must be removed
   d. a and c
7. When text is selected with the selection tool, _____.
   a. the baseline is displayed
   b. the alignment point is displayed
   c. the entire text block can be formatted
   d. all of the above
8. Use the _____ tool to edit the path of a text object.
   a. selection
   b. type
   c. direct-selection
   d. group-selection
9. Text objects can be _____.
   a. manipulated with the transformation tools
   b. edited
   c. painted
   d. all of the above
10. The only way to shorten a text path is to _____.
    a. use the scissors tool
    b. add an anchor point and then delete anchor points
    c. paint it white
    d. a and b

Answers: 1. d; 2. a; 3. b; 4. a; 5. c; 6. a; 7. d; 8. c; 9. d; 10. b

LESSON 9

Typography and Word Processing

OVERVIEW

This lesson concentrates on Illustrator's typographic and word processing functions. You will learn how to set type from the Character, Paragraph, and Tabs palettes and how to use the many text editing functions like the spell checker from the Text filter.

TOPICS

The Character palette
Kerning and tracking
Baseline shift
Horizontal scale
Paragraph formatting
Hyphenating text
Hyphenation options
Word spacing and letter spacing
Hanging punctuation
Space before a paragraph
Setting tabs
The Text filter
Finding and replacing text
Specifying rows and columns
Smart punctuation
Review Exercise
Review Questions

TERMS

baseline
font family
kerning
leading
letter spacing
tracking
word spacing

TUTORIAL FILES

Lesson 9.Text
Lesson 9.Tabs

⌘-I Object/Paint Style
⌘-T Type/Character
⌘-K File/Preferences/General

THE CHARACTER PALETTE

Many of the text attributes accessed from the menu are also available from the Character palette. Like all palettes in Illustrator, when you type a value in any field, you must press the Return or Enter key to execute the value.

The top panel of the Character palette contains fields for font, font style, font size, and leading (Figure 9.1).

FYI

A font family is the complete set of characters in one style for a specific typeface. Palatino, for example, is a font family. Palatino Bold is a *style* of Palatino.

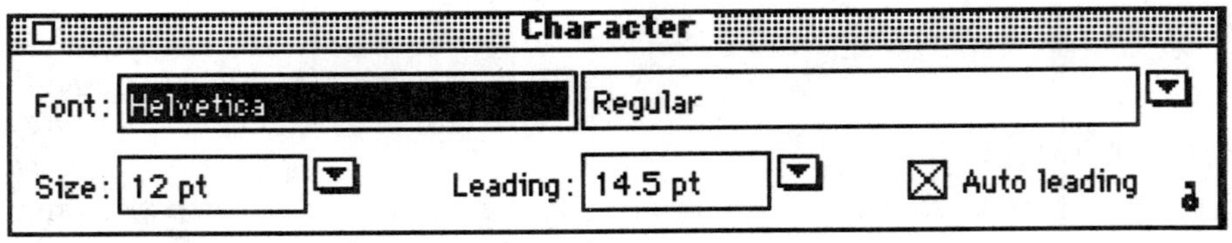

Figure 9.1—The Character palette is accessed from the Type menu.

Tip

To quickly select a font name from the Font menu, type the first letter of the font family to display the font family's name. The default font family in Illustrator is Helvetica. Type *P* and Palatino will be displayed. Type *T* and Times will be displayed—if these fonts are installed in your system.

Any font installed in your system will appear in the Font menu along the Menu Bar at the top of the drawing page and from the Font pull-down menu on the Character palette. The left Font field displays the name of the font family, like Helvetica or Times. The field next to it displays the style of that font family—regular, bold, italic, etc. Use the pull-down menu on the right to select a different font family and font style.

The Size pull-down menu is used to choose a type size for the selected type. If the size you want is not displayed, choose Other. This highlights the Size box where you can type the size you need. Size is always measured in points, but you don't have to type the abbreviation (pt) in the Size box; Illustrator does it for you.

The Leading and Auto leading fields affect the amount of vertical space between the lines of type. Like type size, leading is always measured in points. A common leading value is 120 percent of the type size. For example, if the type size is 10 points, the automatic leading value would be 12 points (10 X 120 = 12).

FYI

If a line of type or a single paragraph contains text characters with different leading values, Illustrator takes the highest leading value and applies it to the line or paragraph.

EXERCISE A

1. Select inches as the Ruler units (Command-K). Click once with the rectangle tool on the drawing page to display the Rectangle dialog box. Type 2 in the Width field; press the Tab key and type 3 in the Height field. Click on OK.
2. Use the Paint Style palette (Command-I) to assign it a fill of None and a black stroke. Choose View/Artwork (Command-E).
3. Click on the area-type tool to select it and click on the top bar of the rectangle to display the flashing cursor. Type *If you see someone without a smile, give him one of yours.* Click on the selection tool to select the entire text block.
4. Display the Character palette (Command-T). Click on the title bar and drag it out of your way.

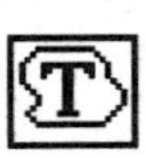

Area-type tool

5. Use the Font pull-down menu to select Helvetica. Use the Size pull-down menu to select 24.
6. Click in the Auto leading field to select it. An X indicates that it is selected. The Leading field displays 29 points.
7. Now *deselect* the Auto leading box and use the Leading pull-down menu to select 36. The increased leading (vertical white space between the lines of type) fits the type in the rectangle (Figure 9.2).

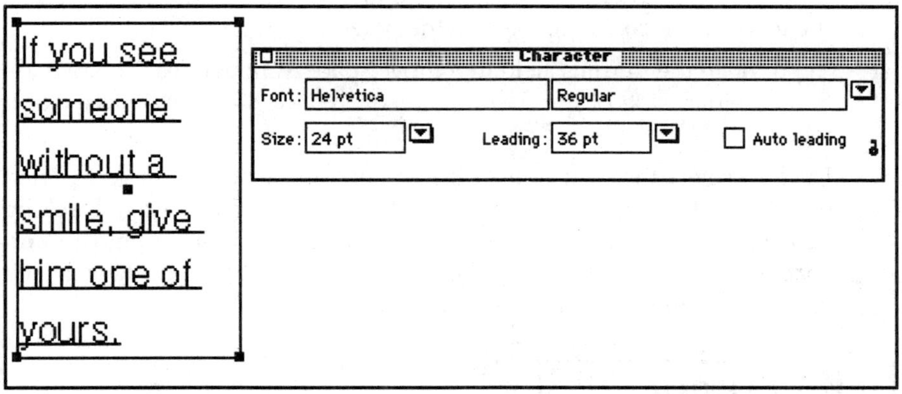

Figure 9.2—A Leading value of 36 points adds enough space between the lines of type to fit it in the rectangle.

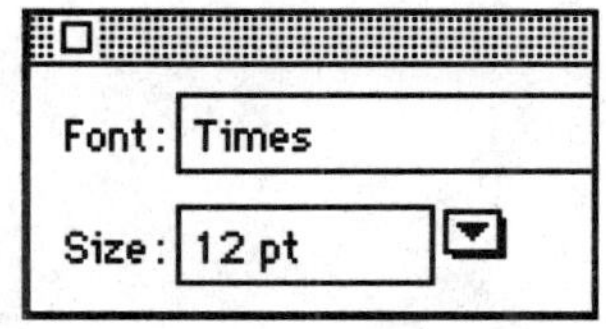

Use the Size pull-down menu to select a size, or type the new size in the Size field and *press Return.*

KERNING AND TRACKING

Kerning is adding or deleting space between two characters. For example, in the word *To*, there might be too much space between the *T* and the *o*. It's frequently necessary to kern type at sizes larger than 14 points.

Tracking applies uniform spacing between *more than two characters* in selected text. Tracking is used to adjust the spacing between all the characters in a word or between all the characters and the space between them in an entire text object.

When you use a positive number to kern or track, you add space; using a negative number removes space. Kerning and tracking values are measured in very tiny units—1/1000 of an em space. An em space is the width of the letter M in the current font. The em dash after the word *units* in this paragraph is the width of the letter M in the Palatino typeface used for this text. If tracking and kerning units are 1/1000 of an em space, then applying a kerning value of 100 adds 1 point of space between two characters in 10-type.

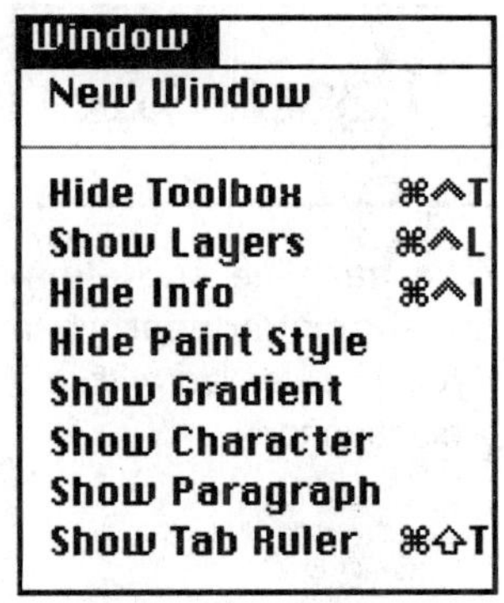

Both the Character and Paragraph palettes can be accessed from the Window menu.

Kerning and tracking values are applied from the lower panel of the Character palette. Click on the lever in the lower right corner of the upper panel to display the lower panel (Figure 9.3).

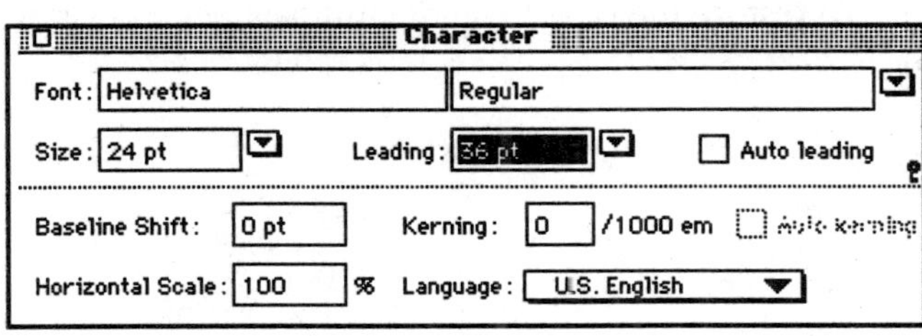

Figure 9.3—Click on the lever to display the lower panel of the Character palette.

⌘-T Type/Character

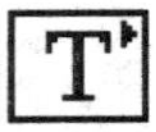

Type tool

Selection tool

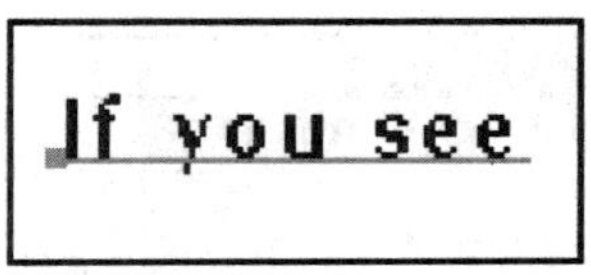

The baseline and alignment point appear when type is selected with the selection tool.

EXERCISE B

1. Use the magnifier tool to draw a marquee around the word *you* in the first line.of the text object you created in the last exercise.
2. Click on the type tool to select it and click between the *o* and the *u* in the word *you* in the first line.
3. Display the Character palette (Command-T) and click on the lever in the lower right corner to expand the palette.
4. Type –80 in the Kerning field to remove space from between the two letters on either side of the flashing cursor. Notice how they move closer together.
5. Drag to select the fifth line, "him one of." Because you have selected more than two characters, the Kerning field changes to the Tracking field in the Character palette. Type 130 in the Tracking field to add space uniformly between all the characters and words in the selected text. Your screen should resemble Figure 9.4.

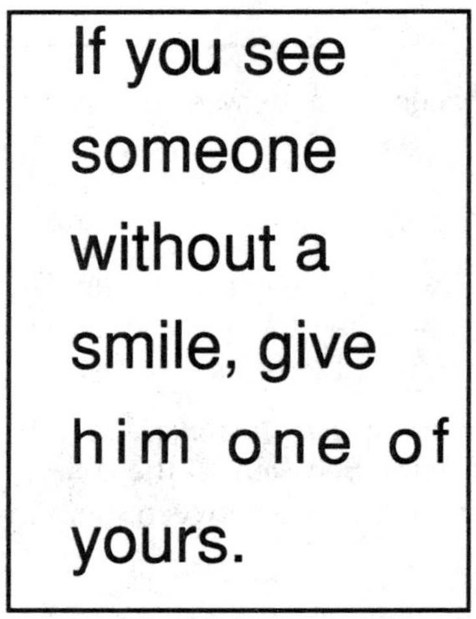

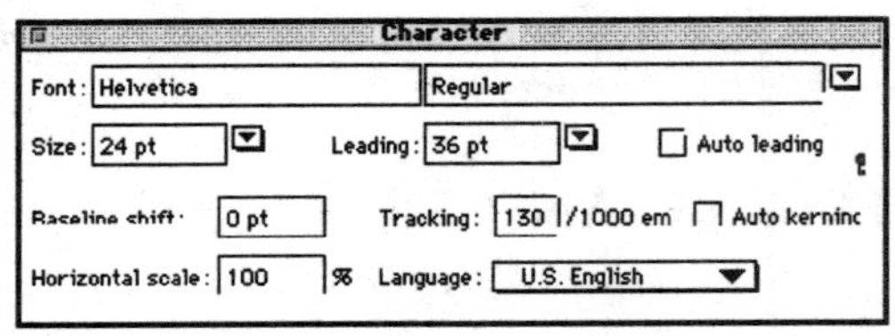

Figure 9.4—Notice the difference in the kerned letters *o* and *u* in the first line and in the unkerned *o* and *u* in *without* in the third line. Adding space between the characters and words in the fifth line spread the line out to the margin.

BASELINE SHIFT

When you first create type and click on the selection tool, the baseline appears under the type. Using the Baseline Shift command, you can raise or lower the type above or below this imaginary baseline to create superscripts or subscripts, or move type around a path for infinite graphic effects.

When inputting values in the Baseline shift dialog box, a positive number raises the selected type above the baseline; a negative number moves the type below the baseline. To restore the type to its default baseline, type 0 in the Baseline shift field.

EXERCISE C

1. Choose View/Preview (Command-Y). Use the oval tool and Option-drag to draw three circles. Use the Paint Style palette (Command-I) to apply a fill of None and a black stroke. Leave the last circle selected.
2. Select the path-type tool and choose Type/Alignment/Center (Command-Shift-C).
3. Click on the top of the circle and type a few words. Use the Font and Type menus to format the selected type with a font and type size. This is the original circle without any Baseline shift commands applied.
4. Use the selection tool to select the second circle. Select the path-type tool, click on the *top anchor point*, and type the same words. Drag to select the words. Choose Type/Character (Command-T) to display the Character palette. Click on the lever to expand the palette.
5. With the type still selected, type 10 in the Baseline shift field. Press Return or Enter. The type moves *up* 10 points above the baseline because you typed a positive number in the Baseline shift field.
6. Use the selection tool to select the third circle. Then use the path type tool to click on the *bottom anchor point* and type the same words again. Select them with any of the type tools. Use the Character palette to select a typeface and apply a type size to the selected type.
7. Type –20 in the Baseline shift field. Press Return or Enter. The type moves 20 points *below* the baseline because you typed a negative number. Your screen should resemble Figure 9.5.

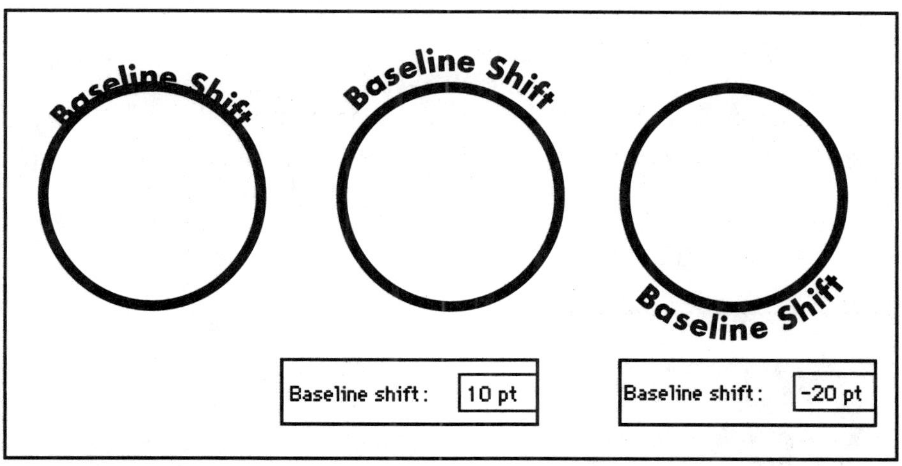

Figure 9.5—The first circle displays the type as it was entered on the path. The center circle displays a Baseline shift value of 10 points. The circle on the right displays a Baseline shift value of –20 points, which causes the type to drop below the baseline.

⌘-Y View/Preview
⌘-T Type/Character
⌘-Shift-C Type/Alignment/Center

Path-type tool

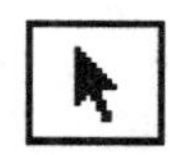

Selection tool

Tip

Click three times with any type tool to select an entire text object.

Another tip

As soon as you finish typing the text, click once on the type tool you used to create the text and the entire text object becomes selected.

⌘-D Arrange/Repeat Transform
⌘-T Type/Character

HORIZONTAL SCALE

When you apply kerning, tracking, or baseline shift values to type, you only affect the *space* between characters and words and the space between type and the baseline. Changing the horizontal scale of type, however, changes the actual letterforms themselves by changing the specified *proportion* between the height and width of characters—not the height of the character.

When you first type a character, its horizontal scale value is 100%, that is, it is horizontally and vertically proportioned the way the fontographer designed it. Typing a number greater than 100% in the Horizontal scale field on the Character palette expands the selected text; typing a value less than 100% compresses the text. To restore selected type to its original shape, type 0 [zero] in the Horizontal scale field.

Oops!

When you first enter text in a file where you have made changes in the Character palette, the new text reflects those changes. If necessary, type 0 [zero] in the Baseline shift field to restore the type to its original baseline or check on the field name to highlight the field.

EXERCISE D

1. Use the type tool to type a short word, then click on the selection tool to select the type and display its baseline.
2. Click on the baseline or on the alignment point and drag the type down, pressing the Option key before releasing the mouse button to create a duplicate of the type.
3. Choose Arrange/Repeat Transform (Command-D) to create a second copy of the original type. You now have three lines of type on the screen.
4. Choose Type/Character (Command-T) to display the Character palette. Click on the lever to expand it.
5. Use the type tool to select one character in the second line of type. Type 200 in the Horizontal scale field of the Character palette. Press Return or Enter to expand the type to twice its normal width.
6. Use the type tool to select any one character in the third line of type. Type 50 in the Horizontal scale field. Press Return or Enter to compress the character to half its original width. Your screen should resemble FIgure 9.6.

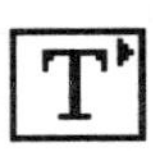

Type tool

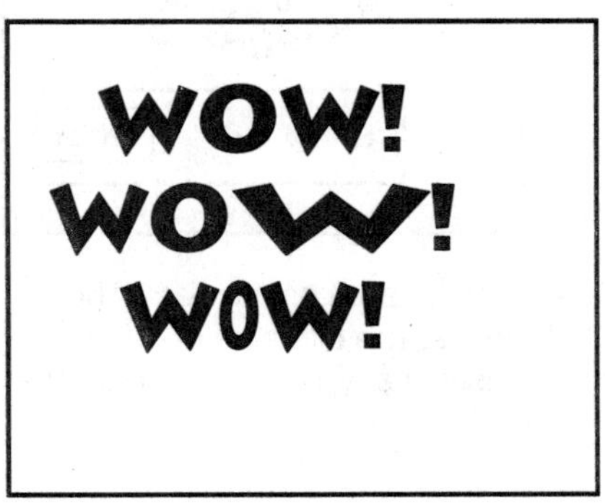

Figure 9.6—The top line of type is the original type (100% horizontal scale). The second *W* in the second line has been scaled to 200% or twice its original width. The *O* in the third line of type has been compressed to 50% of its original width.

PARAGRAPH FORMATTING

The upper panel of the Paragraph palette (Figure 9.7) allows you to apply alignment, indentation, leading, hanging punctuation, and hyphenation values to an entire paragraph. Because all these commands are paragraph-specific, you don't have to select the entire paragraph to apply them; just click anywhere in the paragraph to select the entire paragraph.

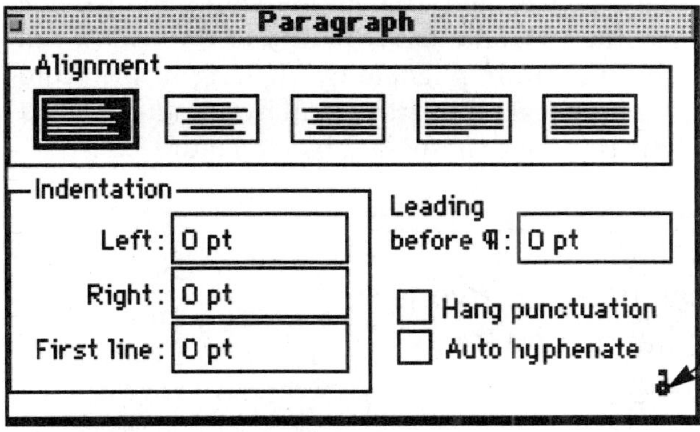

Figure 9.7—The upper panel of the Paragraph palette can be expanded by clicking on the lever in the lower right corner.

EXERCISE E

1. To restore Illustrator's default values, quit the program (File/Quit) and trash the Adobe Illustrator preferences file located in the System folder. Then launch Illustrator again. Select inches as the Ruler units (Command-K).
2. Click on the rectangle tool and click once on the drawing page to display the Rectangle dialog box. Type 3 in the Width field. Press the Tab key and type 4 in the Height field. Click on OK.
3. Select the area-type tool and type the following sentence (no quotes): "During a boring meeting, Charles Dickens once suggested that everyone around the table join hands and try to commune with the living." Click on the selection tool to select the entire text block.
4. Display the Character palette (Command-T) and notice that the text appears in the default 12-point Helvetica.
5. Display the Paragraph palette (Command-Shift-P). With the text block selected, click on each of the Alignment icons at the top of the palette. Notice how the entire paragraph changes from left, to center, to right, to justified, to last line justified alignment. Click on the left aligned icon (first icon) to align the paragraph from the left margin.
6. Choose Edit/Select None (Command-Shift-A) to deselect everything. Use the type tool or the area-type tool to click anywhere in the paragraph. Type 12 in the Left field under Indentation and press Return or Enter to place 12 points of space between the left side of the rectangle and the left margin of the text.
7. Press the Tab key and type 12 in the Right field and press Return or Enter to indent the text 12 points (one pica) from the right side of the rectangle.

⌘-Q File/Quit
⌘-K File/Preferences/General
⌘-T Type/Character
⌘-Shift-P Type/Paragraph
⌘-Shift-A Edit/Select None

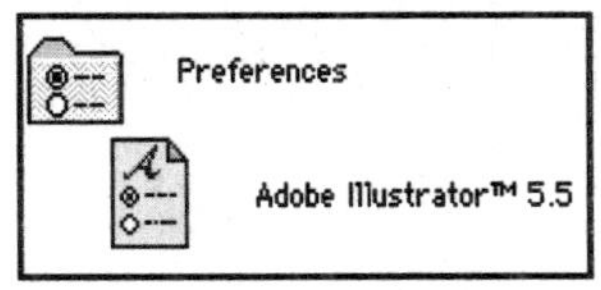

Locate the Adobe Illustrator preferences file in the Preferences folder in the System folder.

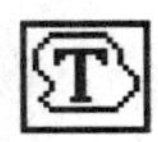

Area-type tool

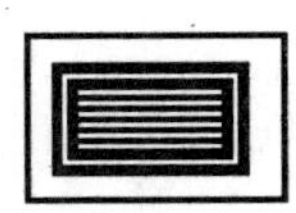

Justify Last Line icon

FYI

Avoid using the Justify Last Line option, because this tracks the last line of text to make it fit between the left and right margins. It is frequently an ugly format—like this.

⌘-I Object/Paint Style
⌘-K File/Preferences/General

8. Now type 0 [zero] in both the Right and Left Indentation fields to restore the text block to its original values.
9. Type 6 in the First line Indentation field and press Return or Enter to indent only the first line, not the entire paragraph, 6 points.

Back to square zero

Click on any field in the Paragraph palette to reset its value to 0; or, in the case of letter and word spacing values, to their default values.

HYPHENATING TEXT

Unless you select the Auto hyphenate check box in the Paragraph palette, Illustrator will not hyphenate the text, and text will drop to the next line in the text block. If you do select Auto hyphenate by clicking in the Auto hyphenate check box until an X appears, Illustrator will hyphenate any text that would extend beyond the right edge of the text block (Figure 9.8).

During a boring meeting, Charles
Dickens once suggested that everyone
around the table join hands and try to
commune with the living.

During a boring meeting, Charles Dick-
ens once suggested that everyone ar-
ound the table join hands and try to
commune with the living.

Figure 9.8—The first paragraph is formatted without Auto hyphenation, causing *Dickens* to move to the second line. The second paragraph is formatted with Auto hyphenation checked, which caused both *Dickens* and *around* to be hyphenated.

HYPHENATION OPTIONS

Unless you specify controls for Auto hyphenation, Illustrator will Autohyphenate words whenever it can and wherever it can. Since this is frequently unacceptable (editors don't like to see more than two hyphens in a row, and, they want at least two, if not three characters before and after a hyphen), use the lower panel of the Paragraph palette to select hyphenation options.

Click on the lever in the upper panel of the Paragraph palette to display the Hyphenation field. Hyphenation options default to two letters at the beginning of a word before a hyphen will be inserted and to two letters at the end of a word after the hyphen. For example, with these values, Illustrator would hyphenate *ab-solute* because there are at least two characters before and after the hyphen. It would not, however, hyphenate *apex* because only one character, the *a*, would appear before the hyphen.

FYI

You can manually hyphenate a word by entering a discretionary hyphen. Press the Control - – keys (Control + minus sign) and Illustrator will override the hyphenation settings and break the word at that point. But be careful! Discretionary hyphens always print, so if you change the type flow, you may have to manually delete the discretionary hyphens.

EXERCISE F

1. Select inches as the Ruler units (Command-K). Click with the rectangle tool on the drawing page to display the Rectangle dialog box. Type 2 in the Width field; press the Tab key and type 4 in the Height field. Click on OK.
2. Use the Paint Style palette (Command-I) to select a fill of None and a black stroke.

3. Click on the area-type tool to select it and click on the upper line of the rectangle. The flashing insertion point appears.
4. Choose File/Import Text. Highlight the Lesson 9.Text file on the Tutorial disk and click on Import. The text appears in the rectangle. Click on the selection tool to select the entire text object.
5. Choose Type/Paragraph (Command-Shift-P) to display the Paragraph palette. Click on the lever in the lower right corner to expand it so that the Hyphenation options are visible.
6. With the text still selected (the baselines are visible), click on the Justify icon in the Paragraph palette to justify the text.
7. Click on the Auto hyphenation check box. Make sure that in the Hyphenation field, the number 2 appears in the letters after… and letters before… check boxes. Press Return or Enter.
8. Notice how the paragraph is hyphenated (Figure 9.9).

⌘-Shift-P Type/Paragraph

Area-type tool

Tip

It's easier to work with type if you magnify the text object.

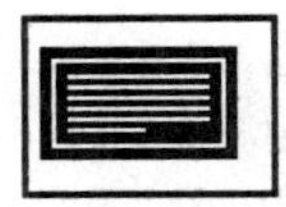

Justify icon

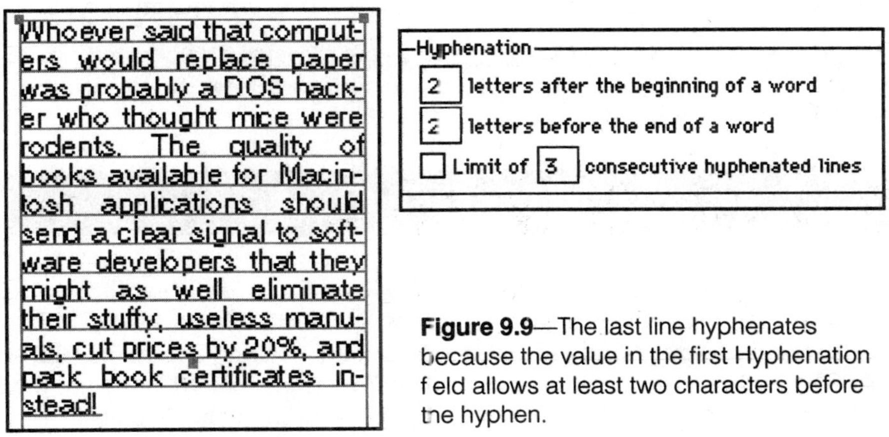

Figure 9.9—The last line hyphenates because the value in the first Hyphenation field allows at least two characters before the hyphen.

9. Now change both values in the Hyphenation field from 2 to 3. Click in the Limit check box to select it and change the value to 2 (consecutive hyphenated lines). Press Return or Enter (Figure 9.10).

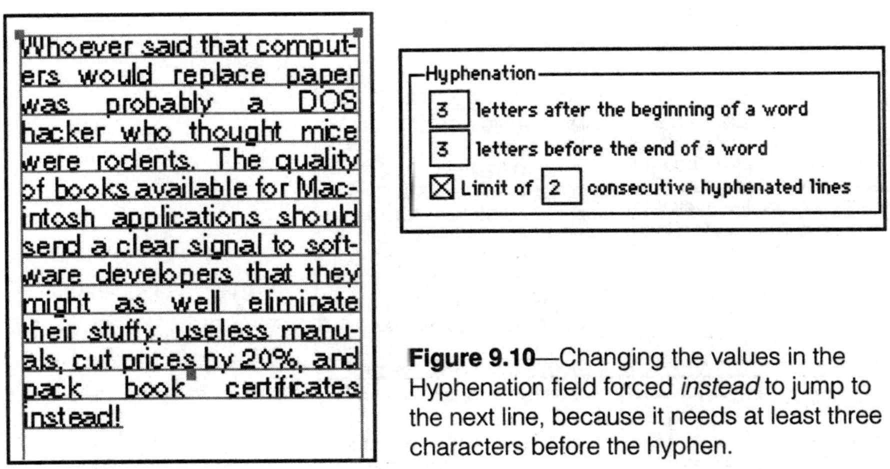

Figure 9.10—Changing the values in the Hyphenation field forced *instead* to jump to the next line, because it needs at least three characters before the hyphen.

10. Because the number of letters at the beginning and end of a word was specified at 3, several words jumped to the next line.

⌘-E View/Artwork
⌘-Shift-O Type/Spacing/Other

FYI

Spacing options are also available from the Type menu. Choosing Type/Spacing displays the lowest panel of the Paragraph palette.

11. Choose File/Preferences/Hyphenation Options to display the Hyphenation Options dialog box. The flashing cursor appears in the entry field. Type a word and click on the Add button. Click on Done. Because the word was added to the Hyphenation dictionary without any hyphens, Illustrator will never hyphenate it. If you add words with hyphens, then Illustrator will override the resident Hyphenation dictionary and hyphenate the word where you specified.
12. Save this file as Hyphens.ai. You will use it in the next exercise.

WORD SPACING AND LETTER SPACING

You probably noticed that the spacing between the words (word spacing) and the spacing between the individual characters (letter spacing) in the paragraph for Exercise F need some attention. The spacing options in the lowest panel of the Paragraph palette allow you to add and delete space between words, between the space between words, and between characters. These spacing options are most helpful when working with justified type.

The word spacing and letter spacing values are measured as percentages of the width of the current type size. Each option allows for minimum, desired, and maximum spacing.

More info

Selecting a paragraph of unjustified type makes only the Desired field available.

EXERCISE G

1. If necessary, open the Hyphens.ai file and choose View/Artwork (Command-E). Use the selection tool to select the text block. Make sure it is 12-point Helvetica. Choose Type/Spacing (Command-Shift-O) to display the lowest panel of the Paragraph palette. Change the number of hyphens to 2 letters after the beginning of a word and 2 letters before the end of a word.
2. To tighten the space between words, type the values under the Word spacing option in Figure 9.11. To tighten the space between the individual letters in a word, type the values in the Letter spacing fields in Figure 9.11. Experiment with these values to change the word and letter spacing options.

Selection tool

Space cadet

The Desired value determines how tight or loose the paragraph should be. Increasing or decreasing a 100% Desired value adds or removes space between letters and/or words. A Desired letter spacing value of 20% inserts 20% of the width of a space created by pressing the Spacebar between each pair of letters in the paragraph. A negative value reduces the space between characters and moves them closer together.

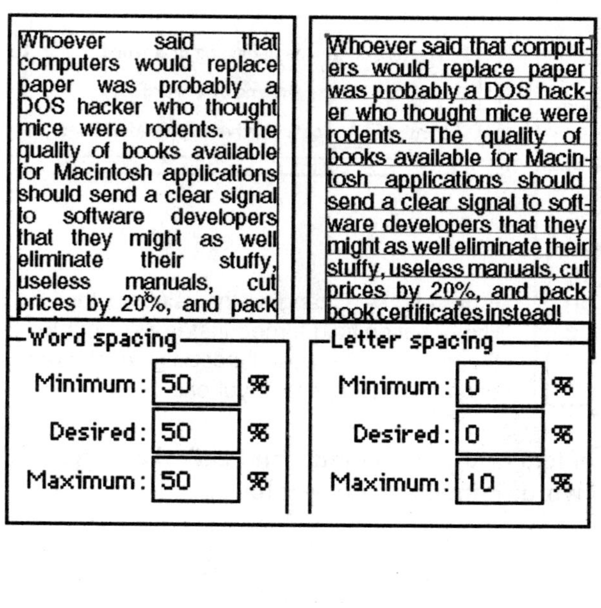

Figure 9.11—Decrease the word spacing values (they don't have to be the same) to tighten the space between words. Increase the Maximum Letter spacing value to decrease space between characters.

HANGING PUNCTUATION

Ordinarily, the first and last punctuation marks in a paragraph, like quotation marks and periods, appear at the edge of the text block. Using the Hang punctuation option in the Paragraph palette will cause them to hang outside the edge of the text block. The edge of the text block is defined by the left margin of the text, not by any stroke applied to the block itself.

⌘-Shift-P Type/Paragraph
⌘-E View/Artwork

SPACE BEFORE A PARAGRAPH

When adding extra space between paragraphs, it's always better to avoid using a paragraph return, because paragraph returns carry text information that can frequently be applied to subsequent paragraphs. To avoid this problem, select the Leading before ¶ command in the Paragraph palette to apply space between the selected paragraph and the paragraph above it.

EXERCISE H

1. Use the type tool to draw a text block about 2 inches wide and 3 inches high. Display the Paragraph palette (Command-Shift-P).
2. When the flashing cursor appears, type (include the quotes) "This is an example of hanging punctuation." Press the Return key to begin a new paragraph.
3. Type *This paragraph has space before it.*
4. Click with the type tool anywhere in the first paragraph and click on the Hang Punctuation check box to select it (an X appears in the box).
5. Click anywhere in the second paragraph and type 8 in the Leading before ¶ field on the Paragraph palette. Press Return or Enter to add 8 points of space *above* the second paragraph. Your screen should resemble Figure 9.12.

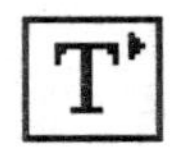

Type tool

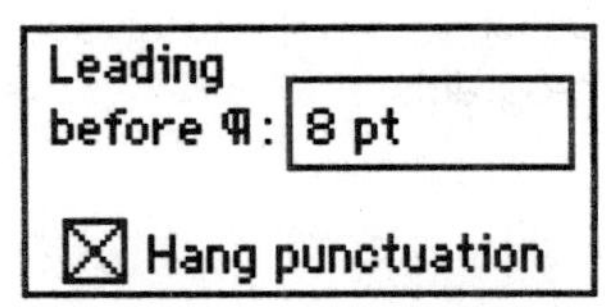

Type a value in the Leading before field to add space before a paragraph. Click to select the Hang punctuation option.

"This is an example of hanging punctuation."

This paragraph has space before it.

Figure 9.12—The opening quotation marks in the first paragraph hang to the left of the text block, and eight points of space have been added above the second paragraph. You can use the Smart Punctuation filter to change the inch marks to curly quotes.

SETTING TABS

The Tab Ruler palette allows you to set left, right, center, and decimal tabs. A visual guide appears in the selected text, so you can tell where the text is flowing even if the text path is rotated or wrapped around another object. Tab positions are measured using the selected Ruler Units measurement in the General Preferences dialog box.

Should you find text disappearing when you press the Tab key, because the text block is too small, deselect everything and select the text block with the

⌘-Control-I Window/Show Info
⌘-T Type/Character
⌘-A Edit/Select All
⌘-Shift-T Window/Show Tab Ruler

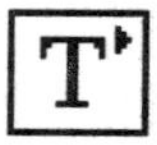

Type tool

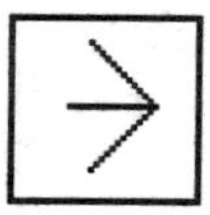

This tab symbol does not appear when you press the Tab key in Illustrator, as it does in word processing and page layout programs.

direct-selection tool. Then use that tool to Shift-select the two bottom anchor points and drag the bottom line down to enlarge the rectangle. Press the Shift key before releasing the mouse button to keep the sides straight.

EXERCISE I

1. On a clean drawing page, choose Window/Show Info (Command-Control-I) to display the Info palette.
2. Click on the type tool and drag to draw a rectangle about 7 inches wide and 4 inches high. Use the Info palette to keep track of the size of the text object you're drawing. When you release the mouse button, the flashing cursor appears.
3. Choose File/Import Text. Go to the Tutorial folder and locate the Lesson 9.Tabs file. Click on Open. When the text appears, click on the selection tool to select it (its baselines appear).
4. Display the Character palette (Command-T) and change the selected type to 24-point Helvetica. Assign a Leading value of 36 points in the Leading field. Press Return or Enter.
5. Use the zoom tool to magnify the text area so you can see the spaces between the words. Press the Tab key where indicated by the tab symbols in Figure 9.13. Depending on the size of the text block, text will move down and possibly out of sight. If the overflow indicator appears (plus sign in a box), use the direct-selection tool to select the bottom anchor points and drag them down to enlarge the text block.

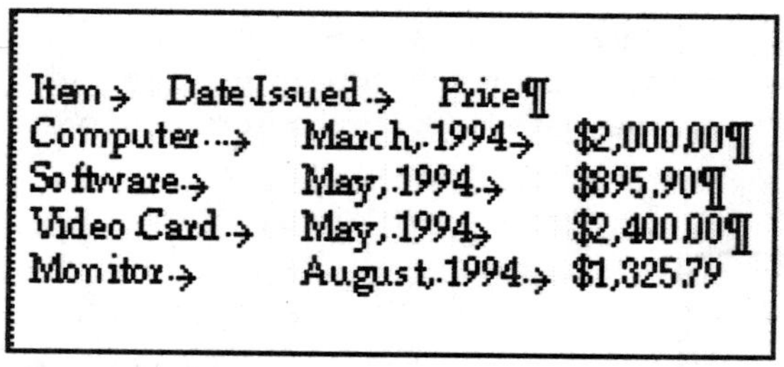

Figure 9.13—Press the Tab key between these items before specifying the tab positions from the Tabs palette.

6. Use the type tool and drag to select the entire text block or choose Edit/Select All (Command-A).
7. Choose Window/Show Tab Ruler (Command-Shift-T) to display the Tabs palette (Figure 9.14). If necessary, click on the Alignment box in the upper right corner to align the Tab Ruler with the left margin.

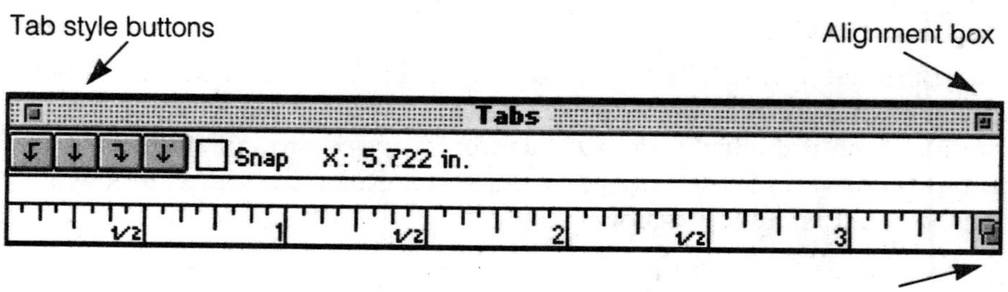

Figure 9.14—The Tabs palette.

8. If necessary, click on the Extend Tab Ruler button in the lower right corner of the palette to extend the ruler.
9. Click in the Snap check box above the ruler to snap the tabs to the ruler units as you drag them.
10. Since you have already placed the tab markers, all you have to do now is position them. With the entire text block selected and the Tabs palette displayed, click on the Left tab icon (the first icon) and click at the 1-inch mark on the Tabs Ruler. Then click on the Decimal tab icon and click on the 2.75 marker on the ruler. As you move a tab marker along the ruler, its position is displayed to the right of the Snap box. Your screen should resemble Figure 9.15.

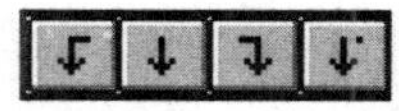

Left-justified, center-justified, right-justified, and Decimal-justified tab icons appear on the Tabs ruler.

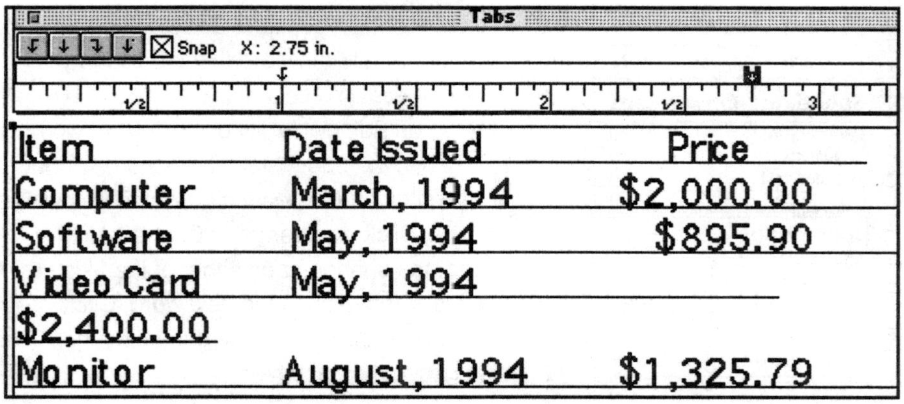

Figure 9.15—Type moves to the positions established by the tab markers. Because the third column was set under a decimal tab, the type aligns under the decimal point.

FYI

To remove a tab marker, click on it and drag it up and off the top of the ruler or to the left and off the ruler.

THE TEXT FILTER

The Text filter under the Filter menu allows you to change the case of selected characters, check the spelling of all the words in a document, export text in a variety of Macintosh and DOS formats, find and replace fonts in a document, find and replace text in a document, set rows and columns, and specify typographic punctuation.

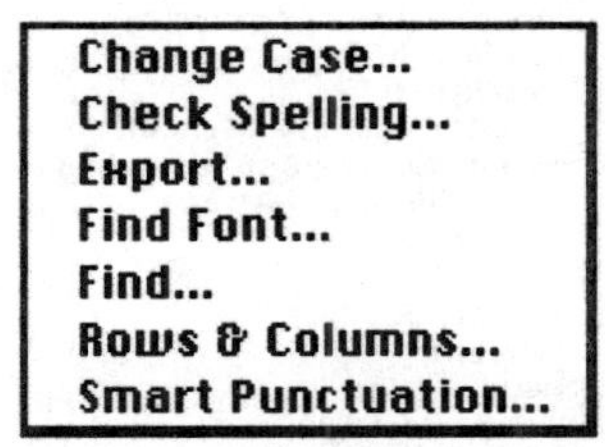

Text Filter options

EXERCISE J

1. On a clean drawing page, use the type tool to type your name. Be sure to capitalize the first letters in each name. Click on the selection tool to select the text block.
2. Choose Font/Helvetica and Type/Size 14.
3. Use the type tool to select the first letter in your first name.
4. Choose Filter/Text/Change Case to display the Change Case dialog box. Click the Lower case radio button and click on OK. The letter is now a lower-case character.

Type tool

⌘-A Edit/Select All

5. Use the type tool and click after your name to continue typing in that text block. Leave a space and type (no quotes) "is wonderfull." Be sure to misspell *wonderful* as *wonderfull*.
6. Choose Filter/Text/Check Spelling to display the Check Spelling dialog box (Figure 9.16).

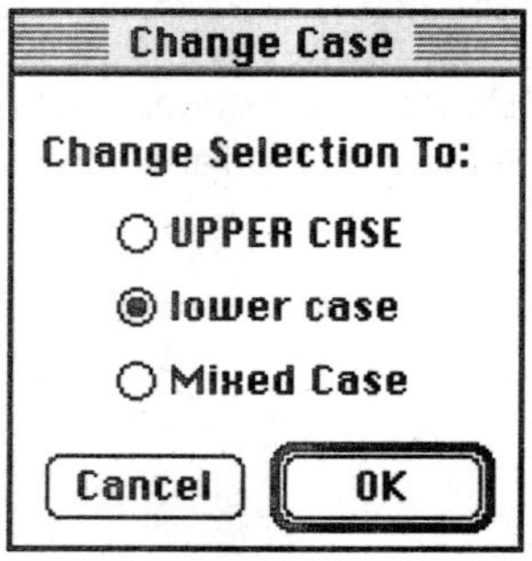

Select an option to change the case of selected text. Selecting the Mixed Case option will set every selected word with a capital letter.

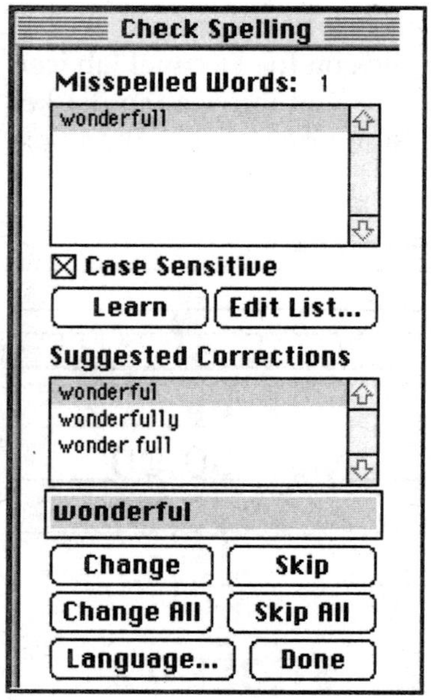

Figure 9.16—If Illustrator finds misspelled words, it displays them in the Misspelled Words window and lists the number of misspelled words in the document. Select or deselect the Case Sensitive option to specify what Illustrator should consider a misspelled word. If you want to add the word to the dictionary, click on Learn. You can always delete it by clicking on Edit List. A list of suggested words appears in the Suggested Corrections window and the first one appears highlighted below the window. Click on Change or Change All to accept the change or on either of the Skip options to move on to the next word. Click Done when you have finished to apply the changes to the document.

7. Click on Change to change *wonderfull* to *wonderful* (the first choice) and click on Done to close the dialog box and apply the changes.
8. Choose Edit/Select All (Command-A) to select the entire text block. Choose Filter/Text/Export to display the Export dialog box.
9. Use the Export pull-down menu to select a format for the file. Click to get to the Desktop and click on the Export button. The selected text now appears in the specified file format on the Desktop.
10. Deselect everything. Choose Filter/Text/Find Font to display the Find Font dialog box (Figure 9.17).

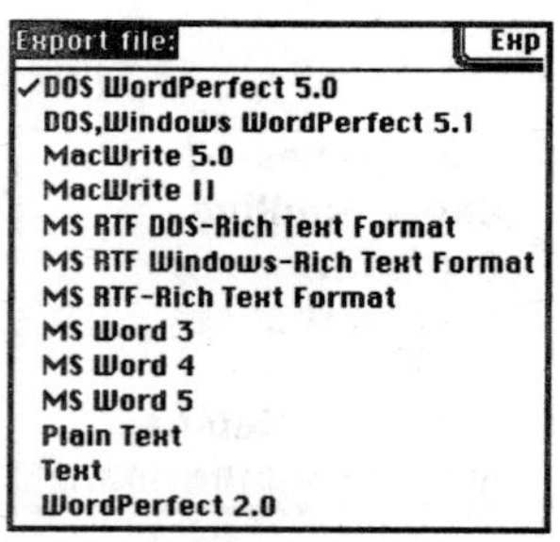

Use the Export File pull-down menu to select a format for the exported file.

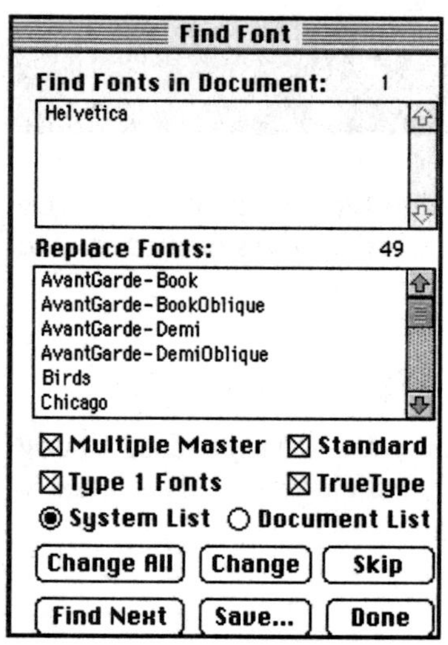

Figure 9.17—The top scroll box displays all the fonts in the current document; the lower scroll box lists all the fonts installed in the system. The check boxes list the kinds of fonts which can be available in any given document. Use the buttons on the bottom to change a font, find the next font, skip changing a font, and so on.

11. Click the check boxes of the kinds of fonts currently present in your system and that might appear in the document. In most cases, clicking Standard and Type 1 Fonts will be enough.
12. Click the Document List button to limit the display to the fonts you have used in the document. Click the Document List button to list all the fonts currently installed in your system.
13. Click on a font name in the upper window. In this example, only Helvetica is used in the document. Illustrator locates the next instance of text formatted in that font in the document. Click Find Next to find the next instance of the font, or click the Skip button to go to the next instance of the font. To change all the text in that font, click on one of the available fonts in the Replace Fonts window and click the Change All button. To replace the font of the selected text, highlight the replacement font in the lower scroll box and click Change.
14. To save a list of all the fonts used in the document, click the Save button. You will then be prompted to type a file name for the font list and a location for that file.
15. When you have finished finding and replacing fonts, click the Done button to exit the dialog box and return to the document.

FINDING AND REPLACING TEXT

You can use the Find function the Text filter to find and replace text anywhere in the document. The replaced text will contain all the formatting commands of the original text.

EXERCISE K

1. On a clean drawing page, use the type tool to type *Let us now praise famous men*.
2. Choose Filter/Text/Find to display the Text Find dialog box (Figure 9.18).

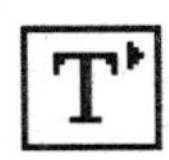
Type tool

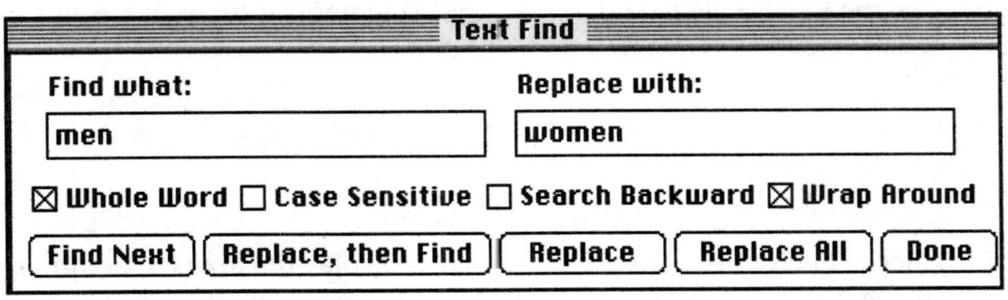

Figure 9.18—The Text Find dialog box.

3. Type *men* in the Find what box. Press the tab key and type *women* in the Replace with box.
4. Click on the Whole Word check box so that Illustrator will find only the word *men* and not words like *mention* or *mentor*.

⌘-I Object/Paint Style
⌘-K File/Preferences/General

5. If you check Case Sensitive, it will match the case of the text in the Find what box. Selecting Search Backward will search the document from the location of the text cursor.
6. Select the Wrap Around check box so that Illustrator will check not only from the cursor to the end of the document, but will also check from the beginning of the document to the position of the cursor.
7. Click on the Find Next button.
8. When Illustrator locates the first instance of *men*, the middle three buttons in the dialog box become available, and you have several options: Click Replace, then Find to replace the selected instance of *men* and locate the next instance; or click the Replace button just to replace the word and do nothing else; or click Replace All to replace every instance of the word.
9. Click on Replace, then Find. Illustrator replaces the one instance of *men* with *women* and beeps to indicate that the search is complete.
10. Click on Done to return to the document.

FYI

To display the Rows & Columns dialog box, the text block must first be selected *with the selection tool.*

SPECIFYING ROWS AND COLUMNS

The Text filter contains a command which changes single-column text blocks and rectangles into blocks of rows and columns. Use the various fields in the Rows & Columns dialog box (Figure 9.19) to change the flow of text within the rows and columns as well as to adjust the height, width, and gutter space between rows and columns.

EXERCISE L

Selection tool

1. On a clean drawing page, with inches as the Ruler units (Command-K), select the rectangle tool and click once on the page to display the Rectangle dialog box.
2. Type 4 in the Width field; press the Tab key and type 6 in the Height field. Click on OK.
3. Use the Paint Style palette (Command-I) to apply a fill of None and a stroke of black.
4. Select the area-type tool and click on the upper line of the rectangle. Choose File/Import Text and go to the Tutorial disk. Locate the Lesson 9.Text file and click on Import.
5. Use the selection tool to select the text block.
6. Choose Filter/Text/Rows & Columns to display the Rows & Columns dialog box. Make sure the Preview check box is selected so you can see the changes applied without exiting the dialog box (Figure 9.19).

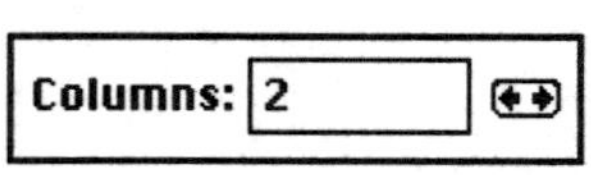

Click on the left arrow to decrease the field value by 1; click on the right arrow to increase the value.

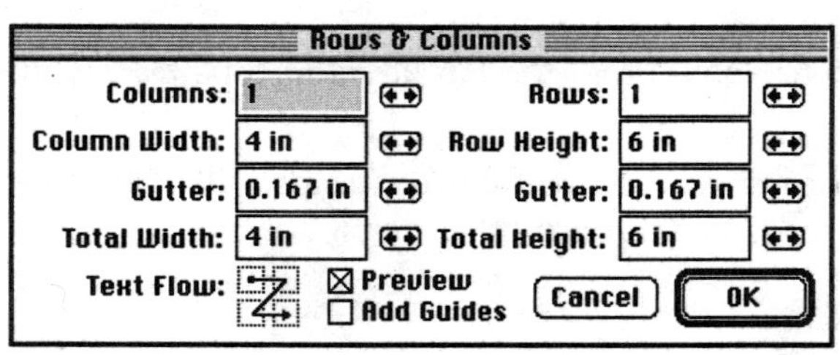

Figure 9.19—The Rows & Columns dialog box.

7. Type 2 in the Columns field or click once on the right arrow next to the Columns field. The text block splits in half with 0.167 inches between the columns. The total width of both columns and the gutter space is still 4 inches.
8. Type 4 in the Rows field or click three times on the right arrow next to the Rows field to divide the text block into four equal rows (Figure 9.20). Click on OK.

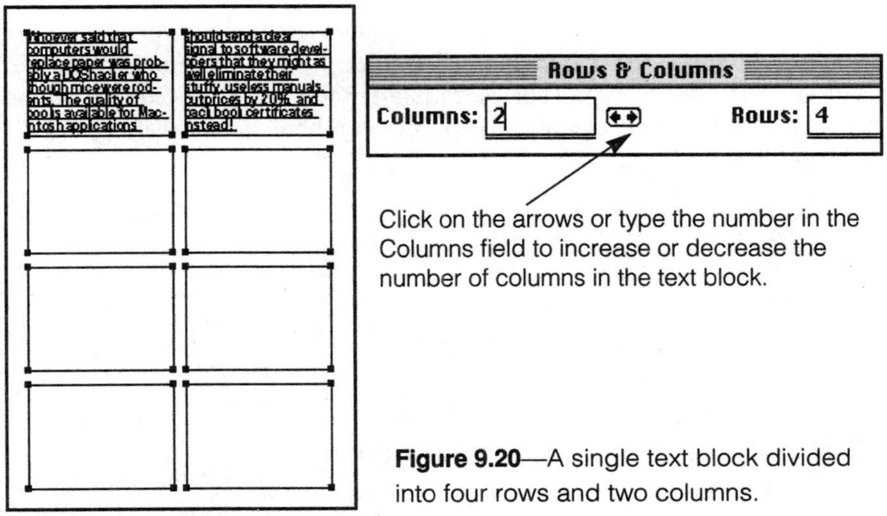

Figure 9.20—A single text block divided into four rows and two columns.

9. To change the direction of the text flow from left to right to up and down, make sure the text block is still selected. Then choose Filter/Text/Rows & Columns again. Click on the lower right box in the Text Flow field. The type flows from the first row in the first column to the second row in the first column (Figure 9.21). Click on OK.

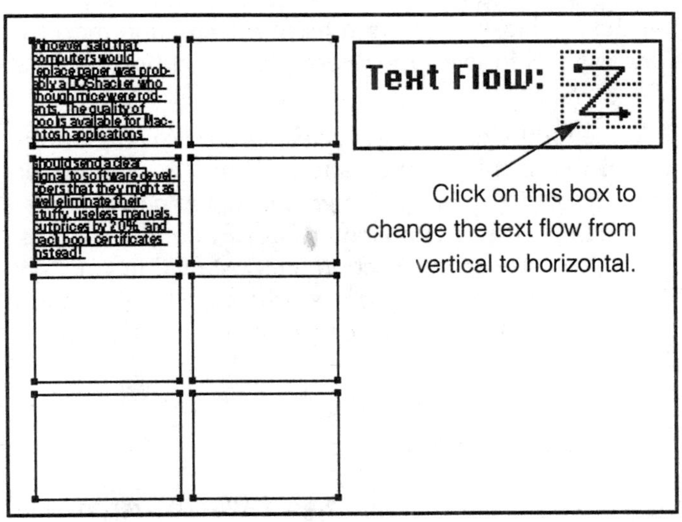

Figure 9.21—Click on the appropriate box in the Text Flow field to change the direction of the text flow.

10. With the text box still selected, choose Filter/Text/Rows & Columns again. Use the control arrows to change the dimensions of the rows and columns. Click on the Add Guides check box to display the guides between the rows and columns. Click on OK.

⌘-N File/New

SMART PUNCTUATION

The Smart Punctuation filter allows you to create type that is typographically correct. You can also use this filter to search for keyboard text symbols and replace them with publishing text symbols.

EXERCISE M

Type tool

1. Choose File/New (Command-N). Use the type tool to type (including the quotes), "Don't flip--listen," I said. "It's...well, something like that." Be sure to type four periods after the word *saw* (three for the ellipse and one for the period) and two hyphens (dashes) after *flipped.*
2. Use the type tool to select the entire text block.
3. Choose Filter/Text/Smart Punctuation to display the Smart Punctuation dialog box (Figure 9.22).

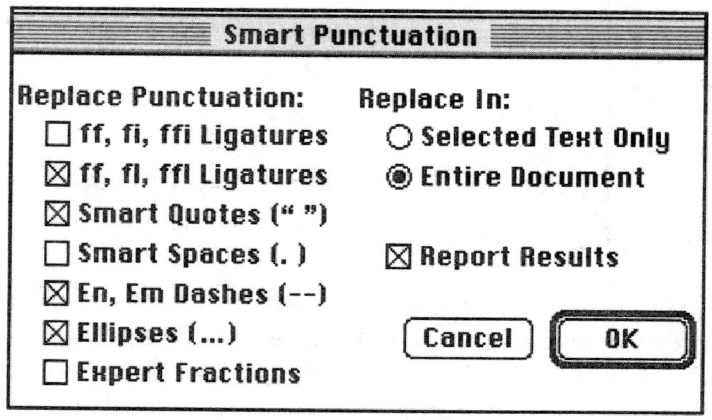

Figure 9.22—The Smart Punctuation dialog box allows you to make text typographically correct.

4. Click to select the options selected in Figure 9.22. Click the Entire Document button in the Replace In field to replace punctuation marks in the entire document. Click to select the Report Results option. Click on OK.
5. Illustrator will do the following: change the fl in *flipped* to a ligature, a single text character that combines the f and l; change the inch marks into printer's curly quotation marks; change the two hyphens into an em dash and change the three periods after *flipped* into a true ellipse (Figure 9.23). If you have the expert fraction font installed in your system, check Expert Fractions and Illustrator will adjust the size and kerning of any fractions in your text to create typographic fractions.

FYI

To replace punctuation marks in selected text, first select the text with the type tool before displaying the Smart Punctuation dialog box.

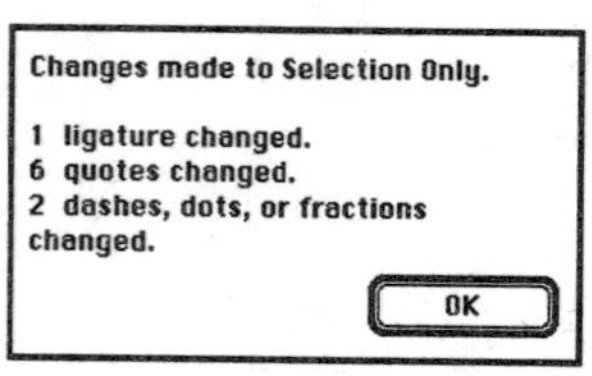

A report on the changes made to the selected text appears if you select the Report Results option. The "6 quotes changed" report includes the two apostrophes.

"Don't flip--listen," I said. "It's...well, something like that."

“Don’t flip–listen,” I said. “It’s…well, something like that.”

Figure 9.23—The report (sidebar) lists the changes made to the punctuation in the original file (top). The same file (bottom) displays the typographically correct punctuation.

⌘-T Type/Character
⌘-Shift-P Type/Paragraph

REVIEW EXERCISE

In this exercise you will create a text block and apply values from the Character palette, Paragraph palette, and Text filter.

1. Use the type tool and drag to create a rectangular text block. Type a few paragraphs in the block, pressing the Return key between each paragraph. If necessary, use the direct-selection tool to enlarge the text block.
2. Use the type tool to select a few lines in the first paragraph. Choose Type/Character (Command-T) to display the Character palette. Use the Character palette to change the typeface, type size, and leading in the paragraph.
3. Click between two characters and apply kerning values (positive and negative) to a few pairs of letters. Triple-click to select a line and apply a positive tracking value to increase the space between all of the selected characters and words.
4. Select a few characters and type positive and negative numbers to move them above and below the baseline.
5. Select the first character in a paragraph and apply a Horizontal scale value of 200% to create an initial cap.
6. Choose Type/Paragraph (Command-Shift-P) and change the indents, alignment, and hyphenation options. Use the Word spacing and Letter spacing options to change those values.
7. Type some columnar material and set left, center, decimal, and right tabs to create columns.
8. Use the options in the Text filter to check the spelling in the document, find and replace text, and change the case of selected characters.
9. Figure 9.24 displays some of these type options. The type was set in Times Roman, 24/50 (24-point type on 35 points of leading). The initial character and the open and close quote marks were enlarged to 36 points and set in Times Bold Italic; their Horizontal scale value was enlarged to 200%. The quotation marks were positioned using the Baseline shift command. *Mae West* was set in 14-point Times Italic, right aligned and moved up using the Baseline shift command. The Hang punctuation option was selected and kerning was applied to make the type visually correct.

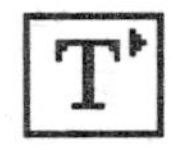

Type tool

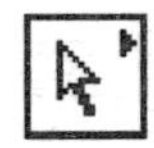

Direct-selection tool

“*I* used to be Snow
White, but I drifted.”
Mae West

Figure 9.24—Many of the commands on the Character and Paragraph palette were applied to this text block.

REVIEW QUESTIONS

Read the following questions and choose the answer which best completes the statement.

1. Type options can be accessed from _____.
   a. the Menu Bar
   b. the keyboard
   c. the Character palette
   d. a and c
2. Adding space between more than two selected characters is called _____.
   a. kerning
   b. leading
   c. tracking
   d. scaling
3. Adjusting the height-to-width proportion of characters affects the _____ of characters.
   a. baseline shift
   b. horizontal scale
   c. leading
   d. a and c
4. To restore Adobe Illustrator to its default values, _____.
   a. relaunch the program
   b. use the Preferences dialog box
   c. trash the Preferences file, then launch the application
   d. buy a new program
5. Hyphenation values are entered _____.
   a. from the keyboard
   b. in the Character palette
   c. from the Format menu
   d. in the Paragraph palette
6. Word spacing and letter spacing applies primarily to _____.
   a. justified text
   b. paragraph-based text
   c. large type
   d. tracking and kerning
7. Before setting a tab marker, _____.
   a. select the line or lines of text to be tabbed
   b. display the Tabs palette
   c. click on the appropriate Tab icon
   d. all of the above
8. Punctuation that extends beyond the left margin of the text block is _____.
   a. created with the Baseline shift command
   b. typographically incorrect
   c. specified in the Paragraph palette
   d. b and c
9. Rows and columns are set up via the _____.
   a. Text filter
   b. Paragraph palette
   c. Character palette
   d. Tabs palette
10. To find and replace text and fonts in a document, _____.
    a. use the Character palette
    b. use the Format menu
    c. make selections from the Text filter
    d. hunt and peck

Answers: 1. d; 2. a; 3. b; 4. c; 5. d; 6. a; 7. d; 8. c; 9. a; 10. c

LESSON

10

Layers, Masks, and Compound Paths

OVERVIEW

How objects are arranged in stacks and layers is covered in this lesson. You will learn how to create and edit layers on which artwork is placed, create masks to protect work from editing, and create compound paths to achieve graphic effects.

TOPICS

Stacking order
Layers
The Layers palette
Creating new layers
New layer options
Moving objects from layer to layer
Layer options from the Layers palette
Layers and groups
Masking objects
Editing masks
Modifying masks
Moving masked objects
Releasing masks
Creating compound paths
Selecting and releasing compound paths
Reversing the fill in a compound path
Review Exercise
Review Questions

TERMS

compound path
layer
mask (masking object)
masked object
stacking order

TUTORIAL FILES

Desert Scene.ai
Layers.ai
Masked Stars.ai
a la Matisse.ai

⌘-N File/New
⌘-Control-L Window/Show Layers

STACKING ORDER

Each overlapping object created in a document is stacked in front of the one previously created. For example, if you draw a circle, then a rectangle over that circle, and then a star on top of the rectangle, the circle is the backmost object in the stacking order and the star is the first object. This arrangement of objects is called the stacking order or painting order.

Objects can be arranged in a file in two ways: they can be stacked on a single layer (like the circle, rectangle, and star in the example above), or they can be placed individually or stacked on different layers in the same document.

LAYERS

A layer is a specific level on which artwork is placed and edited. A layer can be hidden so that the artwork on that level cannot be viewed or edited. A layer can be locked so that the artwork on that layer can be viewed but not edited. Artwork on any layer can be printed or not printed with the rest of the document.

When you first launch Adobe Illustrator, the drawing page appears and Layer 1 is automatically created. To access the layers, use the Layers palette from the Window menu (Command-Control-L).

Tip

The three icons on the Layers palette (one eye, two pencils) can get confusing unless you remember that the Eye icon refers to what is *visible* on the layer, and the Pencil icons refer to what can be *edited* on that layer.

THE LAYERS PALETTE

Use the Layers palette (Figure 10.1) to create, hide, lock, and delete layers. Each layer has its own menu, which allows you to specify the printing and display options for that layer.

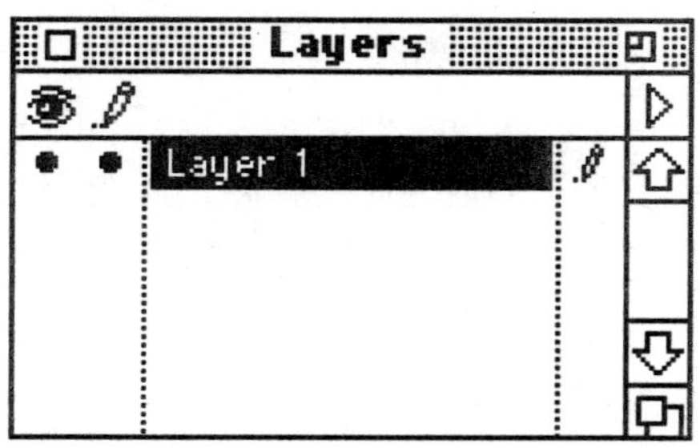

Figure 10.1—The Layers palette as it appears in a new document displays only Layer 1, which is both visible and available for editing.

When you display the Layers palette for a new document, two icons appear to the left of the Layer 1 name: an Eye icon and a Pencil icon. The black dot under the Eye icon tells you that the artwork on that layer is visible (or will be when you draw it). The black dot under the Pencil icon tells you some or all of the artwork on that layer is unlocked and can be edited.

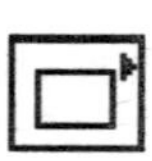

Rectangle tool

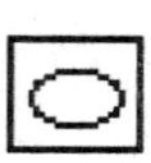

Oval tool

EXERCISE A

1. Create a new document (File/New) and choose Window/Show Layers (Command-Control-L) to display the Layers palette. It appears displaying Layer 1 as visible (black dot under the Eye icon) and editable (black dot under the Pencil icon).
2. Use the rectangle tool to draw a rectangle. Then use the oval tool to draw an oval.

3. With the oval still selected, notice that a black square appears next to the pencil *on the right side of the Layers palette* (Figure 10.2). This tells you that the selected object can be edited. Deselect the oval (Command-Shift-A) and the square disappears.

⌘-Shift-A Edit/Select None

FYI

Icons and dots on the left side of the Layers palette display information related to the entire layer. The Pencil icon and squares on the right side of the Layers palette display information about *selected objects* on that layer.

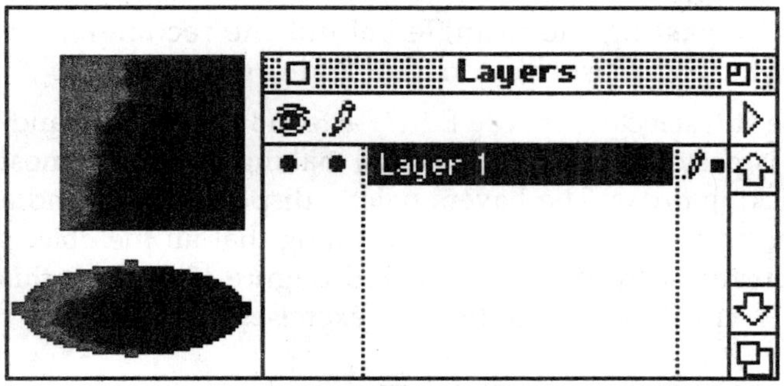

Figure 10.2—The black square on the right side of the palette indicates that the selected object is editable.

4. Use the selection tool to select the rectangle. Choose Arrange/Lock (Command-1). Notice that the black square next to the pencil (editing icon) disappears, indicating that there is a locked (uneditable) object on that layer. The black dot under the Pencil icon on the left side of the palette remains, because there is at least one unlocked, and therefore editable, object on that layer (the oval).

5. Continue to select and deselect, lock and unlock single and multiple objects on Layer 1, while watching the three icons on the Layers palette, until you are familiar with what the dots and squares mean.

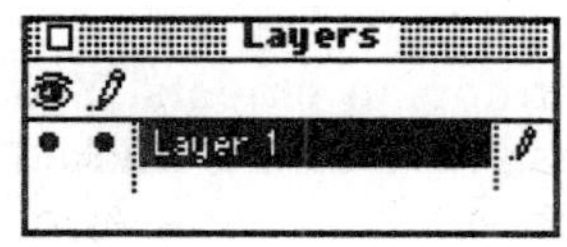

When any object on a layer is locked, the black square on the right side of the Layers palette next to the Pencil icon disappears.

EXERCISE B

1. On a clean drawing page, use the rectangle tool to draw a rectangle, the pen tool to draw a slightly smaller triangle, and the oval tool to draw a circle slightly smaller than the triangle. Use the Paint Style palette to fill and stroke them with contrasting colors (Figure 10.3).

2. Use the selection tool to drag the triangle on top of the rectangle so that half of the triangle extends beyond the right edge of the rectangle. Drag the oval over the triangle so that it extends beyond the edge of the triangle (Figure 10.3).

Selection tool

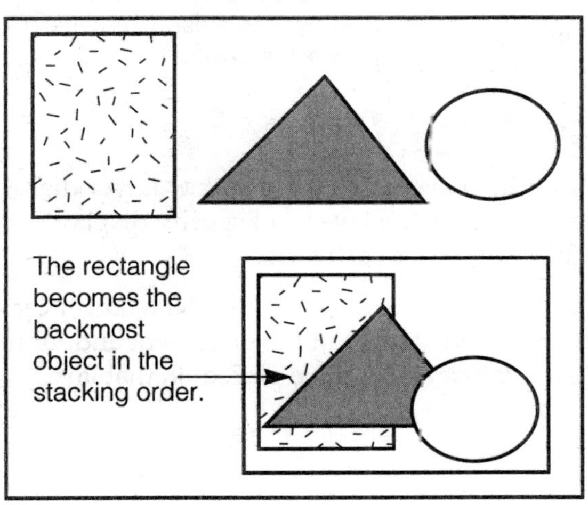

Figure 10.3—Even though the rectangle was the first object drawn, once the triangle and oval are placed in front of it, it becomes the backmost object in the stacking order.

⌘-X Edit/Cut
⌘-B Edit/Paste in Back
⌘-F Edit/Paste in Front

Selection tool

3. Use the selection tool to select the triangle. Choose Edit/Cut (Command-X) to remove the triangle and place it on the Clipboard.
4. Select the rectangle and choose Edit/Paste in Back (Command-B) to place the cut triangle *behind* the selected rectangle. If you had chosen Edit/Paste, the triangle would have been pasted in the center of the drawing page. By pasting the triangle behind the rectangle, the triangle becomes the backmost object in the stacking order.
5. With the triangle still selected, choose Edit/Paste in Front (Command-F). The triangle is pasted in front of the oval, making it the frontmost object in the stacking order. The Layers palette displays circles and a square under the Eye and Pencil icons, indicating that all the objects on Layer 1 are currently visible and unlocked (Figure 10.4). Save this file as Layers.ai. You will need it for the next exercise.

Layer those stacks!

Stacking and layering are two different ways of arranging objects. You can have several stacked objects on one layer or think of it as an individual layer having one or more stacks of objects.

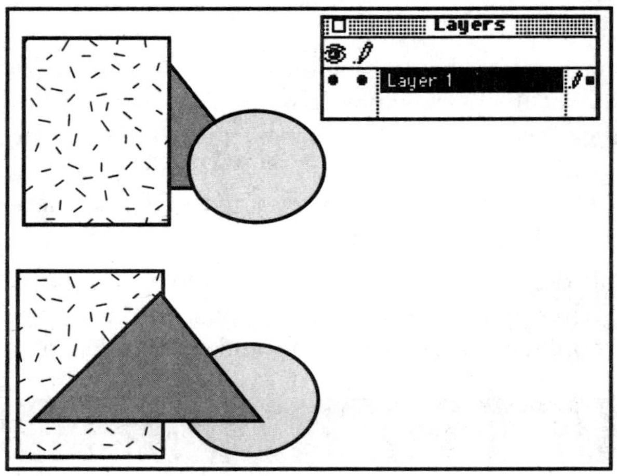

Figure 10.4—The Paste in Back command pastes a cut or copied object behind the last object in the stack, making it (the triangle) the last object in the stacking order (top). When the same triangle is cut and pasted in front, it is pasted in front of the current top object in the stacking order (bottom).

CREATING NEW LAYERS

Click on this triangle and the pull-out menu will display some of the options for the Layers palette.

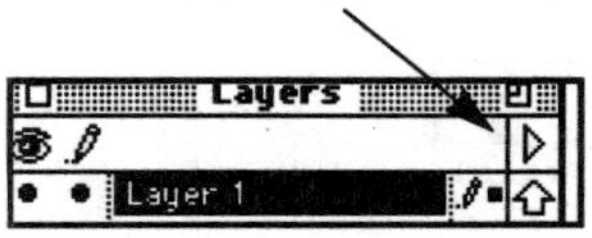

Every new Illustrator document is created with one layer, Layer 1. To add new layers to the document, use the pull-out menu on the Layers palette and drag to select New Layer (Figure 10.5). Once you select New Layer, that layer is created, is named Layer 2, and the New Layer dialog box is displayed.

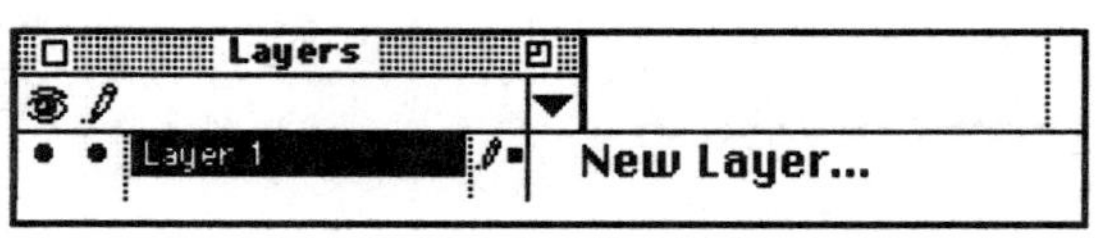

Figure 10.5—Select the New Layer command from the Layers palette.

NEW LAYER OPTIONS

Once you select New Layer from the Layers palette, the New Layer dialog box is displayed. It is here that you name the layer and specify display and printing options for only that layer or level of artwork.

Whenever you create a new layer by clicking on OK in the New Layer dialog box, that new layer becomes the active layer in the document and, until you specify otherwise, any objects you create will be placed on that layer.

MOVING OBJECTS FROM LAYER TO LAYER

Although it's good practice to define the layers in a piece of artwork before you begin drawing, many times we get so carried away by the fact that the drawing is actually looking like it's supposed to look that we end up with many objects on one layer. This makes it difficult to edit and sometimes print the document. Even though the Layers palette is not displayed, objects are being drawn on the currently selected layer (usually Layer 1), so it is frequently necessary to move objects to new layers in the artwork.

To move objects from one layer to another, cut them, select the new layer, and paste the objects on that new layer. Another way to move objects from layer to layer is to use the Layers palette. Select the object to be moved and drag the black dot next to the Pencil icon *on the right side of the Layers palette* up or down to the new layer.

EXERCISE C

1. If necessary, open the Layers.ai file you created in the last lesson (File/Open) or create a new file with three objects on one layer. Choose Window/Show Layers (Command-Control-L) to display the Layers palette. Layer 1 is highlighted, indicating that it is the active layer; any objects you draw will be placed on that layer.
2. Use the selection tool to select an object. Layer 1 remains highlighted, indicating that the object is on that layer.
3. Click on the triangle in the right corner of the Layers palette to display the pull-down menu. Drag to select New Layer. The New Layer dialog box appears, displaying Layer 2 as the highlighted name of the new layer (Figure 10.6).

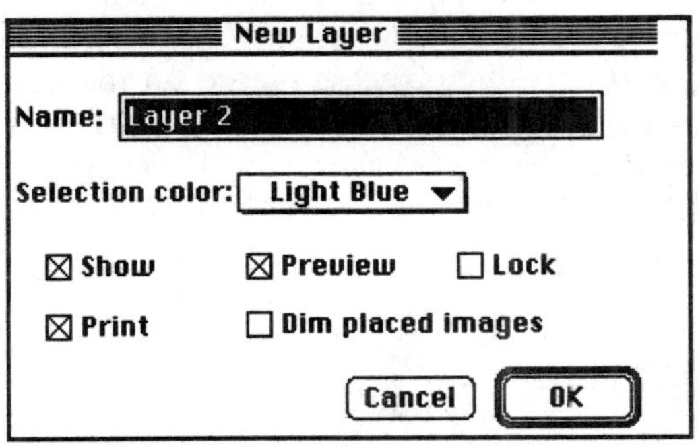

Figure 10.6—Make display and printing choices in the New Layer dialog box.

4. Type (no quotes) "Triangle" in the Name field. Change the Selection color if you like, and make sure that Show, Print, and Preview are checked. Click on OK. The Triangle layer appears as the topmost layer in the Layers palette. However, it does not display any icon on the right side of the palette, because there are no objects on the Triangle layer.
5. Use the selection tool to select the triangle. Layer 1 on the Layers palette becomes highlighted, because an object on that layer has been selected. And because the triangle is available for editing, a black square appears next to the Pencil icon on the right side of the Layers palette.

⌘-O File/Open
⌘-Control-L View/Show Layers

FYI

The Layers palette is saved with the document.

More info

You can select the Paste Remembers Layers option in the General Preferences dialog box or the Layers palette pull-out menu to cut an object on one layer and paste it at the top of the stack on the same layer. If you deselect this option, the object is pasted onto the current layer regardless of what layer from which you cut or copied the object.

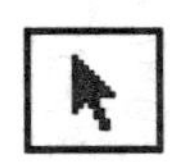

Selection tool

Color code

The Selection color specified in the layer's dialog box determines the color of the squares on the Layers palette.

⌘-X Edit/Cut
⌘-P File/Print

6. Choose Edit/Cut (Command-X). Click once on the Triangle layer to get to that layer and choose Edit/Paste (Command-V). The triangle is pasted on the Triangle layer and, because it is selected and available for editing, a black square appears next to the Pencil icon on the right side of the palette (Figure 10.7).

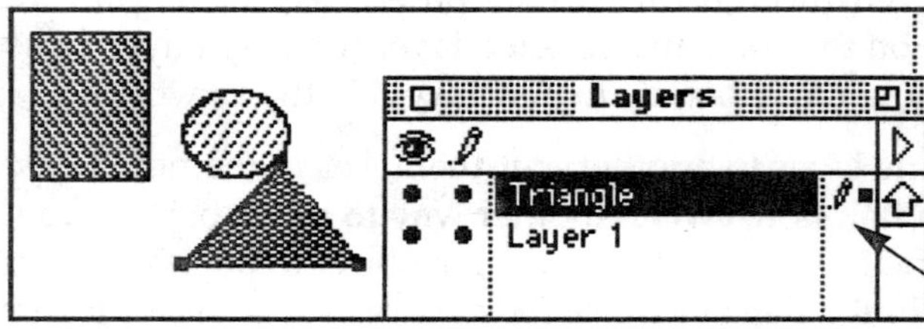

Figure 10.7—The black square next to the Pencil icon indicates that the selected triangle on the current layer, Triangle, is available for editing.

7. Because you selected Show in the New Layer dialog box, all objects on the Triangle layer are displayed. The triangle is displayed with all of its fill and stroke attributes because Preview (viewing mode) was selected, and all the objects on this layer will print when you print the file because Print was selected in the New Layer dialog box.
8. Use the pull-out menu on the Layers palette to create a new layer. Type (no quotes) "Circle" in the name field of the New Layer dialog box. Make sure that only Show is selected. Click to deselect Print and Preview. Click on OK. The Circle layer, now the first layer in the Layers palette, is highlighted, indicating that it is the active layer and that anything you draw will appear on that layer. Notice also the white dot under the Eye icon on the left side of the Layers palette. This tells you that all the objects on this layer are displayed in Artwork mode.
9. Click on the circle, which deselects the Circle layer and highlights Layer 1 because the selected object (the circle) is on Layer 1.

Selection tool

10. Click with the selection tool on the black square next to the Pencil icon on the right side of the palette and drag it up to the Circle layer. A hand appears as you drag, and once the object is placed on the new layer, a black triangle appears where the finger is pointing (Figure 10.8), indicating that the selected object has overcome all transportation hazards and been safely moved through all the layers onto the designated layer.

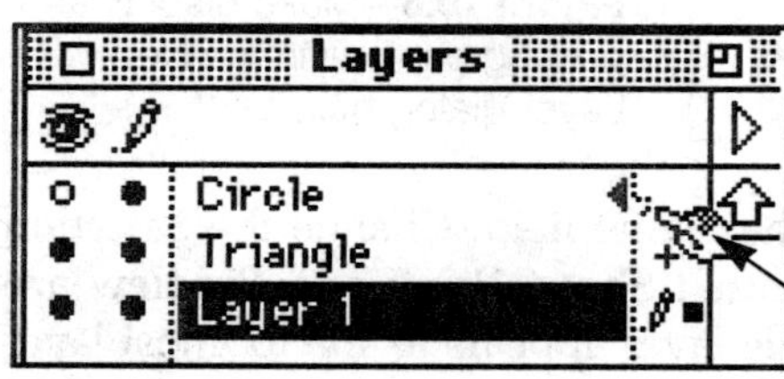

Figure 10.8—Dragging the black square on the right side of the Layers palette to another layer moves the selected object to that layer.

Too much of a good thing?

If you find all these dots, squares, triangles, and fingers too many icons to deal with, use the Cut and Paste commands to move items from one layer to another. It's not uncommon to confuse these icons. You're not dumb; the icons are excessive.

11. Because Artwork mode was designated in the New Layer dialog box, the circle appears on the Circle layer in Artwork mode, even though the objects on the other two layers are displayed in Preview mode.
12. Choose File/Print (Command-P) to display the Print dialog box. Click on OK. Because the Print check box was not selected in the Circle layer's dialog box, only the rectangle and triangle print.

13. Choose New Layer from the Layers palette. Type Rectangle in the Name field, click to select Show, Preview, Print, and Lock. Click on OK. The Layers palette now displays four layers, the Rectangle layer as the topmost layer, the Circle and Triangle layers, and Layer 1. Notice that there is no black dot under the Pencil icon on the left side of the Layers palette. Since the Rectangle layer is locked, no items placed on that layer can be edited (Figure 10.9).

⌘-X Edit/Cut
⌘-V Edit/Paste
⌘-S File/Save

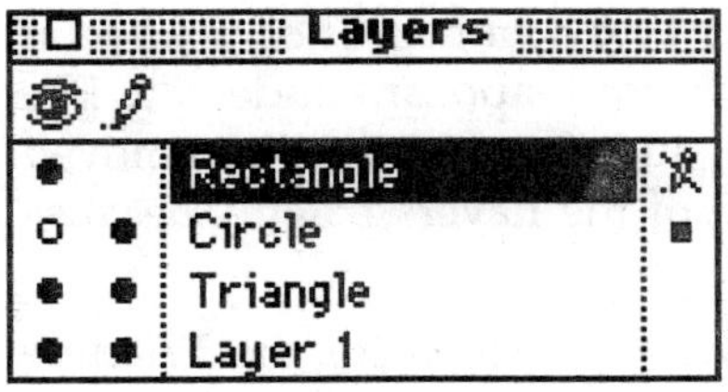

Figure 10.9—The Rectangle layer is the topmost layer because it was created last.

Selection tool

14. Click with the selection tool on the rectangle and notice that Layer 1 is highlighted, because that is where the rectangle is. Choose Edit/Cut (Command-X). Click once on the Rectangle layer to access it, and choose Edit/Paste (Command-V). An Alert dialog box appears telling you that this is a hidden or locked layer. Click on OK to paste the rectangle on the Rectangle layer and to simultaneously unlock the layer.
15. Save this file (Command-S). You will use it in the next exercise.

LAYER OPTIONS FROM THE LAYERS PALETTE

You can view and hide layers, lock and unlock layers, and change any layer's display mode from the Layers palette. Remember: the Eye icon refers to what is visible; the Pencil icon refers to what can be edited.

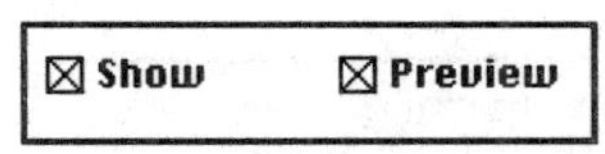

When Show is selected, the items on the layer will be displayed. If Preview is selected, those objects will be displayed in Preview mode.

EXERCISE D

1. If necessary, open the Layers.ai file you worked on in the last exercise or open (Command-O) the Layers.ai file on the Tutorial disk.
2. Display the Layers palette (Figure 10.10). As the file is now, the Rectangle, Triangle, and Layer 1 layers can all be viewed and edited. Those layers are also displayed in Preview mode. The Circle layer can be viewed in Artwork mode and can be edited.

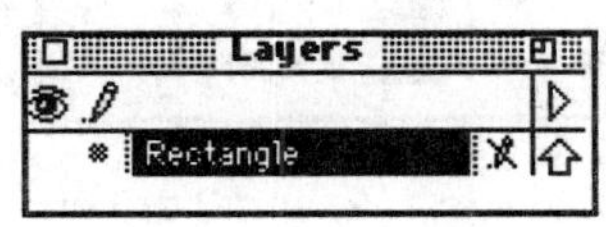

Clicking on the black dot under the Eye icon deselects the Show check box in the layer's dialog box and makes the objects on that layer invisible.

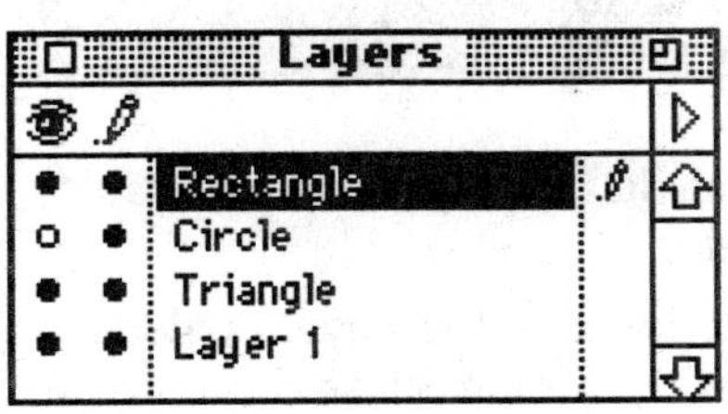

Figure 10.10—The Layers palette for the Layers.ai file indicates that only the Circle layer is displayed in Artwork mode.

⌘-O File/Open
⌘-Control-L Window Show Layers

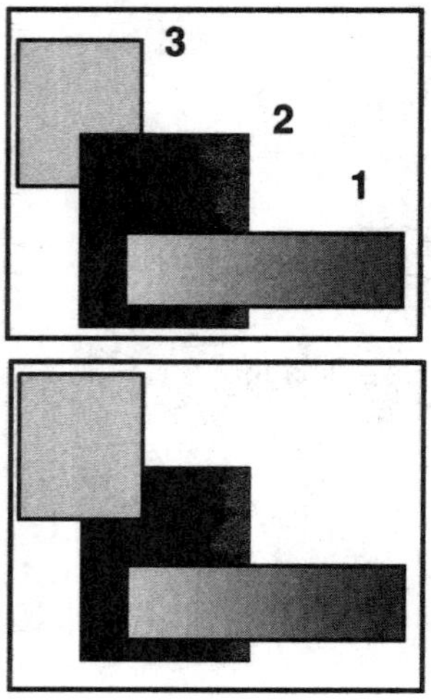

All objects are on the same layer. When objects 1 and 3 (above) were grouped, object 2 was moved behind the group.

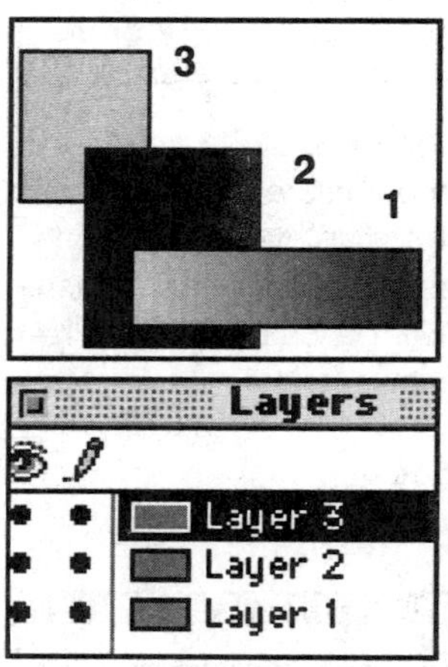

Objects 1, 2, and 3 are on three different layers. When objects 1 and 3 are grouped, the group will be placed on Layer 3 behind any non-grouped object on that layer.

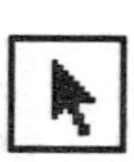

Selection tool

3. Click once on the black dot under the Eye icon for the Rectangle layer. Three things happen: the black dot disappears, indicating that the Show check box in the Rectangle layer's dialog box has been deselected; the black dot under the Pencil icon becomes dimmed (gray), indicating that the objects on the Rectangle layer cannot be edited; and a slashed line appears over the Pencil icon on the *right* side of the palette as another indication that the objects on that layer cannot be edited.
4. Double-click on the Rectangle layer's name to display its Options dialog box, and notice that the Show check box is empty. Click to select it and click on OK. Notice that the black dot reappears under the Eye icon because the layer is now visible, and the slash line is removed from the Pencil icon on the right side of the Layers palette, because items on that layer can now be edited.
5. Click once on the black dot under the Pencil icon for the Triangle layer. Two things happen: the dot disappears, indicating that although the objects on that layer are visible, they are locked and not available for editing; and a slashed line appears over the Pencil icon on the right side of the palette as another indication that the objects on that layer cannot be edited.
6. Double-click on the Triangle layer's name to display its Options dialog box. Notice that the Lock check box is selected, indicating that all the objects on that layer are locked and cannot be edited.
7. Try clicking on the triangle itself, and notice that you cannot select it because it is locked.
8. Click where the dot should be under the Pencil icon for the Triangle layer to restore the black dot and unlock the layer.

LAYERS AND GROUPS

Thus far you have worked with single objects on single layers. The rules change when you are grouping individual objects on different layers. When objects on one layer are arranged in a stacking order, grouping two or more objects results in the non-grouped objects being moved behind the group.

Since all grouped objects must exist on a single layer, if you group objects drawn on different layers, that group of objects is placed on the frontmost (top) layer of the group directly behind the frontmost object on that layer. In other words, the group takes a back seat on the layer.

EXERCISE E

1. Open the Layers.ai file on the Tutorial disk (Command-O). Display the Layers palette (Command-Control-L).
2. Double-click on the name of the Circle layer in the Layers palette to display the Layer Options dialog box. Click in the Show check box to display any artwork on that layer in Preview mode. Click on OK.
3. Use the selection tool to Shift-select both the circle and the triangle (Figure 10.11).

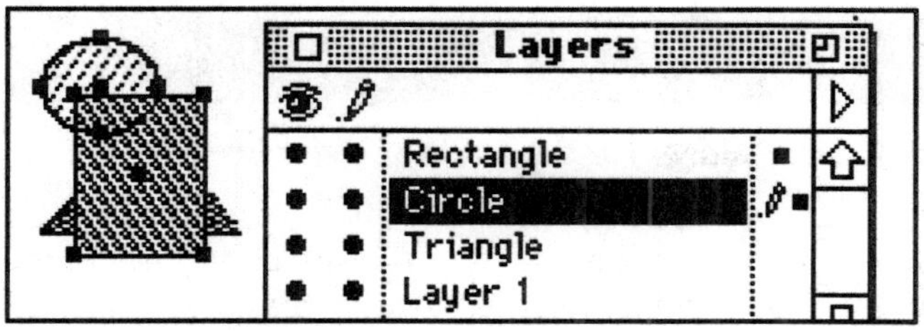

Figure 10.11—Shift-selecting the rectangle and circle displays black boxes on the Layers palette.

⌘-G Arrange/Group
⌘-Shift-A Edit/Select All

4. Notice the black squares which appear on the right side of the Layers palette next to the Rectangle and Circle layers. These squares indicate that objects on those layers are selected.
5. With both the rectangle and circle selected, choose Arrange/Group (Command-G). Both objects are grouped and placed on the Rectangle layer because it is the frontmost layer in the document.
6. Click once on the black dots under the Eye icon for the Circle, Triangle, and Layer 1 layers. Notice that now only the *selected* circle and rectangle group are visible, because the other three layers are now hidden (Figure 10.12).

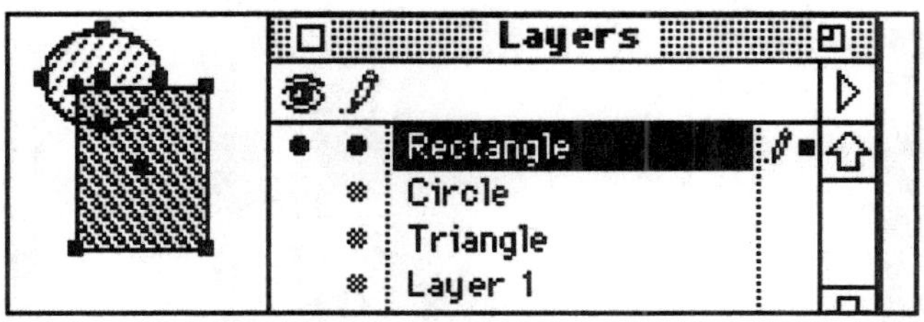

Figure 10.12—The dimmed circles under the Eye icon indicates that those layers are hidden.

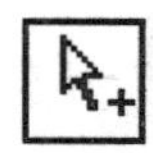

Group-selection tool

7. Choose Edit/Select None (Command-Shift-A) and choose the group-selection tool. Click once on the rectangle and click again to select the second item in the group, the circle. Drag the group around the page.

MASKING OBJECTS

A mask or masking object is an art object placed on top of other artwork which allows only the artwork within its confines to be displayed and printed. When you cover a piece of artwork with a masking object, only the selected artwork within the boundaries of that masking object will be previewed and printed.

When you create a mask, two things happen: any fill and stroke attributes which the masking object displayed are switched to None, and any part of the illustration which appears outside the boundaries of the masking object disappear. Although this sounds like an elegant way to crop an image, you have to be careful. Using complex shapes as masks or creating several masks in a single file can cause problems with printing the file.

Masks pay attention to layers. The masking object must be the frontmost object in the stacking order and must appear on the topmost layer in the illustration. If you create a mask which covers objects on different layers, any objects on the intermediate layers become masked. For example, you might have a four-layer file with a house on Layer 1, shrubbery on Layer 2, cars on Layer 3, and sky on Layer 4. If you draw the masking object over the house on Layer 1, Shift-select the masking object, the house on Layer 1, and the cars on Layer 3, then the shrubbery on Layer 2 will also become part of the mask.

What is that masked object?

The terms *mask* and *masking object* are synonymous. A mask or masking object covers (masks) artwork under it and protects it from disappearing when the Mask command is applied. The artwork that is covered by the mask is called the *masked object.*

Tip

If you can, keep all the objects to be masked on one layer.

⌘-N File/New
⌘-A Edit/Select All

EXERCISE F

1. Choose File/New (Command-N) and open the Desert Scene.ai file on the Tutorial disk.
2. Use the rectangle tool to draw a long narrow rectangle over the illustration (Figure 10.13). This rectangle is the mask or masking object. It doesn't matter what fill and stroke character it has, because they will be stripped from the mask once you choose the Mask command.
3. Choose Edit/Select All (Command-A) to select the mask (rectangle) and the underlying artwork.
4. Choose Object/Masks/Make. Notice that the mask lost its fill and stroke values and that the only visible parts of the illustration are those within the confines of the rectangular mask (Figure 10.13).

FYI

Masks are not limited to rectangles and circles. Any path can be used as a mask. Try selecting one of the cacti and using it to mask another object in the image.

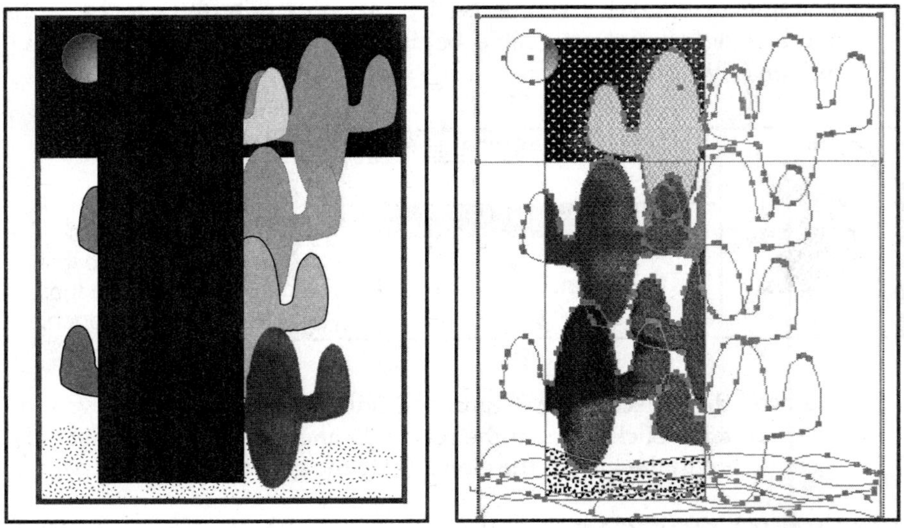

Figure 10.13—The black mask is placed over the artwork (left). The entire image and the mask are selected and the rectangle is defined as a mask from the Object menu. Only the selected artwork beneath the mask is now displayed and printed.

Selection tool

5. Choose File/Print (Command-P). Click on Print to print the masked image. Your printout should resemble Figure 10.14. Save this file as Mask. You will use it in the next exercise.

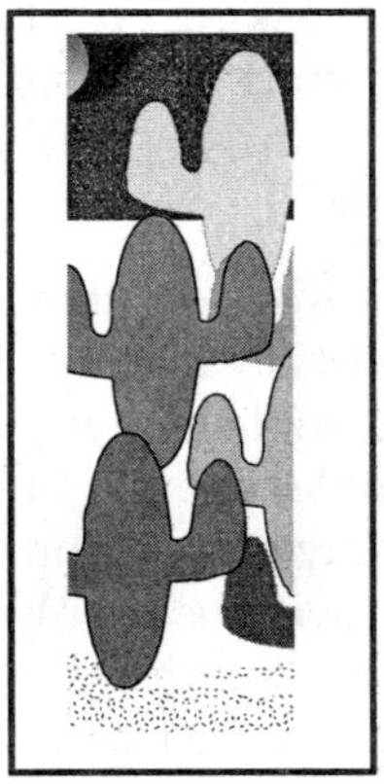

Figure 10.14—Only the selected artwork under the rectangular mask prints.

EDITING MASKS

Once an art object has been converted to a mask, it loses its stroke and fill attributes. Look at Figure 10.13 and notice that the black rectangle lost its black fill. That mask, however, can be copied and pasted and then stroked and filled again. It can also be modified and removed

⌘-O File/Open
⌘-Shift-A Edit/Select None
⌘-E View/Artwork
⌘-C Edit/Copy
⌘-V Edit/Cut
⌘-I Object/Paint Style
⌘-Y View/Preview

EXERCISE G

1. If necessary, open the Mask file (Command-O) that you created in the last exercise. Deselect everything (Command-Shift-A).
2. Choose View/Artwork (Command-E). Use the selection tool to select the rectangular mask. Choose Edit/Copy (Command-C). Then choose Edit/Paste (Command-V). The rectangle appears in the center of the drawing.
3. Using the selection tool, click on the center point of the copy and drag it to the center point of the original mask. The cursor will become white when the two points meet (Figure 10.15).

Selection tool

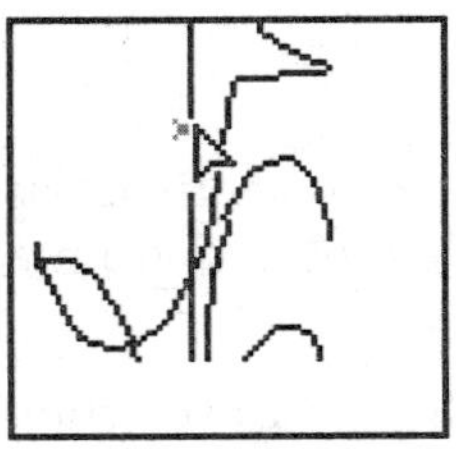

Figure 10.15—The black selection cursor changes to white when the two center points meet.

4. The copy is still selected. Use the Paint Style palette (Command-I) to select a fill of None and a red stroke. Assign it a weight of 6 points.
5. Choose View/Preview (Command-Y) to display the stroked mask.
6. Choose View/Artwork (Command-E). Use the selection tool to select the stroked copy of the mask. Choose Object/Masks. Only the Make command is available, because you have selected a copy of the mask, not the original mask.
7. Press the Delete key to delete only the copy, not the original mask.
8. Select the mask itself. Choose Object/Masks/Release. The entire image is restored and the masking object (the rectangle) appears as an unfilled and unstroked art object. You can fill, stroke, or delete it.
9. Choose File/Revert to Saved and click on the Revert button to revert to the original file. You can also use the Filter menu to select as well as fill and stroke the mask.
10. Choose View/Artwork (Command-E). Chose Filter/Select/Select Masks. The rectangular mask appears selected. Choose Filter/Create/Fill & Stroke for Mask to paint the mask with the currently selected colors.
11. Choose Filter/Create/Fill & Stroke for Mask. An Alert dialog box appears, telling you that the fill and stroke will be based on the currently defined colors in the Paint Style palette. Click on OK to apply the fill and stroke attributes. Your screen should resemble Figure 10.16.

FYI

Before applying a fill and stroke to a mask from the Filter menu, the fill and/or stroke have to be specified in the Paint Style palette.

More info

If anything in the illustration is selected before you choose the Select Masks filter, the filter deselects any of the objects which are not masking objects. If no objects are selected when you choose the Select Masks filter, then the filter selects any and all of the masks in the illustration.

⌘-I Object/Paint Style

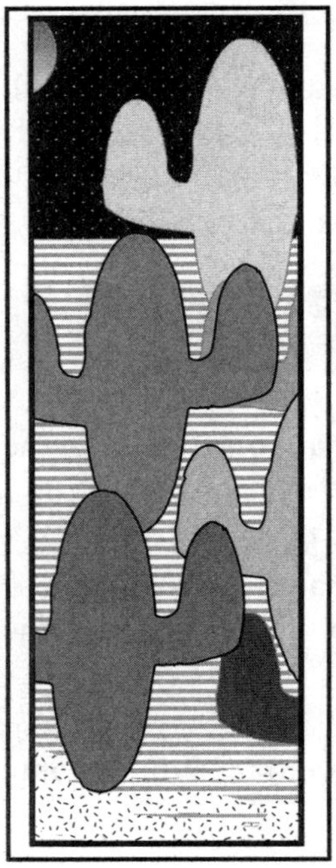

Figure 10.16—The fill and stroke attributes applied to the mask are two separate objects which can be selected and modified.

MODIFYING MASKS

A mask can be modified by changing its fill and stroke characteristics as you did in the last exercise. You can also add and delete objects from a mask, thus modifying it even further.

When selecting a mask with its masked objects, use the group-selection tool. When selecting one or more masked objects, use the selection tool. To reshape the mask itself, use the direct-selection tool.

EXERCISE H

1. On a clean drawing page, choose Filter/Create/Star to display the Create Star dialog box. Type 6 in the Points field. Click on OK.
2. Use the selection tool to select the star and use the Paint Style palette (Command-I) to assign it a fill of None and a black stroke.
3. With the star still selected, Option-drag it slightly to the right. Release the mouse button, *then* the Option key to create a copy of the original star.
4. Select another star and Option-drag it to create another copy. Do this until you have a cluster of stars (Figure 10.17).

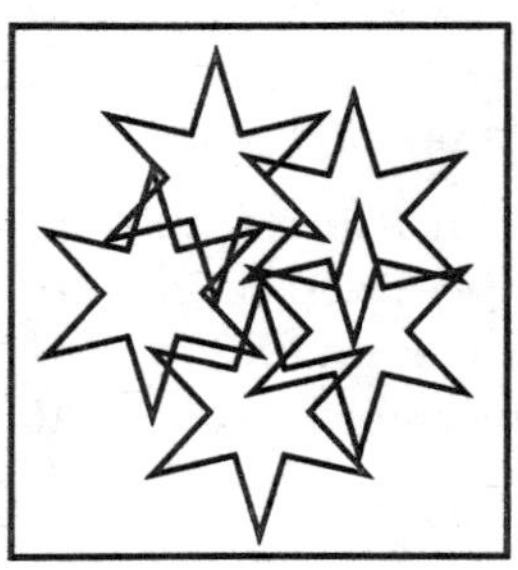

Figure 10.17—Option-drag the original star to create a cluster of stars.

5. Make sure the Ruler units is inches (Command-K). Click on the oval tool and click in the center of the cluster. Type .75 in the Height field. Tab to the Width field and type .75. Click on OK. The circle has the same stroke as the stars.

⌘-K File/Preferences/ General
⌘-E View/Artwork
⌘-Y View/Preview

6. Use the selection tool to move the circle to the center of the cluster of stars, making sure that some of the star points extend beyond the circle. The circle will become the mask (Figure 10.18).

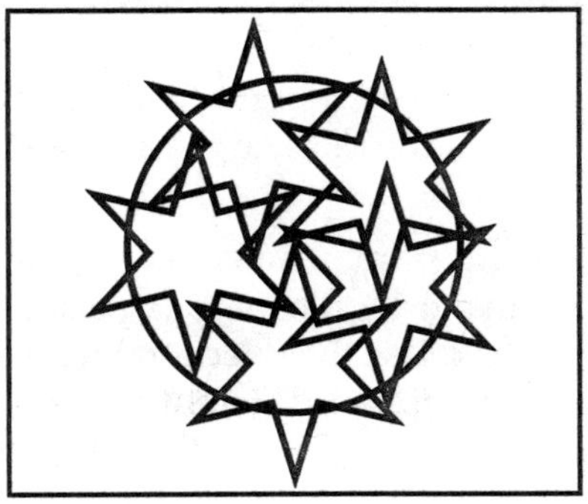

Figure 10.18—The circle is the frontmost object in the stacking order and will mask the cluster of stars.

FYI

Unless the mask is the last object you created, select it and choose Arrange/Bring to Front before choosing the Make Mask command. The mask must always be the topmost object in the stacking order.

7. Choose Edit/Select All (Command-A) to select all the stars and the circle. Choose Object/Masks/Make. Choose View/Preview (Command-Y) and click on an empty area of the page to deselect everything. Your screen should resemble Figure 10.19.

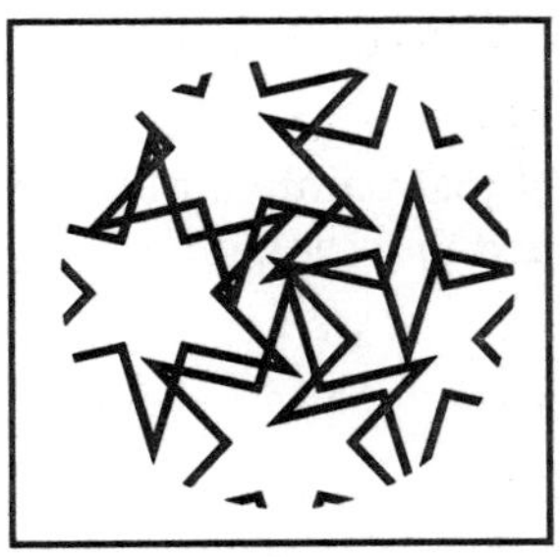

Figure 10.19—Only the star parts covered by the mask (circle) appear. The circle's stroke disappeared when it became a mask.

Easy viewing

Use the New Window command (View/New Window) and choose Preview mode for the new window while you work in Artwork mode in the original window. This allows you to select objects easily and see what is happening at the same time.

8. Choose View/Artwork (Command-E) or use the New Window command. In Artwork mode, use the direct-selection tool to select the mask (circle). Click on the right anchor point and stretch it out. Do the same with the left anchor point to create an oval.
9. Now that the mask has been modified, use the Filter/Select menu to select the mask, the Paint Style palette to specify a fill and stroke color, and the Filter/Create menu to paint the mask.The fill and stroke attributes are applied. Your screen should resemble Figure 10.20. Save this file as Masked Stars. You will use it in the next exercise.

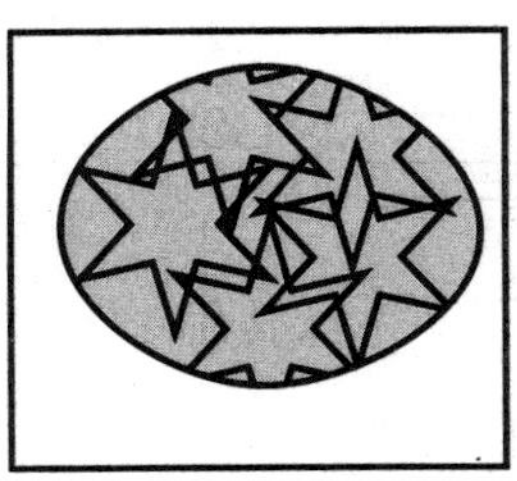

Figure 10.20—The stroked and filled mask.

⌘-K File/Preferences/
General
⌘-F Edit/Paste in Front
⌘-X Edit/Cut
⌘-B Edit/Paste in Back

MODIFYING MASKED OBJECTS

You can add and delete masked objects to and from the mask by using the Cut and Paste commands. An object can be pasted in front of or in back of the mask. If you select an object already inside the mask, the object you cut and paste will be stacked in front of or behind the selected object.

EXERCISE I

1. If necessary, open the Masked Stars file you created in the last lesson or choose File/Open (Command-O) and open the Masked Stars file on the Tutorial disk.

Selection tool

2. Use the selection tools to select one of the stars. Choose Edit/Cut (Command-X). Choose Edit/Paste (Command-V). The star is pasted on the page and is no longer part of the mask. Use the selection tool to move it to an empty area of the page and apply a different fill and stroke to it (Figure 10.21).

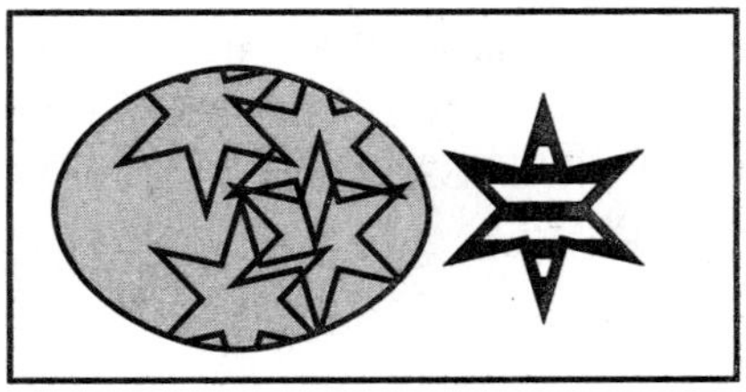

Figure 10.21—One of the stars was cut from the mask, pasted onto the page, and then painted with a patterned fill.

3. Use the selection tool to select the single star you just painted. Move it directly over the mask so that part of the star extends outside of the mask (Figure 10.22).

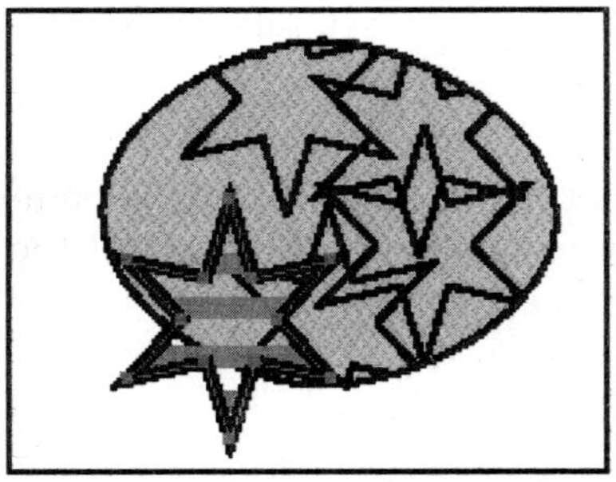

Figure 10.22—Move the selected object over the mask.

4. Choose Edit/Cut (Command-X).
5. Click on one of the other stars to select it. Choose Edit/Paste in Front (Command-F) or Edit/Paste in Back (Command-B). The painted star is stacked in front of or behind the selected star. Your screen should resemble (Figure 10.23).

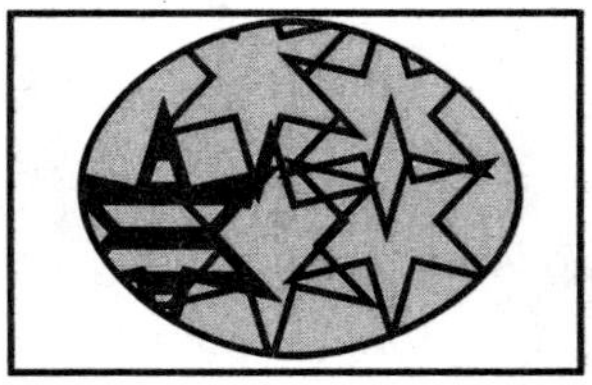

Figure 10.23—The cut star is pasted in front of a selected star and now becomes part of the mask.

RELEASING MASKS

Objects which are made into masked objects can be unmasked. Once the Release command is applied, all the objects, including the mask, revert to their original status as independent art objects. Their original fill and stroke values are not restored.

⌘-O File/Open
⌘-A Edit/Select All
⌘-K File/Preferences/General
⌘-9 Object/Compound Paths/Release

EXERCISE J

1. Open the Masked Stars.ai file on the Tutorial disk (Command-O). Choose Edit/Select All (Command-A).
2. Choose Object/Masks/Release (Command-9). Nothing appears to happen, but actually all the stars, as well as the fill object and the stroke object which formed the mask, have been released from the Masking command.
3. Deselect everything by clicking on an empty area of the page. Then use the selection tool to select each star and move it out of the oval.
4. Choose File/Preferences/General (Command-K) and make sure the Area Select option on the left side of the dialog box is deselected. This will require you to select a filled object by clicking on its outside edge, not on its area fill.
5. Select the oval by clicking on its stroked edge and move it down. Notice that only the stroke object moves; the fill object remains.
6. Click on the edge of the fill object and move the oval outline out of the way. The oval fill is not moved, because it is a filled mask (Figure 10.24).

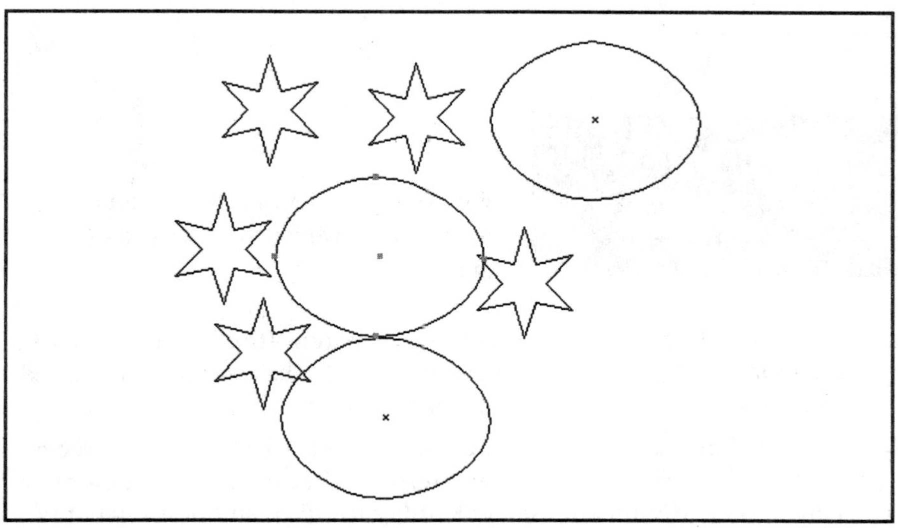

Figure 10.24—If you view in Artwork mode, you will see three oval outlines. One is the original oval, another is the stroke object applied to the mask, and another is the filled oval or painted mask.

⌘-K File/Preferences/General
⌘-Y View/Preview
⌘-I Object/Paint Style
⌘-E View/Artwork
⌘-= Arrange/Bring to Front
⌘-A Edit/Select All
⌘-8 Object/Compound Paths/Make

Type tool

Selection tool

CREATING COMPOUND PATHS

A compound path is a group of at least two paths which overlap so that, in spite of any painting characteristics, the overlapping paths appear transparent. This allows the backmost object to "poke through" stacks of artwork and be displayed.

EXERCISE K

1. On a clean drawing page, with Ruler units set to inches (Command-K), click on the rectangle tool. Click once on the page and type 2 in the Width field; tab to the Height field and type 2. Click on OK.
2. Choose View/Preview (Command-Y). Use the Paint Style palette (Command-I) to paint the selected square a dark color.
3. Choose Window/New Window and move the second window so that both windows are visible. Choose View/Artwork (Command-E) for the second window. This allows you to work in Artwork mode and see the effects of the commands in Preview mode.
4. Click on the type tool, click on the page, and type an asterisk (Shift-8). Click on the selection tool to select the type. Format the type in 120-point Times from either the Font and Type menus or from the Character palette (Command-T).
5. With the type still selected, choose Type/Create Outlines. The asterisk becomes a path. Fill the new path with a light color. Then use the selection tool to drag the path to the top of the square so that half of the object overlaps the square (Figure 10.25).

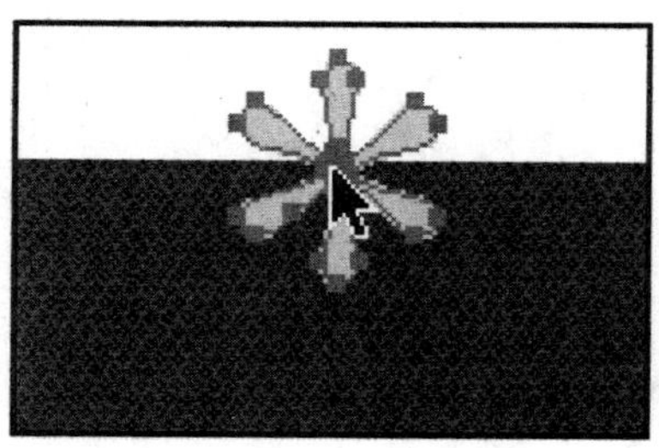

Figure 10.25—Move the type character which was converted to a path to the top of the square.

6. The overlapping object to become transparent (the asterisk) must be the topmost object in the stacking order. With the asterisk still selected, choose Arrange/Bring to Front (Command- =).
7. The overlapping object and the background object must be selected. Choose Edit/Select All (Command-A). Choose Object/Compound Paths/Make (Command-8). Look at Figure 10.26 and notice what two things happened: the part of the object that overlapped the rectangle cut through the rectangle to the white background and the nonoverlapping part of the object assumed the fill attribute of the rectangle. In other words, the Compound Paths command cut a hole in the rectangle, making it transparent, so that the background object (white drawing page) peeks through those "holes."

⌘-= Arrange/Bring to Front

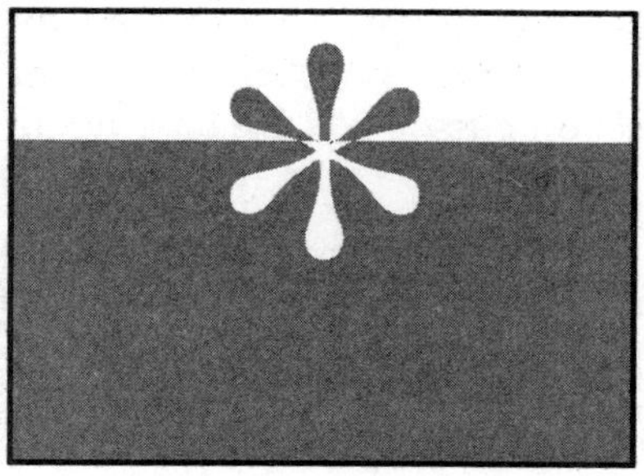

Figure 10.26—Any part of the foreground object (asterisk) that overlaps the background object (square) is made transparent by the Make Compound Paths command.

EXERCISE L

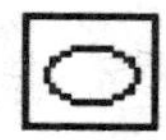

Oval tool

1. On a clean drawing page, use the oval tool to draw a 2-inch circle. Fill and stroke it with any color combination.
2. Use the rectangle tool to draw three rectangles vertically through the circle. The center rectangle should be longer than the outside ones, and both of the outside rectangles should be the same size. Fill and stroke the three rectangles with another color combination (Figure 10.27).

Rectangle tool

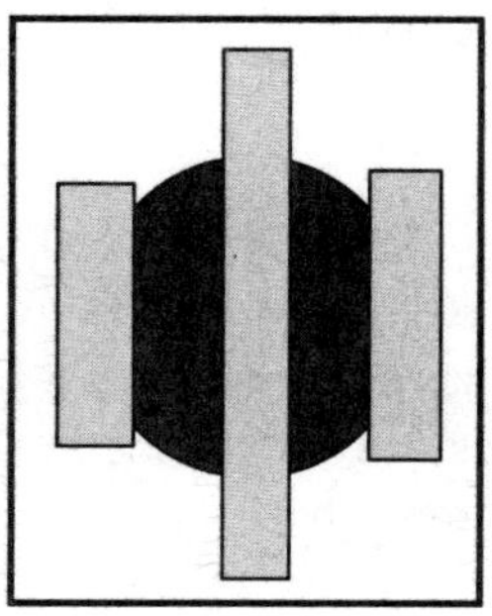

Figure 10.27—The parts of the rectangles that overlap the circle will become transparent when the Compound Paths command is applied.

Tip

To make both outside rectangles the exact same size, draw the first one, then Option-drag to create a copy of the original rectangle.

3. Use the selection tool to select the circle and Option-drag it away from the artwork to create a copy of the original circle. You will use this circle as a mask later in the exercise.
4. Shift-select the three rectangles and choose Arrange/Bring to Front (Command- =).
5. Use the selection tool to draw a selection marquee around the four rectangles and the background object (the circle). Choose Object/Compound Paths/Make (Command-8). Any part of the rectangles (foreground objects) that overlapped the circle appears as white, because the overlapping parts of the rectangle cut "holes" in the circle and reveal the white layer beneath the circle. Your screen should resemble Figure 10.28.

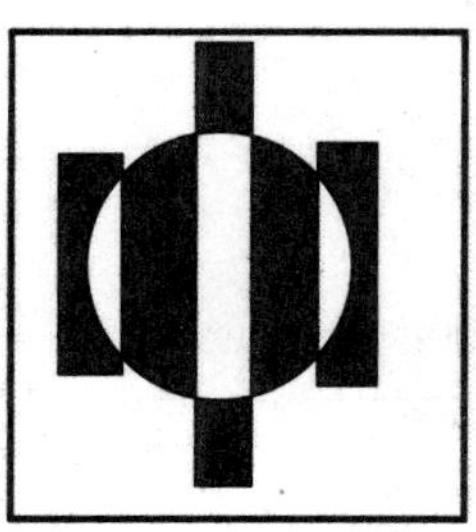

Figure 10.28—The parts of the rectangles that overlap the circle become transparent when the Compound Paths command is applied.

6. Use the selection tool to select the circle you dragged out of the way earlier. Drag it by its center over the circle in the compound path until it is centered over the circle. The selection cursor will become white when it is directly on top of the lower circle.
7. Switch to the direct-selection tool and, keeping the circle selected, Shift-select the three rectangles (Figure 10.29).

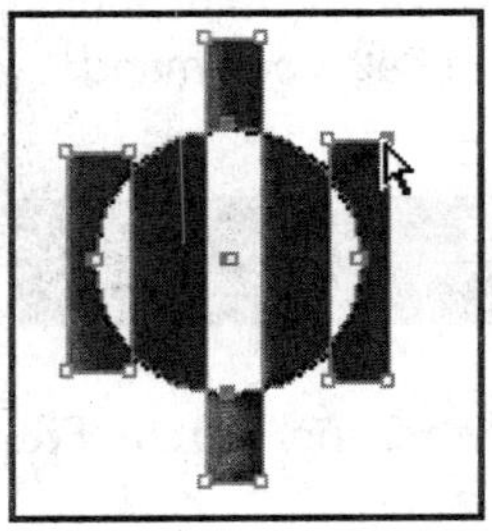

Figure 10.29—Shift-select the mask (circle) and the three rectangles which will be masked.

Tip

When working with compound paths and masks, it's usually easier to create a new window (Window/New Window). Use one window to preview the illustration, but work in the other window in Artwork mode.

8. Choose Object/Masks/Make. The Mask command displays only the objects covered by the mask (circle). Your screen should resemble Figure 10.30.

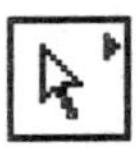

Direct-selection tool

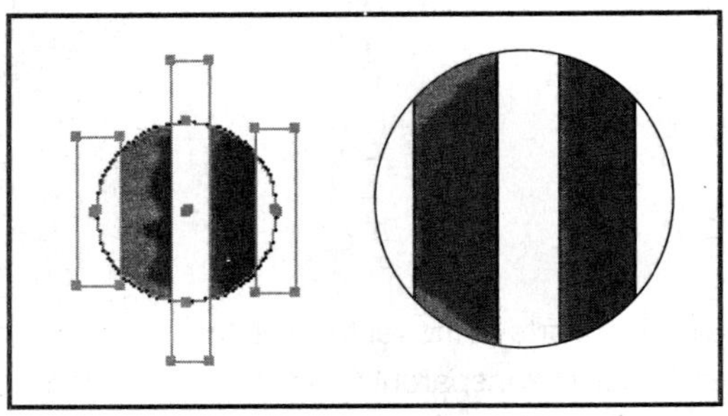

Figure 10.30—The Mask command masks (left) and displays (right) only those parts of the illustration beneath it.

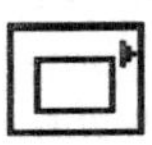

Rectangle tool

SELECTING AND RELEASING COMPOUND PATHS

Compound paths are grouped objects. To select the entire compound object, use the selection tool or the group-selection tool. To select part of a compound path, use the direct-selection tool.

EXERCISE M

1. On a clean drawing page, draw a rectangle. Fill it with a pattern. Draw a smaller rectangle on top of that one and fill it with a color. Draw a circle on top of the smaller rectangle and fill it with a different color. Your screen should resemble Figure 10.31.

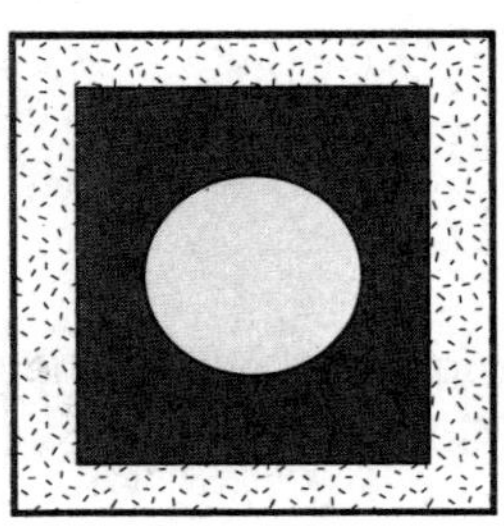

Figure 10.31—With this stacking order, the patterned rectangle is the background and the circle is the front-most object.

2. Use the selection tool to Shift-select the circle and the small rectangle behind it. Choose Object/Compound Paths/Make (Command-8). The hole created by the circle reveals the backmost object, the patterned rectangle (Figure 10.32). The circle and small rectangle are the compound path.

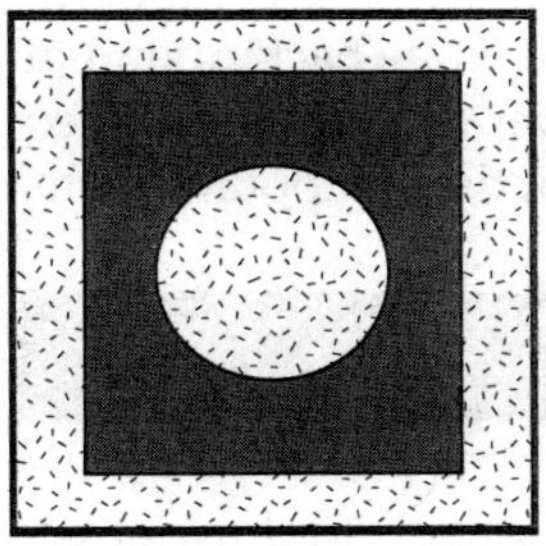

Figure 10.32—The patterned background appears through the compound path.

3. Use the selection tool to select the compound path and drag it off the patterned rectangle.
4. Choose Edit/Undo (Command-Z) to return the compound path to its original position. Deselect everything (Command-Shift-A).
5. Use the direct-selection tool to select the smaller rectangle and drag it to the left. When you do this, only the part of the circle that overlaps the rectangle displays the patterned background. The other part of the circle displays the fill color of the small rectangle (Figure 10.33).

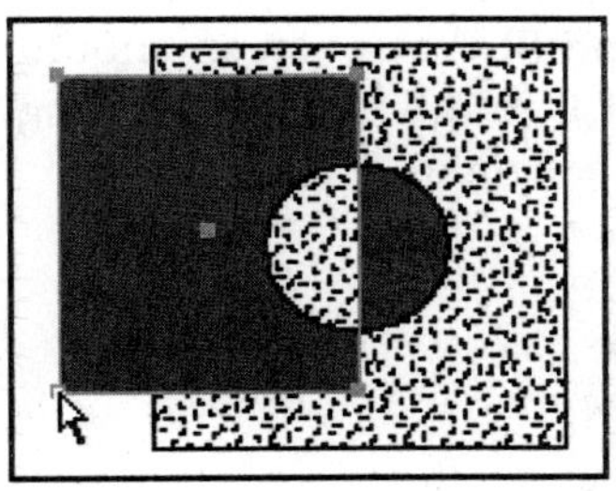

Figure 10.33—With this stacking order, the patterned rectangle is the background and the circle is the frontmost object.

6. Use the selection tool to drag the patterned rectangle away from the compound path. Since the hole created by the compound path displays the backmost object, it currently displays white because the backmost object was removed.
7. Deselect everything (Command-Shift-A). Click on the group-selection tool and click *once* on the circle in the compound path to select just the circle. Move it halfway over the rectangle.
8. Click twice on the compound path with the group-selection tool to select the entire compound path. Drag it over the patterned rectangle to make the pattern visible through the half circle.
9. Make sure that the compound path is selected with either the selection tool or the group-selection tool. Choose Object/Compound Paths/Release (Command-9). The circle is released from the small rectangle and displays the fill color assigned to the rectangle.

⌘-8 Object/Compound Paths/Make
⌘-Z Edit/Undo
⌘-Shift-A Edit/Select None
⌘-9 Object/Compound Paths/Release

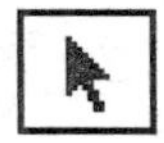

Selection tool

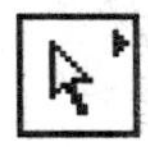

Direct-selection tool

Group-selection tool

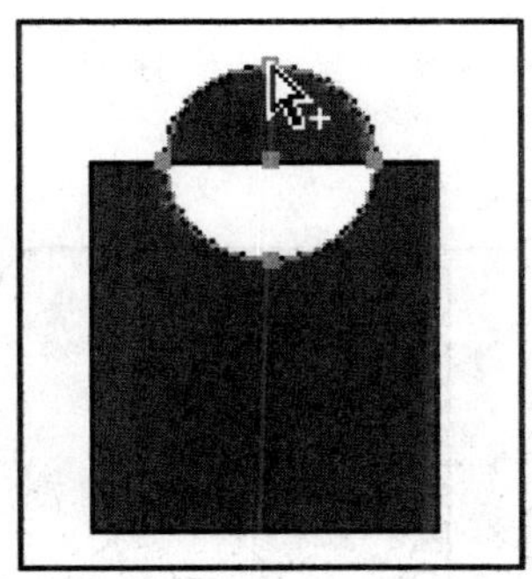

Clicking *once* with the group-selection tool on one path in a compound path selects just that path and allows you to reposition it. Clicking *twice* with the group-selection tool selects all the other paths in the compound path.

⌘-= Arrange/Bring to Front
⌘-8 Object/Compound Paths/Make
⌘-Control-A Object/Attributes

REVERSING THE FILL IN A COMPOUND PATH

Ordinarily, when a compound path is created, the object behind the compound path is displayed through the hole and becomes the fill for the hole. For example, in the last lesson, when the compound path was created with the small rectangle and the circle, the patterned rectangle became the fill for the circle. When the asterisk was joined to the rectangle as a compound path, the overlapping part of the asterisk displayed the white background of the drawing page. You can, however, reverse this order so that the selected path displays not the background color but the color of the compound path.

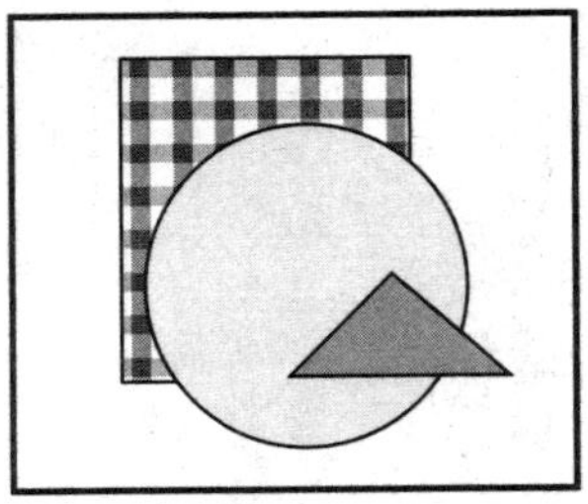

Even when objects overlap each other, the stacking order is maintained. The triangle is still the first object in the stacking order even though it overlaps the circle.

EXERCISE N

1. On a clean drawing page, use any of the drawing tools to draw a rectangle, a triangle, and a circle. Fill the rectangle with a pattern and fill the triangle and circle with different colors. Stroke all the objects.
2. Place the circle on top of the rectangle. Place the triangle on top of the circle. The objects can overlap. With the circle selected, choose Arrange/Bring to Front (Command-=). The circle should be the first object in the stacking order, the triangle the second, and the patterned rectangle the third.
3. Since the triangle and circle will be made into a compound path, the color of the circle becomes the "official color" of the compound path.
4. Use the selection tool to Shift-select the circle and the triangle. Choose Object/Compound Paths/Make (Command-8). Your screen should resemble Figure 10.34, where the hole cut through the overlapping paths displays the object behind them (the rectangle).

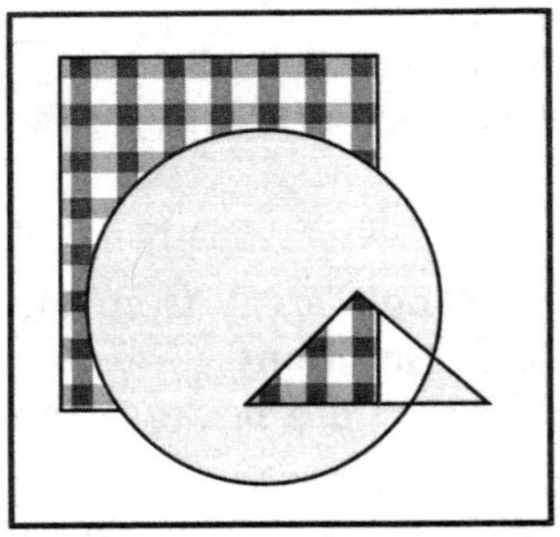

Figure 10.34—The compound path reveals the patterned background.

5. Use the direct-selection tool to select either the circle or the triangle. Choose Object/Attributes (Command-Control-A) and select or deselect—depending on the status of the check box—the Reverse path direction check box. Click on OK. The selected path now assumes the fill color of the compound path. Remember: All the paths in a compound path must have the same fill and stroke attributes.

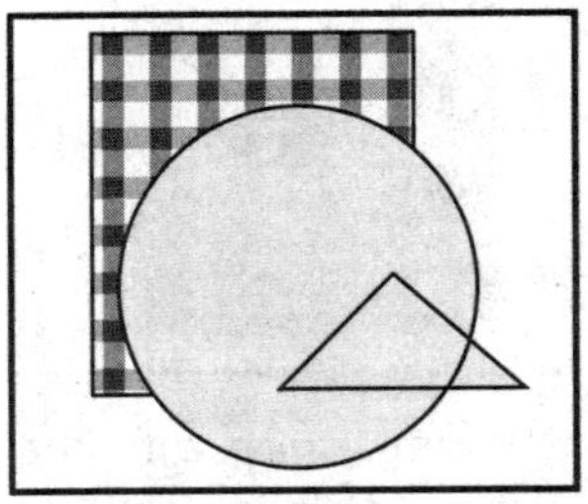

When the Reverse path direction option is selected in the Attributes dialog box, the selected path fills with the compound path fill.

REVIEW EXERCISE

In this exercise you will work with a completed illustration by placing individual paths on different layers, specifying view and print options for those layers, creating a new layer, and combining paths into a compound path. Finally, you will mask several paths in the illustration.

⌘-Control-L Window/ Show Layers

1. Open the a la Matisse.ai file on the Tutorial disk (Command-O). Choose Window/Show Layers (Command-Control-L) to display the Layers palette. The illustration displays five dancers, one on each layer. There is also a background layer.
2. Choose File/Save As and name the file Dancers. Click on the blond dancer on the left to highlight the dancer 5 layer. Double-click on the layer's name to display the Layers dialog box. Type *Pierre* in the Name field. Click on OK. Repeat this process to rename the other four dancer fields.
3. Click on the left boot of the third dancer, the boy in the right corner of the illustration. Notice that it is not on the same layer as the dancer (Figure 10.35). Click and drag the dot next to the Pencil icon on the *right side* of the Layers palette up to the boy's layer.

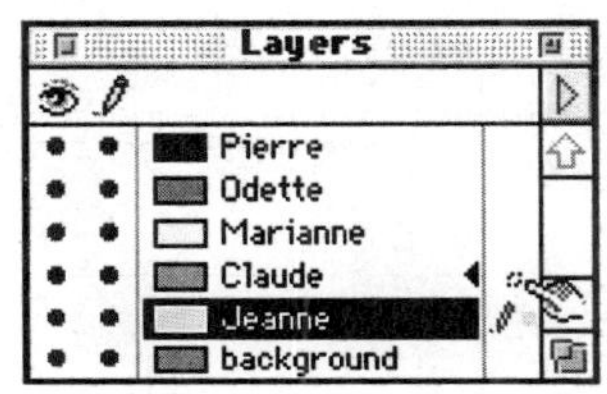

Click and drag a selection to another layer.

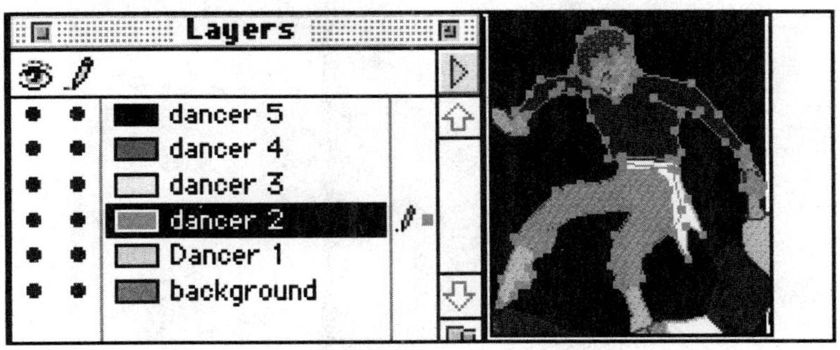

Figure 10.35—All the selected paths of dancer 2 appear on the dancer 2 layer. Only the right boot is on a different layer.

4. Click once on the black dot under the Pencil icon next to the background layer. Notice that you cannot edit the background.
5. Click once on the black dot under the Eye icon for the background layer. The black background disappears and the white drawing page is displayed. Click under both the Eye and Pencil icons for the background layer to restore the display and make it available for editing.
6. Double-click on the layers for the girl dancers and deselect the Show check boxes to display only the boy dancers.
7. Double-click on those same layers again and deselect the Print check boxes. Double-click on the background layer and deselect the Print check box.
8. Choose File/Print (Command-P) to print only the boy dancers.
9. Drag on the Layers palette pull-out menu and highlight Show All to display all the dancers and the background.

⌘-T Window/Show Character
⌘-G Arrange/Group
⌘-I Object/Paint Style
⌘-X Edit/Cut
⌘-V Edit/Paste
⌘-8 Object/Compound Paths/Make
⌘-D Arrange/Repeat Transform
⌘-A Edit/Select All

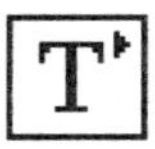

Type tool

A la Matisse, Adobe Illustrator 5.5 illustration, was created by Virginia Asman, Illuminage Art and Design, 1994.

10. Select the type tool and click in the lower center area of the background. Type (no quotes) "DANCE!" and click on the selection tool.
11. Use the Character palette (Command-T) to format the selected type in 72-point Times. Choose Type/Create Outlines to change the type into individual paths. Since all the paths are selected, choose Arrange/Group (Command-G) to group all the characters together.
12. Use the Paint Style palette (Command-I) to assign the type a yellow fill and no stroke.
13. Choose Edit/Cut (Command-X) to cut the type from the illustration and place it on the Clipboard.
14. Choose New Layer from the Layers palette pull-out menu. Type Text in the Name field. Click on OK. The Text layer appears as the first or frontmost layer in the illustration and is selected. Choose Edit/Paste Command-V) to paste the type on the Text layer.
15. Use the selection tool to drag the yellow type over the blue skirt of the dancer. Your screen should resemble Figure 10.36.

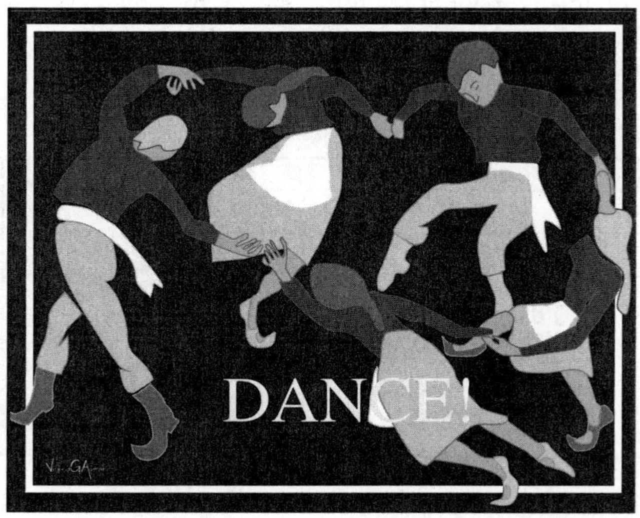

Figure 10.36—The type is converted to outlines and dragged over the blue skirt.

16. Use the selection tool to Shift-select the type and the blue skirt. Choose Object/Compound Paths/Make (Command-8). The type which overlaps the skirt displays the black background color.
17. Use the direct-selection tool to select each text path and move it up or down to create a staggered effect with the type. Because the *D* and *A* have cutouts, you will have to move those paths in two steps.
18. Select the outside of the *D* with the direct-selection tool and move it. Select the inside of the *D* and choose Arrange/Repeat Transform (Command-D) to move the smaller path inside the *D*. Do the same with the *A*.
19. Use the direct-selection tool to Shift-select all the type paths and assign them a 2-point white stroke.
20. To mask several paths in the illustration, first place all the objects on one layer. Choose Edit/Select All (Command-A). Choose Edit/Cut (Command-X).

21. Use the pull-out menu on the Layers palette to highlight New Layer. Type Mask in the Name field. Click on OK. Choose Edit/Paste (Command-V) to paste all the paths in the illustration on the Mask layer. Save the File (Command-S).
22. Use the Oval tool to draw an oval around part of the illustration. Choose Arrange/Bring to Front (Command- =) to make the mask the topmost object in the stacking order.
23. Choose Edit/Select All (Command-A) to select all the objects and the oval mask.
24. Choose Object/Masks/Make. Only those objects covered by the mask (oval) are displayed.
25. Since a mask loses its stroke and fill attributes, apply a new stroke to the mask. On the Mask layer, choose Filter/Select/Select Masks. The oval mask appears selected. Choose Edit/Copy (Command-C) to copy the mask.
26. Deselect the mask (Command-Shift-A). Then choose Edit/Paste in Front (Command-F) to paste the mask from the Clipboard back in its original position. Apply a stroke to the mask.
27. Double-click on the Mask layer. Make sure that the Print check box is selected. Choose File/Print (Command-P). Your screen and printout should resemble Figure 10.37.

⌘-V Edit/Paste
⌘-S File/Save
⌘-= Arrange/Bring to Front
⌘-A Edit/Select All
⌘-C Edit/Copy
⌘-F Edit/Paste in Front
⌘-P File/Print

Tip

When working with masks, it's often easier to work in Artwork mode or to open a new window (Window/New Window) and assign Artwork mode to one of the windows.

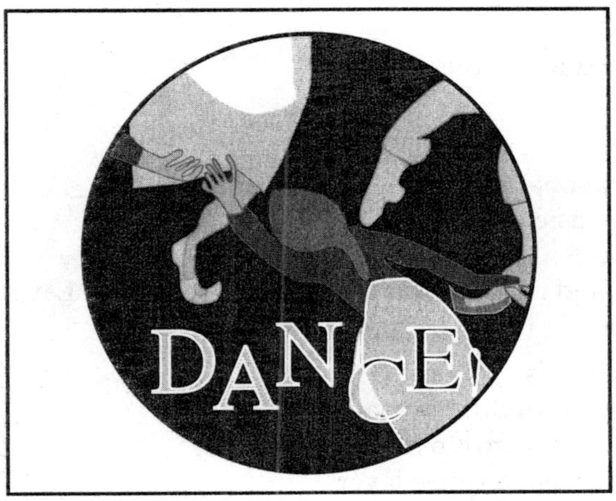

Figure 10.37—The masked objects appear inside the oval mask which has been stroked.

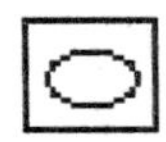

Oval tool

REVIEW QUESTIONS

Read the following questions and choose the answer which best completes the statement.

1. The stacking order of an object in an illustration is determined by ______.

   a. the layer it is on
   b. objects created before and after it
   c. its fill and paint attributes
   d. primogeniture

2. The Layers palette is used to _____.
   a. lock and hide objects
   b. create and delete layers
   c. print and display objects
   d. all of the above
3. An art object which specifies what part of the illustration will be displayed and printed is called a _____.
   a. layer
   b. mask
   c. stack
   d. a and b
4. Which terms are synonymous?
   a. mask and masked object
   b. masking object and masked object
   c. mask and masking object
   d. mask and Lone Ranger
5. Hidden layers _____.
   a. cannot be viewed
   b. cannot be edited
   c. cannot be previewed
   d. a and b
6. Before type can become part of a compound path, it must first be _____.
   a. stroked
   b. converted to outlines
   c. filled
   d. selected
7. To move an object from one layer to another, _____.
   a. cut and paste from one layer to another
   b. delete it
   c. select it and drag the dot on the right side of the Layers palette
   d. a and c
8. Grouped objects _____.
   a. can come from different layers
   b. must exist as a group on the same layer
   c. can come from a single layer
   d. all of the above
9. To edit a mask, _____.
   a. copy and paste it before filling and stroking
   b. select it and paint it
   c. use the appropriate filters
   d. a and c
10. To work in two viewing modes, _____.
    a. use layer options
    b. use the New Window command
    c. buy two copies of Adobe Illustrator
    d. a and b

Answers: 1. b; 2. d; 3. b; 4. c; 5. d; 6. b; 7. d; 8. d; 9. d; 10. d

LESSON 11

Working with Patterns

OVERVIEW

This lesson deals with creating, modifying, and using patterns in an illustration. You will learn how to create custom patterns and apply them as fill and stroke attributes in a document. Printing and troubleshooting when printing patterns are also covered.

TOPICS

Creating patterns
Creating geometric designs from patterns
Repositioning patterns
Editing patterns
Deleting patterns
Transforming patterns
Review Exercise
Review Questions

TERMS

bounding rectangle
pattern
pattern tile

⌘-I Object/Paint Style
⌘- – (hyphen) Arrange/ Send to Back

CREATING PATTERNS

Patterns are designs created from Adobe Illustrator artwork which, when used as fill and stroke attributes, repeat in an illustration. Patterns are constructed from tiles, pattern objects (the artwork) surrounded by a rectangle called the bounding rectangle. Bounding rectangles cannot be rotated and must be the backmost object in the pattern's stacking order.

Once you create a pattern and add it to the list of default patterns which come with Adobe Illustrator, you can apply that pattern from the Paint Style palette just as you would apply any of the default patterns.

EXERCISE A

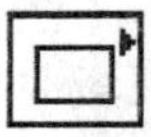

Rectangle tool

1. Select the rectangle tool and click on the drawing page to display the Rectangle dialog box.
2. Type 1 in the Width field; press the Tab key and type 1.5 in the Height field. Click on OK.
3. Use the Paint Style palette (Command-I) to fill and stroke the rectangle.
4. Use the pen tool to draw a closed shape inside the bounding rectangle (Figure 11.1).

Selection tool

Pen tool

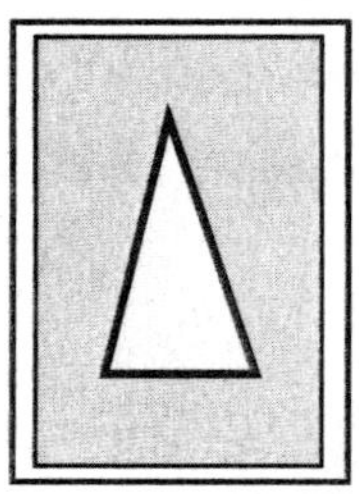

Figure 11.1—Create a drawing in a bounding rectangle. Then send that rectangle to the back. The bounding rectangle can also be filled and stroked, as it is in this figure.

5. Click with the selection tool on the rectangle. Choose Arrange/Send to Back (Command- –). This makes the bounding rectangle the backmost object.
6. Use the selection tool to draw a selection marquee around both the bounding rectangle and the artwork.
7. Choose Object/Pattern to display the Pattern dialog box. Click on New and the pattern appears in the preview box in the upper right corner of the dialog box (Figure 11.2).

TIP

Creating a complex pattern requires that the bounding rectangle be relatively small. The best dimension for a bounding rectangle is one inch square. This allows for faster printing.

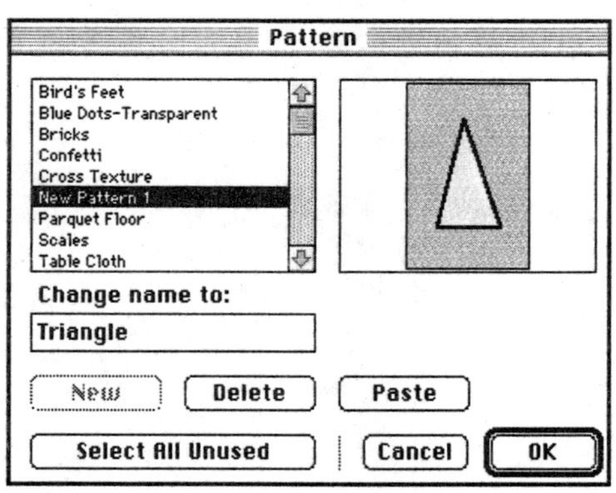

Figure 11.2—Clicking on New displays the selected tile in the Pattern dialog box.

8. Type a name for the pattern. Click on OK. The artwork and bounding box have now become a pattern which can be applied as a fill to any path.

⌘-I Object/Paint Style

EXERCISE B

1. Use the rectangle or oval tool to draw a large closed path. Keep it selected.
2. Display the Paint Style palette (Command-I). Click on the Fill icon. Click on the Pattern icon in the color strip area.
3. The pattern you created appears in the pattern scroll list. Click on it to select it as the pattern fill. It tiles inside the rectangle or oval you drew (Figure 11.3).

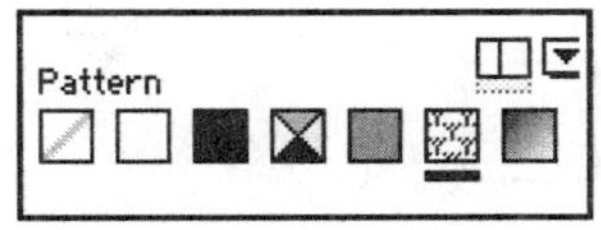

Pattern appears above the color strip area when the pattern icon is selected.

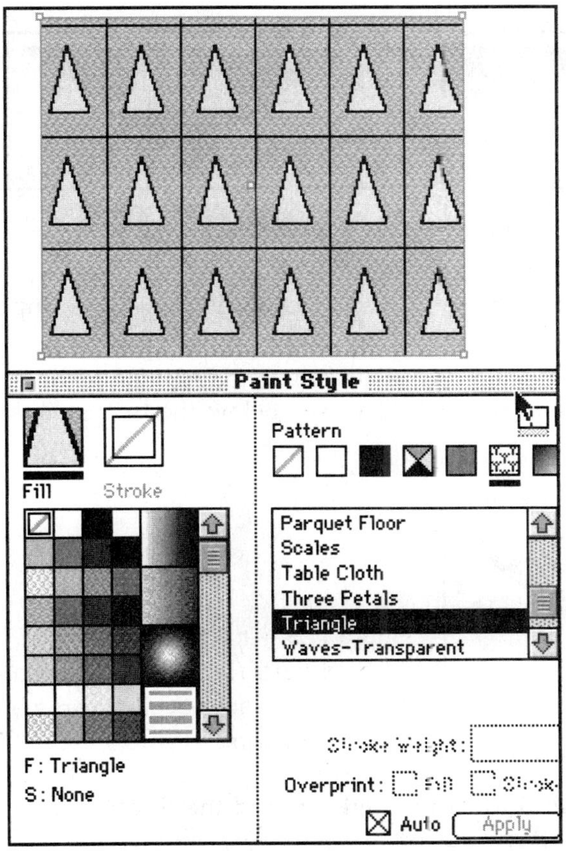

Figure 11.3—When a drawing and its bounding rectangle have been defined as a pattern and named in the Pattern dialog box, that pattern can be accessed from the pattern scroll list in the Paint Style palette. Here, the Triangle pattern is used to fill the selected rectangle.

⌘-I Object/Paint Style
⌘-Y View/Preview
⌘-A Edit/Select All
⌘-G Arrange/Group
⌘- – Arrange/Send to Back

CREATING GEOMETRIC DESIGNS FROM PATTERNS

Once a pattern tile is created, it can be duplicated to create another pattern. This will fill more of the area and allow for more interesting graphic effects.

EXERCISE C

Selection tool

1. Display the Paint Style palette (Object/Paint Style) and select the Fill icon. Click to select a dark fill color. Select None for the stroke. Choose View/Preview (Command-Y).
2. Use the selection tool and Option-drag the object to the right so that the left corner of the copy touches the right corner of the original.
3. Drag-copy another object below the two objects (Figure 11.4).

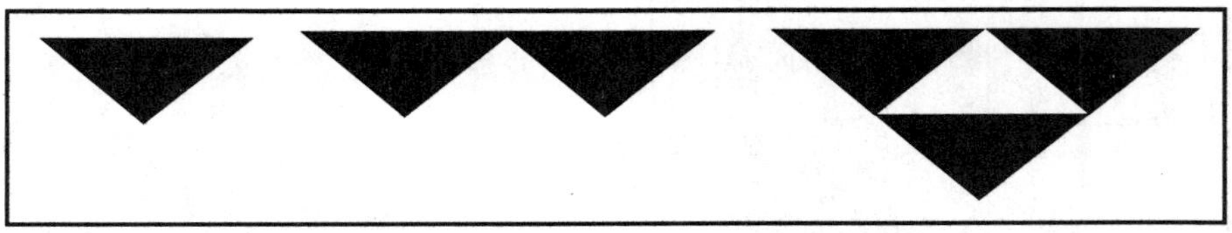

Figure 11.4—Option-drag to create the other units in the geometric design.

Tip

Select the Snap to point option in the General Preferences dialog box and use ruler guides to position the objects. Drag the objects by the anchor point closest to the guide and the point will snap to the guide. This makes it much easier to align objects.

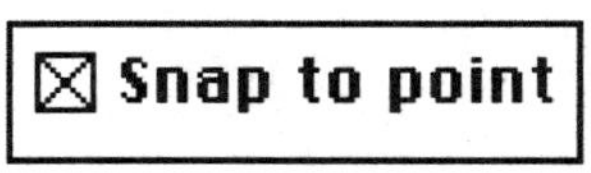

4. Choose Edit/Select All (Command A) and choose Arrange/Group (Command-G).
5. Use the selection tool to Option-drag the group to the right of the original group. Option-drag again to drag a copy below the two groups (Figure 11.5).

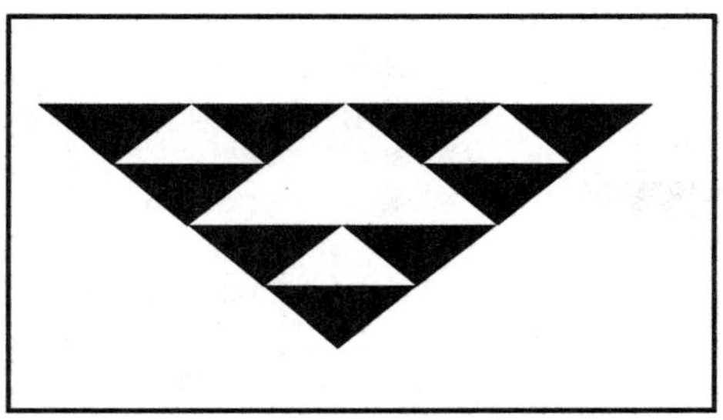

Figure 11.5—Option-drag to copy the single units (groups) and position them to create another element in the geometric design.

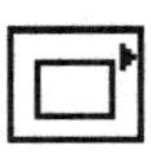

Rectangle tool

6. Use the rectangle tool to draw a rectangle around the three units to complete the pattern tile (Figure 11.6).

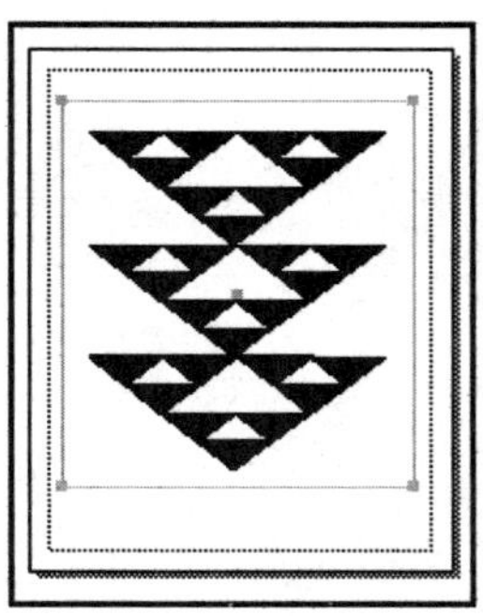

Figure 11.6—The three units are surrounded by a bounding rectangle to complete the pattern tile.

7. Use the selection tool to select both the grouped triangles and the bounding rectangle. Choose Arrange/Group (Command-G).
8. Double-click on the scale tool to display the Scale dialog box. Type 50 in the Uniform % field and click on OK. The smaller the pattern, the more times it will repeat.
9. With the entire unit (group) of three sets of triangles and bounding rectangle still selected, choose Object/Pattern. Click on New. The pattern tile appears in the Preview box. Type a name for the pattern and click on OK.
10. Use the rectangle tool to draw a long narrow rectangle. Display the Paint Style palette (Command-I) and select the Fill icon. Click on the pattern icon in the color strip area. When the patterns load, click on the name of the pattern you just created. If the Auto box is not selected, click on the Apply button. The rectangle fills with the geometric pattern.
11. Save this file (File/Save) as "Patterns.ai" in the Illustrator 5 format. You will use it in the next exercise.

⌘-G Arrange/Group
⌘-I Object/Paint Style
⌘-S File/Save
⌘-O File/Open
⌘-Shift-A Edit/Select None

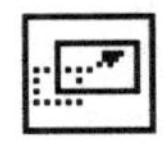

Scale tool

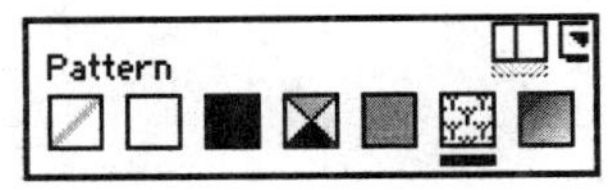

Pattern icon selected in the color strip area

REPOSITIONING PATTERNS

Once you apply a pattern as a fill or stroke, you can then reposition the pattern within the object without moving the object itself. Before the pattern can be moved, however, the filled object must first be selected with the selection tool.

Important info

Before a pattern can be repositioned, it must first be selected with the selection tool. Select it first, *then* press the *P* key.

EXERCISE D

1. If necessary, open (Command-O) the "Patterns.ai" file you created in the last exercise.
2. Use the selection tool to draw a selection marquee around the entire object.
3. Move the cursor into the object, but *before clicking,* press the *P* key while moving the pattern around within the object.
4. If you don't like the way the pattern fits the object, deselect everything (Command-Shift-A) and use the direct-selection tool to select the object.
5. Shift-select two of the rectangle's anchor points and drag the segment between the selected anchor points to enlarge or reduce the size of the rectangle. Be sure to press the Shift key *before* releasing the mouse button, so the sides of the rectangle will still be straight when they are resized.

Selection tool

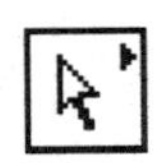

Direct-selection tool

⌘-I Object/Paint Style
⌘-Shift-A Edit/Select None

FYI

Because redefined patterns replace existing patterns in open documents, close any documents containing patterns you don't want updated with the new pattern. You could also save the redefined pattern under another name by clicking on New in the Pattern palette.

Rectangle tool

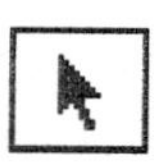

Selection tool

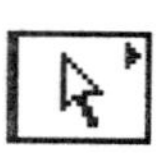

Direct-selection tool

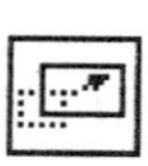

Scale tool

EDITING PATTERNS

Any pattern tile that has been added to the Patterns list in the Paint Style palette can be retrieved and edited. You can leave the modified pattern under its old name or rename the modified pattern, thus creating a second pattern based on the original.

If you redefine a pattern that has been used in any open documents, the newly defined pattern replaces the existing pattern wherever it was applied in the artwork of any currently open files.

EXERCISE E

1. Use the rectangle tool to draw a rectangle. Display the Paint Style palette (Command-I) and click on the Fill icon. Click on the Pattern icon in the color strip area.
2. Use the scroll bars to locate the Three Petals pattern. Click on OK.
3. Deselect everything on the drawing page (Command-Shift-A).
4. Choose Object/Pattern to display the Pattern dialog box.
5. Click to select the Three Petals pattern. Click on the Paste button and click on OK. The pattern is pasted into the document and is available for editing. If necessary, use the selection tool to drag it by an anchor point to an empty area of the page.
6. Zoom in on one of the three-petal clusters. Use the direct-selection tool to select the top petal and group all the anchor points (Command-G).
7. Click on the scale tool and click with the scale pointer on the topmost anchor point of the center petal. Move the cursor away from the point and drag up to enlarge the petal (Figure 11.7).

Figure 11.7—The center petal in the cluster has been enlarged.

8. Use the scale tool to enlarge another petal in another cluster. Modify the petals to create a different pattern.
9. Use the selection tool to draw a selection marquee around the edited pattern tile.
10. Choose Object/Pattern and click on Three Petals in the scroll box to redefine the pattern. Click on OK. The rectangle is filled with the newly defined Three Petals pattern. You can now delete the pattern tile, which is still selected, by pressing the Delete key.

DELETING PATTERNS

⌘-I Object/Paint Style

If you have created patterns and want to delete them, use the Pattern dialog box to select and delete any unwanted patterns. Once you delete a pattern that has been used in an open document, all objects painted with that pattern will be filled with black, and the pattern will be deleted from the scroll list in the Pattern dialog box.

EXERCISE F

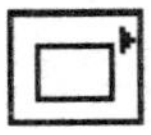

Rectangle tool

1. If necessary, draw a rectangle and fill it with a pattern, or use the rectangle filled with the modified Three Petals pattern which you created in the last exercise.
2. Choose Object/Pattern and click on Three Petals in the scroll box. An Alert dialog box appears, warning you that deleting this pattern will result in all objects in any open document painted with that pattern being painted black. Click on OK. Click on OK again to return to the document, where the rectangle is now filled with black.

TRANSFORMING PATTERNS

Rotate tool

You can use the rotate, scale, reflect, shear, and blend tools to transform pattern tiles. When you display any of the transformation dialog boxes, you can specify whether only the object (rectangle) transforms while the pattern remains stationary; whether the object remains stationary while the pattern transforms; or whether both the object and the pattern transform.

EXERCISE G

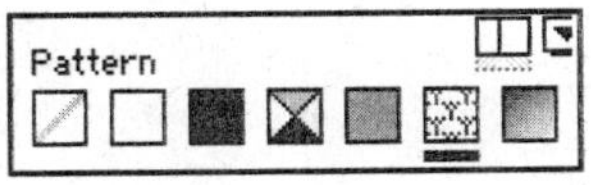

Pattern icon selected in the color strip area.

1. On a clean drawing page, use the rectangle tool to create a rectangle. Display the Paint Style palette (Command-I). Click on the Fill icon.
2. Click on the Pattern icon in the color strip area and select the Transparent Waves pattern.
3. With the rectangle still selected, double-click on the rotate tool to display the Rotate dialog box.
4. Type 45 in the Angle field. Click on the Objects check box to select it. Deselect the Pattern Tiles check box. Click on Copy. A rotated copy appears on top of the original. Use the selection tool to move it to the right.
5. With the original still selected, double-click on the shear tool. Type 45 in the Angle field. Click on Horizontal. Deselect the Objects check box (click until the X disappears), and click to select the Pattern tiles check box. Click on Copy. A sheared copy appears on top of the original. Use the selection tool to move it to the right. Click to select *both* the Objects and Pattern tiles check boxes. Click on Copy.
6. Click to select the first rectangle again. Double-click on the scale tool to display the Scale dialog box. Type 50 in the Uniform % field. Your screen should resemble Figure 11.8.

Shear tool

Selection tool

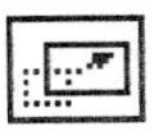

Scale tool

⌘-Q File/Quit
⌘-K File/Preferences/General
⌘-D Arrange/Repeat Transform
⌘-I Object/Paint Style
⌘-E View/Artwork

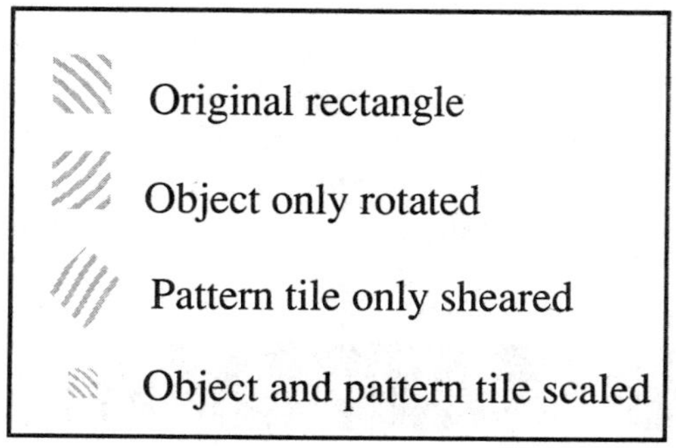

Figure 11.8—The same pattern has been rotated, sheared, and scaled. The bounding rectangles for these patterns have not been stroked.

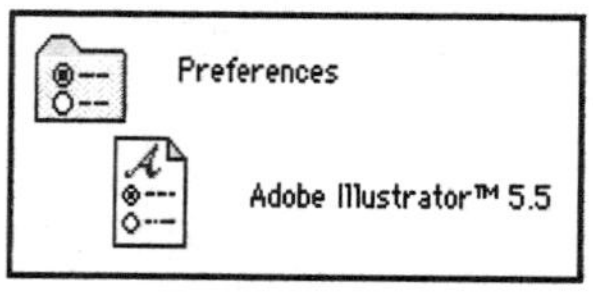

Trash the Preferences file to launch Adobe Illustrator's default patterns.

REVIEW EXERCISE

In this exercise you will create, modify, and edit patterns to create a logo. Since you modified the default patterns in Adobe Illustrator during this lesson, you must first restore those default patterns.

1. If you are in Illustrator, choose File/Quit (Command-Q). Go to the System folder, then to the Preferences folder, and drag the Adobe Illustrator Preferences file to the trash. Empty the Trash (Special/Empty Trash).
2. Launch Illustrator to display a new file. Choose File/Preferences/ General (Command-K) and select inches from the Ruler units pull-down menu.
3. Use the type tool and click in the center of the page. Type *Joy's Fabric Studio.* Click on the selection tool.
4. Use the Font and Type menus to format the text in 18-point Times Roman.
5. Select the rectangle tool and click on the drawing page to display the Rectangle dialog box. Type 1 in the Width and Height fields. Click on OK to create a 1-inch square.
6. Use the selection tool to drag the square to the right while pressing the Option and Shift keys. Release the mouse button, then the Option and Shift keys to create a copy of the rectangle, which aligns next to the original.
7. Choose Arrange/Repeat Transform (Command-D) to create a third square next to the second square.
8. Use the selection tool to select the first square. Display the Paint Style palette (Command-I) and click on the Fill icon. Click on None.
9. Choose View/Artwork (Command-E).
10. Use the oval tool and drag inside the square to create a circle. Once you start drawing, press the Option and Shift keys to create a circle drawn from the center outward. Release the mouse button, *then* the Option and Shift keys.
11. With the circle still selected, click on the Stroke icon and stroke the circle with a 1-point stroke in any color.

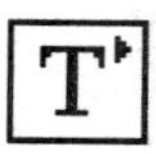

Type tool

Tip

Don't press the Option or the Shift key until you have started dragging an object.

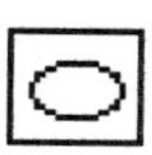

Oval tool

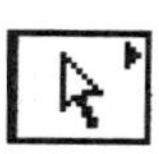

Direct-selection tool

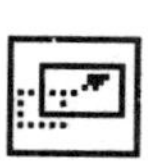

Scale tool

12. With the stroked circle still selected, double-click on the scale tool to display the Scale dialog box. Type 50 in the Uniform % field and click on Copy to create a smaller circle inside the larger one.
13. With the smaller circle still selected, click on the Fill icon in the Paint Style palette and click on anything but a gradient fill. Your screen should resemble Figure 11.9.

⌘-E View/Artwork
⌘-G Arrange/Group
⌘- – (hyphen) Arrange/Send to Back

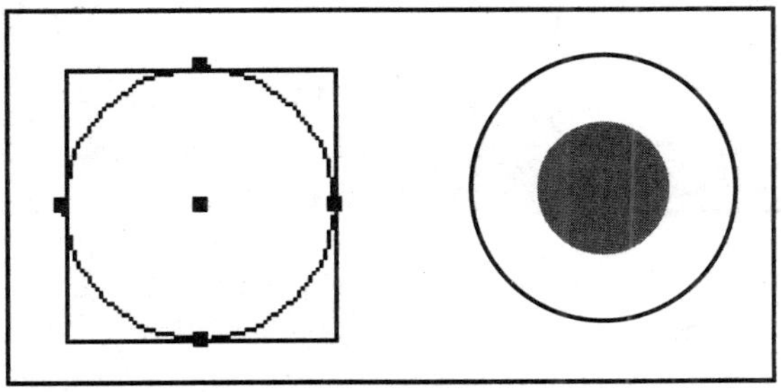

Figure 11.9—The drawn and stroked circle (left) and the scaled, filled copy (right).

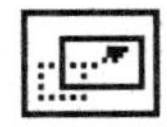

Scale tool

14. In Artwork mode (Command-E), use the selection tool to draw a selection marquee around the square and two circles. Choose Arrange/Group (Command-G).
15. Use the selection tool to click on the group and drag it down, pressing the Option and Shift keys once you start dragging to create a copy directly beneath the original. Align the lower square directly under the upper square.
16. Draw another selection marquee around both the original and the copy. Choose Arrange/Group (Command-G) again.

Selection tool

More info

You can't create a pattern from an object filled with a pattern or with a gradient fill.

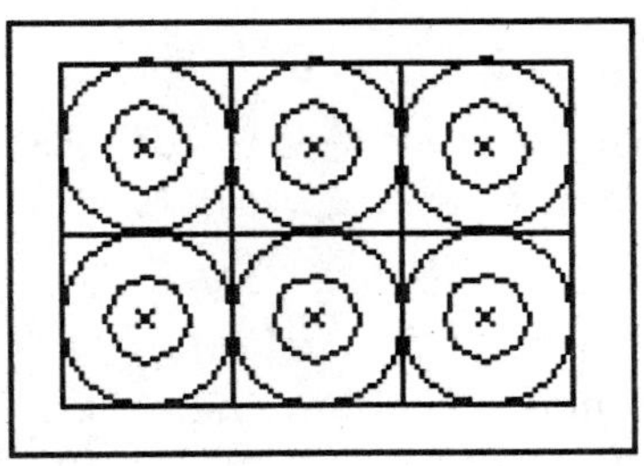

Figure 11.10—Option-Shift-dragging creates the six tiles more easily than drawing each one from scratch.

17. Option-Shift-drag the larger group to the right to create another group whose left sides align with the right sides of the original group. You should have six tiles (Figure 11.10).
18. Use the direct-selection tool to Shift-select the six bounding boxes (squares). Press the Delete key twice to delete them.
19. Click on the rectangle tool and drag to draw one bounding rectangle around the six sets of circles. With only the rectangle selected, choose Arrange/Send to Back (Command - –).
20. Use the selection tool to draw a selection marquee around the entire object—the bounding rectangle and the six circles.
21. Choose Object/Pattern to display the Pattern dialog box.
22. Click on New. The pattern tile appears in the preview box. Type Circles in the Change name to field (Figure 11.11).

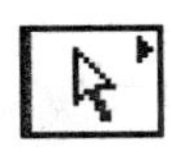

Direct-selection tool

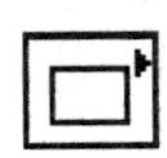

Rectangle tool

⌘-Shift-A Edit/Select None

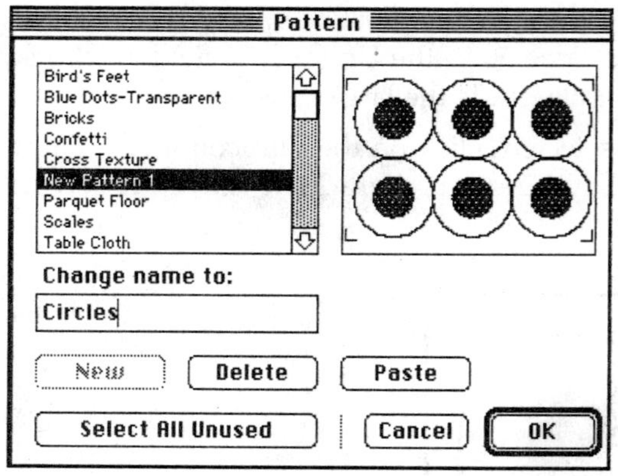

Figure 11.11—The design is named and designated a pattern in the Pattern dialog box.

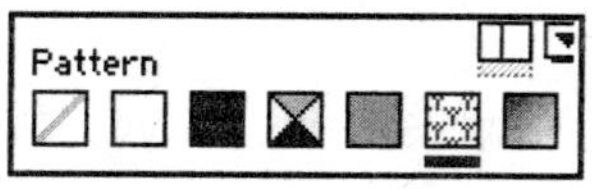

Pattern icon selected in the color strip area.

23. Select the first square. Click on the Pattern icon in the Paint Style palette, and click on the Circles pattern in the patterns scroll box.
24. Deselect everything (Command-Shift-A). Select the second square and use the Paint Style palette to fill it with the Yellow Stripes pattern. Then deselect everything again by clicking on an empty area of the page.
25. Choose Object/Pattern to display the Pattern dialog box. Click on the Yellow Stripe pattern and click on Paste. Click on OK.
26. The Yellow Stripe pattern appears in the center of the drawing page. Use the selection tool to move it to a blank area of the page.
27. Deselect the pattern tile (Command-Shift-A) and use the direct-selection tool to select alternate stripes and change their color (Figure 11.12).

Direct-selection tool

Figure 11.12—Use the direct-selection tool to modify elements in a pattern. Here, the alternate yellow stripes were painted black.

28. Use the selection tool to draw a selection marquee around the pattern tile and choose Object/Pattern. Click on the Yellow Stripe pattern. Click on OK. The pattern in the second square is redefined to match the edited pattern.
29. Click in the third square. Use the Paint Style palette to fill it with the Table Cloth pattern.
30. Double-click on the shear tool to display the Shear dialog box. Type 10 in the Angle field. Click on Horizontal. Click on Pattern Tiles to shear only the pattern. Click to deselect Objects so only the pattern and not the bounding rectangle (object) will shear. Click on OK.
31. Use the selection tool to arrange the three one-inch squares under the text. If you wish, enlarge the type and rearrange the squares. Your screen should resemble Figure 11.13.

Selection tool

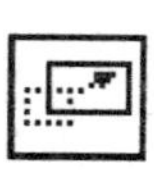

Shear tool

Figure 11.13—The modified and transformed patterns.

REVIEW QUESTIONS

Read the following questions and choose the answer which best completes the statement.

1. The key element in a pattern is _____.
   a. its design
   b. the Adobe Illustrator artwork
   c. its position
   d. all of the above
2. Patterns are defined in the _____.
   a. Paint Style palette
   b. Pattern dialog box
   c. Preferences dialog box
   d. a and b
3. Before a design can be defined as a pattern, it must be _____.
   a. surrounded by a bounding rectangle
   b. named in the Pattern dialog box
   c. scaled
   d. geometric in design
4. Patterns can be _____.
   a. renamed
   b. repositioned
   c. edited
   d. all of the above
5. To edit a pattern, use the _____.
   a. transformation tools
   b. direct-selection tool
   c. selection tool
   d. a and b
6. The last step in defining a pattern is to _____.
   a. paste it into the illustration
   b. edit it with the transformation tools
   c. select it and the bounding rectangle with the selection tool
   d. admire it

7. Pattern transformation can include _____.
    a. the object
    b. the object and pattern
    c. the pattern
    d. all of the above
8. Use the _____ command to display and edit an existing pattern.
    a. New
    b. Paste
    c. Send to Back
    d. Bring to Front
9. Use the _____ command to define a pattern.
    a. New
    b. Paste
    c. Send to Back
    d. Bring to Front
10. The bounding rectangle must be _____.
    a. longer than it is wide
    b. no more than one inch wide
    c. the backmost item in the pattern's stacking order
    d. filled and stroked

Answers: 1. b; 2. b; 3. a; 4. d; 5. d; 6. c; 7. d; 8. b; 9. a; 10. c

LESSON 12

Filters

OVERVIEW

This lesson will explore many of Adobe Illustrator's filters which make exciting graphics options possible. You will learn how to apply filters and how to specify values to change the effect of a filter.

TOPICS

What are filters?
Colors filter
Distort filters
Align filters
Other Objects filters
Pathfinder filters
Divide and Merge filters
Mix filters
Select filters
Stylize filters
Review Exercise
Review Questions

TERMS

backmost object
filter
frontmost object

-Y View/Preview
-I Object/Paint Style

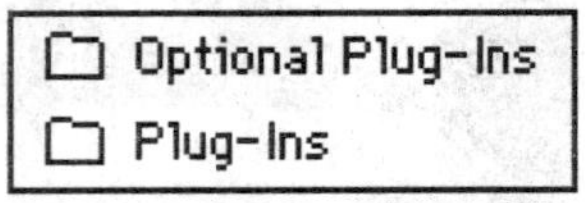

Any filters present in the Plug-Ins folder will be activated when Adobe Illustrator is launched.

No filters?

If your Filter menu is empty, choose File/Preferences/Plug-Ins and scroll to locate the Plug-Ins folder, which should be in the Adobe Illustrator 5.5 folder. Click on Open to activate the filters.

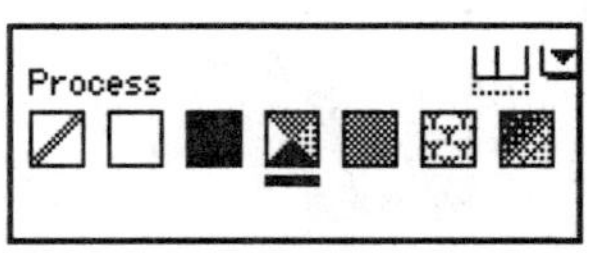

The Process color option selected in the color strip area of the Paint Style palette.

WHAT ARE FILTERS?

Filters are modules which, when accessed by Adobe Illustrator and applied to an illustration, allow you to adjust color and create and apply special effects to an illustration, as well as select, reshape, and reposition objects.

Several filters come with Adobe Illustrator and are automatically placed in the Plug-Ins folder in the Adobe Illustrator folder when the program is installed. Other filters are placed in the Optional Plug-Ins folder, also in the Adobe Illustrator program on the hard drive. To activate the optional plug-ins, drag them from the Optional Plug-Ins folder into the Plug-Ins folder before launching Adobe Illustrator.

Many of the filters will create different effects depending on the kind of object they are applied to. The only way to get comfortable with what a filter can do is to apply it to different kinds of painted and stroked objects and then print the illustration at its eventual resolution. Filters printed at 300 or 600 dpi on a laser printer will look different when printed at 1240 dpi to an imagesetter or film.

COLORS FILTERS

There are nine filters under the Colors submenu (Filter/Colors) which affect the way colors are applied and modified (Figure 12.1). Some of them, like the Blend filters, create a series of intermediate colors based on the stacking order or alignment of selected objects. Others saturate and desaturate (increase or decrease CMYK values of) colors, while the Invert Colors filter creates a negative of a selected object.

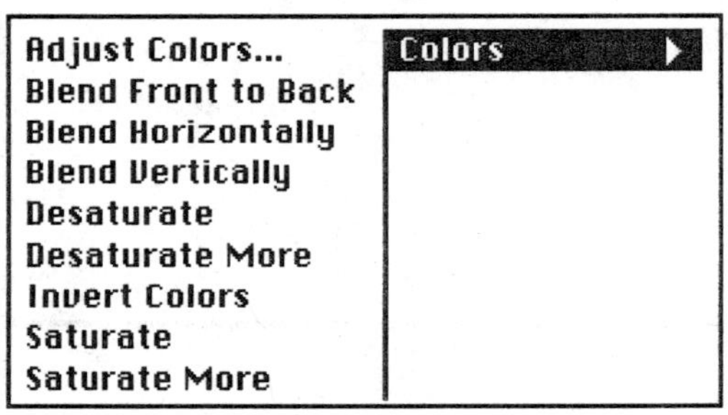

Figure 12.1—The Colors submenu under the Filter menu displays nine filters for adjusting color.

EXERCISE A

1. On a clean drawing page, use the rectangle tool to draw a rectangle. Choose View/Preview (Command-Y). Display the Paint Style palette (Command-I) and click on the Process Color icon in the color strip area to display the process color sliders.
2. Fill the selected rectangle with a process color, any combination of Cyan, Magenta, Yellow, and Black. Make sure that the Magenta value is at least 10%.

3. Choose Filter/Colors/Adjust Colors to display the Adjust Colors dialog box (Figure 12.2).

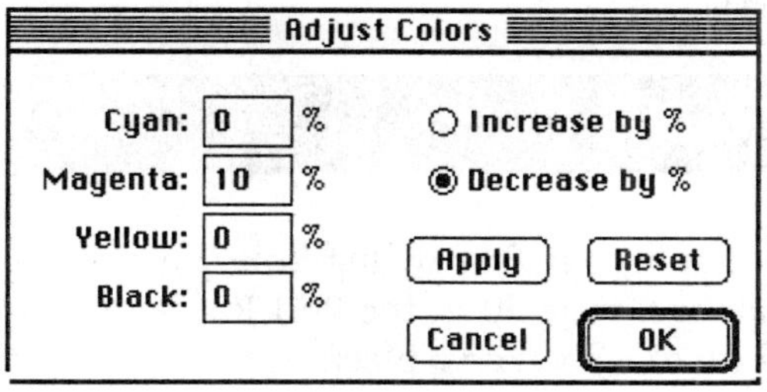

Figure 12.2—Type a value in any of the process color percentage fields and click on Increase by or Decrease by to adjust the colors in an object.

4. Type 10 in the Magenta field and click on the Decrease by button to decrease the percentage of magenta in the selected object by 10%. Click on Apply.
5. Type 15 in the Cyan field and click on the Increase by button to increase the Cyan percentage by 15%. Click on OK to apply the color adjustments.

EXERCISE B

1. Use the rectangle tool to create three overlapping rectangles.
2. Use the Paint Style palette (Command-I) to select the Process Color icon. Select the first rectangle and fill it with 60% Cyan and 10% Yellow, Magenta, and Black.
3. Use the selection tool to select the second rectangle and fill it with 10% Cyan, 66% Magenta, and 10% Yellow and Black.
4. Select the third rectangle and fill it with 10% Cyan and Magenta, 66% Yellow, and 10% black.
5. Shift-select all three items and choose Filter/Colors/Blend Front to Back to fill the middle object with a color which is a blend of the first and third objects' fill colors. Deselect everything (Command-Shift-A).
6. Select the first rectangle, the one with 66% Cyan and 10% Yellow, Magenta, and Black. Choose Filter/Colors/Desaturate. The Cyan value changes to 56% and the other values change to 8%, thereby reducing the intensity of the process color.
7. With the rectangle still selected, choose Filter/Colors/Desaturate More to further reduce the color's intensity.
8. Use the keyboard shortcut to reapply the most recently applied filter by pressing Command-Shift-E. The color intensity is further reduced. Press Command-Shift-E once more to change all the CMYK values to 0 and create a fill of None.

-I Object/Paint Style
-Shift-A Edit/Select None
-Shift-E Filter/Reapply Filter

Nothing changes

Using Command-Shift-E to reapply the most recently applied filter applies that filter with the same values as before. This command does not give you access to the filter's dialog box.

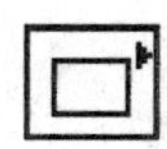

Rectangle tool

FYI

The Blend Horizontally and Blend Vertically filters blend the colors of the left and right or the top and bottom objects in a group of selected objects.

Selection tool

More info

Saturate and Saturate More filters increase the CMYK values for the fill and stroke of a selected object.

-D Arrange/Transform Again

DISTORT FILTERS

The Distort filters do just that—distort the shape of an object by changing the direction of an object's path.

EXERCISE C

Tip

Use the New Window command (Window/New Window) to make viewing and selection simultaneous and easier.

1. Choose Filter/Create/Star to display the Star dialog box. Type 20 in the 1st Radius field; press Tab and type 50 in the 2nd Radius field. Click on OK. Assign the star a fill of None and a black stroke.
2. Use the selection tool and Option-drag the star to create a second star. Choose Arrange/Repeat Transform (Command-D) five times to create a total of seven stroked stars.
3. Select the first star. Choose Filter/Distort/Free Distort. Make sure the See button is selected so you can view the distortion.
4. Move the top right anchor point toward the center. Move the lower left point toward the center to distort the star (Figure 12.3). To revert to the original star, click on the Reset button. Move the points again. Click on OK.

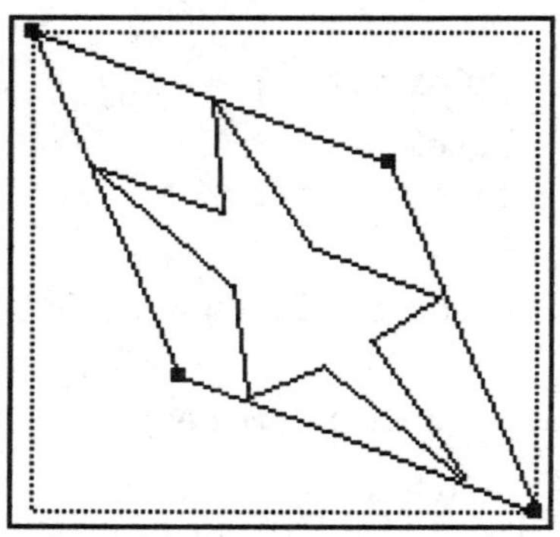

Figure 12.3—Use the four points in the Distort dialog box to distort the object.

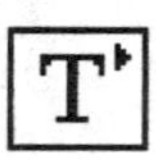

Type tool

5. Select the type tool, click under the distorted star, and type *Free Distort*. Click on the selection tool to select the type, and format it in 10-point Helvetica. Use the selection tool to drag the type by the alignment point directly under the star.
6. Select the second star. Choose Filter/Distort/Roughen to display the Roughen dialog box. Type 10 in the Size field; press Tab and type 5 in the Detail field to specify how many anchor points will be added to each inch of the path segments. Click to select the Jagged option, which will move the anchor points in a jagged direction from the original path by the specified percentage (Figure 12.4). Click on OK.

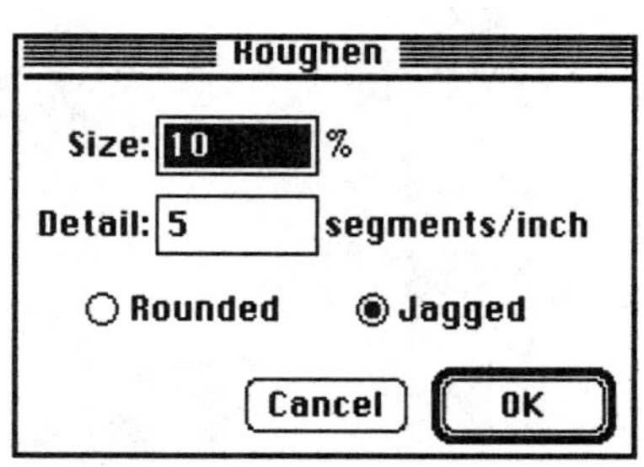

Figure 12.4—The Roughen dialog box.

7. Use the type tool to type Roughen/Jagged and move the text object under the star.
8. Select the third star and apply the Roughen filter (Filter/Distort/Roughen) again, but this time choose the Rounded option. Click on OK. Use the type tool to create a Distort/Rounded label for the star.

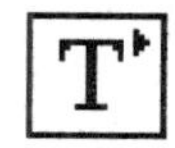

Type tool

9. Select the fourth star. Choose Filter/Distort/Scribble to display the Scribble dialog box, where you specify how the anchor points move in a random direction away from the original path.
10. Type 10 in the Horizontal field; tab to the Vertical field and type 10 again (Figure 12.5). These values calculate the the horizontal and vertical percentage of the longest segment of the object, and specify the distance an anchor point or segment will be moved.

FYI

The Scribble filter does not add anchor points to the object; it only *moves* existing points in random directions.

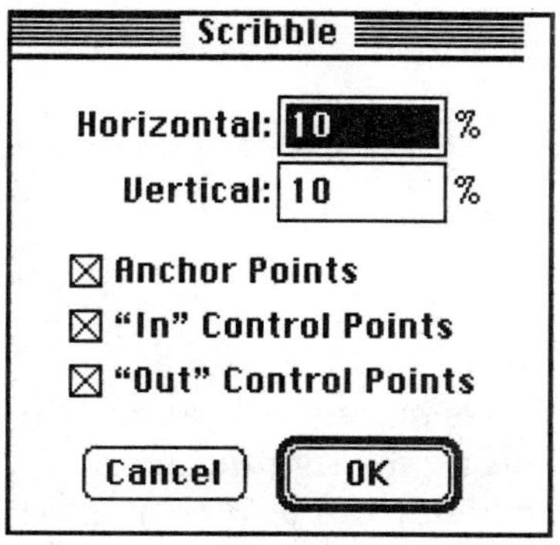

Figure 12.5—Scribble dialog box.

11. Click to select the Anchor Points check box to move the anchor points of the selected object. Click to select the "In" Control Points check box to move all the Bézier *direction handles* associated with path segments going into the anchor point. Click to select the "Out" Control Points check box to move the Bézier direction handles associated with path segments going out from an anchor point. Click on OK.
12. Type a label for this star and move it under the star.
13. Select the fifth star and choose Filter/Distort/Tweak. The Tweak filter moves anchor points by a specific amount. Type 5 in the Horizontal and Vertical fields to move all the anchor points 5 points. Click to select all of the check boxes, which will move the control points that lead into and out of the anchor points on the path. Click on OK.

Selection tool

14. Type a label for the star and move it under the star.
15. Select the sixth star and choose Filter/Distort/Twirl. Type 50 in the Angle field to to rotate the selected object more sharply from its center than at its edges. Click on OK.
16. Type a label for the star and move it under the star.
17. Select the seventh star and double-click on the Rotate tool. Type 50 in the Angle field and click on OK. Notice the difference between rotating an object and applying the Twirl filter.
18. Type a Rotate label for this last star and move it under the rotated star.
19. Your screen should resemble Figure 12.6.

-O File/Open
-A Edit/Select All
-U Arrange/Ungroup

20. Save this file (File/Save) as Star Filters.ai as an Illustrator 5 file. You will need it for the next exercise.

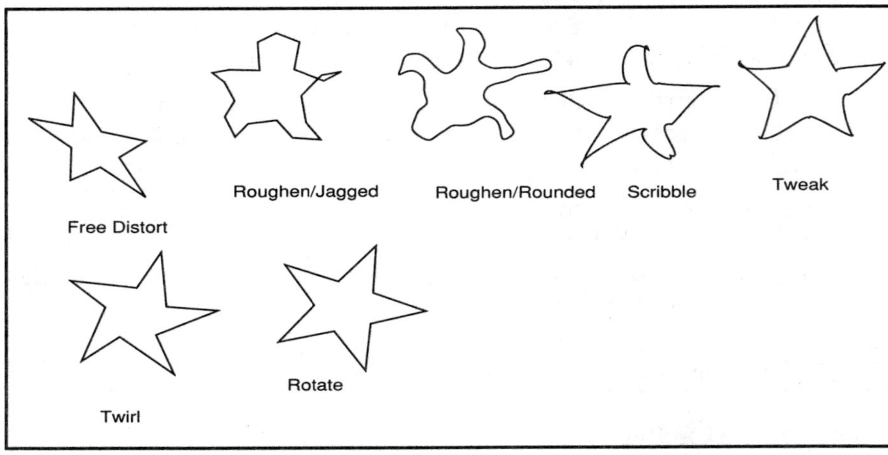

Figure 12.6—The stars with various Distort filters applied.

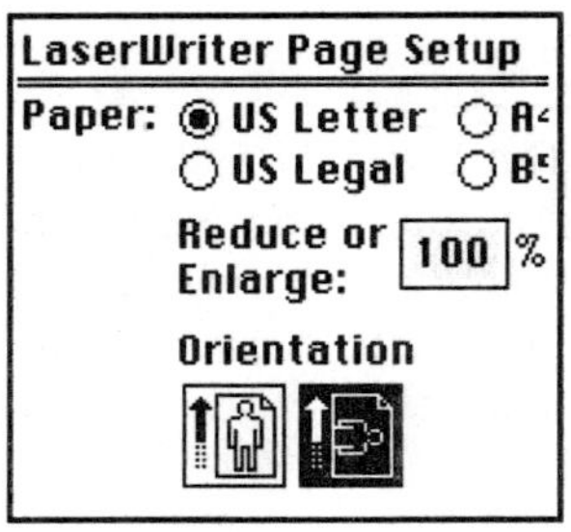

Landscape icon selected in the Page Setup dialog box.

ALIGN FILTERS

The Objects filters include filters for aligning objects horizontally and vertically. Selected objects can be aligned vertically using the rightmost, center, or leftmost anchor points of the selected objects. They can also be aligned horizontally using the topmost, center, and lowest anchor points.

Specify a printer

To specify a printer, select Chooser from the menu. Click the printer icon for the printer attached to your system. Click to highlight its name in the preview box on the right side of the screen. Then click on the Close button (upper left corner of the dialog box) to exit the Chooser.

EXERCISE D

1. If necessary, open the Star Filters.ai file (Command-O) which you created in the last exercise. If you don't have the file, use the Create filter to create a star, duplicate it six times, and apply a different filter to each star. Use the type tool to create labels for the stars as in Figure 12.6.
2. You will align the seven stars and their labels in two rows across the width of the page. Choose File/Page Setup to display the Page Setup dialog box for the printer you specified in the Chooser.
3. Your page is currently set for Portrait mode, that is, the page is placed with the shorter side of the page (drawing area) at the top. Click the Landscape Orientation icon to switch the shorter side of the page to the side. This will give you more room to arrange the stars.
4. Choose Edit/Select All (Command-A) and Edit/Ungroup (Command-U) to ungroup any objects you might have grouped together.
5. Use the selection tool to Shift-select the seven stars. Do not select the labels.
6. Choose Filter/Objects/Align Objects to display the Align Objects dialog box (Figure (12.7).

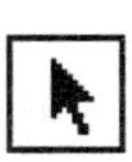

Selection tool

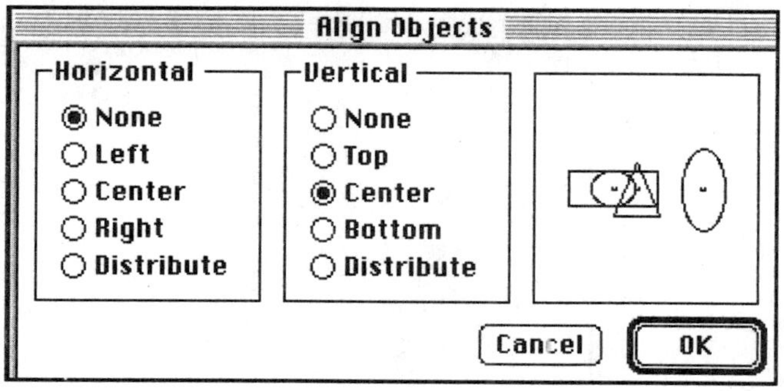

Figure 12.7—The Align Objects dialog box.

-Shift-A Edit/Select None
-Shift-E Filter/Reapply Filter

7. Since you are not aligning objects above and/or below each other, click to select None in the Horizontal field.
8. To align all the selected objects from their centers, click the Center button in the Vertical field. The preview box displays the selected alignment. Click on OK. Your screen should resemble Figure 12.8.

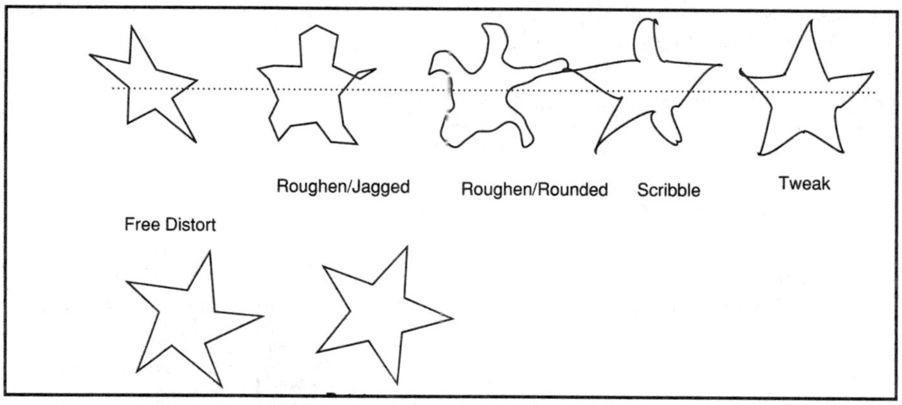

Figure 12.8—The stars in the top row are aligned vertically across the center points.

It doesn't have to make sense!

Objects are lined up horizontally (across) at the same position on the Y (vertical) axis. That's why you select the Vertical options when you want to string objects across the page. The three balls below are at the same point on the vertical axis, that is, they are all, for example, two inches *down* from the top margin.

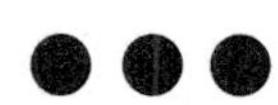

9. Shift-select the five labels under the five stars in the top row. Choose Filter/Objects/Align Objects to display the Align Objects dialog box.
10. Click to select None in the Horizontal field. Click to select Bottom in the Vertical field so that the selected labels will align from their bottom points, in this case, the baseline or alignment point. Click on OK.
11. Deselect everything (Command-Shift-A).
12. Use the selection tool to Shift-select the two stars in the bottom row. Press Command-Shift-E to reapply the last filter, in which you aligned the selected objects from their lowest anchor points. You could also choose Filter/Align Objects, which would apply to the currently selected objects the last alignment filter you applied.
13. Deselect everything by clicking on an empty area of the page or choosing Command-Shift-A.
14. Use the selection tool to Shift-select the two labels under the two stars in the bottom row. Press Command-Shift-E again to align the labels vertically from their lowest anchor points, the alignment points.

Selection tool

-Shift-E Filter/Reapply Filter

15. Shift-Select the first star in the first row, its label, the first star in the second row, and its label (Figure 12.9).

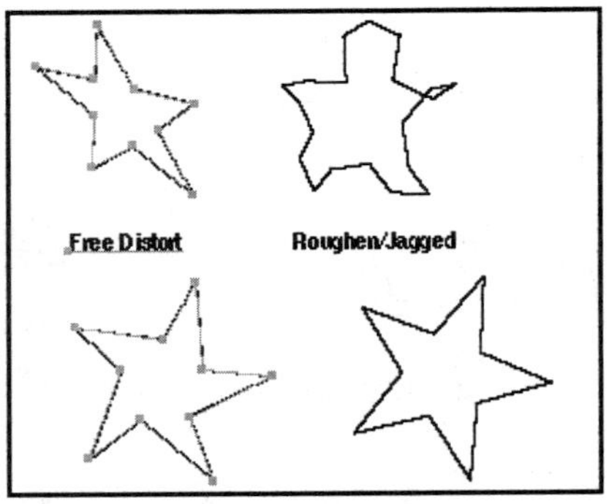

Figure 12.9—Shift-select only the first star and label in each row.

FYI

The Distribute Horizontally and Distribute Vertically filters do exactly what selecting Distribute from the Horizontal field and None from the Vertical field in the Align Objects dialog box does. With the Distribute option selected, objects are evenly distributed between the position of the leftmost and rightmost objects (horizontal distribution) and between the top and bottom objects (vertical distribution).

16. Choose Filter/Objects/Align Objects to display the Align Objects dialog box. Click to select Left in the Horizontal field. This will align the selected objects from their leftmost anchor points. Click None in the Vertical field (Figure 12.10).

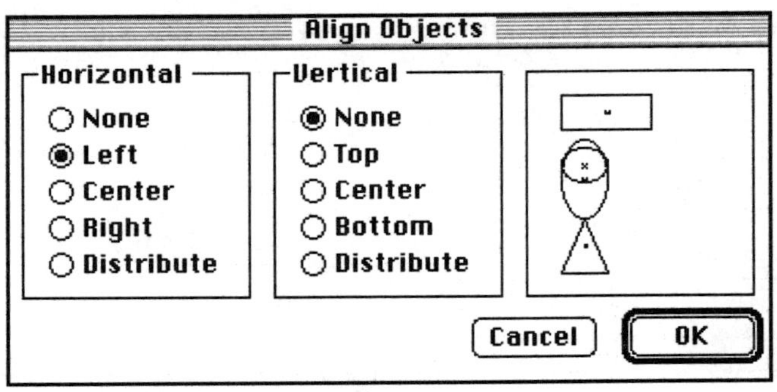

Figure 12.10—The Align Objects dialog box for horizontal alignment from the leftmost anchor points.

17. Click on OK. The four objects (two stars and two labels) are aligned vertically from their leftmost anchor points.

Selection tool

18. Use the selection tool to Shift-select the second star in the top row, its label, the second star in the bottom row, and its label. Press Command-Shift-E to reapply the horizontal alignment values. Your screen should resemble Figure 12.11.

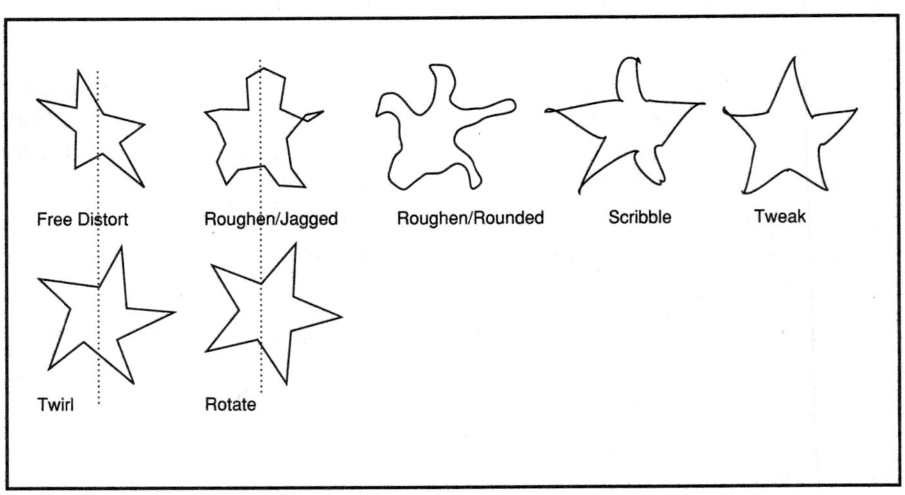

Figure 12.11—Stars and labels aligned vertically from their center points and horizontally from their leftmost points.

OTHER OBJECTS FILTERS

The Add Anchor Points filter doubles the number of anchor points in a selected path by adding a point between each pair of points on the path.

The Move Each filter is similar to the Move dialog box except that the Move dialog box is used to move only *selected points*, while the Move Each filter moves *all the anchor points* in a selection. The Move Each dialog box also includes a Random check box. Selecting this option tells Illustrator to move the selected objects randomly based on the horizontal and vertical values in the dialog box.

The Offset Path filter traces a second path around the selected path. The Outline Path filter, sometimes called Outline Stroke, strokes a closed path with another path, thus permitting you to apply a pattern to the stroke. Both of these filters require that the computer be equipped with a math coprocessor or floating-point unit (FPU).

The Rotate Each filter works with several selected objects and rotates each selected object independently around its center. The Scale Each filter works in much the same way. It scales each selected object in a group of selected objects independently around its center.

EXERCISE E

1. On a clean drawing page, choose Filter/Create/Polygon to display the Create Polygon dialog box. Type 7 in the Sides field and click on OK (Figure 12.12). The 7-point polygon is displayed.

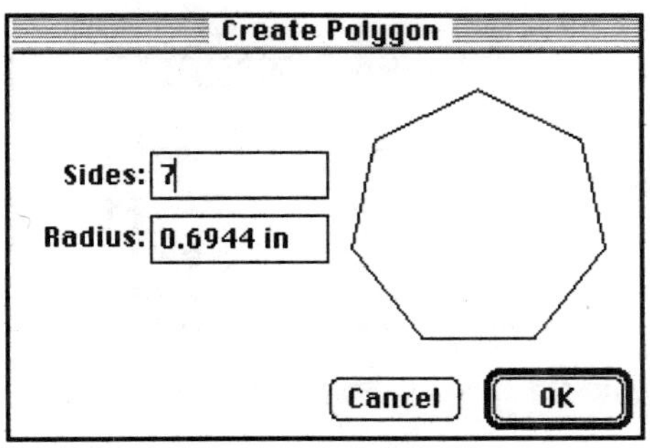

Figure 12.12—The Create Polygon dialog box.

2. Choose Filter/Objects/Add Anchor Points. The 7-point polygon now displays 14 anchor points.
3. With the polygon still selected, apply any fill and a 20-point black stroke.
4. Click on the Patterns icon in the color strip area of the Paint Style palette. Choose File/Open (Command-O) and highlight the Patterns folder in the Adobe Illustrator 5.5 folder on your hard drive. Click on Open. Double-click on Native American to open the Native American patterns. The file containing the patterns is displayed on the screen and the Patterns scroll box now includes all of the Native American patterns.

-O FIle/Open

FYI

Multiple-selected objects do not have to be grouped before applying the Rotate Each or Scale Each filter.

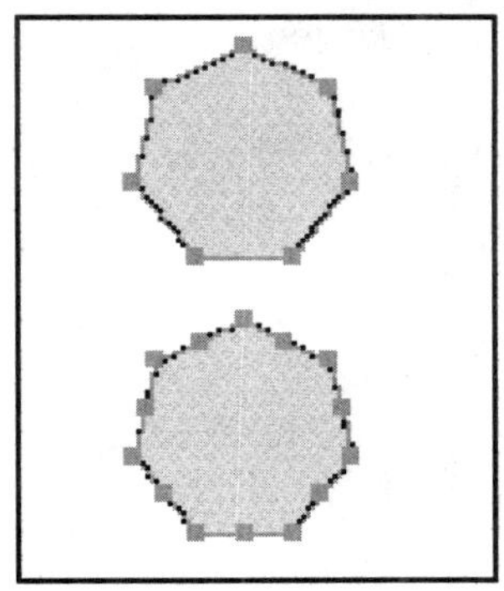

The Add Anchor Points filter doubled the 7-points in the polygon to 14 points.

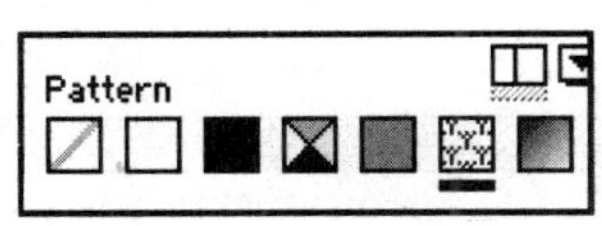

Pattern icon selected in the color strip area.

-E View/Artwork
-Shift-E Filter/Reapply Filter

FYI

You must select the stroke pattern *before* applying the Outline Path filter if you want to fill that new path with a pattern.

Use it and lose it!

Before applying the Outline Path filter, there was only one object, a polygon with a stroke and fill applied. Once you apply the Outline Path filter, that polygon becomes a grouped object, because the new path and the center path are now two separate paths, and must be moved with the group-selection tool.

Selection tool

Pen tool

More info

Typing a negative number in the Offset field of the Offset Path dialog box will offset the new line the specified distance *below* the original line.

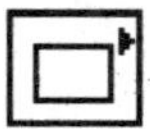

Rectangle tool

5. With the polygon still selected, click on the Stroke icon in the Paint Style palette and click on the Pomo pattern in the Patterns scroll box.
6. The polygon's stroke is replaced with a path. And since, unlike strokes, paths can be filled with a pattern, the new path is filled with the Pomo pattern. Your screen should resemble Figure 12.13.

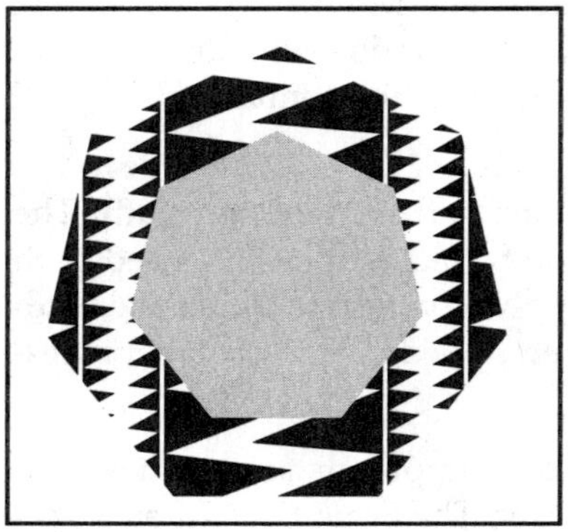

Figure 12.13—The polygon is no longer stroked. Instead, its outline is a path which can be filled with a pattern.

7. On a clean drawing page, use the pen tool to draw a straight line. Assign it a stroke of 10 points. Then select it with the selection tool.
8. Choose Filter/Objects/Offset Path to display the Offset Path dialog box. Type 20 in the Offset field to offset the new line 20 points from the original. Click on OK.
9. Press Command-Shift-E to reapply the filter. Do this a few times until you have about four lines on top of each other. Your screen should resemble Figure 12.14.

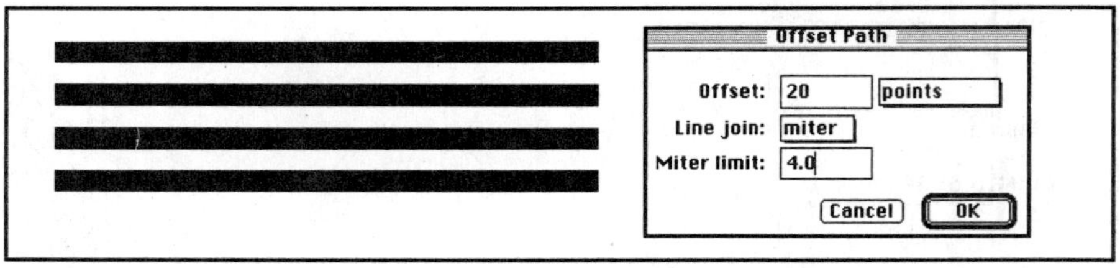

Figure 12.14—Using the Offset Path filter and reapplying it results in duplicates of the original line.

10. On a clean drawing page, use the rectangle tool to draw a rectangle. Assign it a fill of None and a 10-point stroke. Keep it selected.
11. Choose Filter/Objects/Offset Path. Type 20 in the Offset field. Click on OK. Press Command-Shift-E (Filter/Reapply Filter) a few times. Your screen should resemble Figure 12.15.

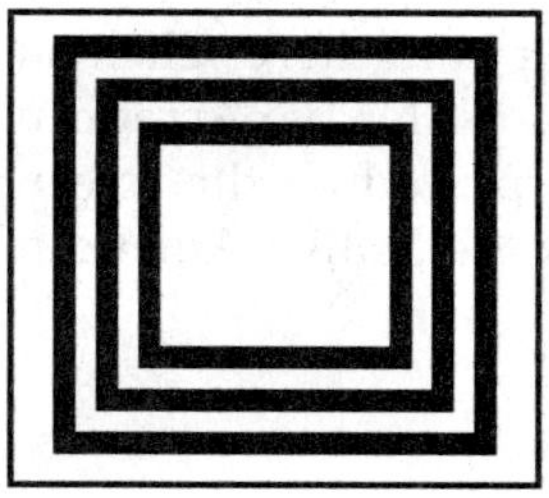

Figure 12.15—A closed path offset 20 points.

EXERCISE F

1. Drag with the rectangle tool to create a rectangle about 4 inches wide and 6 inches high. Fill it with purple.
2. Choose Filter/Create/Spiral. Type 5 in the Winds dialog box and click on the Clockwise option. Click on OK (Figure 12.16).
3. The spiral is displayed as a selected path. Assign it a yellow stroke.

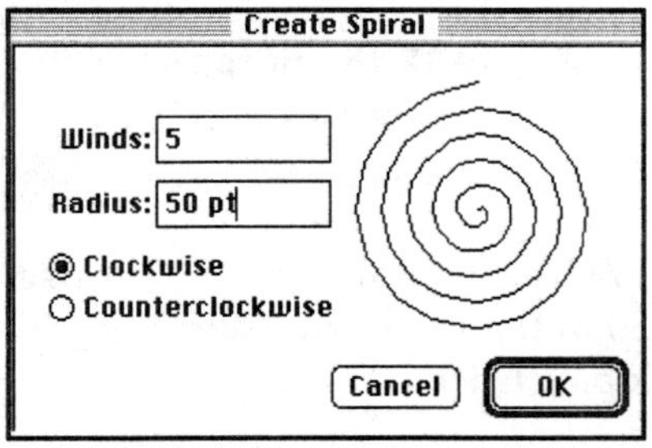

Figure 12.16—Specify the number of winds, the distance between winds, and the direction of the spiral in the Spiral dialog box.

4. Press Command-Shift-E to reapply the filter. A second spiral is placed on top of the original spiral. Use the selection tool to move it away.
5. Continue to use the Spiral filter to create clockwise and counterclockwise spirals with different winds and space between the winds. Then select only the spirals and choose Filter/Objects/Move Each to display the Move Each dialog box (Figure 12.17).

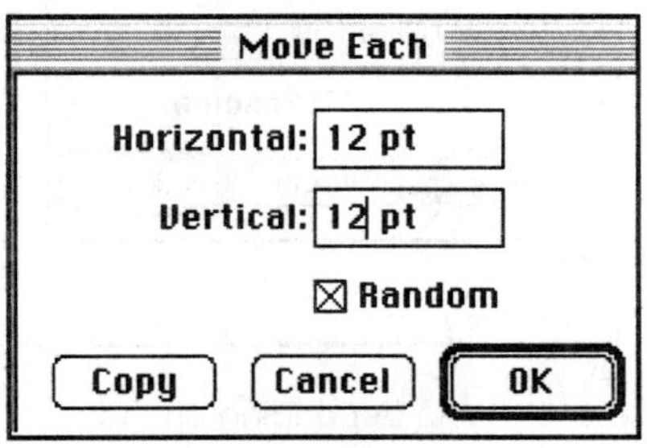

Figure 12.17—Type values for a move's horizontal and vertical distance in this dialog box.

6. Type 12 (points) in the Horizontal field; tab to the Vertical field and type 12. Click on the Random check box to move each spiral randomly within the 12-point horizontal and vertical specification. Click on Copy to create two more spirals.
7. Press Command-Shift-E to reapply the filter. Do this a few times until you are satisfied with the way the spirals are arranged.
8. Choose Filter/Create/Polygon to create a three-sided object, a triangle.
9. Choose Filter/Objects/Rotate Each. Type 15 in the Angle field. Do not select the Random option. Click on the Copy button to create a rotated copy of the original triangle.
10. Press Command-Shift-E to reapply the filter a few times. Then select the whole group and Option-drag it to create a copy of the group. Do this a few times to create a design similar to the one in Figure 12.18.

-Shift-E Filter/Reapply Filter

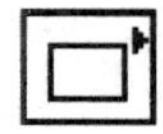

Rectangle tool

Selection tool

FYI

Use the General Preferences dialog box (File/Preferences/General) to select a unit of measure for the filter dialog boxes. You can also override the current unit of measure by typing *in* or *pt* in the dialog box.

- Shift-E Filter/Reapply Filter

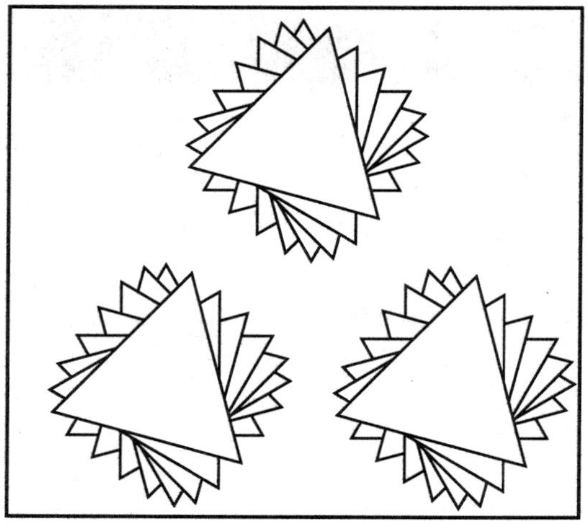

Figure 12.18—Reapply the Rotate Each filter to create a new design.

11. Create another triangle (Filter/Create/Polygon). Choose Filter/Objects/Scale Each and type 150 in the Horizontal and Vertical fields. Do not select the Random check box. Click on OK.
12. Choose Filter/Objects/Scale Each again. Type 50 in the Vertical field and *click on Copy*.
13. Press Command-Shift-E a few times to reapply the filter. Your screen should resemble Figure 12.19.

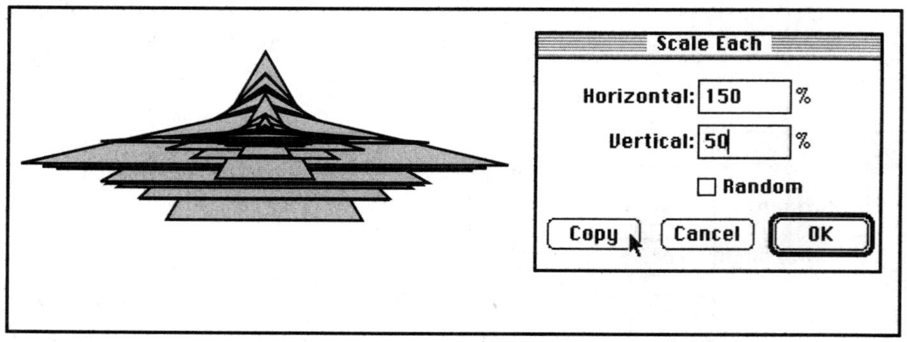

Figure 12.19—The Scale Each filter creates different effects depending on the specifications in the Scale Each dialog box.

FYI

Some Pathfinder filters require a math coprocessor installed in the computer. Unless installed separately, the Macintosh LC, IIsi, Centris, and 610 models do not have the required coprocessor. Neither do the Powerbook 500 series computers.

PATHFINDER FILTERS

Use the Pathfinder filters to join, separate, and subdivide paths as well as to create new paths from the intersection of objects. Many of the Pathfinder filters create compound paths, which create a see-through effect with the overlapping objects.

The first five Pathfinder filters, called the Combine filters, create their effects by tracing the *outline* of overlapping or nonoverlapping shapes. Some, like the Back Minus Front and Front Minus Back filters, are useful in creating knockout areas of the illustration by adjusting the stacking order of the selected objects. Others, like the Mix Hard and Mix Soft filters, are used to create a transparent effect by combining overlapping colors.

EXERCISE G

1. On a clean drawing page, use the rectangle tool to draw a 6-inch square. Fill and stroke the the square.
2. Select the type tool and type an ampersand (Shift-7) in the center of the square. Click on the selection tool and use either the Character palette (Command-T) or the Font and Type menus to format that single character in 300-point Palatino italic—the typeface isn't that important.
3. Drag the character in the square so that it extends beyond the square. While it is still selected, choose Type/Create Outlines to convert the text character to a path (Figure 12.20).

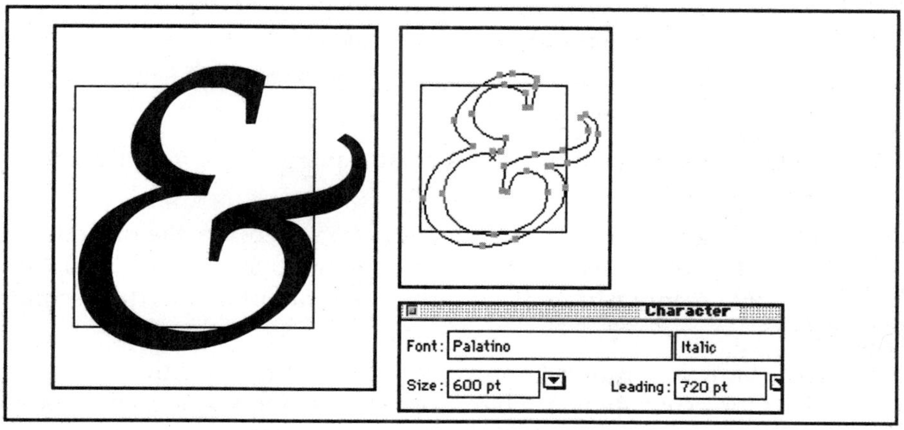

Figure 12.20—A text character is placed over a colored square (left), then converted to a path.

4. Choose Edit/Select All (Command-A) to select both the character and the square. Choose Filter/Pathfinder/Intersect to delete the part of the character that does not overlap the square (Figure 12.21). This filter applies the paint attributes of the frontmost object to the newly created object. Choose Edit/Undo (Command-Z) to restore the original image.
5. Select both the square and the character again (Edit/Select All) and choose Filter/Pathfinder/Exclude (Figure 12.21) to delete any area where the two objects overlap. Again, the paint attributes of the frontmost object are applied to the newly created object. Choose Edit/Undo Command-Z) to restore the original image.

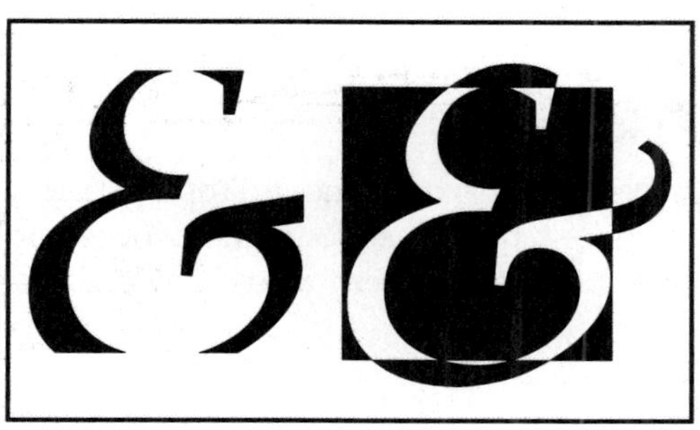

Figure 12.21—The Intersect filter (left) deletes any nonoverlapping areas; the Exclude filter (right) deletes those areas where the objects overlap. They are now independent segments and can be selected with the direct-selection tool.

-T Window/Show Character
-A Edit/Select All
-Z Edit/Undo

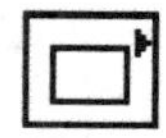

Rectangle tool

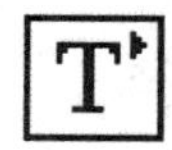

Type tool

-Z Edit/Undo
-A Edit/Select All

6. Select both objects again and choose Filter/Pathfinder/Minus Front to delete any part of the backmost selected object where it overlaps the front object (Figure 12.22). Choose Edit/Undo (Command-Z) to restore the original image.
7. Select both objects again (Command-A) and choose Filter/Pathfinder/Minus Back to delete any part of the frontmost object that overlaps the backmost object (Figure 12.22).

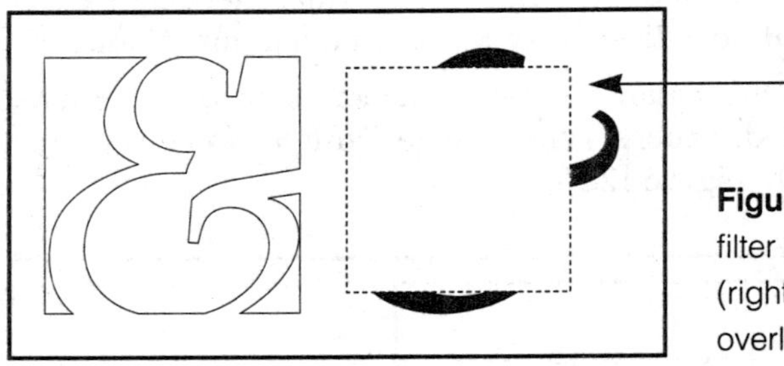

Figure 12.22—The Minus Front filter (left) and Minus Back filter (right) delete the back and front overlapping parts of the image.

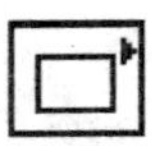

Rectangle tool

8. Use the rectangle tool to draw a small square. Apply fill and stroke attributes to it.
9. Option-drag to create another square diagonally below the first one so that the top left corner of the duplicate intersects the original at its center point. Apply different fill and stroke attributes to the second square.
10. Select both squares and choose Filter/Pathfinder/Unite. The two objects are joined into one object. The overlapping segments disappear and the paint attributes of the frontmost object (the second square) are applied to the newly created object (Figure 12.23).

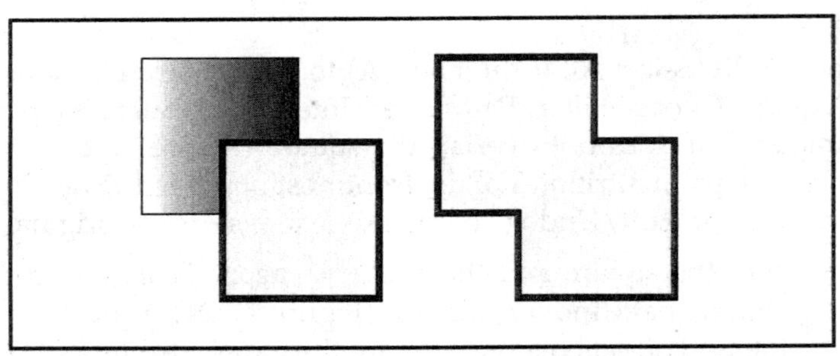

Figure 12.23—The frontmost object (left) has a yellow fill and six-point stroke applied. When the Unite filter is applied, those fill and stroke attributes are applied to the newly created object (right).

DIVIDE AND MERGE FILTERS

The Divide and Merge filters split overlapping and nonoverlapping paths and then merge them into closed and/or open objects. In the process of dividing and merging, fills and strokes are either removed, replaced, or repositioned.

EXERCISE H

1. Use the rectangle tool and Shift-drag to create a square. Use the type tool to type an ampersand (Shift-7) and click on the selection tool to select the text character.
2. Format the ampersand in any size of Palatino italic which will make the text overlap the square as in the Original example in Figure 12.24.
3. With the text character still selected, choose Type/Create Outlines to convert the text character to a graphic object. Fill it with a color that contrasts with the square. Assign it a 2-point stroke.
4. Shift-select both objects with the selection tool and Option-drag to create another pair. Choose Arrange/Repeat Transform (Command-D) five more times. You should have a total of seven pairs.
5. Label one pair as Original. Shift-select the second pair of objects and choose Filter/Pathfinder Divide. The new object keeps its fill colors, but the strokes are removed from both the character and the square. Any area where the character and the square overlapped has become a separate object.
6. Click on one of the overlapping areas and notice that it is a separate path. Fill it with a different color from the Colors palette.
7. Shift-select the third pair of objects with the selection tool. Choose Filter/Pathfinder/Outline. The Outline filter strips the selected objects (they don't have to overlap) of their fill attributes and replaces the stroke attributes with the color of the original fill.
8. Shift-select the fourth pair of objects with the selection tool. Choose Filter/Pathfinder/Trim to strip the stroke attributes from the selected objects. The fill attributes remain the same.
9. Use the rectangle or oval tool to draw an object that overlaps the character and square in the fifth pair. Fill it with the same color as the character. Choose Arrange/Send to Back (Command- –) to make it the backmost object in the stacking order of the three objects.

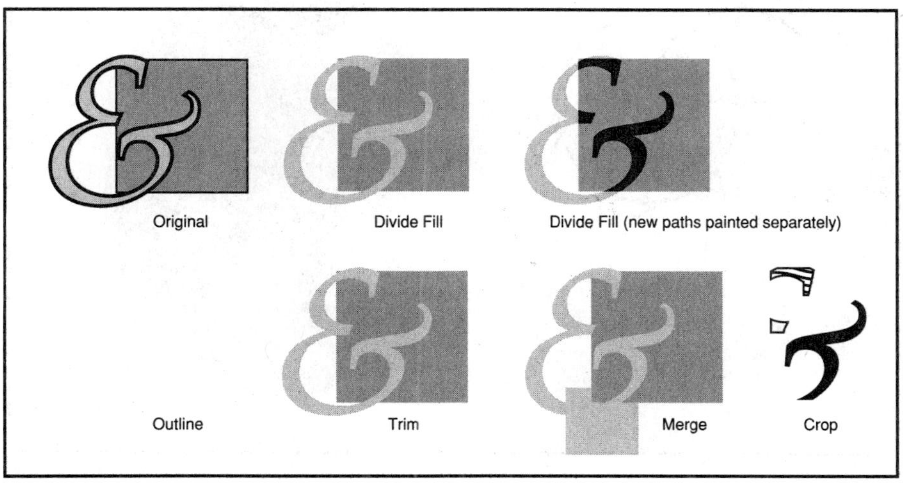

Figure 12.24—Displays examples of the Divide and Merge filters. The segments of the Crop example were selected and filled independently.

-D Arrange/Repeat Transform

- – (hyphen) Arrange/Send to Back

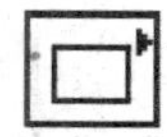

Rectangle tool

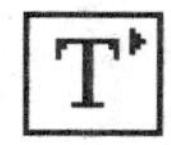

Type tool

Selection tool

FYI

The Trim and Merge filters remove any part of a filled path that is not visible behind another object. The Trim filter does not merge objects with the same fill color as does the Merge filter.

-I Object/Paint Style
-A Edit/Select All

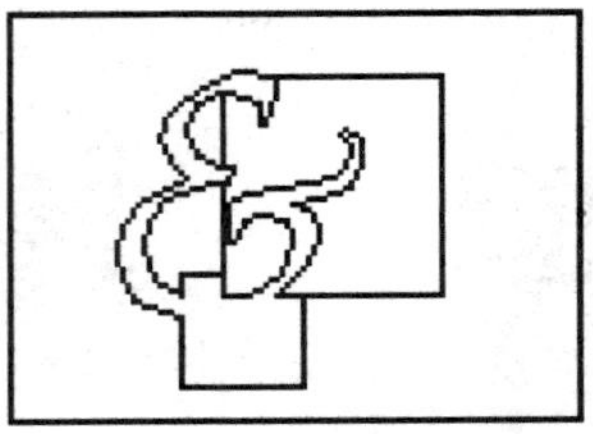

Merge filter applied in Artwork mode.

10. Shift-select the fifth pair of objects and choose Filter/Pathfinder/Merge to remove any part of a filled path that is hidden and merge the overlapping objects filled with the same color.
11. Shift-select the sixth pair of objects and choose Filter/Pathfinder/Crop to delete any part of the selection extending beyond the frontmost object. The resulting object becomes separate paths which can be filled and stroked independently.

MIX FILTERS

The Mix Hard and Mix Soft filters transform the areas created by overlapping objects into separate objects. These new objects are filled with a *mixture of the colors* from the overlapping objects. Stroke attributes, however, are removed.

EXERCISE I

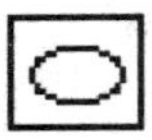

Oval tool

Selection tool

1. Use the oval tool and Shift-drag to create a circle. Option-drag the selected circle a few times to form a cluster of circles (Figure 12.25).
2. Choose Edit/Select All (Command-A) and apply a black stroke to all the selected circles.
3. Use the Paint Style palette (Command-I) to fill every circle with a different color.
4. Choose Edit/Select All (Command-A) and use the selection tool to Option-drag a copy of the circles to another part of the drawing page.
5. Use the selection tool to draw a selection marquee around all the circles in one cluster. Choose Filter/Pathfinder/Hard. The CMYK values with the highest values in each object are mixed in the overlapping areas. Any strokes applied to the selected objects are also removed. Your screen should resemble Figure 12.25.

Tip

To achieve more striking results and interesting effects with the Mix Hard filter, use different or contrasting colors.

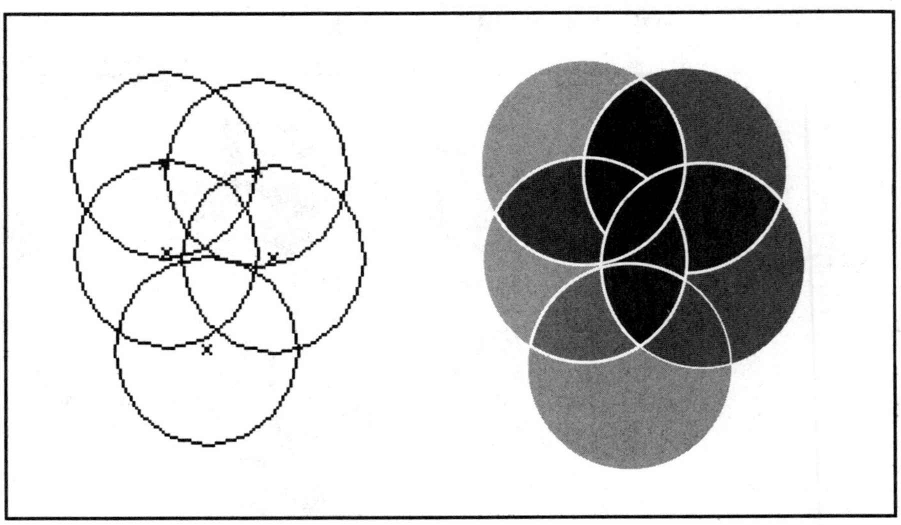

Figure 12.25—The circles in Artwork mode (left) and after the Mix Hard filter was applied. A 2-point white stroke was applied to the segments, which display the new (mixed) colors.

6. Use the selection tool to draw a selection marquee around the second cluster of circles. Choose Filter/Pathfinder/Soft to display the Pathfinder Soft dialog box (Figure 12.26).

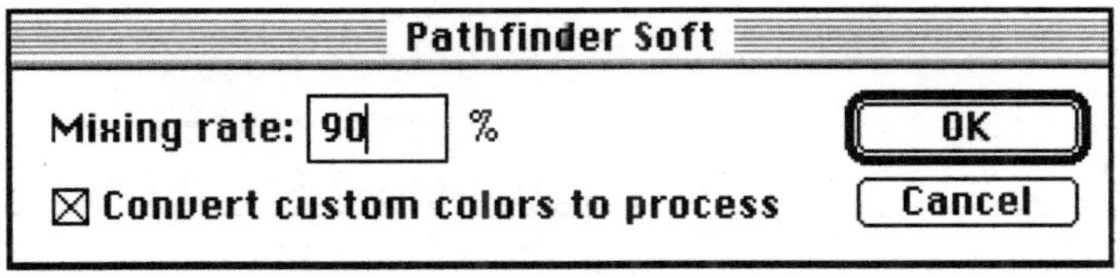

Figure 12.26—The higher the value in the Mixing rate field, the greater the transparency.

7. The higher the value entered in the Mixing Rate field, the greater the transparency of the frontmost objects. Type 90 in the Mixing rate field. Click to select the Convert custom colors to process check box and click on OK. Your screen should resemble Figure 12.27.

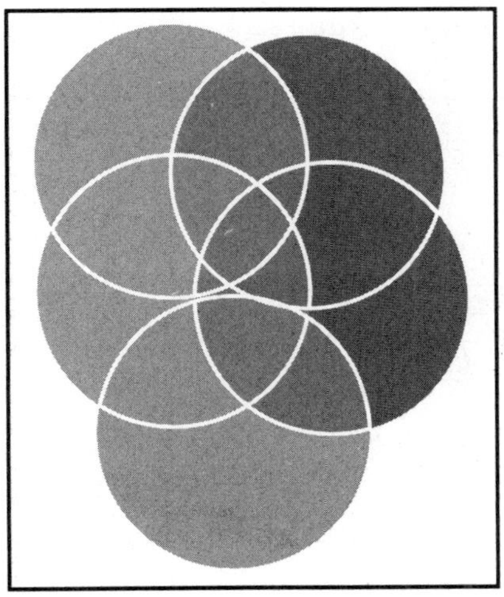

Figure 12.27—The Mix Soft filter makes the frontmost objects transparent. A 2-point white stroke has been applied to the overlapping objects.

Frontmost object (oval) was originally filled with white.

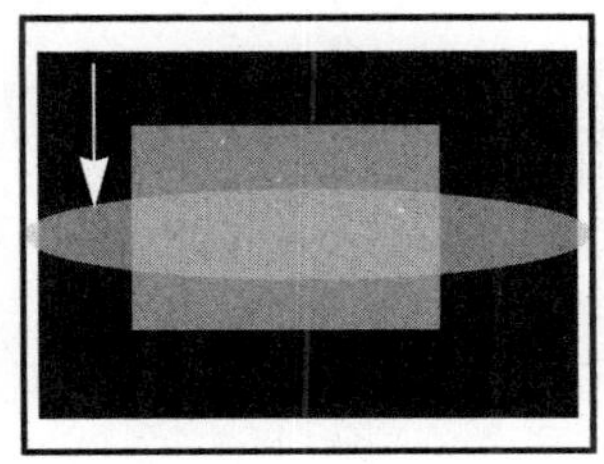

A mixing rate of 80% will make the underlying colors appear lighter when the frontmost object has a white fill.

SELECT FILTERS

Use the Select filters (Figure 12.28) to select objects with the same fill, paint, and stroke attributes. The Inverse filter will switch selections—select what is not selected and deselect what is selected.

The Stray Points filter cleans up anchor points that may be littering the drawing page when you click with the pen tool and then decide to use another tool. This leaves a stray anchor point on the page which you can select with the Stray Points filter and delete.

These filters are handy when you decide that the purple stroke on the yellow birds is too bright. You can select one object with the purple stroke, use a Select filter to select all the other objects with that stroke, and change the color and/or weight with one keystroke.

-Shift-A Edit/Select None

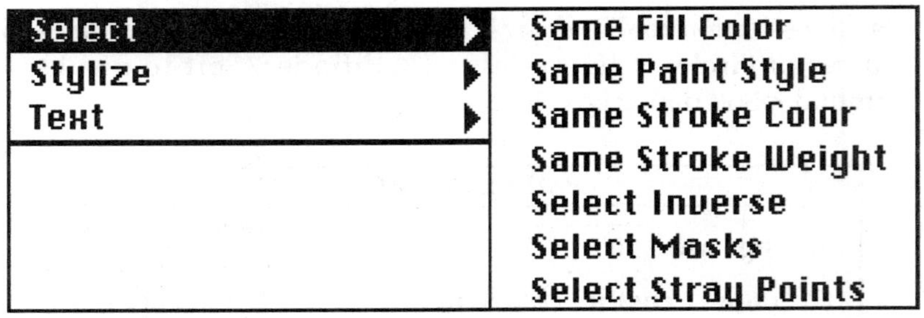

Figure 12.28—The Select filters.

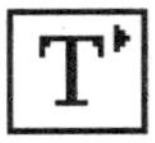

Type tool

EXERCISE J

1. Use the drawing tools or the Create filters to draw four objects. Assign two objects the same fill and stroke attributes. Assign the other two objects different fill and stroke attributes. You now have four objects with two different fill and stroke attributes (Figure 12.29).

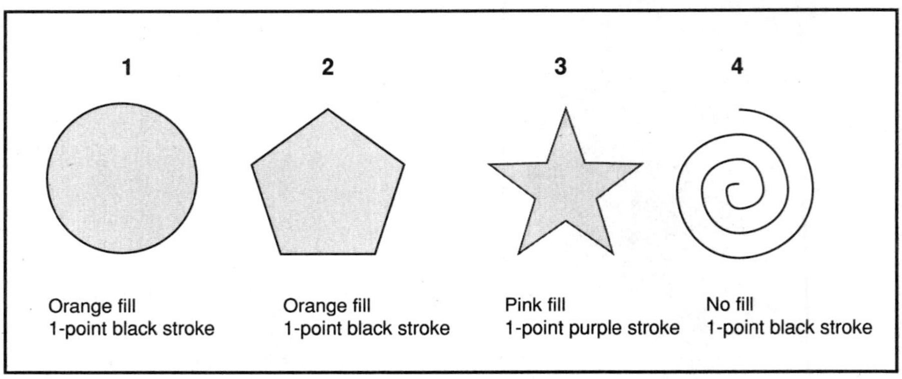

Figure 12.29—Four objects with similar and different strokes and fills.

Bye, bye

The two ways to deselect every object in the illustration are to press Command-Shift-A (Edit/Select None) or to click on any empty area of the drawing page.

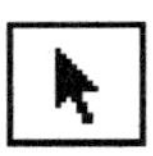

Selection tool

2. Use the selection tool to select Object 1. Choose Filter/Select/Same Fill Color. Both Object 1 and Object 2 are selected because they have the same fill attributes.
3. Deselect everything (Command-Shift-A). Select Object 2. Choose Filter/Select/Same Paint Style. Object 1 becomes selected because it has the same fill, stroke, and stroke weight as the originally selected object (Object 2).
4. Deselect everything by clicking on an empty area of the drawing page. Choose Filter/Select/Same Stroke Color. Objects 1, 2, and 4 are selected because they all have the same black stroke.
5. Deselect everything. Select Object 4. Press Command-Shift-E to apply the Select filter again. Objects 1 and 2 are now selected because they have the same black stroke as Object 4, the selected object.
6. Deselect everything. Choose Filter/Select/Same Stroke Weight. All the objects are selected because they all have the same 1-point stroke. Color is not an issue with this filter.

7. Deselect everything. Use the selection tool to select Object 3. Choose Filter/Select/Select Inverse. Object 3 becomes *deselected* and Objects 1, 2, and 4 become selected. The Select Inverse filter *deselects the selection* and selects every other object in the document.
8. Deselect everything. Choose Filter/Select/Select Stray Points. The single point you created with the pen tool appears selected. Press the Delete key to delete the stray point.
9. Change the paint, stroke, and stroke weight values of the four objects and practice using the Select filters to select similar objects. Once you have them selected, use the Paint Style palette to make global fill and stroke changes.

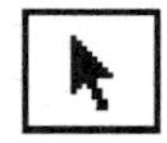

Selection tool

STYLIZE FILTERS

The Stylize filters are used to add special effects to objects. You can create interesting graphic effects with these filters, especially when you use them with text objects which have been converted to outlines.

EXERCISE K

1. The Add Arrowheads filter adds arrowheads to the start, end, or start and end of any selected open path. Use the pen tool to draw a straight line. Apply a stroke of any weight. Keep the line selected.
2. Choose Filter/Stylize/Add Arrowheads to display the Add Arrowheads dialog box (Figure 12.30). Click on the hand arrows to move forward and backward to select arrowhead #20, one of the many installed arrowheads. The selected arrowhead appears in the preview window.
3. Type 100 in the Scale field and click in the Start and End button to make the arrowhead appear at both ends of the open path. Click on OK. Your screen should resemble Figure 12.30.

Pen tool

FYI

An open path must be selected before the Add Arrowheads filter can be applied.

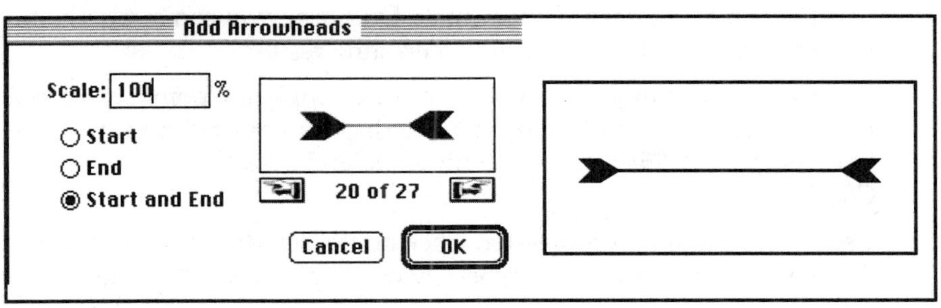

Figure 12.30—This Add Arrowheads dialog box specifies arrowheads for the start and end of the open path.

Tip

Increasing and decreasing the Scale value in the Add Arrowheads dialog box will make the arrowheads larger or smaller.

4. Draw another line, select it, and use the Add Arrowheads filter to create different graphic effects. The path does not have to be a straight line (Figure 12.31) as long as it is an open path.

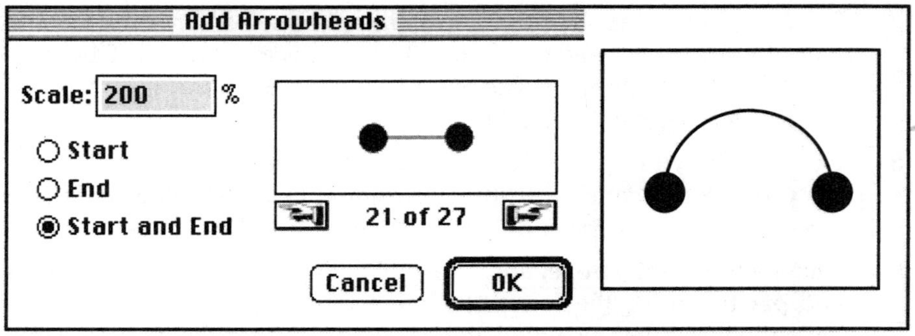

Figure 12.31—Draw a circle and select it. Use the scissors tool to cut the two horizontal anchor points and delete the bottom path. Then select the top path and add the balls to the start and end of the path via the Add Arrowheads dialog box.

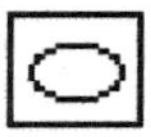

Oval tool

5. Select the oval tool and Shift-drag to draw a circle. Choose Filter/Stylize/Bloat to display the Bloat dialog box. The Bloat filter curves a selected path out from its anchor points at a specified value. Type 30 in the Amount field to curve the anchor points outward by 30%. Click on OK. Your screen should resemble Figure 12.32.

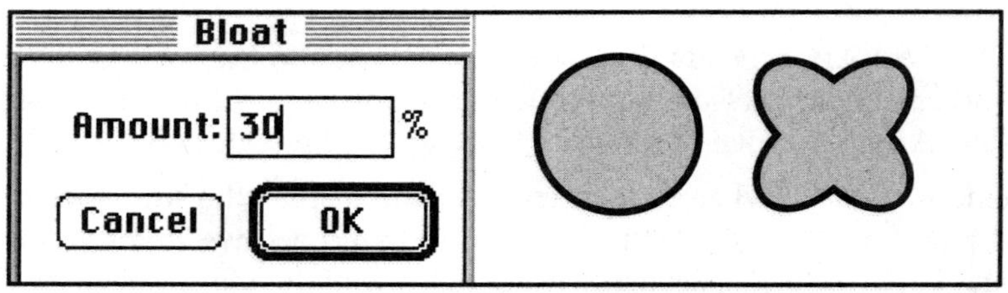

Figure 12.32—The greater the value in the Amount field, the more pronounced the outward curve of the anchor points.

FYI

The Calligraphy filter resembles the Calligraphic option for the brush tool. However, the Calligraphy filter differs from the Brush tool option in that the filter can be applied to an object that is already created.

6. The Calligraphy filter applies a line of varying weight to an open or closed path. Although you cannot apply this filter to text, if you convert the text to outlines (Type/Create Outlines), you can apply the filter to the paths and achieve some interesting results.
7. Use the freehand tool to draw a wavy line. Apply a 6-point stroke and no fill. Choose Stylize/Calligraphy to display the Calligraphy dialog box. Assign a 0.125-inch Pen Width value and a 120° Pen Angle value. Click on OK.

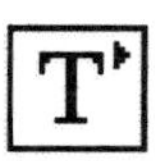

Type tool

8. Use the type tool to type a letter. Click on the selection tool and format the text character in 72-point type. Choose Type/Create Outlines.
9. With the character object still selected, choose Filter/Stylize/Calligraphy. Type 1 (inch) in the Pen Width field. Tab to the Pen Angle field and type 45. Click on OK. Your screen should resemble Figure 12.33.

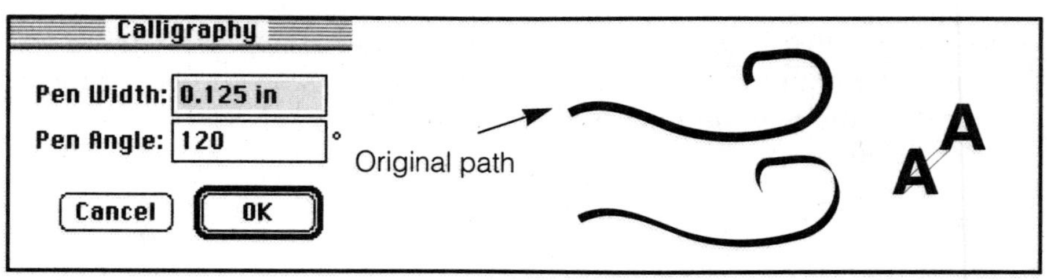

Figure 12.33—The Calligraphy filter applied to an open path and to a text character converted to outlines.

10. Select Points/Picas as the Ruler units (Command-K).
11. Use the rectangle tool to draw a rectangle. Assign it a black stroke and no fill. Choose Filter/Stylize/Drop Shadow to display the Drop Shadow dialog box (Figure 12.34). The value in the X Offset field determines the horizontal distance between the selected object and the shadow; the Y Offset field determines its vertical distance.

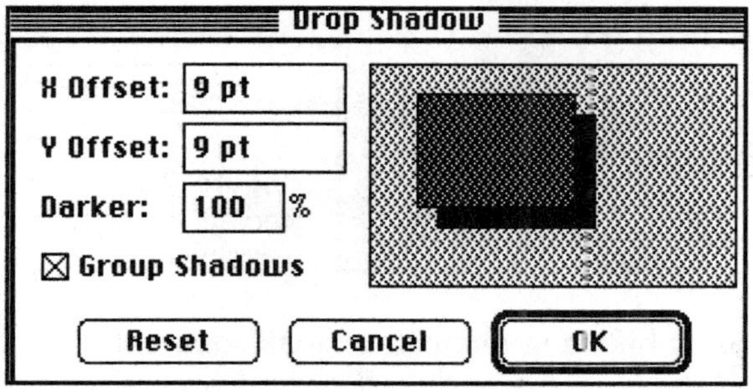

Figure 12.34—The Drop Shadow dialog box.

12. Type 9 in the X Offset field to offset the drop shadow 9 points to the right of the selected object. Press the Tab key and type 9 in the Y offset field to offset the shadow 9 points down from the object. The preview window on the right side of the dialog box displays the effect of the values.
13. Type 100 in the Darker field to make the drop shadow black. Any value below 100% makes the drop shadow lighter than black.
14. Click to select the Group Shadows check box to group the drop shadow with the selected object. Click on OK.
15. Draw another rectangle and choose Filter/Stylize/Drop Shadow. Type –9 in the X offset field to offset the shadow 9 points to the left of the selected object. Type –9 in the Y Offset field to offset the shadow 9 points above the object. Leave the Darker value at 100%. Click on OK. Your screen should resemble Figure 12.35.

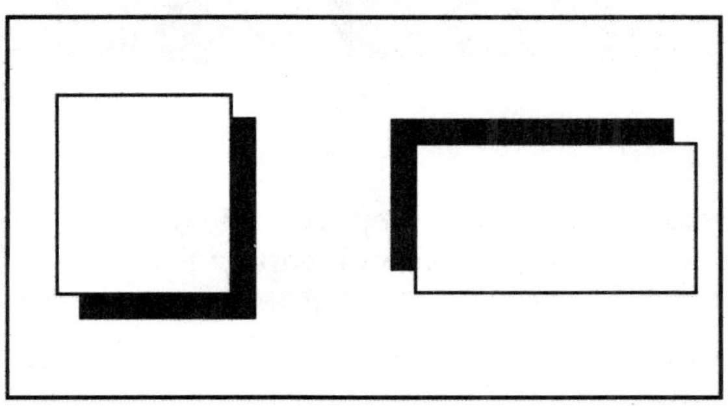

Figure 12.35—The drop shadow on the left displays positive offset values; the one on the right displays negative offset values.

16. Use the rectangle tool to draw another rectangle. Choose Filter/Stylize/Punk to display the Punk dialog box. Type 20 in the Amount field to distort the edge of the selected object and make it jagged. Click on OK. Your screen should resemble Figure 12.36.

-K File/Preferences/ General

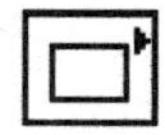

Rectangle tool

Design Tip

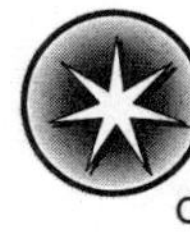

Create drop shadows around different graphic objects like stars and polygons. Save them as EPS files and import them into your page layout program to add a little pizazz to pages.

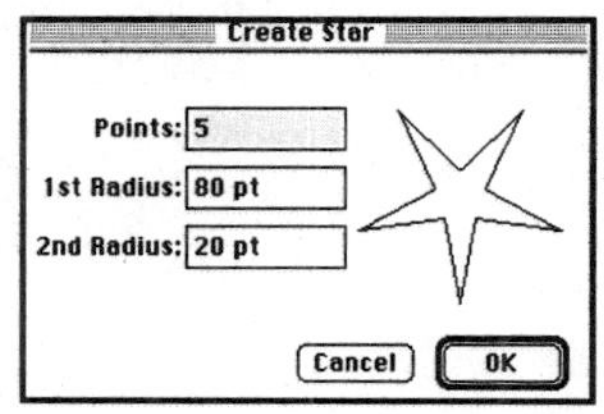

The 1st Radius value affects the size of the star, since this value determines the distance from the center of the star to its outer points. The 2nd Radius value determines the distance between the center of the star and the inner points.

FYI

You can enter a value between –200 and 200 in the Amount field of the Punk dialog box. The higher the number, the more pronounced the distortion.

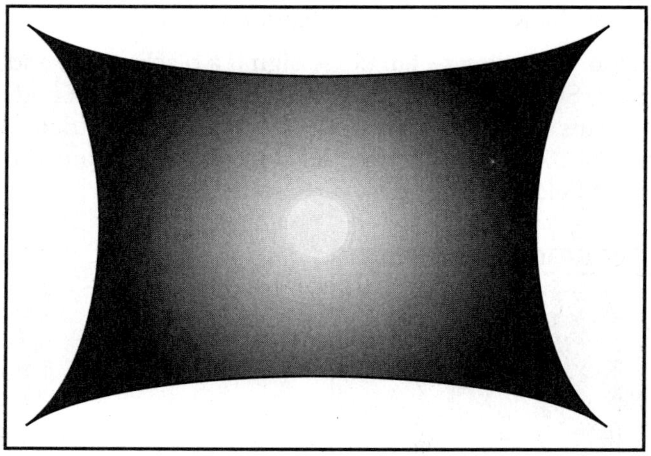

Figure 12.36—A rectangle stylized with the Punk filter.

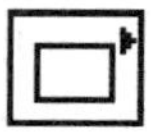

Rectangle tool

17. Use the rectangle tool and Shift-drag to create a small square. Choose Filter/Stylize/Round Corners to display the Round Corners dialog box. Type 60 in the Radius field and click on OK. Your screen should resemble Figure 12.37.

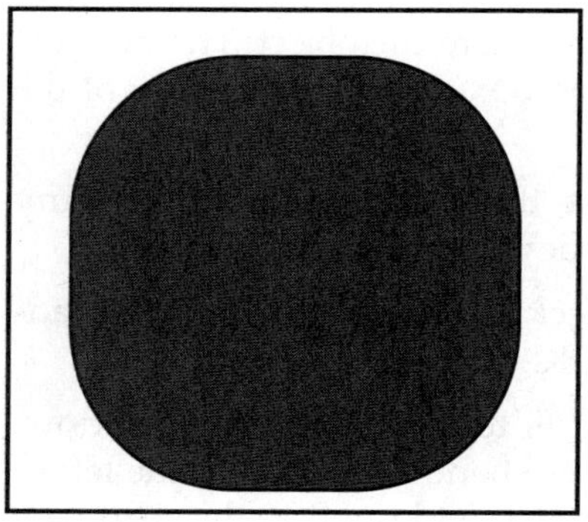

Figure 12.37—A rectangle stylized with the Round Corners filter.

REVIEW EXERCISE

This is a free exercise!

1. Use the Create filters or draw objects and apply various filters to them. Change the values in the dialog boxes and reapply the filters to see how objects can be altered with the different values.

Path-type tool

2. Use the Create command to create a spiral. Then use the path-type tool to type text on the path and the direct-selection tool to stroke the path.
3. Use the Add Arrowheads filter to create different effects with arrowheads on straight or curved *open* paths.
4. Use a wide Pen Width value like 9 or 10 in the Calligraphy dialog box to create a compound path which will reveal the background behind it. Your screen might resemble Figure 12.38.

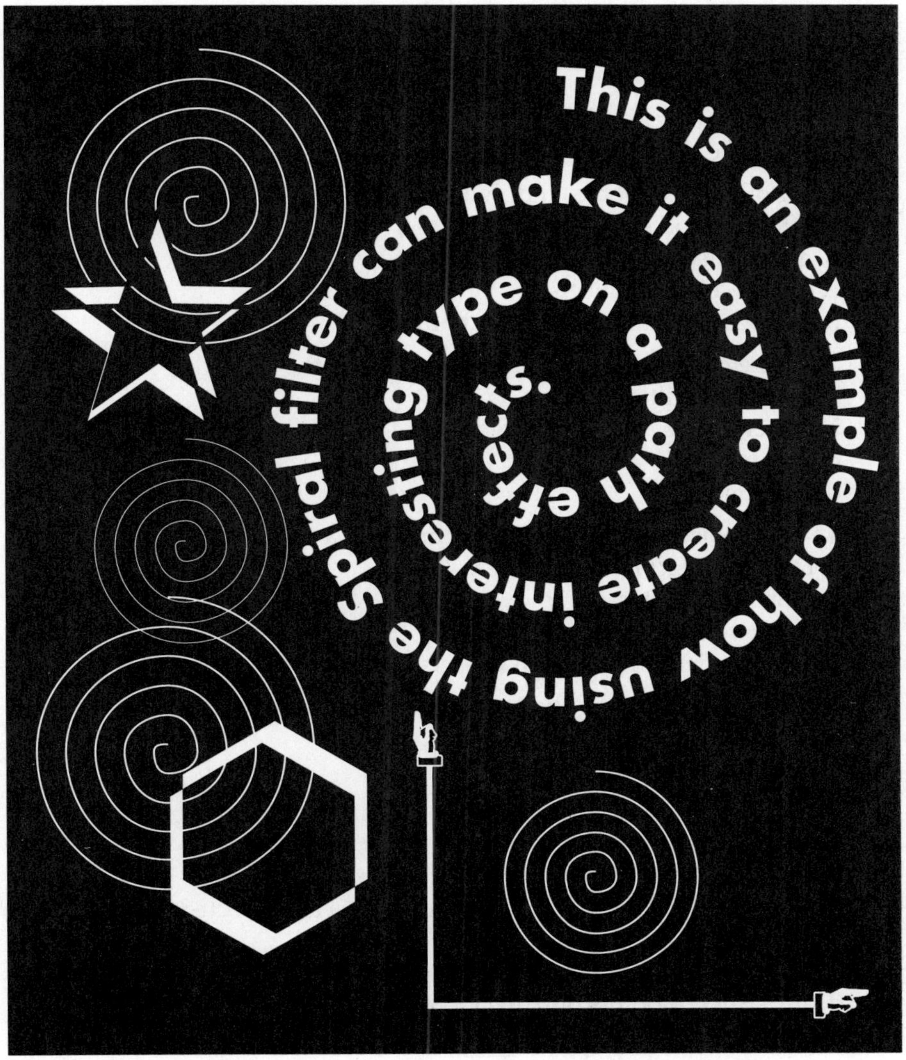

Figure 12.38—Displays spirals; a spiral with text; a star and polygon stylized with the Calligraphy filter and then painted white, which makes their centers transparent; and graphic arrowheads at the start and end of an open path.

REVIEW QUESTIONS

Read the following questions and choose the answer which best completes the statement.

1. The Adjust Colors filter _____.
   a. adds colors
   b. changes CMYK values
   c. saturates colors
   d. changes spot colors to process colors

2. The Pathfinder filters _____.
   a. merge paths
   b. divide paths
   c. affect stroke and fill attributes
   d. all of the above
3. The Roughen, Scribble, and Twirl filters _____.
   a. affect fill and stroke attributes
   b. affect selected anchor points
   c. distort selected objects
   d. can be used only on an open path
4. To make global changes in a document, use the _____.
   a. Pathfinder filters
   b. Select filters
   c. Create filters
   d. Objects filters
5. To align objects at the same point on the X axis, use the _____.
   a. Distribute Horizontally filter
   b. Offset Path filter
   c. direct-selection tool
   d. Vertical field in the Align Objects dialog box
6. Arrowheads and drop shadows are created with the _____.
   a. Stylize filters
   b. Create filters
   c. Object filters
   d. none of the above
7. The Add Anchor Points filter _____.
   a. adds a specified number of anchor points to a selected object
   b. can be applied to text
   c. doubles the number of anchor points in a selection
   d. adds anchor points only to closed paths
8. Pressing Command-Shift-E _____.
   a. doubles the number of selected objects
   b. allows you to enter values in a Filter dialog box
   c. applies a filter to the next selected object
   d. reapplies the most recently applied filter
9. To create transparent effects with overlapping colors, use _____.
   a. the Mix Soft filter
   b. the Blend Front to Back filter
   c. the Invert Colors filter
   d. all of the above
10. Stars and polygons are created with the _____.
    a. Create filter
    b. Stylize filter
    c. Objects filter
    d. Pathfinder filters

Answers: 1. b; 2. d; 3. c; 4. b; 5. d; 6. a; 7. c; 8. d; 9. a; 10. a

LESSON 13

Color Trapping and Printing

OVERVIEW

This last lesson covers converting custom colors to process colors and creating color traps to compensate for misregistration when printing. You will also learn how to print black-and-white files and color separations. How Adobe Illustrator interfaces with Adobe Separator and QuarkXPress is also discussed.

TOPICS

Printing with color
Converting to process colors
Printing to a laser printer
Printing color separations
Adobe Separator
Trapping
Spread traps and choke traps
The Trap filter
Review Exercise
Review Questions

TERMS

choke trap
crop marks
knockout
overprinting
process color
spot color
spread trap
trapping

TUTORIAL FILES

a la Matisse.ai

⌘-I Object/Paint Style
⌘-Q File/Quit

PRINTING WITH COLOR

Color comes in two flavors: spot color and process color. Process color is sometimes called four-color process. Spot color is a single color that is premixed from any number of colors. A custom color like "Banana Yellow," created in Illustrator, is a combination of any percentage of the four process colors, cyan, magenta, yellow, and black. When you apply "Banana Yellow" to an object in Illustrator and print the file through either Adobe Separator or a page layout program like QuarkXPress, a separate plate will be printed for "Banana Yellow." Even though you used two or three or even four process colors to create "Banana Yellow," because you specified it as a custom color, it remains a single color requiring a single plate and only *one ink.*

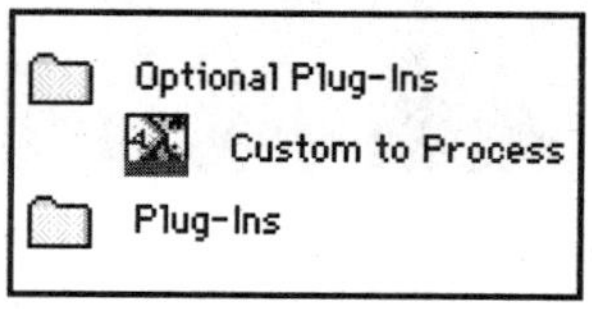

Drag the Custom to Process filter from the Optional Plug-Ins folder to the Plug-Ins folder and quit Illustrator. When you relaunch the application, the Custom to Process filter will be active.

Process colors are also comprised of the four process colors, cyan, magenta, yellow and black. However, unlike spot colors, if you define "Banana Yellow" as a process color made up of 17% Cyan, 21% Magenta, 100% Yellow, and 11% Black in the Paint Style palette (Figure 13.1), *four plates* will print *for each page* on which an object painted with that color appears.

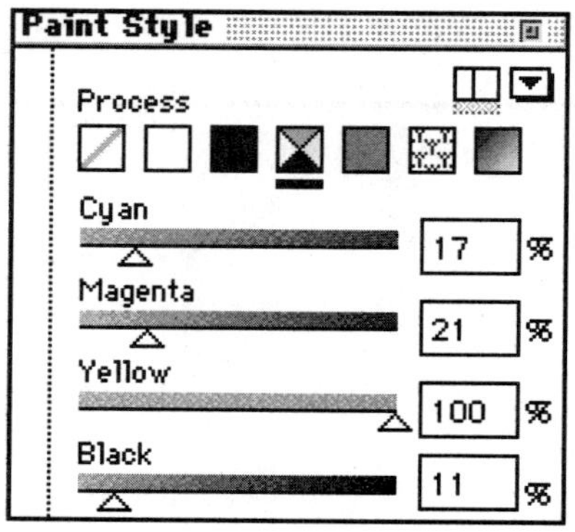

Figure 13.1—The Paint Style palette displays the CMYK percentages for a color named "Banana Yellow."

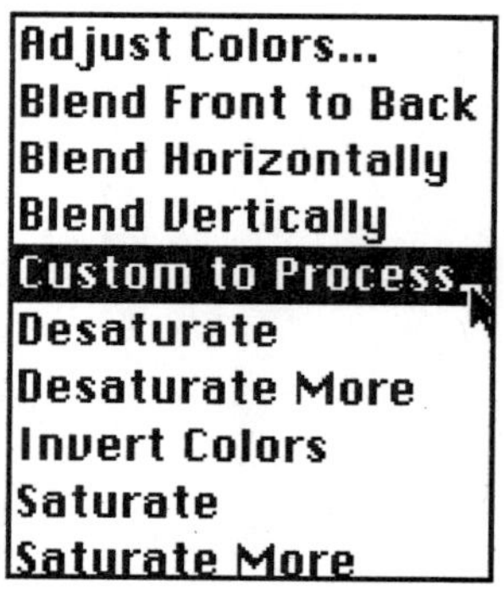

The Custom to Process filter is one of the Colors filters.

Since each spot color requires a separate plate, if you are printing a file with three or more spot colors and black text, it is cheaper to convert the spot colors to process colors so that only four plates will print. Otherwise, a plate will be printed *for each page* on which each spot color is designated, as well a black plate for the text.

CONVERTING TO PROCESS COLORS

The easiest way to convert spot colors to process colors in version 5.5 is to drag the Custom to Process filter from the Optional (inactive) Plug-Ins folder into the Plug-Ins folder. You must then relaunch Adobe Illustrator so that it can initialize the new filter.

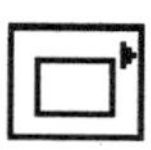

Rectangle tool

EXERCISE A

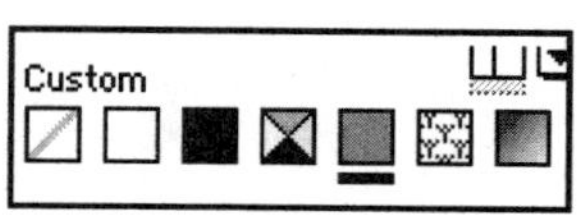

Custom color icon selected in the color strip area.

1. Drag the Custom to Process filter from the Optional Plug-Ins folder to the Plug-Ins folder in the Adobe Illustrator 5.5 folder. Quit Illustrator (Command-Q) and relaunch the program.
2. Draw a rectangle and display the Paint Style palette (Command-I). Click on the Custom color icon in the Paint Style palette and use the scroll box on the right to highlight Gold.

3. Choose Filter/Colors/Custom to Process to display the Custom to Process dialog box. Make sure the Retain Tint check box is selected to keep the custom color tint from the Paint Style palette. Click on OK.
4. The Process color icon becomes selected in the Paint Style palette, and the CMYK sliders display the values used to create a process color version of the custom color, Gold.
5. Choose File Save. Type Process Yellow.ai in the Save this document as field and select Illustrator 5 from the Format pull-down menu. Click on Save (Figure 13.2).

⌘-O File/Open
⌘-P File/Print

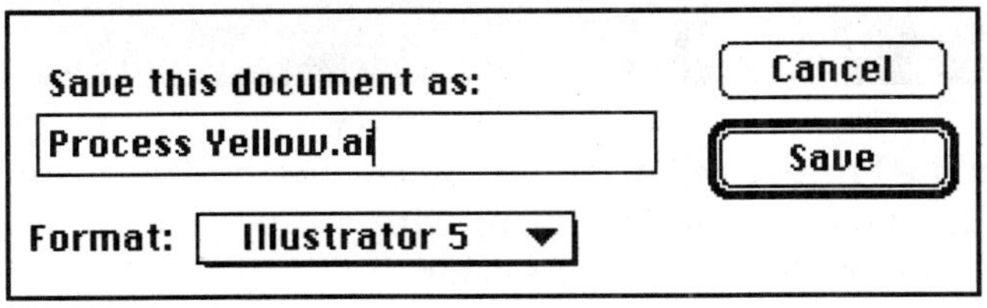

Figure 13.2—Save the file in Illustrator 5 format.

PRINTING TO A LASER PRINTER

Printing to a black-and-white or color PostScript printer is rather straightforward in Adobe Illustrator. You must first specify a printer, make the appropriate selections in the Page Setup dialog box, and then use the Print command.

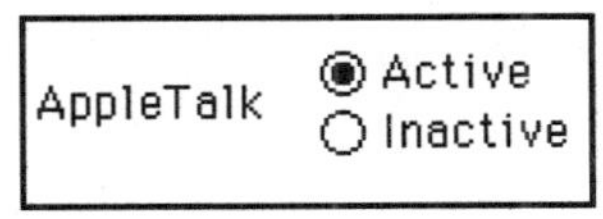

Click to select the Active option in the Chooser dialog box if your printer is on a network.

EXERCISE B

1. *Turn on the printer* and launch Adobe Illustrator. If necessary, open the Process Yellow.ai file (Command-O). Pull down the Apple menu on the extreme left side of the Menu Bar () and highlight Chooser to display the Chooser dialog box.
2. Click on the icon on the left side of the screen for the printer connected to your computer. When its name appears in the right side of the dialog box, click on it to highlight (select) it. If you are on a network, click to make Appletalk active. Click the Close box in the upper left corner of the Chooser dialog box to exit the Chooser and return to Illustrator.
3. Choose File/Page Setup to display the Page Setup dialog box. Click to select US Letter *or* click the Tabloid button and use the pull-down menu to select the printer driver for your *color printer*.
4. Make sure that the Portrait Orientation icon is selected to print the page vertically. None of the other options have to be checked. Click on OK.
5. Choose File/Print (Command-P) to display the Print dialog box. Leave 1 in the Copies field and the All button selected. If you wanted to print only specific pages, you would type values in the From (page) and To (page) fields.
6. Click to select the Color/Grayscale option if you are printing to a color printer, or if you want the colored objects printed in easily distinguishable shades of gray.
7. Click Printer as the Destination and click on OK. (You did turn on the printer, didn't you?)

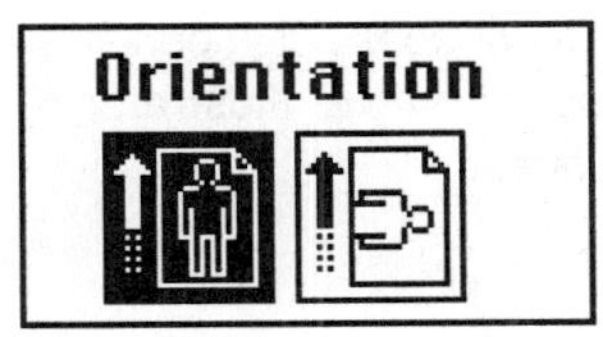

Click to select Portrait orientation to print vertically on the paper.

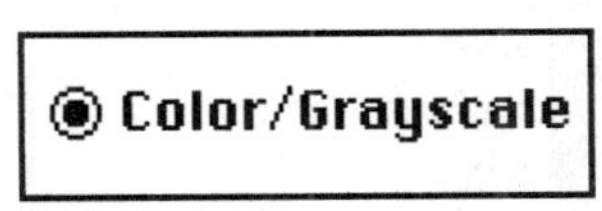

Selecting this option prints the colored objects in the document as different shades of gray so you can more easily distinguish between objects.

PRINTING COLOR SEPARATIONS

There are two ways to print color separations. The easiest way is to save the Illustrator document as an EPS file and import it into QuarkXPress, which will automatically add the process color to its Colors palette *and* separate the color when printing.

The more complicated way to print color separations from Adobe Illustrator is to separate the colors in Illustrator's companion application, Adobe Separator.

Selection tool

EXERCISE C

1. If necessary, open the Process Yellow.ai file you created earlier. If you don't have the file, create a new document with a process color or with a custom color converted to a process color.
2. Select the object. This will display the CMYK values for that object in the Custom Color dialog box. Choose Object/Custom Color to display the Custom Color dialog box.
3. Click on New and type *banana yellow* in the Change Name to field. Click on OK. The new name has now been added to the list of custom colors.
4. Choose File/Save As. Change the .ai suffix to .eps and select EPS from the Format pull-down menu (Figure 13.3). Click on Save.

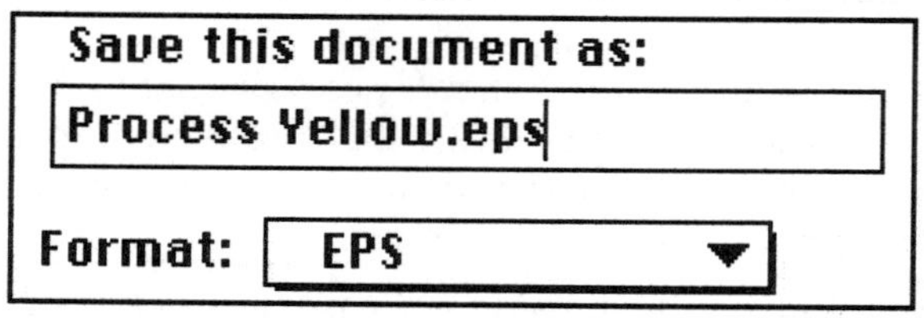

Figure 13.3—Save the file as an EPS file so it can be imported into QuarkXPress.

FYI

The only way to get an Illustrator 5 file into QuarkXpress is to save it as an EPS file in Illustrator. Quark does not import files saved in the Illustrator 5 format.

5. The EPS Format dialog box appears (13.4). Select 8-bit Macintosh for the Preview and Illustrator 5 for the Compatibility options. Click on OK.

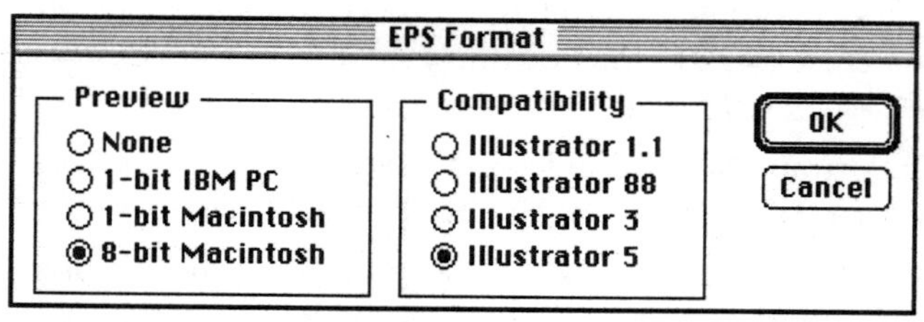

Figure 13.4—Select a Preview option to view the Illustrator file in another program.

6. Launch QuarkXPress, draw a picture box, and choose File/Get Picture. Scroll to locate and highlight the Process Yellow.eps file and click on Open.
7. Choose View/Show Colors to display the Colors palette. Notice that the process color you created in Illustrator, banana yellow, appears in the Quark Colors palette and is now part of the Quark document.

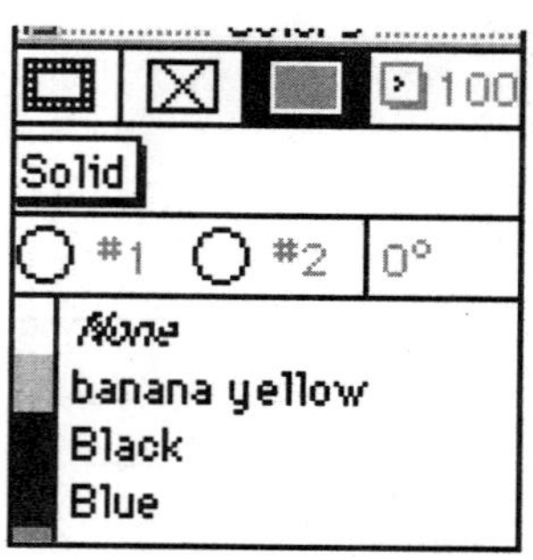

The color created in Adobe Illustrator, banana yellow, now appears in the QuarkXPress Colors palette.

8. Choose Edit/Colors to display Quark's Edit Colors dialog box. Click to highlight banana yellow and click on Edit to display the Edit Color dialog box for banana yellow.
9. Make sure the Model pull-down menu displays CMYK. Click to select the Process Separation check box (Figure 13.5). Click on OK to return to the Edit Colors dialog box. Click on Save to return to the document.
10. Choose File/Print to print the four plates necessary to separate the banana yellow color.

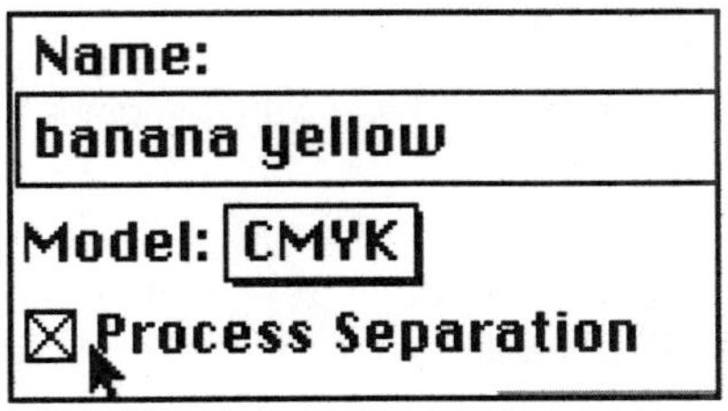

Figure 13.5—Select the Process Separation option to print color separations for banana yellow.

ADOBE SEPARATOR

Adobe Separator is an application which comes with Illustrator and is installed in the same folder as Adobe Illustrator's Separator & Utilities folder on your hard drive. To separate a file in Adobe Separator, it must first be saved in Illustrator as an EPS file with a black-and-white or color Preview option.

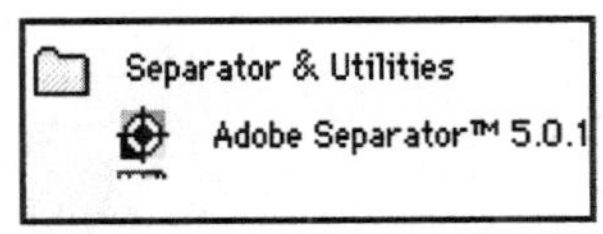

Double-click on the Adobe Separator icon to launch Adobe Separator.

EXERCISE D

1. Locate the Adobe Separator application in the Separator & Utilities folder in the Adobe Illustrator folder on your hard drive. Double-click on the application icon to launch the program.
2. Open the Process Yellow.eps file you created earlier. If you can't find the file, create another Illustrator file and save it as an EPS file with a color Preview format.
3. Scroll to the Adobe Illustrator folder, to the Separator & Utilities folder, and open the PPDs folder. Highlight the PPD file for the target printer or imagesetter which will print the plates for the file. Click on Open.
4. The Setup window appears with a preview of the image on the right and the setting options on the left. Make sure that Orientation is set to Portrait.
5. By default, Separator will print every process and custom color in the illustration. You can, however, specify which colors will and will not print by clicking the Separations button in the Setup dialog box.

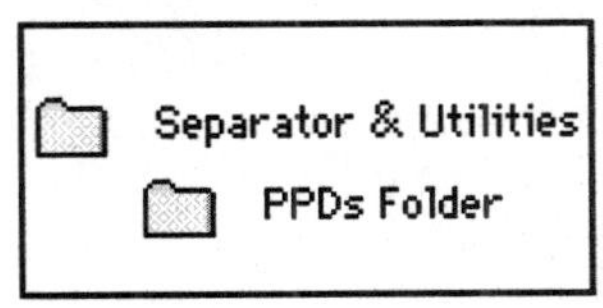

The PPDs folder is inside the Separator & Utilities folder, which is in the Adobe Illustrator folder on the hard drive.

⌘-S Save All Separations

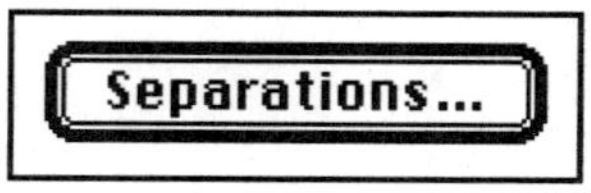

Click on this button in the lower right corner of the Setup dialog box to select colors for printing.

6. Click on the Separations button to display the Separation dialog box (Figure 13.6).

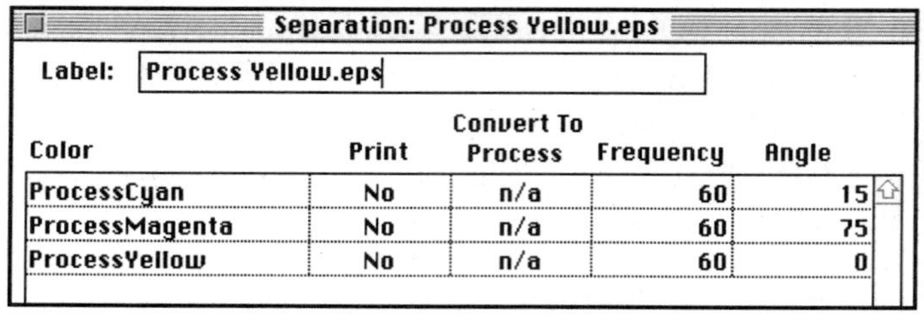

Figure 13.6—Click on No in the Print column to toggle to Yes if you want the color to print.

7. Click on No in the Print column for each color you want to print to toggle to Yes. For this example, toggle all to Yes.
8. If you did not convert a custom color to process color, you could also make the conversion in this dialog box. Since you already converted banana yellow to a process color, this option is not applicable. Leave the other values as they are and close the dialog box by clicking on the Close box in the upper left corner.
9. Pull down the File menu and notice the two Save options, Save Selected Separations and Save All Separations.
10. If you had not specified every color to print, you could now choose to save only those separations for which you indicated Yes in the Print column of the Separations dialog box. You can also choose to save all the separations by selecting Save All Separations, which will save every color in the document regardless of what you selected in the Separations dialog box (Figure 13.6).
11. Choose Save All Separations (Command-S) to save the three colors used in this illustration (cyan, magenta, and yellow) as three separate files.

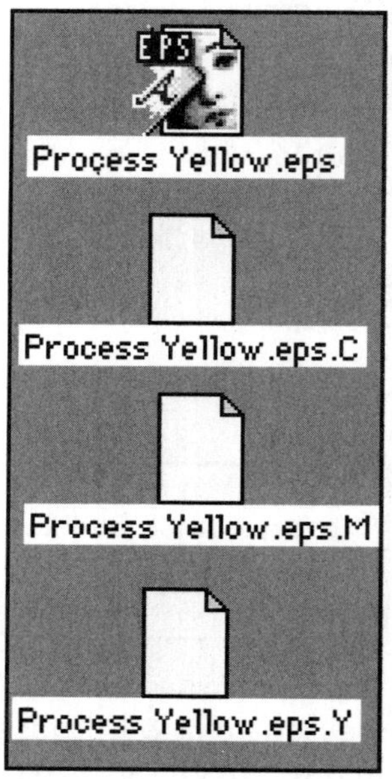

When Save Selected Separations is selected, Separator saves only those separations which you indicated should print in the Separation dialog box.

TRAPPING

Trapping is a method of compensating for gaps which appear when overlapping colors are printed on a printing press. Because presses shift, even slightly, gaps can appear when one color is printed on top of another color. By creating a small area of overlap, this gap between overlapping colors can be eliminated (Figure 13.7).

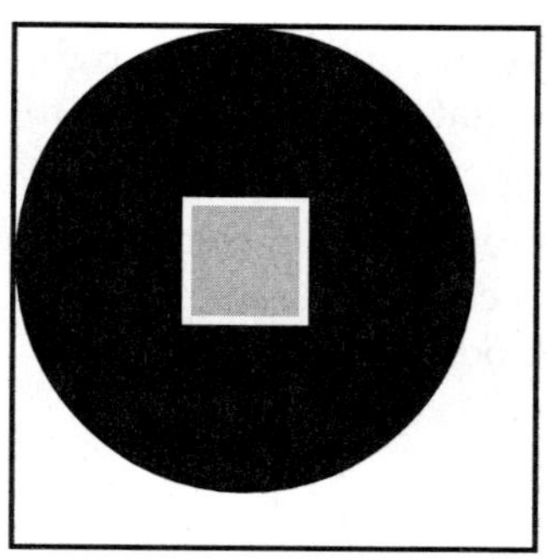

Figure 13.7—Notice the white paper showing through the gap between the black circle and the yellow square. Trapping will eliminate this gap.

SPREAD TRAPS AND CHOKE TRAPS

There are two kinds of traps, a spread trap and a choke trap. A spread trap extends or spreads the lighter color object over the darker background. In Figure 13.7 a spread trap would spread (extend) the yellow square (object) over the black circle (background).

A choke trap extends the lighter background color behind the darker foreground object (Figure 13.8). Regardless of the kind of stroke you apply, the foreground object overprints the background, creating a combination of the two colors where the object and background overlap.

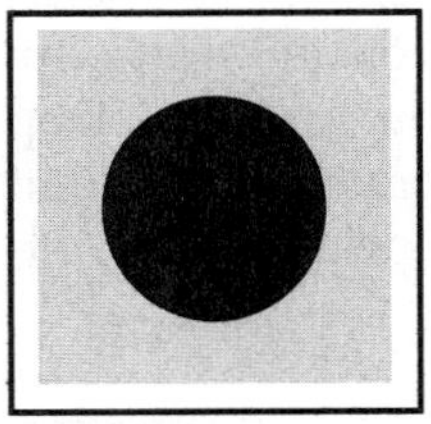

Figure 13.8—A choke trap is used here to spread the lighter yellow background behind the darker object (circle).

EXERCISE E

1. Use the drawing tools to draw a purple rectangle and a yellow oval. Move the oval (object) on top of the rectangle (background). Save the file (Command-S) as Trap Practice.ai.
2. Select the lighter object (oval) and apply a stroke in the same yellow color as the fill. Assume that the printer told you to apply a 2-point trap. Since you should double that value for a trap in Illustrator, make the stroke weight 4 points. Type 4 in the Stroke Weight field. In the Overprint area, click on the Stroke check box to select it. This will place the four-point stroke halfway under the circle so that the extending 2 points will overlap the background and blend with it to eliminate any gap between the objects (Figure 13.9). This is called a spread trap because the trap spreads out of the lighter object onto the darker background.

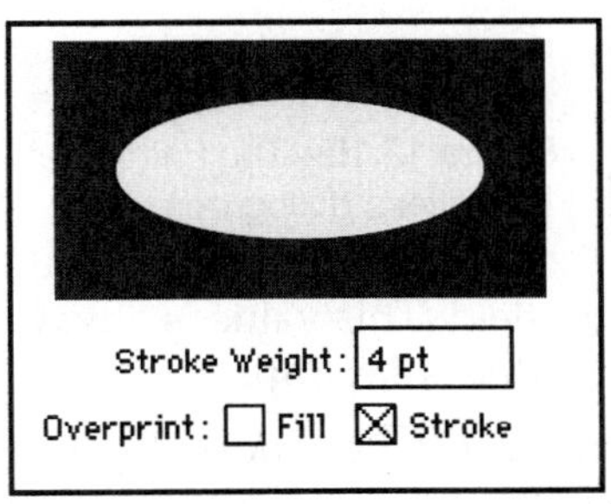

Figure 13.9—Apply a four-point yellow stroke to the lighter foreground object (oval) and overprint it to create a two-point trap which extends into the darker background.

3. Choose File/Open (Command-O) and open the Trap Practice.ai file. This is the file to which no trapping was applied.
4. Switch the colors so that the foreground object (oval) is purple and the background (rectangle) is yellow.

⌘-O File/Open
⌘-S File/Save

Trap on the light side

Try to manipulate the lighter color when creating a trap. If the lighter color is the object, spread it; if the lighter color is the background, choke it.

FYI

Always let the printer tell you how heavy the trapping stroke should be. A common weight is a quarter-point trap.

Traps are not visible on proofs, only on negatives.

Knockout vs. Overprint

When one overlapping color does not overprint the background color beneath it, a knockout results, which avoids mixing the overlapping colors. Instead of the overlapping color appearing on the page and mixing with the background color, the white area where that foreground color should appear—the knockout—is displayed.

Selecting the Overprint option in the Paint Style palette results in the foreground fill and stroke colors printing on top of the background colors, resulting in a combination color where those two colors overlap.

5. Select the lighter object (oval) and apply a four-point stroke in yellow, the same color as the background. Click on Stroke in the Overprint area. You have applied a choke trap because the lighter background (yellow rectangle) now overlaps the oval by half the stroke weight.

FYI

Before any trap can be set with the Trap filter, at least two or more objects must be selected.

THE TRAP FILTER

The spread and choke traps which you set manually must be used for complex artwork like gradients, patterns, and placed objects, since the Trap filter does not work on these kinds of overlapping objects.

Trapping text is also another issue. Avoid trapping text at small point sizes, because both trapping and the slightest misregistration on the press can make the text difficult to read. Also, any text to which you apply the Trap filter must first be converted to outlines, and when you convert small point size text to outlines, you frequently lose resolution when printing to printers with less than 600 dots per inch.

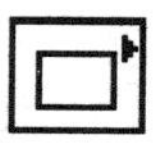

Rectangle tool

EXERCISE F

Type tool

1. Use the rectangle tool to create a rectangle. Fill it with a light color like yellow.
2. Use the type tool and type a few letters inside the rectangle. Click on the selection tool to select the type.
3. Choose Type/Create Outlines. Fill the selected type with a dark color like red or purple.
4. Use the selection tool to draw a selection marquee around both the rectangle and the text to select all the objects to be trapped.
5. Choose Filter/Pathfinder/Trap to display the Pathfinder Trap dialog box (Figure 13.10).

Selection tool

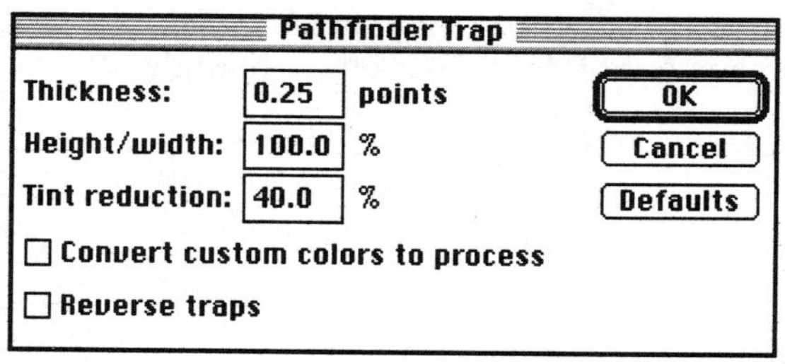

Figure 13.10—The Pathfinder Trap filter's dialog box.

More info

Specify different Height/width values to compensate for any paper stretch on the printing press. Increasing the trap thickness on the horizontal lines without changing the vertical trap is done by setting the Height/width value to more than 100%. Setting it to less than 100% decreases the trap thickness on the horizontal lines without changing the vertical trap.

6. Type the width of the trap in the Thickness field. This value is always entered in points. Leave it at the default quarter-point trap.
7. The Height/width values specify the trap on the horizontal lines of the selected objects as a percentage of the trap on the objects' vertical lines. Leave this value at 100%
8. Leave the Tint reduction value at 40% to create a trap that is a smaller percentage of the CMYK values of the lighter color trapped, and 100% of the darker color trapped.
9. Click to select the Convert custom colors to process colors if you are going to print separations. Click on OK.

REVIEW EXERCISE

In this exercise you will apply trapping values to the objects in the a la Matisse.ai file which you used in Lesson 10.

1. Display the Paint Style palette (Command-I). Display the Layers palette (Command-Control-L).
2. Open the a la Matisse.ai file on the Tutorial disk (Command-O). Click on the Dancer 1 layer in the Layers palette. Use the Layers palette pull-out menu to select Hide Others.
3. Use the selection tool to select the girl's skirt. Click on the Fill icon in the Paint Style palette. Click on the Custom Color icon in the color strip area and select Purple from the color list in the scroll box to fill the skirt with purple.
4. With the skirt still selected, click on the Stroke icon in the Paint Style palette and click on none.
5. Select the girl's apron, click on the Fill icon, click on the Custom Color icon again, and click on Gold in the scroll box to fill the apron with gold.
6. With the gold apron still selected, click on the Overprint box in the Paint Style palette (Figure 13.11).

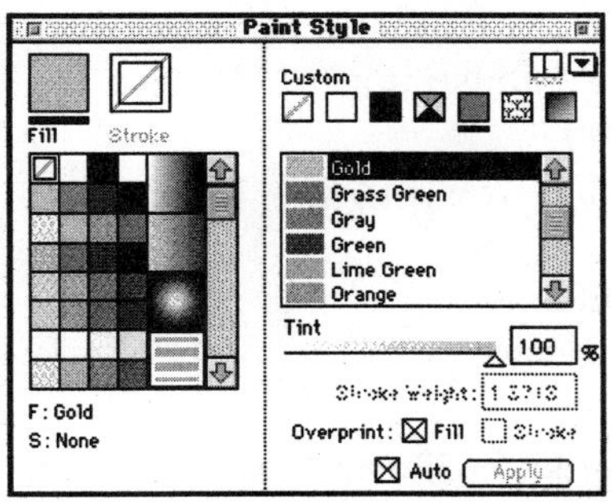

Figure 13.11—Select the Overprint option to avoid a knockout when the file is printed.

7. Use the selection tool to Shift-select the skirt and the apron. Choose Filter/Pathfinder/Trap to display the Pathfinder Trap dialog box.
8. Type .25 in the Thickness field and click to select the Convert custom colors to process colors option. Click on OK to create the trap.
9. Choose Show All from the pull-out menu on the Layers palette.
10. Continue to apply overlapping colors and create traps for other overlapping colors in the illustration. Be sure to select the Convert custom colors to process option every time you create a trap.
11. Save the file as an EPS file (File/Save As) and either import it into QuarkXPress to separate it, following the steps in Exercise C, or separate it in Adobe Separator, following the steps in Exercise D.

⌘-I Object/Paint Style
⌘-Control-L View/Show Layers
⌘-O File/Open

Selection tool

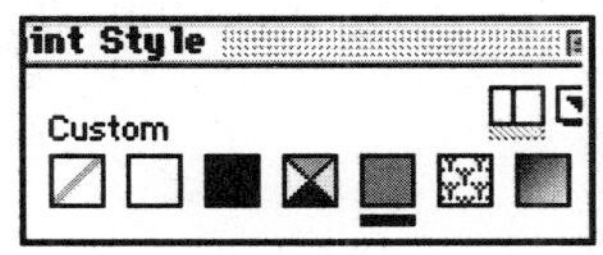

Custom Color icon selected in the color strip area.

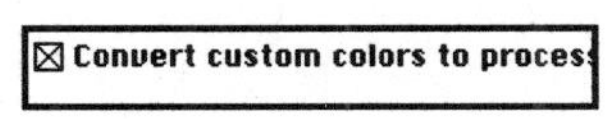

Select this option in the Pathfinder Trap dialog box to convert the custom (spot) colors to process colors.

REVIEW QUESTIONS

Read the following questions and choose the answer which best completes the statement.

1. A color printed with a single ink is called _____.
   a. process color
   b. spot color
   c. gradient fill
   d. b and c
2. A color comprised of cyan, magenta, yellow, and black which prints with four inks is called _____.
   a. process color
   b. spot color
   c. gradient fill
   d. b and c
3. Custom colors are _____..
   a. process colors
   b. spot colors
   c. black or white
   d. all of the above
4. Page orientation is specified in _____.
   a. the New dialog box
   b. Adobe Separator
   c. the Page Setup dialog box
   d. b and c
5. Colors can be separated via _____.
   a. QuarkXPress
   b. Adobe Separator
   c. Adobe Illustrator
   d. a and b
6. Before a file can be imported into a page layout program, it must be saved as _____.
   a. a TIFF file
   b. a PICT file
   c. an EPS file
   d. an Illustrator 5 file
7. Adobe Separator _____.
   a. prints every process and custom color in the illustration
   b. prints only spot colors
   c. prints only process colors
   d. separates EPS files
8. When trapping colors, try to manipulate _____.
   a. the darker color
   b. the lighter color
   c. the foreground object
   d. the background
9. Extending the foreground color creates _____.
   a. a choke trap
   b. a spread trap
   c. a color separation
   d. a and c
10. Extending the background color creates _____.
    a. a choke trap
    b. a spread trap
    c. a color separation
    d. a and c

Answers: 1. b; 2. a; 3. b; 4. d; 5. d; 6. c; 7. a; 8. b; 9. b; 10. a

GLOSSARY

Anchor point—a point at the beginning and end of a segment. When the segment is selected, anchor points are visible. Anchor points appear hollow when deselected and filled when selected.

Area type—type created inside and therefore bounded by an open or closed path.

Auto Trace gap—value from 0 to 2 which defines the number of black pixels the auto trace tool will trace. A value of 0 tells the auto trace tool not to skip any black pixels whose corners touch, even when a white pixel exists between them.

Backmost object—the last painted object in the stacking order on any layer; any object to which the Arrange/Send to Back command is applied. (*See stacking.*)

Baseline—an imaginary line on which type sits. The baseline is displayed when type is selected with the selection tool or when you click on the tool used to create the type immediately after creating that type.

Blend—multiple progression of shapes and/or colors between two open or two closed paths. Objects in a blend are evenly distributed between the two paths in a specified number of steps. When only colors are blended, the result is a gradient fill. (*See gradient fill.*)

Bounding rectangle—the rectangle surrounding artwork designated as a pattern tile.

Cap—a style for the endpoint of a line. Caps can be butt (squared off), round, or projecting.

Choke trap—extending the lighter background color under the darker foreground object.

Closed path—has no apparent beginning or end; has no endpoints. Illustrator calls a closed path a shape.

Coincident points—two endpoints placed directly on top of each other. Using the Join command on two coincident endpoints joins them into one corner, or one smooth anchor point. (*See noncoincident points.*)

Compound path—two or more overlapping paths painted (filled and/or stroked) so that the overlapping paths appear transparent.

Continuous curves—curves connected by smooth points. Continuous curves all curve in the same direction.

Corner points—are created by clicking once with the pen tool. Clicking without dragging with the pen tool creates corner points. Corner points do not display direction handles.

Crop marks—printed marks that define where the printed page will be trimmed.

Custom color—any color you create and name, or any color you select from a color model like the Pantone color models. (*See spot color.*)

Dash/gap fields—in the Paint Style palette where you input values that determine the size of the dashed line (Dash field) and the space between the dashes in a dashed line (Gap field.)

Direct-selection tool—used to select individual segments and anchor points on a path; designated in the Tool palette by a white arrow.

Direction handles—associated with curve points and used to reshape the curve.

Direction points—appear at the end of direction handles and are used to move the direction handles when reshaping curve segments.

Endpoints—anchor points at the beginning and end of an open path.

Fill—paint attributes applied to a closed path. A fill can also be applied to an open path.

Filter—a module separate from Adobe Illustrator which works within Illustrator to create special graphic effects, determine the way objects overlap, select objects, and perform text functions.

Font family—the complete set of characters in one style for a specific typeface. Helvetica, with all its special upper-and lower-case characters, is a font family; Helvetica Bold is a style of Helvetica.

Freehand tolerance—value from 0 to 10 which defines the number of pixels the auto trace tool traces or skips on a template; a value which defines how smooth or jagged is the line drawn with the freehand tool. A value of 0 tells the auto trace tool to trace every pixel in the template. The higher the freehand tolerance value, the smoother the line to be traced or drawn with the freehand tool.

Frontmost object—the most recently painted object in the stacking order on any layer; any object to which the Arrange/Bring to Front command is applied. (*See stacking order.*)

Gradient fill—a graduated linear or radial blend between two or more colors. The gradient fill tool is used to modify the direction and/or the starting and ending point of a gradient fill across single or multiple objects.

Group—two or more objects combined to form a single object. All the objects in a group can be moved and transformed as one unit.

Group-selection tool—used for selecting a group of objects by clicking on any object in the group to select the first object. Click again to select the rest of the objects in the group. Click again to select another entire group of objects in the illustration; designated by a white arrow and plus sign in the Tool palette.

Guide—a nonprinting dashed line pulled up and/or out of the rulers which is used to align objects. If the Snap to Point option is checked in the General Preferences dialog box, an object will snap to the guide if it is positioned at least two pixels from the guide.

Guide object—is a guide created from an object by using the Make Guide command. Guide objects have a fill and stroke value of none.

Join—the way the endpoints of two lines meet. Joins can be mitered where the endpoints meet in a corner; round where the corner formed by the two endpoints is rounded; and beveled where the two endpoints appear to be slit diagonally across.

Join paths—using the Join command creates a single path from two open paths by joining the overlapping endpoints of each path. If the two paths to be joined do not have overlapping (coincident) endpoints, a straight line is drawn between the endpoints. (*See coincident and noncoincident endpoints.*)

Kerning—adding and/or deleting space between two text characters. A positive number in the Kerning field adds space between characters; a negative number removes space.

Knockout—the part of the background object overlapped by the foreground object which does not print on the separations. Knockouts occur when the Overprint option is selected in the Paint Style palette. (*See overprinting.*)

Layer—a specified level in the artwork that allows objects to be displayed, edited, and printed.

Leading—the vertical white space between lines of type. Leading is measured in points from one baseline to the baseline of the line of type above or below it in a selected paragraph.

Letter spacing—the space between text characters in a selected paragraph measured as a percent of the width of a space in that type size. Justified text defaults to 0% Minimum, 100% Desired, and 5% Maximum. The 0% values mean that no additional space is added between letters.

Line—a segment between two endpoints; an open path.

Line attributes—apply to stroked paths and include the stroke or weight of a line, its color, solid or dash status (including gaps between dashes), and its cap and join characteristics.

Mask (masking object)—an object placed over other artwork like a stencil and which prevents any objects not overlapping it from being previewed or printed. Any object covered by the mask (masked object) will preview and print. The mask is always the frontmost object in the stacking order. (*See stacking order.*)

Masked object—any object covered by a mask. Masked objects can be previewed and will print.

Miter limit—a value which determines when the corner's join angle changes from mitered (pointed) to beveled (squared off.)

Noncoincident points—are two endpoints not on top of one another. Using the Join command on noncoincident points creates a straight line (path) between the points. (*See coincident points.*)

Noncontinuous curve—curves connected by corner points. (*See continuous curves.*)

Object—a line or shape that can be isolated and manipulated independently of other objects in the illustration.

Open path—a path with two endpoints. An open path (line) does not have a segment connecting the first and last segment in the path; any segment or segments existing between two endpoints; a line.

Option-dragging—dragging while pressing the Option key and keeping it pressed until releasing the mouse button creates a copy of the object.

Overflow indicator—a plus sign inside a box which appears when you create more type than will fit on or inside a path.

Overprinting—printing overlapping fill or stroke colors of the foreground object directly on top of the background object instead of knocking out the background object. Overprinting results in a combination of the foreground and background colors where they overlap. The opposite of overprinting is a knockout. (*See knockout.*)

Paint Style palette—a floating palette where you create and apply colors as fills and strokes and edit lines.

Path—a single segment or any number of connected segments.

Path type—type that is placed along an open or closed path.

Pattern—a repeating fill and/or stroke Paint Style applied from the Paint Style palette when the pattern icon is selected in the color strip area.

Pattern tile—artwork surrounded by a bounding rectangle and designated as a pattern in the Paint Style palette. A pattern tile repeats to fill the confines of a selected path.

Point of origin—the zero point or intersection of the horizontal and vertical rulers.

Point type—type created with the type tool anywhere on the drawing page; Point type is not connected to any path.

Process color—an ink in which the color is based on a percentage of any or all of the four process colors, cyan, magenta, yellow, and black.

Rectangle type—type created inside the boundary of a rectangle.

Reflect—creating a mirror image of a selected object over a specified axis with the reflect tool.

Rotate—rotating a selected object a specified number of degrees with the rotate tool.

Ruler origin—the zero point at the intersection of the horizontal and vertical rulers; the point from which all measurements are taken.

Scale—enlarging or reducing the size of a selected object with the scale tool.

Segment—a line or curve existing between two anchor points.

Selection tool—used to select a whole path or an entire object by clicking on any point on the path; designated in the Tool palette as a black arrow.

Shape—a group of connected segments; a closed path. Because they are closed paths, shapes do not have endpoints.

Shear—skewing or slanting a selected object horizontally, vertically, or along a specified angle.

Smooth points—anchor points on a straight line between two direction handles. Smooth points connect curve segments; created by clicking and dragging with the pen tool or with the convert-direction point tool.

Spot color—a custom color printed with one ink of that color. (*See custom color.*)

Spread trap—extending the lighter color object over the darker background color.

Stacking order—the order in which objects are drawn, which determines how they are displayed when they overlap. The first object drawn becomes the frontmost object until another object is drawn on top of or overlapping it. That first object then becomes the backmost object in the stacking order and the most recently drawn object becomes the frontmost object in the stacking order. (*See masking objects.*)

Start and stop indicators—triangles at the beginning and end of the gradient fade-out bar which specify where the first color in the gradient fill starts and where the last color in the gradient fill ends. The diamond above the bar marks the point at which the colors are at 50%.

Stroke—paint attributes applied to a line, which can be an open or closed path.

Template—a dimmed PICT or Paint image which appears in the background of the illustration and can be traced with the auto trace tool, or with any of the drawing tools. Templates cannot be selected, edited, or printed.

Text object—any type selected with the selection tool, and which is manipulated or transformed like an art object instead of being edited like text.

Tracking—adding and/or deleting space between all the characters and the space between words in a selected range of text. A positive number in the Tracking field adds space; a negative number removes space.

Trapping—a method of avoiding gaps between overlapping colors which occurs when the printing press misregisters or when paper shifts on the press.

Word spacing—the space between words in a selected paragraph measured as a percent of the width of a space in that type size. Justified text defaults to 100% Minimum, 100% Desired, and 200% Maximum. The 100% Minimum and desired values indicate that no additional space will be added between words.

INDEX